MURDER IN THE PLAYGROUND

THE BURNAGE REPORT

LONGSIGHT PRESS
LONDON

First published in 1989 by Longsight Press,
76 Stroud Green Road, London N4 3EN,
England

ISBN: 1 872417 00 0 Paper
      1 872417 02 7 Cloth

Printed by Biddles Ltd, Walnut Tree House,
Woodbridge Park, Guildford, Surrey,
GU1 1DA, England.

Cover design by Julian Stapleton

DEDICATION

This report is dedicated to the memory of AHMED IQBAL ULLAH who was murdered in the playground at Burnage High School on Wednesday, September 17th 1986.

It is also dedicated to members of Ahmed's family who have pledged that his death shall not be in vain.

TERMS OF REFERENCE

The purpose of the Inquiry is to receive evidence, examine, report on and make recommendations in respect of:
1. The extent to which there was a racial aspect to the circumstances and events leading up to and surrounding the death of Ahmed Iqbal Ullah at Burnage High School in September 1986.
2. The extent to which there are racial aspects to the problems of violence and discipline in Burnage High School and other Manchester schools.
3. What can be done to eliminate or reduce racial harassment, racial violence and racism in schools.

THE PANEL

The Inquiry was headed by Ian Macdonald QC, a senior barrister in London who has a particular expertise in immigration and race relations law.

He had three assessors sitting with him. They were:

Lily Khan – a former Commissioner with the Commission for Racial Equality and Co-ordinator for the Bangladeshi Homeless Families Project in the Inner London Education Authority.

Gus John – Director of Education, London Borough of Hackney, and formerly Deputy Director of Education (Post Schools) in the Inner London Education Authority. He is the author of a national study funded by the Department of Education and Science on youth and race in the inner city.

Reena Bhavnani – Education Consultant, trainer and freelance researcher. She is a specialist in development work on women's issues and on women's education rights.

ACKNOWLEDGEMENT

A great number of people, far too many to mention, collaborated with us from the moment Ian Macdonald was commissioned to conduct the Inquiry, throughout the course of the Inquiry and during the production of our report. We thank them all for their time, their patience and, above all, their courage.

Foremost among them are the Ullah family, and in particular Mrs and Mr Ullah and their daughter Selina. Their willingness to re-live the pain and devastation of the murder of Ahmed was second only to their determination that his death shall not be in vain.

We are grateful to Nigel de Noronha and Salma Ahmed who carried out research on our behalf and acted as a source of advice, and to Dr Elinor Kelly of the Extra Mural Department of Manchester University whose independent research was commissioned on our behalf by Manchester City Council. Her report, produced under great pressure, is set out in Chapter 26.

We cannot name the many employees of Manchester City Council who have made our task easier, particularly those from the Education Department and the Town Clerk's Department. Ruby Khan has now left her employment in the Education Department and we would like to express our appreciation of the tremendous work she did behind the scenes on our behalf, not least in making available to us mountains of relevant documents from the Education Department.

The City Council also provided two clerks to the Inquiry from their staff, Moira Suringer and Martin Lugsdin, and appointed Yasmin Hasvad to be our personal assistant and cope with the secretarial work of the Inquiry. We are grateful for all their work. Throughout the Inquiry, Marguerite Russell acted as counsel to the Inquiry and prepared a summary of the evidence. She was indefatigible throughout. She was instructed by Jack Thornley (until he resigned) and by Robert Lizar, both experienced local solicitors. Forewarned of the enormity of the task Robert Lizar appointed three talented interviewers, Airinne Ryan, Carol Micah, and Hilary Somerlad, with secretarial assistance from Margaret Irving. They were the engine room of the Inquiry and carried out their respective tasks with great skill and professionalism.

We would also like to thank all those who gave evidence to us. Some are named in the report, but many more asked to remain anonymous.

ACKNOWLEDGEMENT

We have respected their wish and have not included a list of witnesses in our report.

Apart from the particular help we received from Manchester City Council we would also like to acknowledge their courageous decision to set up the Inquiry and to allow us to have full autonomy from them whatever conclusions we might reach.

FOREWORD[1]

Involvement in discussion, starting with people from where they are and moving forward with them, informed the whole of our Inquiry. The non-publication of our report has resulted in the opposite happening, where nothing is discussed. There has been no public meeting at Burnage High School to discuss our report. The council forbids such a meeting. The teachers asked for a meeting with us. We want to have a meeting with the teachers. We asked the council. They said 'No'.

Many parents and students want to know what is happening, but the parents and students of Burnage High School only find out what is going on at their school by reading about it in the *Machester Evening News* or some other paper, or by watching it on the television, and that has been their history since at least 1985, and probably since the incident involving the son of the Bangladeshi Deputy High Commissioner in 1982.

Now, the way that we started this Inquiry, the way we worked this Inquiry, and the way we had hoped that things would follow through is quite important. Let me start at the beginning and say how we came into existence. On the day after the murder, there was a very large meeting held at Bangladeshi House which is a community centre, a mile from the school. It was an overflow meeting rather like the meeting here tonight. Many people who came to that meeting came with the memory of the incident of the Bangladeshi Deputy High Commissioner's son in 1982 at the front of their minds.

A lot of people who came were students or had recently left school, and they immediately saw the murder of Ahmed as a metaphor of their own lives and experience, living in Manchester, and they were disturbed and angry. On the platform, the community elders and community leaders had lined up the Chief Education Officer, a Chief Superintendent of Police, and other important people.

The Chief Superintendent arrived late. Maybe he had not time to guage the feelings of the meeting. When he spoke he created an angry outcry by repeating what the police had already told the press on the day of the murder – there was no evidence of any racial overtones to the killing. When the youth in the hall reacted, he went on to warn them that they should not be saying things about the murder because it was now *sub judice*. To the youth it was as if they were being told 'your

ix

feelings aren't really legitimate, your experience isn't legitimate and if you discuss this thing, watch out for contempt of Court'.

The youth went away angry and disgruntled and formed their own organisation, the Ahmed Ullah Memorial Committee, and it was an organisation with a lot of ups and a lot of downs, and eventually it petered out just after the trial. It was an organisation which based itself on the experience of other Asian youth movements in Southall, in Newham and in Bradford, and they organised around the slogan 'self defence is no offence'.

Well you can imagine that the community elders and leaders were very worried about this mobilisation and the threat it posed to their own standing. They did two things.

They said to the council: 'you have got to have a public inquiry into this business' and they said to the police with whom they had ongoing relations: 'you have got to retract what you have said'. They entered into a spirited correspondence with the police and obtained some success in getting them to retract, but that is another story. The other thing (positive or negative, only history will tell) was that I became the embodiment of the Public Inquiry. I don't think I was the original idea for the Public Inquiry but I was the eventual idea and I was approached in November 1986.

At that time we couldn't do anything because of the trial of Darren Coulburn. After his trial was over in February 1987 I got down to business and met Ahmed's family and as many community organisations as I could. I met all the teacher trade unions, the National Association of Headteachers, and other representative bodies. I met various members of the council and their officials. There were two matters which I discussed with all of these people. One was the panel, and two was the terms of reference.

Draft terms of reference were submitted to the council by many of those organisations. I then took the drafts and knocked them into a shorter form and held further discussion to see that the terms of reference suited them and that they agreed with them. The eventual terms of reference were put to the principal organisations, unions and individuals, and agreed by them.

I went through the same process with the procedures for the Inquiry – whether it should sit in public (my original idea) or private, and so forth. That was the way I intended to work and the way that the Inquiry in fact worked. We did everything as a result of discussion and, wherever possible, by consensus and agreement.

All our procedures, including our decision to hold it in private, were

arrived at in consultation with representatives of community organisations and of the teacher trade unions, including the National Association
of Headteachers. Originally I had gone along, saying, 'I think we'll hold
a public inquiry.' The community organisations said, 'well our people
won't give you any evidence'. One instance shows how frightened
people were. A young Bangladeshi student had given an interview on
television shortly after the murder, and his parents were so frightened
that he was flown to Bangladesh immediately afterwards. That was the
level of fear within the community. If people had to talk to us publicly
about their experiences, there was no question of them coming to give
us evidence and they made that clear.

As for the teachers, I went along to a meeting with them and said,
'O.K. these are the procedures.' There were about 40 people round the
table. The teachers trade unions are a formidable lot when they get
together. They said, 'no, no no. You will not get one single one of our
members giving evidence to you if you hold this in public.'

So all these procedures were agreed.

When we came to hold our Inquiry, we held it in Longsight library
and again, a lot of the people who came and spoke to us only came after
prior meetings and discussions about the inquiry, its procedures and
what it was about. For example, there was a lot of fear among the
teachers at Burnage High School, because of the whole history of that
school, and, let it be said, because of the particular management style at
that school. The panel went down there to talk to staff. At that stage no
one was coming forward, not a single teacher.

At the meeting the hall was packed. About 70 out of a staff of 100
turned up. I got up to address them and explain why we needed their
evidence. Other panel members spoke. No one moved a muscle. No one
moved their eyes. No one moved their head. People stared stonily at us.
We were getting absolutely no reaction, nothing. Then at the end of the
meeting two teachers came up when we were leaving the hall and when
they thought no one else was looking. That broke the ice. Then we had
meetings. We had to. People wanted to discuss the process of giving
evidence before they eventually came. We had no powers of subpoena.
We were not like the Cleveland or King's Cross Inquiries. If people
were going to give evidence they could only give evidence because they
wanted to, and because they trusted what we were likely to do with that
evidence, and how we would use it.

We took evidence in formal session from 165 witnesses during the
months of May, June, July and September 1987. We had statements
from some 200. We met people on an informal basis, or, part of the

panel did, in youth clubs, on the streets. We had two people who did separate interviews of young Asian students – boys and girls. We interviewed individuals. We commissioned a general survey, an attitudinal survey, where 900 students in three different schools (none of them Burnage) were interviewed in their classrooms.

So a lot of people came and put into this Inquiry their thoughts, feelings and experience, as well as their accounts of what had happened. Then we sat down and we wrote our report. We tried to distil that evidence and make some sense of it. We tried to give some kind of analytical framework, so that after the inquiry was over, those same people who had participated in it (and I use the word 'participated' quite deliberately) could continue their participation in the things they were trying to do as part of the whole school community

Our report was seen by us very much as a campaigning document. We were not sitting in judgement. We were trying to produce a document which people could use.

When we told the council of our recommendations in a confidential briefing on 14 January 1988, we asked if we could have a launching conference and invite all those groups and individuals who had participated in the Inquiry. The idea was that they should come armed beforehand with a copy of our report, unexpurgated, unedited, with all the purple passages. We have never seen ourselves as delivering the last word. We have seen our report as a beginning of a discussion and participation, and involvement – an involvement of the whole school community. But that was not to be so.

So now we have decided after all the shenanigans, the toings and froings, that if Manchester won't publish it, if Mr Baker won't publish it, then we will.

We feel confident about the integrity of our report. We feel that where we have criticised people we have criticised them fairly. We have criticised them based upon the evidence that we have received. We believe that our criticisms are justified in every single case and we are prepared to put our personal assets behind that view. That is a dangerous thing for anyone to do, but we feel that there is such enormous public interest in what we have to say, that we will be fully justified and that we will have the widespread public support that we need.

We publish, not because we are claiming to have discovered a new recipe, but because we believe that by putting into our report the feelings and experience of hundreds of people from Manchester schools, we can all take the struggle against racial violence and racial harassment forward to a new stage and can use positively the lessons of Burnage.

In particular we can learn from the death of Ahmed Ullah, because, as far as we are concerned, a very strong motivating force for us throughout this Inquiry has been that Ahmed Iqbal Ullah shall not have died in vain.

FOOTNOTE

[1]Edited transcript of Ian Macdonald's speech at the public meeting on the Macdonald Inquiry at Southall Town Hall on 29th July 1988

'PRINT NOT'

by Laurie Bullas, Manchester Evening News

There was always a clear understanding on all sides that Manchester City Council would publish the findings of the Macdonald Inquiry. So from the time it ended on September 30 last year I regularly asked the Town Hall Public Relations Office for the date of publication.

Month after month passed, but a date was finally fixed and a press conference arranged for Wednesday, March 30. It did not take place. Two days before it was due I learned that the council had scrapped the launch. I was also told by the council that Mr Macdonald and his panel were to go ahead with the Press conference and publish their summary and conclusions independently. Then that possibility was ruled out.

At that stage I felt I had no alternative but to publish information I had already had about the content of the report, and this provided the Manchester Evening News with a front page lead which also revealed the row over publication. There was widespread criticism of what was then taken to be simply a delay caused, the council said, by the length of the report and late alterations to the text.

Panel members had briefed council leader Graham Stringer and chief officers on the report's contents, conclusions and recommendations on January 14 and insisted that the complete report was with the council little more than two weeks later. In the controversy non-publication inevitably caused, the council emphasised the changes made to the report after that date. But there was never any satisfactory explanation for the lost weeks between January 30 and March 14, when the council's principal legal officer, Mr Roy Ingham, had an 'initial sight' of the crucial final chapter. The parting of the ways between the council and the inquiry panel came at a stormy private meeting on March 25. As it turned out, there was more at stake than delay in publication.

According to a report which went to the council's policy committee, Mr Ingham expressed concern about the content of the chapter and, on advice from counsel, suggested alterations which were accepted by Mr Macdonald. Then at the meeting on March 25 the council insisted that further advice from specialist defamation counsel was needed. In the meantime, Mr Macdonald was instructed not to publish and warned that the council would accept no liability for the consequences.

On April 20, with the local council elections in full swing, Councillor Stringer said the council could not publish the report because of advice given by leading libel lawyers Mr Richard Hartley, QC, and Mr Richard Walker. A major concern was that, in the face of such legal advice, elected members could be personally surcharged for damages and costs in the event of a successful libel action. Any such action can be defeated if the words complained of can be proved to be true or to be honest comment on a matter of public importance. But counsel pointed out that the inquiry had taken evidence in private and had locked it away until the year 2,000.

In correspondence with the council, Mr Macdonald – by now himself a QC – raised two crucial questions. Would anyone sue? Were the allegations true? He insisted that any action could be successfully defended and complained that at no time had the panel been given the opportunity to help assess the risks involved in publication.

A demand by the overwhelming majority of teaching and non-teaching staff at Burnage for publication of the report was followed swiftly by an anonymous leak of its final conclusions and recommendations, Chapter (33) to the Manchester Evening News. The chapter appeared in full on April 25 in a special supplement which was widely praised and was, until now, the only substantial public source of information on many of the report's recommendations. Coincidentally, the city education committee met on the day of the Manchester Evening News publication and decided to give preliminary consideration to the full report in private at its meeting on May 17. Despite all the previous delays, members of the committee by that time had copies of the report released to them under qualified privilege – protection from libel action unless malice can be proved. Other members of the city council, Burnage governors and certain officers also received copies on the same basis. But public access was restricted to 11 chapters and three out of eight appendices, all cleared by lawyers of any possible risk of libel action.

Mr Macdonald and other panel members attended the May 17 education committee meeting, but the four-hour debate behind closed doors was concerned almost entirely with the ban on publication rather than the content of the report. The Labour-dominated committee, and the full council the following day, confirmed the decision not to publish, although it did acknowledge the "professionalism and competence" of the inquiry.

As a result, the panel revived the idea of independent publication, although it welcomed the council's request to Education Secretary Mr Kenneth Baker to publish the report under the protection of Parliamentary privilege. When Mr Macdonald raised the possibility of independent publication in a letter to the council, Mr Ingham replied with a repeated instruction not to publish and a renewed warning that the council would accept no responsibility for any consequences.

The city council's letter to Mr Baker included its constantly repeated insistence that it wished to see the report published in full and its offer of freedom to publish to anyone who would guarantee to meet the cost of any libel suits. On June 17, Mr Macdonald wrote offering a personal indemnity from himself and his three colleagues on the inquiry panel. The letter said: "We have considered very carefully the advice given to Manchester City Council by Counsel and in particular what they have to say about the defences of justification and fair comment. As a panel we feel confident about the factual basis of our report and that we would have a good defence to any action in defamation."

Shortly afterwards, Mr Baker formally announced what he had previously trailed – that he would not use his power to publish the report in a way which would prevent legal action. So the panel was left with no alternative but to leave the full report beyond public reach or put their personal assets at risk.

THE MEDIA COVERAGE

On Monday April 25th, under an 'Exclusive' label, Manchester Evening News published in full the chapter of conclusions in the Macdonald Inquiry report. The front page banner headline was: 'BURNAGE: THE WHOLE STORY'. Under that headline, the education correspondent, Laurie Bullas, gave a summary of the Inquiry's conclusions, which included the following passages:

'. . . The report concludes that the murder of 13-year-old Ahmed Ullah was racist, although it says there is no evidence that race-hate was killer Darren Coulburn's prime motive.

. . . And its wider inquiry into racism and violence in Manchester schools suggest a murder could have happened elsewhere.

. . . The report is highly critical of Burnage headmaster Dr Gerry Gough and his two deputies and it recommends that they should be moved elsewhere.

. . . It claims (Dr Gough's) application of doctrinaire multi-culturalism and anti-racism has been an 'unmitigated disaster', achieving the opposite of what was intended.

. . . Instead of exercising the common sense and judgment schools usually bring to sticky situations, the dogmatism results in confusion and lack of logic, the report says.

. . . The report draws attention to an anomaly between schools in deprived white working class areas and those serving districts with large black and Asian populations.

. . . It expresses support for the view that equal opportunities policies ought to cover class for the benefit of 'the white working class majority'.

In that same edition, the *Manchester Evening News* printed an 8-page special 'pull-out' report, giving, word for word, the concluding chapter of the Burnage Report. On the front of that report, Bullas again highlights the panel's conclusion that:

'there was no evidence that the murder would have happened if Ahmed Ullah had been white or of some other ethnic origin. In our view, the situation in which the two boys met in fatal combat would not have taken place if Ahmed had been white. *Racism was one of the vital ingredients that brought the two boys together*'. (Our emphasis).

In addition to Laurie Bullas' comments on the conclusions and to the chapter of the conclusions itself, the paper carried the following editorial:

BURNAGE REPORT: WHY WE PUBLISH

Today, the *Manchester Evening News* publishes – in full – the conclusions and recommendations of the Macdonald Inquiry into Racial Violence in Manchester Schools.

This is the inquiry, following the murder of Ahmed Iqbal Ullah at Burnage High School, that inquiry chairman Ian Macdonald QC is unable to publish and which Manchester City Council is unwilling to publish.

The Evening News is publishing it because we feel that the pupils, parents and teachers at the school deserve to read the report; and also because we feel that the report makes a major, constructive contribution to the understanding and therefore the obliteration of racism in our society.

The inquiry's recommendations deserve close attention, and – if they are not shelved as Mr Macdonald fears – they will make an important contribution to easing the racial tensions which clearly exist in our towns and cities, and therefore our schools. Tensions that could well be increased as an Asian community perceive the white "establishment" covering up their own faults by suppressing the report.

The report concludes that the murder of 13 year old Ahmed Ullah by a white boy could have happened anywhere.

But we hope the city council will act on the inquiry's proposals for Burnage, which has suffered a dramatic drop in its intake following this and other controversies in recent years.

It is a great tribute to the quality of the staff – and the report gives them high praise – that parents with boys there now still express satisfaction with the teaching.

It would be surprising if there were unanimous backing for the Macdonald analysis of Burnage's problems or its solutions for them. But we believe they will command widespread respect and support. They offer hope for the future.

Burnage clearly needs a new start and the governors and the city council – even if they cannot accept the report's conclusions – should cooperate in making it possible.

Two aspects of the report deserve special attention – not only in Manchester but nationally.

The report suggests that schools in deprived white working class areas need the kind of special help available to those with large numbers of black and Asian pupils.

And it claims that the particular approach to anti-racism adopted at Burnage is fatally flawed and has achieved the opposite of what was intended.

For all the problems surrounding the report the city council deserves credit for commissioning it.

The report praises the council's efforts to promote multi-cultural and multi-racial policies and draws attention to much good work.

So we are puzzled as to why the council has not done what we have done – and published.

Macdonald says that everyone connected either directly or indirectly with the school should get a summary of his report.

We have done this: The council should have done this.

Manchester Evening News readers, at least, were left in no doubt as to the Macdonald Inquiry findings and their relevance to education in Manchester and elsewhere.

The Attack on Anti-Racism

But Manchester Evening News is a provincial newspaper with a local readership. The national media had been alerted, with the full knowledge and co-operation of the Manchester City Council, to the fact that Manchester intended to publish the full report on March 30th, but had had to live with the news of a delay in publication at the last minute. Their appetites had been whetted by an earlier leak of two of the report's findings in the week that Machester City Council cancelled the planned publication.

What did they make of the Manchester Evening News scoop?

Between April 25th and May 9th, the national media published a whole number of stories backed up by editorial comment which either stated categorically or implied that anti-racism and anti-racists at Burnage High School were to blame for Ahmed Ullah's murder. They proceeded to mount a sustained attack on anti-racism, anti-racist policies, "looney left" Councils with such policies, and anti-racist approaches in education and schooling.

"Burnage" was suddenly writ large as a question-mark against anti-racist education. The findings of the Inquiry panel, the concerns of the panel members, of the Ullah family and of the Burnage High School community were converted, at a stroke, into the media's obsession with the very notion of 'anti-racism' and with those who encourage policies and practices in relation to it.

The same evidence Laurie Bullas scrutinised to write his reports was available to the national media. With the findings printed only in the Manchester Evening News, however, they were at liberty to distort the facts, substitute myth for reality, and project to the nation an image of a demonic anti-racist crusade sweeping through our cities and placing "the British people" at risk.

The day after the Manchester Evening News report appeared, the Daily Mail blamed anti-racism for causing Ahmed Ullah's death and condemned 'this dangerous obsession' with race which was 'endemic to certain left-dominated education authorities'. It invoked Raymond Honeyford (on whom the British media has bestowed the dubious honour of being a 'martyr' to anti-racism) and quoted him as saying: "the sort of policies this head was following were precisely the same as they tried to force on me. The report shows that they are a disaster".

Other pundits of the right wing were also invoked, including Rhodes Boyson who claimed that the Burnage report should serve as a lesson for areas like Brent "which has similar anti-racist policies which do not seem to have helped".

The daily heavies weighed in as well, adding their own commentaries which bore little resemblance to what the Manchester Evening News had reprinted from our report. The Daily Telegraph stated categorically the day after the conclusions were leaked: "Anti-racist policy led to killing". The Times blamed "left wing ideas" at the school for engendering 'tension', and, in its editorial column pointed to a number of 'malign consequences arising from the fanaticism of those who march under the banner of "anti-racism", using public money for their campaigns'. Ahmed Ullah's murder was seen as the latest in a string of these malign consequences.

Peter Wilby, education editor of the 'Independent', called into question the policies operated by Bradford, Berkshire, ILEA and other such education authorities, suggesting that supporters of such policies had suffered 'a serious setback' from the Burnage Inquiry report. As far as Mr Wilby was concerned, 'anti-racist' education itself had proved 'A disaster'.

Peter Wilby's 'Viewpoint' article provoked much panic in education offices and in town halls across Britain. A number of education officers who for years had resisted any notions of multi-culturalism let alone anti-racism, were liberally handing copies of the Wilby article and "The

xx

Times" editorial to their middle management colleagues and to those advisers and teachers who had constantly cajoled them to take those issues on board. Such education managers considered their position vindicated. Here, at last, was an official endorsement of their view that anti-racist education was dangerous . . . It had even "led to a killing".

Disturbed by the media coverage and by the obvious glee of some of their colleagues, other education managers and practitioners sought urgent clarification from members of the Macdonald Inquiry Panel as to what we did and did not say. The Guardian provided an opportunity for a member of the Panel, Gus John, to comment on the Burnage story and challenge the interpretations the media had provided of what the report concluded. Those people in education departments who had so eagerly distributed the 'Independent' and 'Times' articles could not be persuaded to do the same in relation to the Guardian article.

Such was the extent of media misunderstanding of our findings and of the preoccupation with the role of anti-racist education in the events at Burnage High School, that we felt it necessary to hold a press conference and deal with the media coverage the report had been receiving.

The Macdonald Inquiry Panel issued the following press statement on May 5th 1988, embargoed till the press conference on May 9th.

PUTTING THE RECORD STRAIGHT

Macdonald Inquiry Rejects Demands for Secretary of State Investigation of Lea's Anti-Racist Education Policies

One year ago, May 1987, Manchester City Council set up an Inquiry into circumstances surrounding the murder of 13-year-old Ahmed Iqbal Ullah by a 13-year-old white pupil at Burnage High School in September 1986. The two students met in fatal combat because Ahmed had intervened to stop Darren Coulburn's racist bullying of smaller Asian boys.

The Inquiry was led by Ian Macdonald QC assisted by Lily Khan, Director of Asian Studies at Tower Hamlets Adult Education Institute in the East End of London, Reena Bhavnani, a sociology lecturer at Ruskin College, Oxford, and Gus John, Assistant Education Officer in the Inner London Education Authority, and former Vice-Principal of Community Education in North Manchester. Manchester City Council had undertaken to publish the Inquiry report, and received a confidential briefing on the Inquiry's findings in January of this year. A publication date was set for March 30th but was cancelled because printed copies of the report could not be produced in time, and because Manchester City Council became concerned that parts of the report were defamatory and might expose the Council to libel action.

On Monday March 28th, two days before the aborted launch of the report, the Manchester Evening News (M.E.N.) ran a story in which they leaked two of the main findings of the Inquiry. On Monday April 25th, the M.E.N. printed the whole chapter of conclusions and recommendations from the report.

The report, as leaked in M.E.N. criticises the senior management of the school for applying 'moral', 'symbolic' and 'doctrinaire' anti-racism, and for failing to involve the whole school community, including white students and parents, in their strategies to tackle racism.

The report dealt with the background to the murder and the school's handling of the aftermath of the murder. Particular attention was paid to the polarisation along racial lines which took place after the murder and which resulted in a series of flare-ups in the school in March 1987. The report concludes that polarisation was due in large measure to police denials that the murder was racist, as well as to the clumsy and inept way in which the aftermath of the murder was managed by the school.

We conclude that the school failed to act sensibly and responsibly when, in 1982, a Bangladeshi student suffered serious facial injuries in an unprovoked attack by white students. Even if one were prepared to give the school the benefit of the doubt and go along with their view that that brutal atack had no racist motive, there is no evidence that the school found such a sudden and mindless outbreak of violence sufficiently disturbing to involve the whole school community in working to create a less violent learning environment. We received no evidence either that a programme of monitoring was introduced to detect whether or not black students tended to be the victims of racial attacks, racist bullying or racist name-calling that may or may not result in fights.

The school pacified the injured student's family and the Bangladeshi community. Nevertheless, a residue of anger and much anxiety remained within the Bangladeshi community and particularly amongst school students and young adults. Following Ahmed's murder, that community immediately recalled the 1982 incident and the lack of robust action on the part of the school and local authority. This lack of action, they claimed, contributed to the climate in which young Asian students continued to be harassed and attacked, and in which bigger students such as Ahmed felt impelled to intervene.

An effective anti-racist policy should have eliminated that climate, and the issue of violence in general and racial violence in particular should have been tackled in a forthright manner, both as a discipline and a curriculum issue. Similarly, if the school had been operating an effective anti-racist policy, the polarisation which occurred in February/March 1987 could have been prevented.

In saying so, we are clearly not suggesting that racism does not exist, or that it is some mythical invention of 'left wing' Councils, or that anti-racist policies and strategies have no place in schools. Nor do we suggest that because anti-racist policies were applied in a senseless and counter-productive way in that particular school, all anti-racist policies should be abandoned or considered suspect.

It is because we consider the task of combatting racism to be such a critical part of the function of schooling and education that we condemn symbolic, moral and doctrinaire anti-racism. We urge care, rigour and caution in the formulating and implementing of such policies because we consider the struggle against racism and racial injustice to be an essential element in the struggle for social justice which we see as the ultimate goal of education.

School and local education authorities, therefore, are invited to ask themselves, to what extent does their particular brand of anti-racist policy and the manner of its application result in even worse conditions for black people, and earn the policy makers ridicule from those on the right?

We urge Manchester City Council to publish the full Inquiry report because it is our view that it will greatly assist schools and local authorities in re-appraising their own policies and practices. . .

SHOULD MR KENNETH BAKER INTERVENE?

We say 'yes', and make suggestions as to how he might do so.

Following the Manchester Evening News leak, the tabloid press led the rest of the media up a 'colour-blind' alley, invoking Raymond Honeyford, Rhodes Boyson and other exponents on the right, and arguing that now, at last, even a panel of people with 'impeccable left-wing credentials' had condemned anti-racist policies. That lobby concluded from their reading of the Manchester Evening News report that anti-racist policies in Burnage High School resulted directly in the death of Ahmed Ullah and in the violent incidents in and around the school in February/March 1987. Those events are thus added to the other causes celebre such as the Honeyford issue, the McGoldrick issue, etc. That lobby have also called for the Secretary of State to intervene and 'investigate' the anti-racist policies of those L.E.A.'s who have them.

We repudiate totally any suggestion that the anti-racist education policy in Burnage High School led either to the death of Ahmed Ullah or to the disturbances in March 1987. Far from suggesting that Burnage High School and other schools should abandon strategies for combatting racism and adopt a 'colour-blind' approach, we state emphatically that the work of all schools should be informed by a policy that recognises the pernicious and all-pervasive nature of racism in the lives of students, teachers and parents, black and white, and the need to confront it. We further emphasise that this is not only a task facing schools in inner cities or in what some people still insist on calling 'immigrant areas'. It is incumbent upon schools and colleges everywhere to tackle the issue of racism in the same way as they recognise the need to accept the technological revolution and prepare students to be technically competent in an age of new technology.

We welcome the suggestion that the Secretary of State reads the full report which is with Manchester City Council. We trust that having done so he would rule against local authorities and individual schools adopting a 'colour-blind' approach, or soft-pedalling on the need to develop strategies to combat racism. The report will provide the Secretary of State with ample evidence that racism cannot be wished away, and does not go away voluntarily if ignored. The report also points out how dangerous to the well-being of black students and to the social development of white students a 'colour-blind' approach to racism is. Such an approach is much more a recipe for disaster than any badly applied anti-racist policy could ever be.

Now that the Home Office has accepted that racial attacks are not a figment of black people's imagination, and now that the Department of Education and Science is aware of the growing body of evidence of the vast extent of racial harassment in schools, evidence that includes the recent Commission for Racial Equality publication "Learning in Terror", it is to be hoped that the Secretary of State for Education would see fit to give a national lead in terms of the responsibility of all local education authorities and all schools to develop effective measures for arresting this growing menace.

If Mr Baker chooses to 'reform' British education in this single aspect, Ahmed Ullah will not have died in vain.

xxiv

Unfortunately the media failed to report the Inquiry team's clarification of issues in the Burnage story with the same vigour with which they spread their original distortions.

Subsequent to that press conference, thousands of copies of the press statement were distributed to organisations and groups across the country, as were equivalent numbers of the Manchester Evening News special report, originally published on April 25th.

CONTENTS

CHAPTER 1

Burnage High School

On the morning of Wednesday 17th September 1986, Ahmed Iqbal Ullah was murdered in the playground of Burnage High School. That tragic event was to lead to the setting up of this Inquiry.

One of the Inquiry's terms of reference relates specifically to Burnage High School. The major part of this report, therefore, focuses on Burnage.

What sort of school is it?

The school lies about five miles south of the centre of Manchester. It is a split-site school, with the Lower School housing Forms 1, 2 and 3, and the Upper School Forms 4, 5 and 6. The two halves of the school are about ½ mile apart, with a busy major road running between them.

Burnage caters for boys aged between 11 and 19.

At present, Burnage is an eight form entry school, with 240 boys joining it each year. Some 1,500 boys are at the school, of whom 150 are in the sixth form. The boys are expected to wear school uniform.

Of the total student body, one-third or some 530 are of 'New Commonwealth and Pakistan origin'. This is a slightly higher proportion of black students than is suggested by statistics available for the local catchment area, unlesss one looks specifically at Longsight. The following table (see page 2) gives a rough indication of changes in the racial composition of the population and of the level of poverty in the approximate present catchment area of Burnage High School from 1971 to 1981. It also gives a comparison with figures for the rest of Manchester.

The 1981 figure almost certainly understates the black population, since it does not include households where the head of household is black, and was born in the United Kingdom. This is also true of the 1971 figure, but the distortion of the figure is likely to be very much less than now. However, what is clear from the figures is that there has been a significant increase in the population of New Commonwealth and Pakistani origin since 1971.

Burnage has about 100 full-time teachers, of whom one is an Afro-Caribbean woman who teaches drama, and one a South Asian woman

1

	Burnage High School Catchment Area		All Manchester	
	1971	1981	1971	1981
Students aged 5 to 15 years as a percentage of whole population	16.3%	15.6%(a)	17.6%	15.7%
Economically inactive	6.8%	16.0%(b)	8.4%	17.3%
Parents born in New Commonwealth/Pakistan	5.9%	12.5%(c)	4.1%	7.9%
Households living at density of more than one person per room	9.2%	6.2%(d)	9.4%	5.7%
Population decline from 1971 to 1981		(12.6%)		(17.5%)

(a) This figure varies from Withington (13.3%) to Longsight (18.5%)
(b) This figure varies from Withington (11%) to Longsight (23.6%)
(c) This figure varies from Burnage (2.8%) to Longsight (30.6%)
(d) This figure varies from Withington (4.0%) to Longsight (10.9%)

---

who teaches physics. Although about 35% of the student population is black, the figure for full-time teaching staff is only 2%.

The school also employs a black reprographics technician, full-time, and the following part-time staff, all black:

2 peripatetic teachers of Urdu
2 peripatetic teachers of Music
1 Library Assistant
1 School Meals Supervisor

Most, if not all, of those staff have been engaged in the last 3 years.

Brief History of Burnage

Burnage High was formed in 1967 as a comprehensive school for boys.

The original grammar school amalgamated with Ladybarn Secondary Modern to form Burnage High.

The school now occupies buildings that are over fifty years old, on its two sites.

In 1986, a review of secondary school accommodation noted that both buildings were then deficient, for teaching purposes. Since then some improvements have been made. One of these was the construction of a new art building at the Lower School. However, despite this start, a major construction scheme has never been fully implemented. The major part of the teaching accommodation at Burnage High has thus remained untouched since 1967. The 1985 Inspectorate report noted that the school buildings reflect the impact of several years of cutbacks by central Government, particularly cutbacks on local authority expenditure.

Where does Burnage draw its students from?

Between 1972 and 1982 the school drew children from an area within a three mile radius of the school. Schools filled their places by applying this formula:

> A third to half of the available places went to children with a brother or sister in the school.
> A further third of the places went to children within the catchment area.
> Some 20% of the intake would be chosen by random selection from among those who had applied and who had not gained places under the other two entry criteria.

Before 1982, therefore, Burnage High could draw its intake from a greater potential number of students. Parents outside the three mile radius were choosing Burnage. Most were attracted by its grammar school ethos which it retained despite being a comprehensive. Others who had had other children at the school continued to send their boys there, even though they might not be in the catchment area.

Catchment Area 1982 to date

In 1982 the system was changed to a feeder school system. Burnage has twelve feeder schools.

> Acacias Primary (Burnage)
> Alma Park (Levenshulme)
> Birch Primary (Burnage)
> Chapel Street Primary (Levenshulme)
> Crowcroft Park (Longsight)
> St. Agnes C.E. Primary (Longsight)
> St. Andrews C.E. (Levenshulme)
> St. John C.E. Primary (Longsight)
> St. James C.E. Primary (Rusholme)
> Old Moat Primary (Withington)
> Mauldeth Road Primary (Withington)
> Ladybarn Primary (Withington)

3

Primary schools are feeders for more than one secondary school. The feeder school system does, however, define a catchment area for the majority of students at Burnage.

Manchester re-organised its secondary education in 1982. Schools which were not considered viable were closed, and the re-organised schools were assisted in reviewing their curriculum and the systems they operated. They also had significant changes in their staffing.

Keith Joseph, then Secretary of State for Education, declared Burnage a school of 'proven worth'. It was thereby exempted from the re-organisation that was going on around it. As a result, it avoided the need to carry out a curriculum review, and the staff remained more or less the same as before.

Burnage thus had a large proportion of its teaching staff who had spent many years there, and whose only experience of teaching was at Burnage.

Those teachers were mainly responsible for the prevailing ethos within the school, which many parents found attractive, not least because it reflected the old grammar school.

The 1982 re-organisation led to the formation of 11–16 schools, and of separate 6th form colleges. Burnage, however, fought to keep its 6th form, and succeeded with a little help from Keith Joseph.

A 'ringed fence' was placed around those Manchester schools which formed part of the re-organisation. This meant that staff could apply to transfer from one re-organised school to another, or for higher posts within the re-organised schools. They could also apply for posts in schools outside the 'ringed fence'. Thus, Burnage gained one of its deputy leaders, Peter Moors, who moved from Levenshulme High School at re-organisation. On the other hand, Burnage teaching staff were more limited in their ability to move from Burnage to posts inside of the 'ringed fence'.

1982 was significant for Burnage in another respect. Following the departure of the permanent headteacher in the middle 1970s, Burnage experienced a succession of temporary headships until the appointment in 1982 of Dr Gerry Gough.

On his appointment, Dr Gough faced many challenges. He inherited a school where corporal punishment was still very widely used, and with a long-serving staff who had their origins in the tripartite system of education, a system that favoured streaming and the application of traditional curriculum methods.

In 1982 also, Manchester Education Committee was pressing ahead with a number of policy initiatives, and providing in-service training

4

and inspectorate support for management and staff in schools and colleges to take those policies forward. Among those were the abolition of corporal punishment, and the adoption of multi-cultural policies in education.

These policy initiatives coincided with the new feeder system for the admission of students to the school. The stage was thus set for the whole school community at Burnage to face a number of challenges and take the school forward under the leadership of a new Head and Deputy Head.

In later chapters, we explore the relationship between these policies, the manner in which they were implemented at Burnage, and the circumstances surrounding the murder of Ahmed Iqbal Ullah.

CHAPTER 2

Murder in the Playground

By Monday 15th September 1986, the new Autumn term at Burnage Lower School had only just begun, but already the behaviour of one of the students in Form 3H was causing concern. Form 3H was a mixture of two 'special needs classes' which had formerly been called 'slow learners'. Such classes were being phased out, and 3H contained students considered not ready for mixed ability classes in the mainstream of the school. It was accepted that these students had low self esteem and tended to be more disruptive.

On the 3rd September, the very first day of term, Darren Coulburn had been involved in a breaktime incident, when he and another boy had bullied a junior school student from Ladybarn School. The boy's face was slapped and drink taken from him. He was kicked and punched. Within two days of the start of term, Sue Raddings, the form teacher for 3H, had Darren Coulburn under observation. He was the biggest boy in the form, and he was bullying smaller Asian students. He was quite subtle in his bullying: he ordered them around; he did not give them letters that everyone else had been given; if he collected up books, he would put their books at the bottom of the pile; most worrying of all, he would sneak kicks at them when he passed their desks. Having spoken to Darren without success, the form teacher spoke to the Head of Department, Mr K Mann, who told her to report the incidents to the Deputy Head, Peter Moors. On 5th September, Sue Raddings spoke to Peter Moors about Darren's behaviour.

Peter Moors referred Darren Coulburn's problems to Mike Ellis, the Senior Advisory Teacher concerned with disruptive students. Mike Ellis saw Darren and tried to talk to him about bullying. He also spoke to the form teacher, and, on observing the students, saw that they lined up on racial lines – smaller Asian boys on one side, larger whites on the other. Mike Ellis and Sue Raddings were concerned at the possible racial overtones and so both of them spoke to Lesley Aisthorpe, the head of Community Education. Was Darren bullying because of size? Was he bullying because of race?

Lesley Aisthorpe informally contacted an educational psychologist, Ken MacIntyre, who was concerned with problems of racism. The decision taken was to observe the class for a period.

In another series of meetings, the social worker for Darren attended the school on 8th September 1986. A possible placement for Darren was discussed at the suggestion of Jackie Hill, the senior teacher at the school.

The school was not sent the Report from the Intermediate Treatment Centre, where Darren had gone at the end of the Summer term. None of the staff was aware of this report, which spoke in positive terms of a violent response by Darren Coulburn during assessment.

'There seemed to be no urgency'.

Yet this was not the first time that Darren Coulburn had caused concern at Burnage. In fact he had quite a history. He lived alone with his father, who had suffered three heart attacks, and in September 1986 was awaiting a heart by-pass operation. In class, Darren Coulburn had often been disruptive. He was involved in a number of incidents of bullying and extortion of money from other boys – Asian and white – always smaller than himself. Darren also had a history of truancy and lateness. Neighbours used to 'phone the school, complaining he was hanging around the streets or being a nuisance or annoyance. On one occasion he was brought into school by the police, who had caught him knocking on doors and behaving suspiciously. He was in the Juvenile Court twice in the Autumn term in 1985. On the first occasion it was for stealing a motor cycle. The second occasion was for burning down the school's art block, which he had entered with another boy in order to steal some lighting equipment.

There was also the worry that if Darren Coulburn was still able to remain at Burnage, after a serious act of arson, other boys might believe that similar breaches of discipline would also go unpunished so far as the school was concerned.

His attitudes on race are not clear cut. The other boy involved in burning down the art block was Asian, and Darren used to get into trouble with another boy who was Afro-Caribbean. We were told that he used to call Asian students 'Paki' and did not particularly like Asian children, but this was not an aspect of his behaviour which was seen as problematic. On one occasion Darren came into school drunk. There was a young Indian woman on the school switchboard. Darren called her a 'Paki' and made rude pelvic gestures.

After he was arrested he was sent to Red Bank Approved School to await his trial. He told other boys at the remand centre that he was there for 'killing a Paki' (South Manchester Reporter 13th Feb 1987). Later, we look at the words he used at the time of the murder and shortly afterwards.

8

The burning of the school art block was done during the school holidays and something like £40,000 damage was caused. It only became known to staff several months later, as a result of Darren telling other boys about his involvement. Darren was sentenced to 24 hours at an Attendance Centre.

The Court had dealt with Darren Coulburn, but what should the school do? Burning the art block down, even if done in the school holidays or out of school hours, is a pretty massive event and the charred remains stood testimony to the act long afterwards. It was there to be seen from balconies and corridors by everyone, every day, on arrival at the school, at break times, changes of class and on departure at the end of the day. Everyone knew that Darren Coulburn and the other boy were the culprits. The teacher most directly responsible for him thought that he should move to another school. It would be to his benefit and the benefit of the other boys in his class.

On 3rd December 1985, the matter came before a governors' meeting. The item was put on the secret part of the agenda. No advance notice of the item was given. A request to have the matter deferred was swept aside. Darren and his friend had already been punished by the Court and should not be punished by the school a second time. This was the Headteacher's considered view, and one which the governors were invited to endorse. The argument won the day. With hindsight, one governor told us that if the matter had been more carefully considered, with further teacher input, the decisions would probably not have been any different, but the Governors might have requested that they be notified if either of the boys showed further signs of disturbance.

Darren Coulburn showed further signs of disturbance in the Winter and Summer terms of 1986, but his behaviour was never brought to the attention of the Governors – at least not until after the murder that no-one imagined was to follow.

After the Governors' meeting, Darren's Head of Year, Mr Williams, was told of the outcome by Mr Moors. Then he came back and said: 'that information that I gave you is confidential. Could you make sure you do not tell anybody else?'

Earlier, Mr Williams had issued a memorandum to Darren Coulburn's form teacher, with copies to Mr Moors and Dr Gough, giving the results of his court case. This was issued on November 25th. Nothing was said until December 13th, when Dr Gough attended a meeting in the Head of Year's room and announced to the meeting, without addressing any complaint to the Year Head himself, that such memos were not to be sent in the future, as the result of a court appearance

9

should remain confidential. He thought that Darren had been punished enough. According to our evidence it was public knowledge at Burnage High School that Darren Coulburn had burnt down the art block and public knowledge that he had been arrested and taken to Court for it, but his form teacher was not to be officially told of the outcome.

This is one indication of a management style at Burnage School which will feature again and again throughout this report. Indeed, there are elements in the school's dealings with Darren Coulburn which we have found disturbing. As a result, staff who had to deal with him were not kept in the picture and their views were never made known to the school governors. One thing has puzzled us. At a press conference after the conviction of Darren Coulburn, the Vice Chairman of Governors, Dr Glaizner, was reported as saying:

'After the burning of the art block, as far as I know, Darren was monitored by Education Department Assessors, and they found no evidence to have him placed in a special school.'

The evidence given to us was that Mr Hewitt, the Deputy Head responsible for pastoral care within the whole school, was asked to monitor Darren Coulburn's progress in January 1986. According to him all reports on Darren came to him at his request. However, none of the teachers more directly responsible for Darren Coulburn knew anything about this monitoring and our perusal of all the internal memoranda suggests that not all reports of incidents were passed on to Mr Hewitt. We have found it very surprising and somewhat disturbing that, apart from Mr Hewitt, who is clearly a very conscientious man, no other member of staff, no Educational Welfare Officer, Educational Psychologist or Social Worker knew of any monitoring being carried out on this particular boy.

Mr Hewitt, however, was present at a further meeting held to discuss Darren Coulburn's future on 19th February 1986. Also present was his Social Worker, who had recently informed the school that Darren was the subject of a one-year Supervision Order by the Court, Mr Williams, his Head of Year, and Darren's father. Darren's father expressed concern that Darren was being picked on by other boys because of the fire and because he had recently broken the glass on the school fire alarm and set it off. There was discussion about whether Darren could be moved to another school. Mr Williams was hoping the father would move him. Mr Hewitt was not sure it would be a good thing. It was left that the father should discuss it with Darren.

Mr Hewitt suggested after the meeting that a pre-referral form for the opinion of the Educational Psychologist be prepared. This was done, but when Mr Hewitt saw the form he took the view that no urgent referral was needed. Darren Coulburn was not referred to the Educational Psychologists.

But his behaviour did not improve. On 24th February he was excluded from the school after admitting throwing stones and breaking a window in the school building. In may he was caught by the police house breaking. A week later he was brought into school by two police officers for suspicious behaviour while playing truant. By June the Social Worker had found a placement, and in July Darren went to Penrith Arrow Intermediate Treatment Centre for one month leading up to the end of term.

At that time there was great feeling amongst some members of staff against Darren Coulburn being admitted back into Burnage. The Educational Welfare Officer, Mr Trevor Houston, advised a fresh start in another, smaller school, which could give him more individual attention than at Burnage. Darren's Social Worker took a different view. This was his first adolescent case since he qualified in September 1985. He said the reports from Penrith were very good indeed and everything was OK now, and he saw no problems at all. Since no one at the school had seen the Penrith report, his view prevailed. This is what an important section of Darren Coulburn's assessment at Penrith had to say:

'Monday 1:   Arrived . . . Happy and relaxed, confident enough to push staff member into the river during swimming session.

Tuesday 2:   Darren was being picked on by J . . . at every opportunity. Very soon whole group was involved. Soon stamped out by staff then Darren withdrew into himself . . .

Wednesday 3: Little scuffle with J . . . first thing . . . again being subject of everyone's jokes etc. Didn't let it bother him.

Thursday 4:   Canoeing Derwent Water. Eventually Darren came out of his shell by thumping J . . . on two separate occasions, with the support of Group, causing J . . . to run off. After talk with John G they agreed to try and get on better . . .' (Our emphasis). '. . . still Darren keeping very much himself to himself.'

11

Darren Coulburn's violent display is there portrayed as a welcome contrast to his previous withdrawal. The reaction to this apparent encouragement of violence in a deeply disturbed boy with a history of bullying was sharp. 'Absolutely frightening', 'insane', 'it has cut me to the quick', 'trying to contact Darren and trying to encourage him to find other ways after that . . . is going backwards with your eyes closed.' It was stated very clearly to us that if staff had known of Darren's Penrith experience when the first incidents of bullying were reported at the beginning of the Autumn term, there would have been a quite different reaction. As one teacher put it: 'I would have pushed the panic button, and I just could not have been contained at all. . . I would have called in about every service that I could possibly imagine. I would have communicated with my seniors within a minute of having read that – this is something which is beyond the school's ability to cope with, and this kid is clearly a child in need of desperate help, and I just could not cope with that'.

'There seemed to be no urgency.'

How did Ahmed Ullah experience Burnage? He was a big strong lad, bright, intelligent and good at running. He also had a strong sense of justice and did not easily tolerate injustice.

His sister, Selina, describes how he was happy and made good progress in his first year, but in the second year he appeared to be losing interest in school and in academic life. As the year wore on he seemed to be becoming involved in a number of fights at school. His year head and other teachers seemed satisfied that Ahmed had not been responsible for causing the trouble, but invariably ended up defending himself. Selina states:

> 'Ahmed was a tall youth, and I believe that because of this he was singled out by the English boys as a "leader" of the Asian boys in the school. They seemed to want to provoke trouble with him because he was in a sense representing a challenge to them.'

In that second year, the family also detected a gradual deterioration in Ahmed's confidence in the staff at the school. Selina remembered that he would be very reticent about incidents which happened at school, and that the family would have to press him very strongly in order for him to give any details about incidents which had occurred. However, when he was pressed he would say that there was no point in complaining to the teachers over harassment or attacks, as even some of the teachers appeared to be unsympathetic to Asian youths at the school. She remembered Ahmed telling her that he felt that Asian boys were being 'held back' particularly during sports lessons whilst English boys were given preference and encouragement at their expense. Ahmed felt this to be particularly annoying in view of the fact that he had great sporting prowess himself. He also felt that Asian boys were occasionally 'picked on' by members of staff. He mentioned one incident in which he himself had accidentally opened a door to the wrong classroom, and apologised and left. The teacher, however, apparently called him back and chastised him and apparently also reported him to senior members of staff with the allegation that he had been constantly opening the door and running away, which was not true.

Once, a teacher had to bring Ahmed home from school after he had been taken to hospital to have stitches inserted in his eye. Selina Ullah couldn't recall at what point during the year this was, but she remembers that the teachers told her parents that the incident had not been Ahmed's fault, and they stressed that he had been attacked by a group of other boys and had not provoked any trouble.

Ahmed's third year at Burnage High School began in September 1986. In the first week back at school and also in the second week there were a large number of fights between different racial groups in the school. In one incident, a group of Afro-Caribbean youths attacked a group of Asian boys, and a bus driver taking children home was also attacked. All the other buses in the area were stopped and had to be called to the driver's assistance. The police were also called and the boys were delayed for an hour or so while the matter was controlled. This was simply an example of a series of incidents which occurred at the start of term, although from what Ahmed told his family, the majority of them were smaller day to day incidents involving only individual students rather than large groups.

On Monday the 15th of September 1986 the new Autumn term at Burnage had only just begun, and four Asian lads were playing football in break. Darren Coulburn came up, took their ball, and threw it on a roof. Only when the lads threatened to report Darren to Mr Moors, the Deputy Head, did Darren Coulburn grudgingly return their ball, but not before he had threatened M.A., the boy whose ball it was. 'I'll beat you up after school'.

As M.A. left to go home by the gap in the railings by Ladybarn Park, Darren Coulburn lay in wait. He punched M.A., and knocked him down, split his lip, and began to torment and humiliate him, making him stand up, sit down, and say 'Sorry, Master'. The bully was enjoying himself.

Ahmed Ullah, too, was going home across the park that afternoon. Ahmed saw the bullying and did what he always did when he saw

13

smaller boys being bullied; he intervened. He had done so in the past and now he did so again. Now it was Darren Coulburn's turn to be humiliated. Ahmed made Darren stand up and sit down just as he had ordered the Asian lad to do.

The next day, 16th of September, rumours were running around Lower School 'there's going to be a fight in the park after school.' Ahmed and Darren were to have a showdown. A crowd gathered in the park, encouraging them. The proceedings began. Ahmed bled, but then fought back. Ahmed was winning the fight and Darren Coulburn, like all bullies, retreated. Ahmed pursued him, but then older students intervened. Teachers became aware of the incident and the boys dispersed. The fight was over.

Ahmed Ullah went home victorious, but with cut lips and bruises. He told his mother about the fight; he told her Darren Coulburn had threatened to kill him. When his mother became anxious, Ahmed laughed it off. He had won the fight; he was confident that he could handle everything.

At around 7 p.m. that same evening, Darren Coulburn was playing around on bikes with friends. Someone asked about the fight in the park. 'What was it about?' Darren Coulburn said, 'just a fight'. Then he added, 'let him start again and I'll stab him'. A friend replied, 'Don't be daft'. Darren repeated the threat.

Next morning, Wednesday the 17th of September, Mrs Ullah did not want Ahmed to go to school before she had had a chance to speak to his teacher about the fight, but Ahmed had his new Adidas shorts and football boots which his parents had bought him in the holidays. He wanted to take them to school and show them to his friends. He told his mother he was fine, not to worry for him. His mother knew how miserable he would be if she kept him home. She relented; after all, she was going to the school to speak to the teacher, and there had never been trouble before school started in the morning. Trouble usually occurred after school. Ahmed left for school with his football boots and shorts.

As Darren Coulburn was walking to school that Wednesday, he met some other boys, and was talking to them about the fight he had lost the day before. Then he took out a knife and boasted that if Ahmed started on him again he would stab him.

Darren Coulburn and Ahmed Ullah met by the language classrooms in the corner of the playground by the gap in the railings.

The same sort of crowd of boys as in the Tuesday fight collected around them. Darren appeared to be avoiding the fight. Ahmed was

14

keen. Ahmed pushed Darren. Darren then turned and bent over – the next instant he stabbed Ahmed in the stomach, the blade came out covered in blood. Ahmed staggered away and fell. As he did so one eyewitness heard Darren Coulburn shout 'Do you want another one, you stupid Paki; there's plenty more where that came from.' Another remembers 'you want it again, Paki?' before Darren ran off. A few minutes later he was seen by fourth and fifth year students at the gates of the Upper School, freaking out, running about and saying 'I've killed a Paki'.

Ahmed lay in the playground. Darren had run off. It was approximately 8.30 a.m.

As Chris Hanson, Head of Languages, crossed the playground towards the language classrooms, boys ran to him, shouting that there had been a stabbing. Chris Hanson found Ahmed lying on the ground outside room 52. Ahmed was moaning, there was a small bloodstain on his shirt. It became abvious that Ahmed could not be moved, Chris Hanson sent two boys to the office for assistance. When Jackie Hill, the senior teacher, arrived at the scene at 8.40 a.m., she saw Chris Hanson and a group of boys standing around. Other staff arrived, the first being a young teacher, Tobias Redman. It was 8.42 a.m. Tobias Redman tried to comfort Ahmed. None of the staff could judge how serious the wound was, so Jackie Hill returned to the school office to speak to Mrs Simpson, one of the school secretaries, who had had first aid training. Graham Williams arrived and began to try to get boys into their classrooms. Mr Moors, the Deputy Head, arrived at the scene at 8.45 a.m. Mrs Simpson arrived from the office. According to Mr Moors he thought an ambulance had been called for. Mrs Simpson understood that she confirmed an ambulance was necessary. Whichever was correct, Mrs Simpson returned to the office and called to Mrs Ashton, the secretary, to call the ambulance. It was 8.45 a.m. according to school records.

The ambulance service logged the call at 8.48 a.m. At 8.49 a.m. the control operative who took the call spoke to the Belle Vue Ambulance Station and activated an ambulance, which at the time was mobile in the Clayton area, some way from the school. This was a mistake and an ambulance at Sharston Station, much closer to the school, should have been chosen instead. The mistake was spotted by a senior officer, who then alerted the nearer vehicle at 0903 hours, and it arrived at the scene 0909 hours, too late to take Ahmed to the hospital.

Nick Brown, another senior teacher, had arrived with Peter Moors at 8.45 a.m. Teachers were posted at the gates to look out for the ambulance, which did not come. By now Ahmed was in severe pain, calling out and becoming delirious. Tobias Redman and Peter Moors tried to comfort him. Alan Hill, another senior teacher, arrived at 8.50 a.m. He formed a circle of students around Ahmed, facing away from the dying boy, so that other students would be kept away when the 8.55 a.m. bell went. No ambulance arrived. Mrs Hill had returned to the playground with a blanket, which was put over Ahmed.

Senior teacher Mike Ellis saw this scene and went toward the school office with the intention of collecting witnesses, when Val McKenzie, a member of staff, called to him. Val McKenzie pointed toward the school gate on Briarfield Road and there, walking around the side of the building, was Darren Coulburn. Mike Ellis approached Darren Coulburn, who was walking with his arms stiff down by his sides, his mouth open, face pale. Darren Coulburn's eyes were fixed – he just kept looking at Mike Ellis – 'through him'. Mike Ellis asked Darren Coulburn where the knife was. Darren Coulburn told him it was down a drain. As Mike Ellis took hold of Darren Coulburn and walked him back into the school to await the arrival of the police, he could hear Ahmed's cries. It was a scene that was to haunt him.

It was nearly 9 a.m. By now the teachers with Ahmed and waiting at the gates were getting desperate for the ambulance. It still had not come.

The police arrived at the school at approximately 8.58 a.m. Mrs Ashton told them the ambulance had still not come, so the police radioed to see what had happened to the ambulance. Mrs Ashton was 'phoned by the ambulance service five minutes later. She was told that the intercom system had not been working properly, but that an ambulance would be arriving within a few minutes. Police had looked at Ahmed's injuries when they arrived at 8.58 a.m., but apart from radioing the ambulance again at 9.01 a.m., they had not rendered first aid assistance. Nick Brown spoke to them about speeding up the process, and one of the police suggested that Ahmed might be taken to hospital in a traffic car.

At approximately 9.05 a.m. the police and others lifted Ahmed into a car. Peter Moors went with him to the hospital. They arrived at the hospital at 9.10 a.m. On examination by Dr Michael Cork, Ahmed was clinically dead. Resuscitation attempts were made for 45 minutes. They were not successful.

There is no doubt that there was considerable delay in getting Ahmed to hospital, delay before the ambulance was called, delay waiting for the ambulance, delay which might have been avoided if Ahmed had been put in someone's car and driven straight to hospital – a journey which would have taken about 6–8 minutes. A number of witnesses and commentators have asked:

'Would it have made any difference?'

This is an important question which ought to be answered. But it is not within our Terms of Reference and we did not hear any evidence from doctors or pathologists, which might throw light on it.

CHAPTER 3

Aftermath of the Murder

A. The Family

At 9.10 am on the 17th of September, Jackie Hill telephoned Ahmed's parents. Ahmed's sister Selina answered the 'phone. Selina's memory of the 'phone call was that the caller asked the family to go to the Withington Hospital, but that there was no need to worry; another boy and a knife were involved. The family assumed the incident had just taken place, and after waiting for a taxi, Mr and Mrs Ullah left for the hospital.

Mrs Hill's recollection of the call was that she told the family that Ahmed had been stabbed, that he was in the Withington Hospital, that she had asked them to go there immediately, and that "the school had no knowledge of how serious the wound was." A few minutes after the first call Mrs Hill 'phoned again. According to Selina, she expressed concern that Ahmed's parents had not yet arrived at the hospital. Selina explained that her parents had in fact already left by taxi. According to Selina, Mrs Hill said "that's OK then", and put the 'phone down.

Selina Ullah took a third 'phone call that day. This time it was the hospital. She was told her parents would like her to come down to the hospital, and so, taking her younger sister, she too went to the Withington Hospital. As she sat in the taxi, it crossed her mind that it might be that a blood transfusion was needed, or something.

As the sisters arrived, they were directed into a small room to the right of the entrance by a nurse who would not reply when asked how Ahmed was. In the room Selina and her sister found their parents crying. It was their parents who told them of Ahmed's death.

The family faced another ordeal at the hospital. Lesley Aisthorpe had visited Mr Nur-ul-Islam Choudhury, a parent and voluntary freelance interpreter, and asked him to attend the hospital, to act as interpreter for the family.

Mrs Ullah, Selina Ullah and other members of the family were fluent in English. In addition, there were other relatives present. Nonetheless Mr Choudhury remained at the hospital. The police officer in charge turned to Mr Choudhury when the question of identifying the body arose, the police thinking that this should be an all male occasion and

19

that only Ahmed's father and Mr Choudhury should be allowed to go to the morgue to identify the body. Ahmed's father who has since had a heart attack, was not crying like his wife or daughters. The police did not seem to want emotion when the identification was made, and obviously thought it far better for Mr Choudhury to go with Ahmed's father, even though Mr Choudhury had never met Ahmed, than to have his mother and sisters weeping over him.

To Selina Ullah, who had been refused access when she first tried to see the body "because there was no interpreter," this attitude caused additional and unnecessary anguish. Her uncle was with them, and he spoke English; she was there, and she spoke English. This treatment of the Ullah family raises a number of questions. Why was it assumed that the family needed an interpreter? Why was the interpreter kept at the hospital when it became clear that apart from Mr Ullah all of the family were fluent in English? Would a white family have been treated in the same way if a white boy had been murdered?

Ms Aisthorpe contacted Mr Choudhury at the request of Mr Moors the Deputy Head who 'phoned from the hospital. At the time she didn't know whether the family needed an interpreter, nor apparently did Mr Moors. She acted merely as messenger and was not party to the decision to have an interpreter. She did not know where the idea came from. She thought that those who did make the decision felt that under stressful circumstances it would be more appropriate if the family were able to speak in their first language and that that facility should be made available to them.

Mr Moors gave no such explanation. He accepted that when a tragedy happens to any one of us, normally the first line of support is from those who know us. So why had Ms Aisthorpe, rather than the Head of the Year been contacted? He accepted that the Head of Year would probably know the family far better and might know whether they had a particular friend in the community. Instead Ms Aisthorpe was contacted because she knew Mr Choudhury. "Forgive me", said Counsel, "you may not have needed a Bengali speaking person if you had checked with the Year Head?" Anwser: "I accept that we may not have done, but it was a decision I made at the time."

We have found the assumptions made about the family insensitive. First, it was assumed that they needed an interpreter without anyone having taken the trouble to find out if this was true. Secondly, it was assumed that, in grief, communication in the first language is wanted even if it involves the presence of a complete stranger. Thirdly, it was assumed that a strange Bengali speaker is better than no-one at all. The family might have preferred to have been left to cope on their own, but they were never given this choice. We are quite sure that if a white family had lost a son in similar circumstances, they would have been asked if there was any special friend they wanted or if they wanted to be left alone. A stranger would not have been foisted on them willy nilly, just because he or she was English, or Scottish, or Irish, or French. In short they would have been seen as an individual family in grief. There would have been no lack of respect for their grief and their problems would not, as here, have been seen as the problems of the Bagladeshi community rather than ones of family.

B. The Teachers

Ahmed Ullah was dead. Darren Coulburn had been arrested. For the staff who had been directly concerned with these events, the school day continued.

Chris Hanson went to his lesson, where the boys were very agitated. He calmed them and continued. As the day went on he felt bewildered and angry. Tobias Redman went to his class very upset, but he had to carry on as usual. Mike Ellis spent the day with the students who had witnessed the stabbing. He experienced deep feelings of sorrow and a sense of loss. Sue Raddings, Darren Coulburn's form tutor, who had seen Ahmed lying there moaning and who had waited at a gate in vain to direct the ambulance, found it hard to keep control emotionally. She felt numb and just seemed to walk around in a state all day.

During the course of her second lesson Sonia McCann saw a man taping off an area outside the classroom. When she went to inquire what he was doing, he told her he was a plain clothes police officer, and that they had to cordon off the area because the boy had died. She returned to her class and tried to continue the lesson normally. She did not know how she carried on. Alan Hill, who had been shocked by the murder, went to spend the time with the police and students who were witnesses.

Nick Brown drafted a letter to parents, telephoned the Education Department, and arranged a meeting with the school inspector, Michael Molloy, and management. Jackie Hill, after making the 'phone calls to the family, attended the meeting, with Michael Molloy and Dr Gough. Jack Hewitt and Peter Moors, the deputy heads, and Alan Hill were also at the meeting. One of the first issues of the meeting was to brief staff. It was also decided at some stage that the school was to be responsible for communication to the family and that lessons should

21

carry on as normal. Liaison also had to be made with the police, and teachers had to deal with students, and with the press who were already on the scene. This was all achieved in conjunction with members of the Education Department, in particular Roy Jobson, the Senior Assistant Education Officer (Schools), who had arrived on site mid-morning.

C. The Pupils

An announcement was made at 11 a.m. after 2nd break that anyone who had witnessed the stabbing but who had not yet given their names to the police should go to Mrs Hill's office. There were about 13 boys in this group; there is no doubt that some who witnessed it did not go to Mrs Hill's office. Some of them sat in a geography lesson, deeply concerned about Ahmed. Their concern was felt by many students; some who had seen Ahmed lying there were visibly shaken. They resented the school continuing normally while their friend lay injured or dying in hospital. One boy, who was a good friend of Ahmed and who formed part of the circle around him while he lay dying, directed feelings of anger at some of the teachers because he felt that they were not concerned enough about his friend. Lessons went on. The first lesson was French, in which the teacher acknowledged the stabbing by saying it was a stupid, mad thing to do and that the teacher regretted it. After the last period Ahmed's death was announced in a matter-of-fact way. One of Ahmed's good friends thought this was the best way to handle it, but he did feel shocked.

One white friend of Ahmed's (whose older brother was to be concerned in the February/March incidents at Upper School at Burnage) said that the day felt like a horror story. He had seen his friend Ahmed being stabbed in the playground. That day he came home from school upset and crying, and needed to be calmed and reassured by his parents. For another white friend of Ahmed, the shock and grief began and was to continue. One year later he still could not speak to his parents about the murder and loss of his friend.

Another Asian student at Burnage felt that most of the white students seemed unbothered by the tragedy. He felt that it was the Asian and Afro-Caribbean boys who were upset and shocked, and only a few white boys.

The rest of the boys in Darren Coulburn's form (apart from one who asked whether Darren Coulburn would be expelled now), seemed to experience guilt by association, a feeling of form responsibility and fear. They needed to be reassured. They were in deep shock.

22

Large numbers of students were absent from school in the days that followed.

D. *The School*

A school is an institution, part of a larger bureaucracy. In all institutions there is a subculture which evades the bureaucratic process, so throughout the morning of the 17th of September 1987, rumours had flourished and circulated amongst staff, amongst students, the grapevine extending out into the community.

The first institutional response to the stabbing came at lunchtime; Dr Gough addressed the staff at Lower School, while Michael Molloy went over to Upper School with Jack Hewitt, the Deputy Head based in Upper School, to brief staff there. These briefings took place just before the start of afternoon school. A prepared notice was handed out to be read to students in their forms at 3.15 p.m.

To all Form Tutors

17th September 1986

From Dr Gough

Please read this notice to your form at 3.15 p.m. and reassure them as far as possible.

Before school this morning an incident occurred in Ladybarn Park between two third year boys which resulted in one of the boys being fatally injured. He died on the way to hospital.

It is important at this time to behave as normally as possible.

If anyone other than your parents should ask you about this incident – say nothing.

Some teachers felt unable to withhold the information until 3.15 p.m. and told the students the truth at afternoon registration.

For one member of staff, who herself had lost a daughter, the task of reading the death notice was too emotionally difficult. She had to get a colleague to do it for her because she was so upset.

The school's decision was that the school was to be responsible for contact with Ahmed's family. On that day no one from the school went to the Ullah family's home. No one from the Education Department went to the Ullah family's home. No one from the City Council went there either.

23

E. The City Council

Councillor Richard Leese, Chair of the City Council's Education Committee, first learned of the murder in a telephone call from Gordon Hainsworth, the Chief Education Officer, some time after 10 a.m. on the day of the killing. As a result a meeting was organised with Gordon Hainsworth, David Davis, his deputy, the Chair of the Equal Opportunities Committee, and other Council members.

Various priorities and courses of action were decided upon. Manchester City Council issued a statement of regret for what had happened. The Councillors asked the department officials to ensure that a senior Education Department official was at the school, so that the councillors could know what was happening at the school and could then deal with anything that happened as a consequence of the killing. They were informed that Roy Jobson was already on site.

The Councillors decided to send letters to the Governors of Burnage informing them of what had happened, asking the Governors not to make public statements or get involved in public debate, and telling them that they would be kept informed of developments. They also decided that a letter should be sent to Ahmed Ullah's family on behalf of the Education Committee.

F. The Education Department

About 15 minutes after Ahmed was taken to hospital, the Headteacher, Gerry Gough, telephoned Roy Jobson in the Education Department to inform them that there had been a stabbing in the school grounds. Roy Jobson conferred with Gordon Hainsworth and then drove to the school. He arrived at about 9.45 a.m.

To Roy Jobson, it appeared that the Headteacher and other senior members of staff were in a state of shock. There was, according to Roy Jobson, a certain amount of panic and confusion. Accordingly, he asked that the Education Department could either make decisions or give strong advice to those taking decisions. The first Michael Molloy learned of the murder was a message relayed to him on a course he was attending. The message said: "Please 'phone the CEO.; desperately urgent." Michael Molloy telephoned at some time around 10.30 a.m. or 11 a.m., learned the news, and hurried to the school.

When he arrived at the school, Roy Jobson's first reaction was to find out what the role of the police would be particularly in respect to the boys in the school. Roy Jobson specifically requested that the police should not interview students without either their parents being present or at least some representative from the school. As a result, some boys whose parents could be reached by telephone were taken out of school to be interviewed in their homes. Others were taken to a classroom, where senior teacher Alan Hill supervised the interviews.

Roy Jobson thought he should try to get meetings of "community" representatives of some kind, somewhere, to begin to try and explain as much as the school knew. Roy Jobson's view was that members of the Bangladesh Association, particularly, should know as soon as possible. Gordon Hainsworth, the Chief Education Officer, agreed with this view, and either he or Roy Jobson suggested a meeting. So they made telephone calls between noon and 1 p.m. to try and get community representatives to the school. It was very much an 'ad hoc' affair with far greater consequences than either of them could have foreseen.

G. Meeting the "Community"

A school is part of a larger bureaucracy; the City education bureaucracy had decided to have a meeting with the "community."

At 2 p.m. on the 17th of September, the school and the Education Department assembled with the community in the Head's office.

At that meeting the community was represented by Mr Azad of the Manchester Council's Race Sub-Committee; Mr Kabir Ahmed, Mr Abdul Uddin, Mr A. T. T. Choudhury, all of the Greater Manchester Bangladesh Association (GMBA); and Mr S. M. Ahmed and Mr John Tummon of the Manchester Council for Community Relations (MCCR). Forming a link between community and school at that meeting were Mr Jamal, a governor of the school and Mr N. I. Choudhury, (who had been at the hospital and was soon to become one of the School's governors). The school was represented by Dr Gough, Peter Moors, Head of the Lower School, Lesley Aisthorpe, Head of Community Education (Secion 11), and Ben Glaisner of the school's governors. The Education Department was represented by Gordon Hainsworth, Roy Jobson and Michael Molloy.

So far as the school was concerned, the purpose of the meeting was to give information to the community about what had happened, and to reassure representatives of the community. By the time this meeting started the police had still not finished interviewing, the school had no complete picture of events, and Darren Coulburn had not yet been charged with murder.

No formal agreed minutes were taken at this meeting. The only written record is found in a memorandum which was made on the 18th

25

of September 1986 by John Tummon of MCCR, who had made notes at the meeting. So far as relevant, the memorandum reads as follows:

MEMORANDUM
TO: The Principal Community Relations Officer
FROM: The Public Education Officer
RE: The death of Ahmed Iqbal Ullah at Burnage High School
DATE: 18th September 1986

"In accordance with your request, I submit my record of the meeting which we both attended yesterday afternoon in the Headmaster's Study at Burnage High School at 2.00 p.m.

Those present:
Mr Gough, headmaster
Mr Moors, head of Lower School
A female Section 11 teacher at the school
Mr Jamal, a school governor
Mr Hainsworth MEC
Mr Jobson MEC
Mr Azad, City's Race Sub-Committee
Kabir Ahmed
Abdul Uddin
ATTM Chowdury, GMBA
Mr S M Ahamed
Mr J W Tummon
Three others – unknown

The meeting had already begun before our arrival together with the GMBA shortly after 2.00 p.m.

"Dr Gough explained what he knew of the incident which had taken place that morning, and informed us that the police were engaged in interviewing a number of pupils in the presence of their parents or teachers.

"In response to questions, Dr Gough told us that three white pupils, including the one now in police custody, had attacked Ahmed Iqbal Ullah the previous (Tuesday 16) night after school. He also mentioned that the boy in police custody was known to the school to have taunted Asian pupils in the past.

"Again in response to questions, Dr Gough stated that in the middle of last week a teacher had reported racist taunting of Asian pupils at the heart of lessons. The Section 11 teacher gave more

26

details on this, telling us that a second year teacher had noticed that Asian children were extremely reluctant to get into line outside their classroom until the arrival of the teacher, and seemed to be reluctant because of fear. The teacher had also noticed that certain white pupils, when collecting books from their fellow pupils, had quite openly and defiantly placed the exercise books belonging to Asian children to the bottom.

"I then asked the Section 11 teacher if she or anyone else in the school had filed a racist incident report over these developments. The teacher replied that no such report had been filed, because it takes time to find out all the details of incidents. She continued that she had taken the matter up with the head of Second Year and an Educational Psychologist with a view to finding a long-term strategy to deal with the problem. I stated that the long-term initiatives such as anti-racist education, Race Awareness Training and multi-cultural curriculi were and should be kept separate from responding to racist incidents, and could not be substituted for such a response.

"A gentleman with glasses who I do not know then asked me what the school could possibly have done 'to stop a madman'. Dr Gough had stated earlier that the boy in police custody was known to have problems with his home life which had brought about a noticeable instability, and had in fact spent the previous two or three nights outside his family home. Kabir Ahmed had responded to this statement by asking why such a boy had been allowed to continue attending school, especially since he was known to be taunting Asian children, and said that he wanted to know if the school had suspended any pupils for bullying. Dr Gough confirmed that suspensions had taken place because of bullying at school.

"I complained that describing the boy in police custody as a 'madman' was an attempt to run away from the racism which clearly lay behind Ahmed's death, and that there could never be any progress in dealing with racist incidents unless all concerned shared the starting point of acknowledging racism as the underlying cause.

"Mr Moors then intervened to say that not all of the boys subjected to bullying were Asian. I replied that this was irrelevant, since white friends of ethnic minority pupils were clearly targets for bullying from other boys who regarded them as 'nigger lovers', and repeated my insistence that the school should not continue avoiding the acknowledgement of racism as the underlying cause.

"Mr Jamal told the meeting that he had received information about racist bullying over a week previously, and was ashamed now

27

that he had failed to report it. He added that one of the problems was the disinterest amongst Asian parents in the school and in the Asian parents' organisation established at Burnage. Kabir Ahmed hotly disputed this statement with Mr Jamal.

"It had emerged earlier in the meeting that a black parents group and Asian parents group had been established at the school two years before.

"At the suggestion of myself and Mr Azad, Dr Gough agreed that school assemblies the following day would feature one minute's silence for Ahmed Iqbal Ullah. It was further agreed by all concerned that anyone of us contacted by the press would state that the death had occurred because of racism.

"Shortly afterwards the meeting ended.

"The above is a record of the major points made in the discussion. Obviously, there is an emphasis on those parts of the discussion in which I was personally involved, which are easier for me to recall."

From the evidence, it is quite clear that the atmosphere of the meeting was very emotional. Whatever might be said to the contrary, the "community" had made up its mind that the murder was a racist murder. In the evidence Dr Gough said that the memorandum was incorrect in two places. He did not tell the meeting that three white pupils had attacked Ahmed, and according to his account there was no agreement by all concerned that if anyone was contacted by the press they would state that the death had occurred because of racism. That was stated by Mr Tummon, but it was not agreed.

His evidence is contradicted by that of Mr Moors, who said there was an agreement by all concerned that they would tell the press that the death had occurred because of racism.

Our view is that the memorandum is probably correct and that this conclusion was almost inevitable, given the composition of the meeting and the information fed to it by Dr Gough and Ms Aisthorpe. She was there because she knew about racism. Teachers who had taught Darren Coulburn or had direct dealings with him were not invited and information that Darren Coulburn was known to be a very disturbed boy, who had committed major arson at the school in company with an Asian lad, and that his exclusion had been discussed but rejected by the school governors, was withheld from the meeting on the ground that "these were confidential matters concerning a student".

In our opinion the meeting was ill conceived in every way. We accept that the ostensible purpose of the meeting was to allay the fears of the

Bangladeshi, Pakistani, and other communities, but it is clear that neither the school nor the Education Department was in any position to do so. Clearly, none of them had taken the time or trouble to obtain the necessary information from police, teachers or students. They had not done their home work, either on the events or on Darren Coulburn. Secondly, the meeting was unrepresentative. At most it might be in a position to allay the fears of some sections of the Pakistani or Bangladeshi communities, although this is doubtful, but it certainly could not allay the fears that white parents or students might have about bringing their children to school the following day. Thirdly, all the people who had been invited to the meeting, including Ms Aisthorpe, the school's "specialist" on race, had been invited on the assumption that the murder was racist, or at least would be seen as such in the Asian community. Yet no attempt was made, on the assumption that the murder was racist, to bring into the meeting level headed white parents to check out their response, and seek their involvement in dealing with the aftermath of the killing.

The meeting had long term repercussions. It set the seal and established the agenda for dealing with the murder in Burnage High School. It committed the school and the Department of Education to a view of the murder which was partial, incomplete and misleading. For reasons we explain below, we take the view that the murder was racist, but it was more complex than that. It is one thing for Asian students to highlight the racism of the murder, because that focuses on a central part of their daily experience. In our view it is another thing for a school or local education authority to jump to such a conclusion, or for a police force to reach the opposite one. Neither the school nor the Education Department can avoid or neglect that other equally important issue – that Darren Coulburn was a highly disturbed boy with a long history of difficult, delinquent and anti-social behaviour in and out of school; that he was a known bully; that the carrying and use of knives in school was not unknown – indeed one student surrendered his knife to a teacher immediately after he heard of the stabbing; that violence of this kind might be the product of an all male environment and the power structure based on it.

The commitment made by the school to a particular view of the murder at that initial afternoon meeting also led the school authorities to ignore the experience and feelings of the white students, for whom Darren Coulburn was someone quite separate, someone with whom they could not identify and with whom the majority would not wish to be identified. To them, Darren Coulburn was a trouble maker and a bully, someone who was disturbed. With about one exception, none of the white witnesses, boys or parents, who spoke to us or made statements saw the murder as racist. That is their truth, and, in our opinion, the school and the Department of Education had a responsibility to acknowledge and accommodate that view. We see nothing difficult or contradictory for an institution like a school to accept that for Asian students the murder was first and foremost a racist murder and to white students it was merely the work of a nutter and not racist at all. That is the starting point of both groups and unless the school could deal with both points of view it could not possibly begin to allay the fears of either group – Asians afraid of further racist attacks and whites afraid of an Asian backlash. Without such acknowledgement, there was little chance of the school dealing with the racism of the white students, other than by repressing it, or pretending that if it was ignored, it would go away.

In our view, ignoring the white reaction is as objectionable as ignoring the black. It sows the seeds of disillusionment among white students and must be a factor in the polarisation of students into racial groups during the latter events of March 1987.

Later we will deal with the police reaction to the experience and feelings of the Asian community. We suggest that they are the flip sides of the same coin – well-intentioned responses to racism which are themselves racist. The community had expressed its view and had made it known in no uncertain terms that they felt it of vital importance that the school and the education authority acknowledge immediately that racism lay behind the killing. That afternoon there was a senior management team meeting. Ms Aisthorpe was asked to attend on the basis of what she had heard from the community representatives at the earlier meeting. She produced the following note to be handed out to staff the following day:

"to all staff

re: Ahmed Ullah – Tutor Group Discussion

Discussions with students following the death of Ahmed Ullah will be difficult for all of us and form tutors will, undoubtedly, wish to deal with this sensitive subject in their own way.

It may be helpful, however, to consider an approach which stresses the positive steps which we, as a community might take together to prevent such a tragedy happening again.

Some points which might be raised by way of an introduction are:

1. Ahmed Ullah died as a result of racism. The dispute leading to his death happened as a result of his attempts to protect younger students from racial abuse.

2. Racism seems harmless at first, but if unchallenged can lead to terrible consequences, ie. racist jokes – name calling – insults – bullying – racist attacks.

3. Racism is not something which only happens in far away places. It happens here and it happens frequently.

4. We are all shocked and horrified that such a dreadful tragedy should take place at our school involving people we know.

5. We have a school policy on racism which tells us that everyone in this school deserves equal respect and that no one should have to tolerate abuse or bullying of any kind. If we see name calling or bullying going on and stand by and do nothing we must all share the blame even if we are not personally involved.

6. It is our joint responsibility to take care of other students, particularly those younger than ourselves.

7. What can be done?

Pupils should be informed of procedures for reporting harrassment of themselves or others, eg. confidential report to teacher/parents' telephone call to school.

All incidents should be reported. They will be noted down in the official log book which details all racist incidents.

Pupils may wish to discuss measures which might be taken by us as a community.

18.9.86   P MOORS

Although this notice was signed by Mr Moors, it was prepared by Ms Aisthorpe. Once more it committed the school to a particular view of the murder. Ms Aisthorpe later changed her mind. She told us:

"It was not until later that I heard evidence that made me doubt the situation again, when I heard that, in fact, Darren Coulburn had attempted to stop the dispute when he was obviously beaten, but that Ahmed appeared to have started it up again the following day. Then I became rather concerned as to whether I had actually understood the situation properly at the time."

CHAPTER 4

Aftermath of the Murder

The Second Day

On the 18th September 1986 Ahmed Ullah was dead; Darren Coulburn had already been charged with Ahmed's murder and awaited his eventual trial; and Ahmed's family grieved. At the same time they had to cope with the practicalities that surround any death.

That day, Selina Ullah again telephoned the police about the release of her brother's body: in Muslim custom, just as in Jewish custom, quick burial is essential. The police gave her the impression that it might be weeks before his body could be released. Selina Ullah sought help from an Asian Law Centre worker.

No-one from the school had yet visited the Ahmed family, although neighbours came to them to share their grief and to offer practical help.

However, two educational welfare officers were asked to be in the playground for extra help for students. They were not announced as such to students and may have been mistaken for plain clothes police as a result.

That day, the school held its special assemblies in the morning and had a minute's silence in memory of Ahmed. The students, having heard via the media that the police considered the killing to be a non-racist incident, now heard at the assemblies that the school considered it to be a racist killing. These apparent contradictions were to have their effect on Asian and white students alike.

Many of the staff also were still in shock. Some of them felt that the school should be closed for at least a day, if not for a week. The notice to staff, which had been prepared by Leslie Aisthorpe the previous day following the senior staff meeting, was distributed to teaching staff at the morning staff briefing in Upper and Lower School. Some of the non-teaching staff did not receive this or any other notice; they had to rely on information gleaned from colleagues.

Some time that day, Ethel Milroy, Senior Secondary Staff Inspector for Manchester Education Authority, arrived at Burnage High School and became aware that no-one from the school had visited Ahmed's family. She advised that this should happen, and went with Dr Gough, Peter Moors and Lesley Aisthorpe to the home.

Mrs Ullah refused to see them: "What was the use of seeing them now." Selina Ullah, however, did receive them. The first she learned of the proposed visit was a phone call from Mr Rashid of Birch Lane. This seemed to her another example of the authorities avoiding direct contact with the family, instead of arranging the visit with the family themselves. When Dr Gough, Peter Moors, Lesley Aisthorpe, and Ethel Milroy did visit she felt that Dr Gough and Peter Moors felt guilty, and that only Lesley Aisthorpe seemed to respond with real sympathy. Selina felt that this visit was an attempt to pass off Ahmed's death as arising out of a schoolboy dispute. She found the tone of the visit to be insulting and upsetting.

Later that day the school sent out its first official communication to parents:

"BURNAGE HIGH SCHOOL

DRB/SP-84-DR G GOUGH
18 SEPTEMBER 1896

Dear Parents,

It is with regret that I write to inform you of the tragic death of Ahmen Ullah before school started on Wednesday morning, 17 September. I am sure you share the deep sense of shock and sorrow which staff and students feel and join us in our mourning.

The staff and boys joined together today in an act of collective mourning and remembrance.

The incidents leading to the tragedy had occurred outside school hours and resulted from a quarrel in Ladybarn Park. The police have charged a boy with murder. My colleagues and I wish to express our deep sense of grief and outrage caused by this event.

At this stage I wish to allay any fears you may have about the welfare of your son at Burnage High School. Pupils are supervised from the time they are admitted at 8.35 a.m. until they have left the premises at the end of the day. Additional help is also on hand from welfare officers, and the police have offered their assistance outside the school.

I am sure you would wish to be associated with us in expressing sorrow and condolences to Ahmed's family in the great grief they are experiencing.

Yours sincerely,

DR G GOUGH
HEADTEACHER"

Some parents did not receive this letter. Even when they visited the school to find out what had happened, they left feeling none the wiser. Other parents who did receive this letter felt that it was grossly misleading. It left them feeling angry and confused.

When this letter was drafted, Dr Gough apparently wrongly assumed that the stabbing had taken place in the park. Later he was unable to say what he had based that assumption on, but he did deny any intention of misleading the parents.

On the evening of the 18th September 1986, Education Department officials held a meeting with the Greater Manchester Bangladeshi Association (GMBA) in Longsight. Present at the meeting were Councillor Richard Leese; Ms. Fanny Underhill, Head of the Administration Branch; Councillor John Nicholson; Gordon Hainsworth, Chief Education Officer; Roy Jobson, Senior Education Officer; and David Gibson, Principal for the Central Area of Community Education. About 150 to 200 other people, including students from Burnage, attended this meeting.

Gordon Hainsworth and Roy Jobson asked the people at the meeting for feedback along the following lines: "Okay, this is a tragedy. What can we do? Have you got any suggestions to make about steps we can take?" Those at the meeting did try to make positive suggestions, one of which was the setting up of a "hot line" for parents. The following letter was eventually sent out as a result of this discussion at the meeting:

"BURNAGE HIGH
SCHOOL

Ref: DRB/SP-84-DR G GOUGH
    25 SEPTEMBER 1896

Dear Parent,

In the wake of last week's tragic events, I have come to understand from some parents that there may be occasions when parents might not feel comfortable in raising concerns about their children with the school.

I wish to reassure parents that we are always available for consultation and that we do encourage frank discussion and partnership between parents, teachers and students. If, however, some parents do have reservations, then these reservations must be overcome. I have discussed the matter with the Governors and the Chief Education Officer. We are agreed that in these circumstances

35

parents can get in touch directly with an officer of the Education Department at Crown Square.

If on any occasion you should wish to take up this offer of direct contact in the Education Department please, in the first instance, telephone –

Mr Andrew Cant
Assistant Education Officer
Schools Branch
Telephone No: 234 7155

If Mr Cant is not available, please leave a message with his secretary, Mrs Armstrong (234 7154), and he will telephone you back. If you would like the assistance of an interpreter please leave a message for Mr Cant and he will make the necessary arrangement.

I do hope that this information will be of help to you.

Yours sincerely,

G GOUGH
HEADTEACHER"

The "hot line" was not a success. Over the whole period of its operation only four calls were received. Full documentation was kept, but there was no system of registering the race or colour of any callers. We were shown all the documents and it is clear that only one of the cases was of any substance. Perhaps this is not surprising, since the Education Department is a rather remote institution and parents are much more used to dealing with the school.

There was, however, another side to this meeting on the 18th September 1986. The meeting was held in such a small room that there were people standing down the stairs. It was absolutely jammed packed. One of the things that had caused most anger amongst those at the meeting had been the official police statement to the press on the day of the murder: "There was no evidence of any racial overtones to the killing". We now know it was put out by Chief Superintendant Sherratt, in charge of Longsight Police Station. It had been printed in the local and national press. He was present at this meeting. He had arrived late, got up and made a statement that reiterated what had been said in the Press, that it was not a racist murder. The reaction to this was a lot of shouting; there was an angry outcry from those present. The tone and manner in which this statement was made genuinely shocked Roy Jobson; he felt that if he was shocked as a white person in the room, he did not know what the Bangladeshi community felt. The officer then went on to warn students speaking about the incident, that they should not be saying things there about the murder because it was now "sub judice", and that anybody else who had anything to say had better come forward and make a statement to the police.

The police officer's behaviour gave the people at the meeting the impression that the young people were being strongly criticised by the police, because the matter was "sub judice", and that criticism was being levelled at them for opposing the police view that the killing had nothing to do with race. To Roy Jobson, it appeared that the officer had come to a cut and dried decision that the murder was not racist. The effect of the police intervention at the GMBA meeting was threefold.

First, the introduction of the "sub judice" rule had a gagging effect on discussion of the tragedy at Burnage. So far as we can trace, the first time the rule was invoked was at this meeting. How exactly it was introduced into the school is unclear. It may have come from a staff briefing. It soon lodged itself in the minds of staff who had to deal with the students who had witnessed the tragedy. Then it seems to have spread its tentacles to the discussion of the tragedy by students who had not witnessed it themselves, but whose friends had. The effect was dramatic. Effectively, it silenced concerned and traumatised people as well as those who were just curious, and prevented a meaningful discussion of the terrible impact Ahmed's death had on his friends, fellow students and teachers.

A contrast can be drawn with the death in November 1986 of a second year boy, Asim Malik, who was run over and killed on a road near the school. There was no press involvement, no criminal investigation, no outside forces saying, "this is what it is", or "it is not that", no fear, no guilt and, above all, no "sub judice" rule. In his case, his teacher was quite free to lead any discussion and the boys in his class were quite free to sit down and write about all the things they remembered about Asim. In contrast to Ahmed's death, everyone was able to own the tragedy and to express their grief fully.

We understand the reason for the "sub judice" rule and how important it is that teenage witnesses in a forthcoming murder trial should not discuss the evidence they are going to give. But in the case of Burnage, the "sub judice" rule was invoked too often and too much. It undoubtedly hindered the grieving process, a necessary and proper discussion within the school of what had happened. We find it extraordinary that the police should put out a statement that Ahmed Ullah's death had nothing to do with racism, repeat it at a public meeting, and then attempt to use the "sub judice" rule to prevent discussion of the statement.

By the time of the GMBA meeting, Darren Coulburn had already been charged with murder and the matter was already "sub judice"; a fact that could not possibly have escaped that senior police officer.

Secondly, the effect of Chief Superintendent Sherratt's adamant refusal to accept that racism was involved in the murder alienated the Asian youth from the police and boosted their mobilisation into self defence organisations. All evidence given to us indicates that the meeting was an emotional one and highly charged. Ahmed's sudden and tragic death brought out great feelings of vulnerability based on a shared experience of racist name calling, racist abuse and in many cases racial violence. Many of those at the meeting have shared their experiences with members of the panel, formally and informally.

What is more, Ahmed was now added to that long list of Asian people who have lost their lives in brutal and senseless racist killings. That knowledge is part of the consciousness of the black community at all times. The effect of the police intervention at that important first meeting was: "your feelings and experiences count for nothing." This did not allay fears but aroused anger. To the Asian youth it was the clearest possible statement that they could only rely on their own organisation and on their own self defence. That is exactly what happened. From the time of the police intervention we can detect the beginnings of a polarisation of Asian students, a polarisation which was to make its biggest impact in the events of March 1987 at Burnage.

Thirdly, the combination of the police statement and the ensuing mobilisation and radicalisation of Asian youth pushed the leaders of the Asian community, particularly those in the GMBA, into a flurry of activity designed to get the police to back track. They were partially successful as the letter from Chief Superintendent Merricks to the Chairman of the Greater Manchester Bangladeshi Association shows:

"I write in connection with the circumstances surrounding the tragic death of Ahmed Iqbal Ullah and to confirm the genuine concern of Greater Manchester Police for the family of the deceased and the Bangladeshi Community here in Greater Manchester. There is much sympathetic understanding within the Force of the problems faced by the Bangladeshi Community and in particular for the family of Ahmed Iqbal Ullah.

Turning to the matter of the press statement attributed to a police spokesman and published in the Manchester Evening News on Wednesday, 17th September 1986, I have made enquiries and it is highly unlikely that this statement emanated from a police source. However, I dissociate the Greater Manchester Police from the statement because that evaluation of the circumstances surrounding the crime should not have been made and clearly would be unacceptable to the Bangladeshi Community.

I now turn to the meeting held the following evening at Bangladeshi House. It is a matter of regret to me that the representative of the Greater Manchester Police in a verbal statement tended to confirm the press statement and his view did not reduce the level of anxiety and anger felt by those members of your community who attended the meeting. Whilst I am convinced that the officer acted in good faith and with the best of intentions, it appears that his comments did not reassure those present.

Bearing in mind the long standing relationship between the Bangladeshi Community and the Greater Manchester Police which is being assisted by the Manchester Council for Community Relations, together with the efforts and concern shown by the police during the enquiry into the death and the funeral arrangements, I very much hope that the two issues mentioned above do not harm the good relationship that exists between yourself, members of the Bangladeshi Community and the Greater Manchester Police."

(In later correspondence, the Chief Constable of Greater Manchester disassociated his force from the contents of this letter.)

At the same time these things caused the Council to issue a counter statement to that of the police. They put out their own press release, stating that they recognised the strong view of several communities served by the school that the tragedy had racist origins. However, they were thwarted in their efforts to get it published. They were told by the local media, including the Manchester Evening News, that the press would not print such a statement because the matter was now "sub judice". Despite repeated attempts by the City Council to issue this press release, this remained the Press position until after the trial of Darren Coulburn. (See Chapter 10.)

CHAPTER 5

Interpretation of the Murder

The murder of Ahmed Ullah by Darren Coulburn raises two questions:

1 Should Darren Coulburn have been in the school in September 1986?
2 Was the murder racist, and, if so, in what way?

We deal with each of these questions before moving on to the later events.

First, Darren. We have summarised his history in Chapter 2. From the information given to us it would appear that he was severely disturbed, had an unhappy family life, living with a father who was unable to cope, was virtually bringing himself up, was known as a truant in his neighbourhood, was a petty offender well known to the local police, had been involved in the fire in the school art block, and had a history of disrupting class and bullying boys smaller than himself.

It is also clear that the school did not bring together all the facts until after the murder. Mr Hewitt, the Deputy Head, who was responsible for pastoral care in Burnage, produced a very long and comprehensive report in November 1986. He told us that he had been asked to monitor Darren Coulburn in January 1986, presumably at the request of Dr. Gough, but no other staff knew of this. Therefore, no other staff effectively contributed their knowledge of the boy to the monitoring exercise. It is clear that information about him was not shared amongst those with primary responsibility, such as the Head of Year, form teacher, Pastoral Head of Lower School or even the social worker. So, when the suggestion was made in February 1986 to do a pre-referral form for possible reference to the education psychologists, there was insufficient evidence on the school's accepted criteria for acceptance to justify a referral.

In July 1986 Darren was sent to Penrith Training Centre, but this was not the result of any co-ordinated discussion of his particular needs. At the time of the murder, the school was concerned about his behaviour in class, but no one at the school had seen the Penrith report.

Three times, teachers or the Educational Welfare Officer expressed the view that Darren Coulburn would be better off elsewhere. The first time was after his conviction for arson of the school art block in November 1985. The second time was in February 1986 when staff from the school and his social worker met his father, and the third time was

41

at the end of the Summer term 1986, when he went off to Penrith. By the summer of 1986, despite the growing number of incidents in which Darren Coulburn was involved, that option had effectively been taken off the agenda and ruled out. Why? Because it had been brought before a governors' meeting in December 1985, after the burning of the art block, and had been rejected.

At that meeting, the governors felt that there were sufficient grounds for expelling Darren Coulburn for his part in setting fire to the art block. The decision was taken on the basis that he should not be punished twice for the same offence. We have been unconvinced by this as an argument. It ignores the effect on school morale and discipline. Other boys might believe that similar breaches of discipline would also go unpunished if nothing happened to Darren or his companion. It ignores the harmful effect on the boys concerned in the arson, the inevitable taunts and ridicule they would face if they remained at the school. It is also like saying that a police officer convicted of serious assault on a member of the public should still remain in the Police Force or that an employee who is convicted of stealing from his or her employer should never be dismissed because this amounts to double punishment.

We have also been unconvinced by the manner in which the governors reached their decision. The evidence makes it clear that Dr Gough and Mr Moors knew of the staff disquiet about Darren Coulburn remaining in the school, but they did not fully report this to the other governors. By not giving adequate notice of the item on the agenda, they effectively stifled any informed discussion. The teacher governors in particular felt that they would have been able to make a more meaningful contribution if they had had more time. We cannot say whether this was done deliberately or not. We cannot say if the decision at the governors' meeting would have been any different if there had been more time, fuller information and fuller discussion. To us it is one of many examples of the management style of Dr Gough and Mr Moors. Dr Gough got his way, but created a further layer of staff resentment. In the process, it became much more difficult for the school to deal effectively or realistically with Darren Coulburn.

With hindsight, he should have been removed from Burnage before the beginning of the September term. In our view no one can go further. There was certainly no basis for removing Darren Coulburn from Burnage High School because he had shown a propensity to be violent or had given any indication at all that he was likely to commit murder or other serious injury.

Was it a racist murder? In answering this question we have tried to keep to certain working defintions of racism and racialism, which we drew up at the start of our inquiry. These are as follows:

Racial discrimination   To treat one particular group of people, or individuals belonging to that group, less favourably than others on grounds of race, colour, nationality or ethnic or national origins, and unequally with other groups in society – perhaps through laws or social policies only applied to them; also by exercising discretion in the application of rules which clearly differentiate between people, based upon their origin or skin colour.

Racial prejudice   Unfavourable opinion or feelings of and towards particular groups or members of those groups based on the individual or groups' race, colour or ethnicity. Prejudice is not innate, but is learned through socialisation and is encouraged by an environment that has itself been shaped by history, social and economic.

Racialism   Refers to prejudiced beliefs and behaviour based on race, colour or ethnicity. Someone who acts in a racially prejudiced way based on those beliefs is a racialist.

Racism   The doctrine that an individual or his or her behaviour is determined by stable inherited characteristics deriving from separate racial stocks, having distinctive attributes, and usually standing in relations of "superiority" and "inferiority".
Racism is more than just a set of ideas or beliefs. When these become systematised into a philosophy of "race" superiority, and when this then becomes a part of the way in which society as a whole is organised, then the term "racism" is used.
A society whose most powerful economic and social institutions are organised on, or in effect act on or reflect, the principle that one race is superior to another is racist.

Racial Group   A group defined by colour, race, nationality or ethnic or national origins.

Ethnic Group   A group with a long shared history and a cultural tradition of its own, having a common geographic origin, a common language, a common literature and a common religion. In *Mandla Dowell Lee* [1983] 2 AC 548, the House of Lords ruled that Sikhs were an ethnic group based upon those criteria.

We do not claim that these working definitions are either full or comprehensive, but they do indicate the basis upon which we approach our task. We draw a distinction between racism and racialism. Racialism involves a motive and prejudice, but there can be racism

43

without either of these. Thus racism starts out as a doctrine or set of ideas, which then become fixed and embedded into the very structure of society. There comes into being an effective racial hierarchy with one race in charge and others at or nearer the bottom of the hierarchy. The hierarchy is both real and perceived. The "uppety" black person is someone who is perceived as having aspirations above his or her alloted station.

An individual can properly be described as a "racist" if he or she subscribes consciously or unconsciously to the doctrine of racism. Behaviour can properly be described as "racist" if it is based on the doctrine of racism or reflects the racist structure of society. Behaviour may be consciously or unconsciously "racist". Consciously racist behaviour may also be described as "racialist" if the behaviour is motivated by racial prejudice.

A murder comprises the unlawful act of killing someone and a mental element – either an intention to kill or to cause serious injury. The motive for killing may be anger, jealousy, revenge, greed and so forth. A murder may properly be described as "racialist" if, but only if, it is done for a racialist motive, out of racial prejudice, for example because the victim is black.

We have no doubt at all that the murder by Darren Coulburn was not racialist. There is no evidence that he stabbed Ahmed Ullah because he was Asian or because he was looking for a "Paki" to kill. This was not that sort of case at all. On the contrary we have felt it necessary to keep clear the complex motivations behind Darren Coulburn's response to these events. He was a highly disturbed boy, a bully, and a person of low self esteem, who had no doubt been humiliated by Ahmed on the previous day. He may also have felt jealousy – he was in the remedial class, and Ahmed was in the top stream.

While there is no evidence that the murder was racialist, it is equally true that there is no evidence that it would have happened, even if Ahmed had been white. Indeed, we are quite sure that if Ahmed was white, there would not have been this murder.

So was it racist? A murder may be racist if the culture and context in which the killing takes place mirrors the relative positions in society of black and white students or reflects the racist hierarchy in which we live and perceive ourselves. Here we need to look at the culture and context in which Darren Coulburn acted and the audiences to whom he was appealing after the stabbing for support and vindication of what he had done. We find:

44

1 That in the incidents prior to the murder Darren Coulburn was picking on smaller Asian boys who appealed to Ahmed Ullah for help.

2 Ahmed offered his help to those boys in the context that he and they were Asian students who had experienced racism on a day to day basis. His sense of justice was informed and no doubt sharpened by the daily injustice of racism experienced in school and in the community, by the "Paki" label, the jokes about pork and curry, and so forth.

3 Darren Coulburn was very much part of the racist culture of Burnage School, in which Asians were more often identified by white students as "Pakis" than by their individual names, and were called "Paki", even if they were Sikhs or came from Bangladesh. This culture is so firmly embedded that many students and teachers who made statements to us or gave evidence to us did not regard the conduct to which it gives rise as unusual or offensive.

4 At the moment of truth when the knife entered Ahmed's body, he became a "stupid Paki" in the eyes of his killer. After the murder there is evidence of Darren saying to white students "I've killed a Paki". It is as if he is appealing to them for support and vindication of what he has done. It is significant that he did not say: "Ahmed thought he was strong and could deal with me. I showed him who is boss round here." That would be the utterance of a defeated bully getting his own back by playing dirty. But he does not even say: "I killed Ahmed." He depersonalises him. "I've killed a Paki" depersonalises Ahmed and turns him into a thing which is known to be downgraded and fair game within the culture of racism in the society. To "kill a Paki" should earn stripes rather than condemnation. What comes across is a tacit hope and expectation on Darren's part that the white boys he tells cannot possibly react as he would expect them to if he said he had killed a white boy. But there is no evidence that his words found any echo from his audience.

So although it was not a racialist murder in the sense that Darren Coulburn's motive was to kill someone of another race against whom he felt prejudice, it was a racist murder in the light of the culture and context in which it took place. Racism was one of the vital ingredients that brought these two boys together in that fatal encounter. Racism was a factor which led Darren Coulburn to bully the smaller Asian boys in the Ladybarn Park; racism was behind their appeal to Ahmed for help, and his response; racism no doubt fuelled Darren Coulburn's bitter response to his own humiliation by Ahmed and added potency to his vow for revenge; and in the fatal moment Ahmed lost all individual identity and became a symbol of his race – a "Paki".

We emphasise that we are not talking here of marauding gangs of National Front in the neighbourhood, of whom Darren Coulburn is one. Nor are we dealing with some logical progression from racial insults to racial harassment to racial violence to racial murder, as is implied in the notes prepared for tutor group discussion by Ms Aisthorpe. On the other hand, if the murder is not seen in the racist culture in which we live in Britain, we deny the full significance of what has happened. If we do not deal with the racism of the murder, we do away with the need to examine, and, if necessary, change the racial structures which make Asian boys a suitable target for the attention of bullies, which imbue boys like Ahmed Ullah with a particular sense of injustice, and which produce the tragic response of a Darren Coulburn.

By failing to recognise or acknowledge any racism in the crime at all, the police outraged the whole Asian community and denied their reality. On the other hand, by giving racism as the only explanation, the school shut its eyes to the full complexity of the event and failed thereby to make the necessary and significant distinction between Darren Coulburn and his white peers. There is nothing in the evidence to suggest that a murder of this kind could only have taken place at Burnage High School. It could have happened in any number of other schools in Manchester or the United Kingdom. What singles Burnage out is the aftermath of the tragedy. Because of a failure to understand the racist context in which the murder took place, neither the school nor the police were capable of dealing with the great ripple effects that flowed from it. The events of March 1987 are peculiarly Burnage events and we take the view that they flow directly from the handling of Ahmed's murder.

The note prepared by Ms Aisthorpe for tutor discussion totally misses the point. By the terms in which it is expressed it encourages each side to see everything in partial terms and put everything in a racial context. It thus helps to polarise the school along racial lines – whites to take on the guilt of what Darren Coulburn has done, and Asians to feel victimised and further afraid. But there is more. The tone of the document is complacent and self congratulatory. It is almost as if it is directed towards Dr Gough's opposition on the teaching staff, suggesting that the tragedy of Ahmed's death is a good reason for liking his anti-racist policies. It implies that Ahmed's death legitimises these policies.

On the evidence presented to us it is quite clear that the murder was used as a metaphor for the feelings and experiences of all sections of the Asian community, particularly of the youth. Although, as we shall see, much of the expression used by them was hyperbole and seemed to be way over the top, yet it had poignancy and indicated the depth and strength of feeling. It enabled people to bring together their experiences, to explain and to begin to come to terms with the tragedy of Ahmed's death. Unfortunately that, as we shall see, had to be done outside the school and at times in opposition to it. But that is the subject of a later chapter.

CHAPTER 6

The Funeral

When a child dies there is a special grief. When a child is murdered there is a special anger. Ahmed's family, in their special grieving, had to do what any family has to do when confronted with a death – they had to arrange a funeral.

For Ahmed's family in their special grieving there were special problems. The first problem was to convince the police to release Ahmed's body. It took many 'phone calls before the police told them that Ahmed's body would be released. The Coroners' office told them by telephone they would need an undertaker. Ahmed's family contacted a local firm.

For the Ullah family in their special grieving there were special problems. The second problem was that political groups that had become involved tried to take over, saying "You should do this or that". The Imam and some others from the Victoria Mosque came to see the family. They said, "OK, we'll do everything; you don't have to worry, we will get a Muslim undertaker". Weakened by grief, Ahmed's family agreed. For Ahmed's family in their special grieving there were special problems. The third of these was a dispute within the Victoria Mosque: the Mosque was not in fact going to arrange the funeral. This was discovered two days before the funeral was to have taken place. Selina Ullah had been trying to organise it. Never having organised a funeral before, her mother and father too grief stricken to give much assistance, she found herself overwhelmed. Kabir Ahmed of the Greater Manchester Bangladeshi Association then, with what Selina felt was his knack for taking over completely, did exactly that: he took over. The funeral was again out of the control of the family. They were not ungrateful for this help, but neither were they completely happy with it. At least the funeral would take place.

Despite the last minute uncertainties in the funeral arrangements Ahmed's friends in school along with all other students received a letter on the 22nd of September to give to Burnage parents, informing them of the funeral arrangements.

49

BURNAGE HIGH SCHOOL
DRGG/PM/SJS
22nd September, 1986.
Dear Parents,

re: the funeral of Ahmed Iqbal Ullah.

The funeral of Ahmed Iqbal Ullah will take place at Platt Field Park tomorrow Tuesday 23rd September at 2.00 p.m.

As a mark of respect to his family, friends and community, Burnage High School will be closed on Tuesday for the whole afternoon from 1.00 p.m. The arrangements will enable all the many friends of Ahmed amongst the students and staff of the school to pay their respects to his memory by attending the funeral service.

Transport for all those who wish to attend the funeral will be arranged from both schools to the Park. If you wish your son to attend the funeral service as a representative of the school, then please fill in and return the slip printed below on Tuesday morning.

Yours sincerely,

(signed) G. Gough
Headteacher

....

BURNAGE HIGH SCHOOL
The funeral of Ahmed Iqbal Ullah.

I give permission for my son _____ (name) of _____ (form) to attend the funeral of Ahmed Iqbal Ullah at Platt Fields Park on Tuesday 23rd September at 2.00 p.m.

Signed _____
Parent/Guardian

....

By the morning of the 23rd of September 1986, buses had been arranged to take staff and students of Burnage to the funeral. One member of staff had had the foresight to telephone a Muslim parent to find out what would be acceptable dress, and so on. Other members of staff had thought attendance at the funeral was voluntary. When they arrived at school, they found that attendance was required of all staff when an announcement was made that form tutors would be on buses with their forms. Michael Molloy, the District Inspector, had arrived at school

50

early on. While having a conversation with Peter Moors, the Deputy Head, Lesley Aisthorpe told them that some of the women teachers were worried that they were not going to be properly dressed for the funeral. After a brief conversation, Michael Molloy suggested that they go out and buy 15 headscarves, which Lesley Aisthorpe did. To Michael Molloy, this demonstrated that the staff at Burnage School had actually felt uncertain about the role they were to play in relation to the funeral.

By lunchtime on the day of the funeral, white, Afro-Caribbean and Asian students at Ducie School, which Ahmed had attended for a short while, prepared to go to the funeral. Officials at Ducie School had telephoned Ahmed's family about attendance at the funeral, and had been told: "Please don't stop anybody from going because any of Ahmed's friends are welcome".

Robert Raikes, a white parent, made his way at lunchtime to Platt Field Park for Ahmed's funeral. He expected to see his son, a Burnage student, there too.

By lunchtime, the boys at Burnage had been told to assemble in the hall. People were milling around, as the staff and students of Burnage waited to get on the buses. Ahmed's friends – one of whom was Robert Raike's son – prepared to go to the funeral. Moments before they were due to get on the buses, Peter Moors, the Deputy Head, came in to make an announcement. He looked upset. Michael Molloy, the District Inspector, was there; he knew nothing of the announcement before it was made. The staff were there; they knew nothing of the announcement before it was made. A decision had been taken: "Only Asian boys were to go to the funeral." "On information received" it was considered unsafe for white or Afro-Caribbean students of Burnage to go to the funeral of their school friend. Michael Molloy's understanding subsequently was that it was the police who had advised the school that it would be unsafe for white and Afro-Caribbean youngsters to go to the funeral.

According to Dr Gough's account, the police were not involved at all. The first reaction to the announcement was a stunned disbelief. To the staff assigned to get on buses with students, already distressed while waiting, there was no time to discuss the announcement.

The Asian students left with teachers for the funeral. Other teachers volunteered to stay behind with the white and Afro-Caribbean students. Again there was uncertainty. The teacher who had telephoned the Muslim parent to find out about acceptable dress, found it difficult to understand the decision, because she had been told in clear terms by that parent that the Asian community "will have their people under control."

51

The students also found it difficult to understand the decision. As one white student was to say, "it was not fair", because they knew Ahmed had a lot of white friends in his class as well as in the other classes.

At Platt Field Park, the buses drove up, the students and staff got out. When the hearse came, the coffin was carried up a slope onto a dais. The boys stood very quietly in line along the grass verge. During the service, the boys filed by the open coffin. About 1,500 people attended. Amongst the people there were community leaders; local schools; Bangladeshis from the Mosque; and a number of individuals, white and black, young and old. There was no trouble at the funeral – only grief.

No-one at Burnage was unaffected by the decision to allow only Asian students to attend the funeral. That morning, it had stunned and surprised. Robert Raikes felt angry, as he waited at Platt Field for his son to arrive with the school party. His son, Ahmed's friend, never arrived; because Robert Raike's son was white, he never got the opportunity to say goodbye to and mourn his friend. Ahmed's family did not make any distinction between Asian, White, or Afro-Caribbean, they wanted all boys at the funeral.

The decision separated white and Afro-Caribbean students from Asian students. If linked with the leaflet sent out to staff for discussion in class (saying that the murder is racist) the decision must have reinforced a feeling amongst white students that they were somehow to blame. It puts them in the same category as Darren Coulburn. It is a further link in a chain which leads to polarisation of the students at Burnage along racial lines. The polarisation would finally surface in the events of March 1987.

There are no guidelines for sudden deaths of any sort existing in the Education Department. The Education Department does not seem to have advised the school or to have given full consideration to the matter of the funeral. The school management did not seem to have found out even basic facts concerning dress and protocol prior to the funeral. There were no staff briefings or discussion on the implications of such an event prior to the funeral.

The evidence given to us on the decision to exclude white and Afro-Caribbean boys from the funeral is somewhat bizarre. One witness told us that the decision was taken by Dr Gough alone. Mr Moors said he and Dr Gough took it together and Dr Gough was ambivalent.

The reason for the decision is also bizarre. Whether it was taken by Dr Gough alone or by both him and Mr Moors, the evidence suggests that both had had a meeting with Mr Jamal, a school Governor, who says he had informed Dr Gough and Mr Moors that some Asian taxi drivers had visited him on the morning of the funeral, they had sticks with them and were talking of revenge. Mr Jamal said he told Dr Gough and Mr Moors that he thought there would be retaliatory action by Asians against whites at the funeral.

Mr Moors says that he was told by Mr Jamal that things were "tense in the community." He added that he and Dr Gough were influenced by Mr Jamal. Dr Gough painted a much more elaborate picture, but refused to reveal whether he had been given the vital information that there would be trouble at the funeral by Mr Jamal. This is his account:

"When it [the funeral] was to be held in Platt Fields, we knew that what would take place might be quite unlike any other Asian Funeral that any of us had ever attended. From the date of the murder, right through until the week – perhaps a fortnight – after the funeral, we had had continual telephone calls from people such as, 'I live next door to a Pakistani family and they have just told me there is a group going to do this, that and the other', and then one would have suggestions from the other side, that there were white people who were going to do this, that and the other. We knew that there were activist groups involved around this. There had been a call, for example, for an Asian boycott of the school for a week, and there were calls for demonstrations, and a demonstration had finally taken place, although after the funeral. There was one rumour circulating that there was going to be a demonstration either at or after the funeral. We were warned by a member of the Asian community that there was likely to be trouble at the funeral. In this fairly uncomfortable situation, a decision had to be taken, and much as I wanted everyone to go to the funeral, one's prime responsibility is for the students, and in the end a decision was taken that Asian students should go, and that white students should not. It was taken at the very, very last minute, based on information that came very, very late . . ."

"The funeral itself – there were activist groups there, literature was being distributed. I had a worry that perhaps somebody might choose to provoke fights between students – white and black students – I don't know . . . given the massive tensions and the sort of 'phone calls that we had been receiving, and knowledge that activist groups were involved, and the contact from *somebody significant* [our emphasis] in the Asian community to say that we must expect trouble, that decision was taken. At the time of taking it, we knew that we were on a hiding to nothing."

Q. "It was, I think, the information from the particular member of the Asian community that tipped the balance?'
A. 'Yes."
Q. "And are you not anxious to reveal the name of that person because of his position in the community?"
A. "No."
Q. "Is it someone that you regard as very responsible?"
A. "Yes, he is. The information was given in confidence, and I cannot reveal the name of the person."
Q. "Not the sort of man who would needlessly spread alarm or anything like that?"
A. "No."

Dr Gough was then informed of the evidence which both Mr Moors and Mr Jamal had given and after a short adjournment, his solicitor informed the Panel as follows:

"In the near future, during the course of this week, Dr Gough will speak to the source of his information and enquire whether that person is willing to release him from his obligation of confidentiality. If he is, he will write to the tribunal and inform them of the name."

No letter has been forwarded to the Panel.

What is clear from Dr Gough's account is that police played no part in his decision. We infer from all the evidence that the Asian to whom he referred was in fact Mr Jamal and that it was on his last minute information that Dr Gough took the vital decision. It was clearly a panic decision, taken, no doubt, with the best of motives, but taken very much in isolation. We find it a little surprising and disturbing that, for such an obviously vital decision affecting so many people, at a time of great grief and emotion, Dr Gough did not make any obvious consultations. The Chief Education Officer was available; Mr Molloy, the Inspector, was available and was actually at the school at the critical time; he could have consulted with the Ullah family, with the Greater Manchester Bangladeshi Association, with the MCCR or with the Heads of neighbouring schools. He must have known that representatives from Ducie were going to be at the funeral. As a matter of fact, we were told by Ducie High School that they had informed Dr Gough that they were bringing their students (including white and Afro-Caribbean) to the funeral. If he had consulted with any of these people we are quite sure that a different decision would have been taken and Dr Gough would not have panicked.

It was a decision that deepened a special grief. It was a decision that caused a special anger.

CHAPTER 7

The Politics of the Murder

The Community Leaders had become involved on the day of the killing, September 17th 1986 as had the City Council. Three days after the murder, Ahmed's family were visited by Tariq Mahmood of the Pakistani Workers Association. He asked them what action they were taking over Ahmed's death. Selina Ullah and the family had not thought of "taking action". Selina Ullah pointed out that the family could not take any action on their own, that they would need support from others. Tariq Mahmood promised to help obtain support for the family, and said it would be wide support. The family felt the need of support and backing from the Bangladeshi community. They expected to get it.

On the basis of this first discussion a meeting was to be arranged for Sunday September 21st 1986. Selina Ullah had suggested Bangladeshi House as an appropriate place for the meeting, but when Tariq tried to book it, explaining who was to use it, and the fact that Pakistanis and Afro-Caribbeans would be attending, permission was refused because Bangladeshi House would not give permission for Afro-Caribbeans to attend the meeting. When Selina Ullah heard this, she told Tariq to invite Afro-Caribbeans anyway, and that they should go on the Sunday to make sure that they were let in. This in fact is what happened. The room was filled with well over a hundred people. One prominent community leader apparently later informed the MCCR that there were only about twenty people at the meeting and that these were merely "children." Indeed, according to one witness, the established community leaders who were present attempted to exclude all people under sixteen from the meeting on the grounds that it was better for the elders to decide what their children could or could not do. About fifteen of these leaders were present. They asked who was to chair the meeting. Selina Ullah took the Chair. This, too, met with the disapproval of the leaders, according to the same witness. They held it up as a sign of weakness to have a woman chairing the meeting. Her view (and that of the rest of Ahmed's family) was that there should be a steering group that included as many of the various organisations as possible.

Some people at the meeting suggested that Afro-Carribeans were "as bad as the whites", in that they, by themselves, or in collaboration with whites, often make Asians the victims of racial abuse, verbal and physical, and that Asians, therefore, should work alone. To Selina it seemed that some members of the Race Sub-Committee and some of the community leaders intended to thwart the establishment of a wide-based steering committee. Appeals for unity fell on deaf ears as Selina was accused of allowing herself to be manipulated. Every time a proposal for a demonstration of the community's anger was made the established leaders accused the proposer of being a communist, set on causing a race war in order to develop their own beliefs. Every call for effective action was stifled, according to one witness. The meeting was effectively disrupted by this dissension.

Selina Ullah and other members of the family who were at the meeting realised that if the community leaders could not be in control, they would drop the family. Selina Ullah thinks it may have been this meeting which led the religious leaders at the Mosque to stop making the funeral arrangements.

For Selina Ullah and the rest of Ahmed's family there was no going back on the attempt to take public action around Ahmed's murder. A further public meeting was arranged for the following Saturday, and in the course of the week of the funeral the Ahmed Iqbal Memorial Committee was founded. The Committee met every day that week. Between 30–40 people attended. Leaflets were organised and distributed, mainly by fellow students of Ahmed. The Saturday meeting was held at Longsight Library. It was attended by about 300 whites, Asians, and a few Afro-Caribbeans, who crowded into the lecture hall. The form of the meeting was simple: people were told about Ahmed, told about the problems of racism and violence in schools, and were asked for support for the demonstration that was organised for Monday, September 29th. Only one person attended from Bangladeshi House. After the demonstration, Selina was told by someone who was afraid of being victimized that the community leaders had actively discouraged participation.

Another witness told us that the community leaders spent most of the weekend between the Saturday meeting and the Monday demonstration trying to ensure that the demonstration failed. We were told that they had gone round the houses calling on parents and trying to dissuade them from allowing their children to take part.

After the meeting, the organisers contacted the Chief Education Officer for Manchester by letter and by telephone, and asked that school students be allowed to attend the demonstration. The organisers also asked that schools should be closed on that day. The Council denied the request, saying that the notice was too short and there was not enough time to notify parents. One teacher, however, did ~ay that they had been told that students who did attend the demonstration would not be marked off as truanting or absent.

The first demonstration took place on Monday, September 29th 1986. About 1,000 people, mainly school students, attended. Because of the Council's decisions only the most committed students left school to go to the demonstration. The students who attended from Burnage were mainly Asian, but white and Afro-Caribbean students attended as well. They included a number of Ahmed's friends who had been prevented by Burnage School from going to the funeral.

The organisers had also requested that the demonstration be allowed to start from the school playground. This request was also refused, so the demonstrators left from outside the school and followed a 6 mile route to the Education Department in Crown Square. There, the organisers presented a list of points to the staff worker at the main desk. No one from the Council or from the Education Department came out to meet the demonstration, nor did the Council or the Education Department ever acknowledge receipt of the list of points or answer any of the issues raised in them. The demonstration was peaceful and well organised.

The Memorial Committee continued to meet following the demonstration. The number was much smaller than before but included a number of youths from local schools and colleges who met on a regular basis. One of the primary aims of the organisation was to encourage the development of self defence amongst the youth, who continued to face daily abuse of a racist nature and regular attacks in the schools and on the street. The committee, we were told, developed a clear understanding of the inadequacy of the anti-racist policies operating in Manchester schools. Another of the Committee's functions was monitoring Burnage School by meeting with students involved.

By late September and early October, it appeared to these students that despite a superficial lull, the Asian students were in fact very much on edge.

Selina Ullah and others had become concerned about the Manchester Council's complete lack of response to the entire sequence of events. They went to see Kath Robinson of the Council about this complete lack of response. Although Kath Robinson had not been directly involved, she was very sympathetic, and put Selina in touch with

Councillors Val Stevens and John Nicholson. As a result, a meeting was arranged for October 14th – Ahmed's birthday.

At the meeting two issues were raised: the lack of support for the demonstration, and the failure to contact Ahmed's family? The Councillors said that the Council had not supported the demonstration because they did not know who was organising it, the time was too short, it was not planned properly, and the demonstrators had been insensitive in routing the demonstration past primary schools. When asked about the lack of contact with Ahmed's family, they said that they had been dealing with the community leaders at 19 Birch Lane, who had told them they were keeping the family informed. Ahmed's family had in fact received no information, so Councillor Nicholson asked the council press secretary to send all future press releases, together with copies of all those already issued, to the family direct. The family did receive the backdated releases, but none of the future ones were sent until Selina contacted the Council just before the trial. Although the Councillors told Selina to let them know of any future requests, she felt that this was a token gesture. She felt that the Concillors, like the community leaders, were simply behaving in accordance with a particular political stance.

The community leaders also held a meeting after the demonstration to deal with concerns expressed in the community that there was a lack of information about what was happening. On October 1st 1986 the GMBA produced a leaflet headed "DEATH OF A BANGLADESHI BOY". It, too, was an angry leaflet. It stated:

"Ahmed opposed the racial harassment of younger Asian students and was stabbed to death for his action. It is disgraceful and disturbing that on the morning of his death, adults were busy in attempting to conceal the truth . . . what little that has been reported by the media implies that no racial motive can be attributed, though the school, Education Department and the City Council have admitted that Ahmed was the victim of a racist assault."

The leaflet went on to summarise some of the GMBA's findings at Burnage:

1. "The recent report on the high level of violence in schools was ignored.
2. Anxious parents have on occasions been turned away from the school for not making a prior appointment.

60

3. Asian children have been advised by the staff not to discuss racism in the school, either with their parents or others.

4. Section 11 teachers concerned with the problems were powerless to act.

5. The school allowed Asian students to leave 15 minutes earlier than the white children, without the knowledge of the Education Department.

6. The governing body either ignored the problems or were ignorant of them.

7. The life of Ahmed may possibly have been saved if the school had rushed him to hospital.

8. The Headmaster was unable to implement fully the policy of the Education Department, either because of personal resistance to those policies, or pressures exerted by some members of the staff/governing body."

The leaflet then contained a demand that the following steps be taken immediately:

1. "Set up an independent judicial inquiry to investigate racism in Manchester schools, Burnage in particular. The Terms of Reference of the Inquiry are to be outlined by the Greater Manchester Bangladeshi Association.

2. Set up a Memorial Fund in the name of Ahmed Iqbal Ullah, to be used in fighting racism.

3. Set up an affirmative action programme in all the educational institutions in the City, to expand the limited opportunities of employment of Asians (particularly Bangladeshi) who form 2/3 of the ethnic minorities in the City. The programme should aim to achieve a proper racial balance in the workforce. This will give Asians the opportunity and benefits that have been denied to them for years."

The community leaders also pointed to the meeting of September 17th as something that they had "done" after Ahmed's death, and they raised various other matters to reassure the people of the community, including the suggestion that Ahmed's family were in some way ungrateful for the help they had been given. The Memorial Committee felt that the proposal for a Public Inquiry and a memorial fund were meaningless gestures.

There is grief that comes after a death.
There is political capital to be made from a murder.

61

About a week or so before Darren Coulburn's trial, the Memorial Committee met again to discuss the organisation of a meeting prior to the trial and picket of the Court. The meeting was planned to be a public meeting on 31st January, at Longsight Library. However, on Friday, 30th January the Committee received a letter from the Acting Director of Cultural Services of Manchester City Council saying that the Memorial Committee was banned from using all City Council premises because of the "sub judice" provision of the Law. All other Council facilities were taken away, including photocopying and reprographic facilities at Council premises and the Committee's meeting place at Longsight Library. As a result, the Memorial Committee held their public meeting outside the library and about 80 people attended.

The leaflet produced for the picket of the Court has been much criticised and commented on. We, therefore, produce it in full.

AHMED IQBAL ULLAH

Memorial Committee
c/o 584 Stockport Road
Longsight
Manchester

On Wednesday 17th September 1986, Ahmed Iqbal Ullah was brutally stabbed to death by a racist white youth in Burnage High School. On February 3rd 1987, the trial of the racist murderer begins.

Since the murder a conspiracy to cover up the racist nature of this barbaric attack has taken place. The police made statements immediately after the murder, saying that it was not racist. The murderers solicitor had made similar claims and received wide coverage in the media. The Headmaster of the school has gone so far as to send letters saying Ahmed was not murdered in the school. The latest in this conspiracy to cover up the racist nature of the barbaric attack is an attempt to gag up any dissenting voice by raising the bogey of "Contempt of Court".

BANNED
A meeting called by the Ahmed Iqbal Ullah Memorial Committee at Longsight Library of Saturday 31st January 1987 was banned by the City Council by denying the use of the hall or any other hall or premises of the City Council. The letter banning the meeting arrived the day before the meeting was due to be held. The motive behind this move is clear. When we are murdered by racists, we must keep

quiet. Least of all we must not call a racist murder a racist murder. However, it is safe to lie and deny racism. The bogey of "Contempt of Court" had not been raised against those who have stated that racism played no part in this barbaric murder. Furthermore, this action by the City Council is a serious attack upon the rights of black people, and all those who wish to fight against racism. We shall not be intimidated!

What happened to Ahmed?

On Tuesday 16th September 1986, Ahmed went to the assistance of a fellow Asian student who was being bullied by a group of racist white youths. On the way home from school he was attacked and threatened that he would be killed the next day. At 8.30 am the next morning Ahmed was fatally stabbed by a racist white youth, who immediately after the stabbing started boasting that he had "Killed a Paki. . .".

Whilst Ahmed lay bleeding to death, the school authorities at first refused to listen to his screams. By the time assistance was offered, it was too late . . . Ahmed had bled to death.

Organise against RACIST ATTACKS

Ahmed's murder is clearly racist. The purpose of our protest is to make this fact known as widely as possible and to smash the conspiracy of silence. All over this country attacks are on the increase. Not only are we attacked on the streets and in our home, but our children are being murdered in school. The murder of Ahmed is a reflection of a deep-rooted racism within British society. Racist attacks and attackers will not go away by being ignored. The solution lies in the organisation of our own Self-Defence.

Self-Defence – The ONLY WAY

Ahmed's murder has once again shown that the authorities in general and the police in particular are neither capable nor willing to defend us. Therefore we must defend ourselves. The only way that our children can be safe at school is for them to organise their own Self-Defence.

We call upon all black people and anti-racist white people to show their solidarity by coming to the protest outside the Crown Court, Deansgate beginning 3rd February 1987 at 9.30 am.

PROTEST

CROWN
SQUARE
near Deansgate
Tuesday
3rd Feb
9.30 am

Don't
Let
Ahmed's
blood
be in
vain!

ORGANISE
Self-Defence
NOW

The picket began on the first day of the trial. Estimates of attendance at the first day's picket ranged from about 200 to about 50 people. These included students from Burnage and Whalley Range. The protest was loud, but peaceful. Although the police presence seemed to be "average" and there were no arrests, we were told that the police did harass some of the pickets and confiscated their leaflets. That day the leaflets were shown to the trial judge and banned as being in contempt of court and prejudicial to the trial, mainly because they asserted that the killing was racist and that Ahmed's blood should not be in vain.

On the very last day of the trial the picket was the largest. Around 250 people awaited the verdict.

We heard a number of witnesses who had been involved with the Memorial Committee or who had filmed their demonstrations. We also spoke to many students who had taken part in their activities. However, the Pakistani Workers' Association refused to have anything to do with the Inquiry or to give evidence to it.

What is striking about the evidence in this chapter, is the reaction to the attempts of the Asian youth to create their own independent organisation. They were either treated with open hostility or ignored. The established community leaders were openly hostile. They castigated the leaders of the Memorial Committee as communist agitators who were trying to use Ahmed's death for their own revolutionary ends. The

Council leaders were indifferent, later pleading ignorance and lack of time. The City Council was both indifferent and hostile. The Memorial Committee's letters were unanswered, information was refused or simply not given and later all the Council facilities were withdrawn on the flimsy pretext of "sub judice".Dr Gough almost became apoplectic over the contents of a particular part of their leaflet and expressed himself as most concerned that the Panel might give credence to anything that the Memorial Committee had done. Why this hostility?

Their protests were loud and noisy, but they were never violent. With one exception, their message was no different from what the established community leaders were saying, or indeed, the leaders of the Council. Both complained of delay; both complained of racial violence and harassment and said that the murder was racist. But the established community leaders' response was to have an independent judicial inquiry, a Memorial Fund and more jobs for Bangladeshis in the Manchester education service. How these proposals would reduce the violence or harassment is not spelt out. The Memorial Committee on the other hand made no bones about their position. Given the lack of success of the police in dealing with racial attacks and their history of indifference and hostility to any kind of self organisation among Asian youth, there was only one answer – self defence. The Memorial Committee and the Asian youth draw hostility or indifference because they put the finger on all the other organisations and institutions which should be dealing with the problem but are not. It is too easy to attack them on the grounds that they are too young, too revolutionary, too hasty, too angry or too outspoken. There is no doubt that their leaflets were angry; they exaggerated; and the tone was intemperate. But the bald fact of the matter is that no one esle was attempting to address the issue with a similar honesty or commitment. What is clear is that neither they nor any one in the GMBA or other established organisations had sufficient breadth of vision or experience to bridge the gaps which existed and which could have created a new and important organi-sational voice for Asian youth in Manchester. That task still remains to be done.

The second reason for the opposition was the perceived threat from the budding self-organisation of Asian youth to more established organisations and institutions. Any independent self-activity amongst any relatively powerless section of the population always arouses the anger of those who hold the existing reins of power. They feel instinctively threatened. They feel a need to control and channel the fledgling organisation.

Labelling the organisers of the Memorial Committee as outside agitators and communist revolutionaries was a classic response. It ignored the fact that many of the young Asians wanted to use the murder of Ahmed Ullah as a metaphor for their own feelings and experiences about racism. In our view this is neither bandwagoning nor crude opportunism of the sort that one often sees when the disarrayed white left attempt to respond to similar events.

There is also no doubt that the push for an inquiry by the established community leaders was an attempt to channel the response of youth away from demonstrations and marches and into the more established legal channels. The push came after the elders had failed to control the response of the young people who gathered at the first meeting held on Saturday the 21st of September at Bangladeshi House, in Birch Lane. Similarly, when the first demonstration at the end of September 1986 was organised, the established community leaders made a very clear point of discouraging students from joining in.

Then there was the issue of racism. The students did not argue the question of racism. For them it was already settled. They drew on their own experience. Ahmed's death was for them the high moment, the culmination of that experience, and they wanted to do something about it, in order to demonstrate their anger and to organise into self defence groups to stop themselves becoming victims of that racism.

The established community leaders wanted no part of this action, but they did want to argue the question of racism. The police statement that race was not involved in the murder gave them all the ammunition they wanted. It enabled them to enter into a spirited correspondence with the police, the MCCR and Council leaders, and of course while you are still debating the issue, it is always premature to do something about it. We have no doubt that there would have been less ferocity in the debate over racism, if it was merely a response to the police and not also in answer to the calls for demonstrations and self defence by the fledgling youth organisation. In truth, the debate over the racism of the murder was a debate within the established bodies as to how best to control the activities of the youth.

The police motivation in saying that it was not a racist murder was put very openly and frankly by Chief Superintendent Sherratt – it was to prevent warfare on the streets. The police were clearly afraid of a white backlash. If Asian youth organised to defend themselves against racial violence, who knows what might happen. It might even lead to the white backlash joining forces with the Asian self-defence against the police themselves. Autonomous self-defence organisations in 1980s Britain are clearly bad news for any police force. The surprising thing to us is the huge but short lived success of the GMBA in getting the police to backtrack as much as they did over their statement about the racism involved in Ahmed Ullah's death.

The community leaders, on the other hand, were afraid of their own youth getting out of control. By combining the race card and the call for an inquiry they were no doubt hoping to redirect the anger and energy into more established legal channels.

New political movements very rarely realise all their potential and this was true of the Memorial Committee. As an organisation it largely petered out after the trial of Darren Coulburn. But the notion of self-defence did not. It has a much older history and had already caught the imagination of Asian youth in Southall, Bradford, Leeds and East London. From the time of Ahmed's killing it had clearly taken root in the youth in Burnage High School and came to fruition in the events of 1987 in a way that no outside agitator could have planned.

CHAPTER 8

The Management of the Tragedy

A tragedy had occurred at Burnage High School. It was a tragedy for students and staff no less than for parents, black and white alike. What was important was not just an intepretation of what caused the tragedy. It was equally important to deal with the issue of grief, of emotion, of trauma in the school community.

Students do not kill one another in schools every year, let alone every day. The majority of teachers and education officers go through a life-long teaching career without having to deal with the situation that Burnage High suddenly faced on September 17th, 1986. How does a school community deal with the shock, the emotion, the grief, and the intense anger?

Large numbers of students were absent from school in the weeks following the murder. Some parents were actively seeking transfers for their children to get them out of Burnage. Young students were confused, frightened and uncertain when life in their school would return to normal. Many had not experienced deaths within their own families, and many more had never been associated with the death of one so young, killed by someone his own age.

While the event became the subject of great politicking in the community, with press, police, community leaders and local government officials busily engaged in contests and debates, young students re-lived the event of Ahmed's stabbing day and night. Others would not, could not, talk about it. Teachers were equally confused, especially as they were reading about their school almost daily in the local press, and yet were not openly talking amongst themselves, nor having regular briefings from the senior management of the school.

On October 2nd 1986, the Chief Inspector, John Taylor, and Michael Molloy, met a young black probationary teacher at Burnage. Michael Molloy's evidence was that:

"Mr S ... was really upset as a teacher and felt that he could no longer teach in Burnage High School, really because of the murder and his own personal thoughts about that. What we arranged to happen was for him to go and teach in another school, and he went and is now teaching in another high school."

Whether it was Roy Jobson or Mike Ellis who made the suggestion, the Schools Psychological and Child Guidance Service was requested to help with bereavement counselling. As a result, Maria Heffernan, District Senior Educational Psychologist, and Pauline Collier, Educational Psychologist, arranged to go into Lower School on September 22nd, 1986.

For Pauline Collier, this was a visit to a school she had known well some years before, between 1979 and 1982. At that time she had found it a harsh "male culture", and she felt that the potential for violence that the culture of all-male institutions generated was a problem that deserved attention.

By the time she visited in September 1986, she could detect a change in the atmosphere. The atmosphere was noticeably "softer", and she felt that the staff, to whom she and Maria Heffernan spoke, were able to focus their discussion on the emotional needs of the students and teachers who had been most closely involved with the tragedy.

Maria Heffernan and Pauline Collier briefed the staff at a session on October 3rd, 1986, and left them with some guidelines to assist them in dealing with students who required counselling and support.

As will become clear in later chapters, we have concluded that the manner in which the school managed the event of Ahmed's killing determined to a large extent the future course of events in the school and in the community. For this reason, we examine what the school community was or was not assisted in dealing with, through its access to the Educational Support Services.

At the session on October 3rd 1986, Maria Heffernan and Pauline Collier shared the following ideas with teaching staff at Burnage:

"BURNAGE LOWER SCHOOL. October 3rd, 1986

Death is something that can produce our deepest and most profound feelings and the grief that comes with it can be extremely intense. It affects our emotions, it affects our bodies and it affects our lives.

Emotionally grief can start with numbness that can last from a few minutes to a few days, but gradually as the reality of what has happened is let in bit by bit it becomes a mixture of very raw feelings such as sorrow, anguish, anger, regret, guilt and fear.

Physically grief may be experienced as exhaustion – it may also be experienced as emptiness, tension, irritability, sleeplessness or loss of appetite. Grief affects all our lives because it reminds us of our own vulnerability and mortality in a way that makes us re-examine our own personal reationships and our own personal priorities.

The way death occurs obviously has a very powerful effect on the way we feel. The death of a child which seems the most unnatural of deaths is often the most anguishing to face. Sudden deaths, especially violent or accident deaths, can in fact provoke our greatest shock, our greatest anxiety and our greatest distress.

Violent deaths make us feel vulnerable and frightened and often provoke anger and rage at the injustice of it all. Sudden deaths more than any other drive us into hours of preoccupation with if only's – if only he had not come into school, if only a member of staff had been passing, if only we had known what was going on. People in fact can go through hours of torment in this way.

The important thing to remember, of course, is that all those feelings are perfectly natural and perfectly normal, but it takes courage to face them and to feel them and let them in because, of course, it is painful. Many of us fear that if allowed in, grief will overwhelm us indefinitely but the truth is that grief that is felt and experienced does dissolve. The images of death that are so immediately powerful do fade in time.

Most of you will remember the assassination of President Kennedy which was a sudden, unnatural and violent death. What followed was that on T.V. we saw images of Kennedy, his life, the circumstances of his death and his funeral over and over again. People talked to each other about it and read about his life and this, of course, is the essential process of grieving, repeating again and again the images and feelings about the person who dies. In this way the grief ends, the fear retreats, the anger retreats and the guilt retreats. The only grief that does not end is the grief that has not been fully faced.

Grief is painful but it is healthy and surmountable and perhaps most important of all it can provide a unique opportunity to look at what we are doing in an honest way and in a way that produces constructive change. Not to do so is in a sense the biggest waste of all.

Bereavement is about the loss of a close personal relationship and most of you here and most of the boys will not have had a close personal relationship with Ahmed so the immediate shock of what happened may well have dissipated within a few days and normal life resumed. The ones most vulnerable are the ones who did know him, both staff and boys. Also those who had some responsibility for him or were closely involved with what happened and especially vulnerable

71

are those both boys and staff who have suffered other bereavement or loss of some sort in the recent past. It is only natural that a loss such as this re-awakens other losses that we have suffered.

I will just finish by saying that several factors are important in facing death.

1. Knowledge is an important factor in fighting fear. Seeking information is an essential part of adapting to a crisis situation. That is why we have put the first question because asking questions is healthy and it is important that boys' questions are dealt with honestly because you may find an emotional maturity in some of them that will surprise you. On the other hand you may find inappropriate emotions and emotional confusion because after all we bring our boys up not to show feelings; big boys do not cry, and the result of this is, according to research, that by the end of primary school many boys are cut off from their feelings and prefer to talk about other things, such as football matches, BMX bikes etc. They also have difficulty identifying feelings and emotions in others in an accurate way. In fact boys find it difficult relating to each other in a caring way because their usual relationships with each other are based in competitiveness.

2. For some a personal belief system is important whether this is Muslim or Christian. Personally I don't have a belief system and I don't know a great deal about other people's.

3. Perhaps most important of all though, are our personal support systems which includes the network of people and activities that fill our non-working lives. Most of us know the strength or weakness of our own personal support systems but we do not know the strength of the support systems of most of the boys and if you are concerned about any of the boys in particular then I feel that in the first instance personal contact with the parents to assess that support system is crucial.

Reference – *The Courage to Grieve* – Judy Tatelbaum."

Not all staff attended those sessions with the educational psychologists. Some staff carried on as normal.

For the students, however, there was no direct contact with the educational psychologists, and most of them were unaware that some of the staff had felt the need for bereavement counselling. They were unaware of their teachers' own grief.

Maria Heffernan and Pauline Collier discussed a number of issues

72

with the staff, including the support needs of the Ullah family. They indicated that it was perhaps more appropriate for staff from the school to visit the family in view of their needs.

The educational psychologists were assisted in identifying nine students who were principal witnesses to Ahmed's death; these included both Ahmed's and Darren's friends. The psychologists' role, however, was confined to supporting the staff who would work with those students.

The psychologists were in no position to tell us whether the students were ever made aware that the staff needed assistance from them as a service in relation to grief or coping with the tragedy.

Asked whether they thought it would have been important for the whole school to own the tragedy, and for staff to be very upfront about the fact that they were distressed and expected the students to be as well, Maria Hefferenan replied:

"If the school had felt that was something they wanted to share with students, I think that would have been a very positive thing. What we were responding to, at the invitation of the school, was a request to support and advise them in their work; which is slightly different from giving a prescription of what they ought to do in a very directive way."

Q. "How does [sharing the guidelines listed above] become different to recommending that as part of this whole process the school owned the tragedy, and in terms of coping with the relationships and unifying the school, it was necessary for teachers to demonstrate, "yes, we too are vulnerable".

A. I think that would have been a positive thing to suggest at the time. What we were aware of was that individual members of staff were, in fact, sharing their feelings and concerns with their own tutor groups, and were, I think, sharing the feelings that they were having, but there was not, at least in terms of what we did with the school, the kind of presentation that you are suggesting would have been a good thing to advise from our point of view, although we did suggest that it would probably be helpful if the school were to share the plan that we had sort of discussed with them, with the parents."

Q. "Did the sharing with the parents actually happen, to your knowledge?"

A. "I do not know."

Q. "Could I go on then to the question of keeping in touch with, and visting, Darren's parents and being concerned about the feelings and

73

anxieties of his friends. Were you able to monitor the extent to which that actually took place?"

A. "No. Our involvement with the school was not a close involvement over that period. Our involvement was on very much an advisory level, and I think it is fair to say we did not have a close monitoring role."

Miss Collier: "I think the whole thing was made particularly difficult because information was sub judice and people had been told not to talk about things, and that did make it difficult because, obviously, part of grieving and dealing with the pain of that involves discussing it, it involves acquiring information about that, and to balance that against the instruction that it was not to be discussed was very tricky indeed."

The Chairman: "Could I ask you, was the question of what exactly is meant by 'sub judice' ever discussed?"

Miss Heffernan: "No."

Miss Collier: "I think we discussed with each other, because we felt, or I felt, it was permissible to discuss the feelings about what had happened, whilst being careful about the actual facts, if you like, which we did not, in a sense, know anything about."

We received no evidence as to whether the plan discussed with the staff was aired with parents. Certainly, none of the white parents who gave evidence to us spoke of being "brought in" by the school to collaborate with it in taking collective responsibility for unifying the student body and rebuilding the school community.

The Ullah family received much valuable support from white parents, especially those whose sons were Ahmed's friends and who were as deeply affected by the tragedy as were their children.

The school's apparent failure to recognise that fact and build upon it was to have some important consequences in the months to come, as we explore later.

CHAPTER 9

The Trial

Ahmed Ullah did not live to celebrate his fourteenth birthday on the 14th of October, 1986. Darren Coulburn turned fourteen on the 22nd of December, 1986, as he awaited his trial. The trial began on February 3rd, 1987 in the Crown Court. Darren Coulburn was not unfamiliar with courts; he had already appeared in the juvenile court, as we have seen, for other offences. The juvenile court is, however, very different from a Crown Court. In the juvenile court, the case is decided by magistrates who wear ordinary clothes, the public and the press are not allowed in, and the proceedings are kept as informal as possible. This was a Crown Court with a High Court Judge in red robes. This was a Crown Court with barristers in wigs and gowns, and a jury. This was a Crown Court with a public gallery and the press ready to note every word.

It was not only Darren Coulburn who had to face this array. Waiting in the wings were fifteen Burnage students and one member of staff who were going to give evidence from the witness box. It was not just the picket that awaited the eventual verdict: the whole school, the Education Department, the City Council, and the community waited.

The trial began. The first witness was the forensic pathologist, who had examined the body. The most important of his findings was the indication that internally there was a double track to the wound. This meant that Darren had thrust the knife into Ahmed twice.

The next group of witnesses was very different from the forensic expert. The next fifteen witnesses were students from Burnage. Although it was quite clear that Asian students had been present at the time of the stabbing, this group of students from Burnage was predominantly white. Indeed the only Asian student in the witness group – the student that Ahmed had defended the day before Darren killed him – had not seen the stabbing, and no other Asian students were called to give evidence.

Why were all the other students who testified white? The answer is not altogether clear. A group of nine students was gathered together in Mr Ellis' room almost immediately after the stabbing. Eight were white and one was Afro-Caribbean. Later a team of detectives took statements from students under the care of Mr Alan Hill. He was aware of white, Afro-Caribbean, and Asian students giving statements, but found it difficult to say in what proportions. Possibly there was an under-representation of Asian students, but he never questioned it at the time. How the students who made statements were collected was never made clear to us. No-one seemed to know. We have some evidence that Asian students who had seen the stabbing were reluctant to come forward. We do not know whether they were frightened or discouraged. We do not know how many did make statements, or what those statements said. We are not, therefore, able to say whether the Prosecution had decided it was a better tactic to use white students against a white defendant, or to select, so far as possible, Darren's friends, in order to improve the chances of obtaining a conviction in a case, which on any view must have been difficult to conduct.

A charge of racism in the selection of witnesses cannot be proved. Racism did, however, mar the conduct of the trial itself. During the course of the trial, Counsel for both the prosecution and the defence used the phrase "Pakistani boys" so many times that the jury sent a note requesting counsel to use proper names for witnesses rather than calling Asian boys simply "Pakistani boys". Ahmed Ullah was of Bangladeshi origin. So were many of the other boys at Burnage.

An element of the racism involved in the murder also emerged in the evidence against Darren Coulburn. It was suggested that one of the things that Darren Coulburn said to Ahmed was, "Do you want it again you dirty Paki?" We have already dealt with this in Chapter 4.

After the fifteen Burnage students had given their evidence, the statements of Jacqueline Hill and Christopher Hanson were read to the jury. They were not called to give evidence; indeed, the only member of staff who gave "live" evidence was Michael Ellis, who had found Darren Coulburn immediately after the stabbing. After Michael Ellis returned home from court, no one telephoned him from the school to give him support, or to ask him how he had got on. He found the experience traumatic. So, too, did the student witnesses, particularly one who was handed the murder weapon, without warning. This caused deep concern to his father who watched in horror as his thirteen year old son was handed the knife and asked to demonstrate how the stabbing had occurred.

The trial continued. The police gave their evidence. The forensic scientist who had examined Ahmed's clothing and the knife gave evidence. There was no evidence about the ambulance that arrived too late. The prosecution case was over.

None of the student witnesses who described Darren Coulburn as using the description "Paki" was asked whether this was, in fact, racist abuse. Instead, the presentation was of Darren as a schoolboy bully, calling schoolboy names, fighting as a schoolboy. "Boys will be boys". This was not a trial about why boys are violent with one another and bully each other and fight. This was not a trial about racism. These issues are too wide for a murder trial.

Darren Coulburn agreed to give evidence on his own behalf at the trial. Darren Coulburn could talk about the fights. Ahmed Ullah had been silenced by the fight. Only Ahmed's family and the school knew of the name calling, fights and bullying that had gone on before, with other white boys picking on Asians – incidents at bus stops, at lunchtime, and on the way home from school. Ahmed was silent as to why he had had to fight for the young Asian boys.

On February 6th, 1987, the jury returned a verdict of murder. They added a rider to their verdict, that they had concluded that Darren Coulburn had committed murder with the intention of causing some really serious bodily harm. Darren Coulburn received the only sentence possible at his age on conviction for murder: he was to be detained at Her Majesty's pleasure under Section 53 of the Children and Young Persons Act. In November 1987 his appeal was dismissed.

The trial was over. Darren Coulburn was convicted. Ahmed Ullah was buried. Crucial questions remained unanswered. Some are part of our terms of reference; some are not:

"Why did the ambulance take so long?"
"Had the teachers reacted fast enough?"
"Was the murder racist?"
"Did Darren's guilt reflect on the other white students?"
"Was his conviction a "triumph" for the Asian Community?"
"Why are male students so violent?"

A criminal court seeks to establish only whether the prosecution have proved a person's guilt of an offence so that a jury can be sure of that guilt. The only issue the Court was concerned with was whether Darren Coulburn had murdered Ahmed Ullah. It was not concerned with all the layers of experience that made Darren Coulburn what he was and Ahmed Ullah what he was. These things were not relevant to the criminal proceedings.

The trial was over, the waiting was over. 250 people waited on the outside, and then they went home. But before they did so, Selina Ullah

77

spoke to them and gave them her verdict: "The result is not a victory for us, we have lost a son. We must use our power to ensure that it can never happen again."

CHAPTER 10

Setting up the Macdonald Inquiry

The verdict had been returned. Guilty of murder. What did that verdict mean? A verdict of guilty does not provide a reason for death. A verdict of guilty gives no meaning to murder. Amongst the pickets there was euphoria, but not for Selina Ullah, who stood watching the police. They seemed to be more concerned with the pickets than with a National Front contingent standing by. The community leaders who had attended the trial suddenly wanted to protect Selina and the family from the pickets. They told her not to speak to them, but she did. Later at her solicitor's office a call came through from the "community leaders" who asked that they should "work together" in the future. The family went home, but received a visit in the evening from the community leaders wanting to build bridges. The family was too tired.

Throughout September and October there had been meetings arranged by Burnage School with various parents' groups. When the verdict was returned in February, there were no special meetings, no special briefings, no involvement of the Inspectorate, no special visits by senior officials of the Education Department to assist teachers in dealing with the impact of the verdict on the students.

Selina Ullah wanted to visit the school after the trial was over to thank students for their support and to speak to them. Dr Gough refused this request.

The trial had decided who had killed Ahmed Ullah, but the public wanted to know why? The *Manchester Evening News* concluded that the murder was not racist and that the police statement to that effect on the day of the stabbing was proved right (MEN 09:02:87). A line by line rebuttal of this point of view was signed by Councillor John Nicholson and thirty four others and was printed in the *Evening News* on the 16th of February:

"Dear Editor,

The editorial of February 9 claims that the *Manchester Evening News* is not racist. Let us consider this:

1. On September 17, 1986, Ahmed Ullah was killed in Burnage. The *Evening News* published the police statement that this death was not racist.

2. On September 19, the *Evening News* did not publish the (legally checked) council and community statements that the issue should not be prejudged in this way.

3. During October and November the *Evening News* published the white boy's solicitor's statement that both he and the Bangladeshi boy's family's solicitor agreed that the death was not racist. The *Evening News* did not publish denials of the latter or apologies for the former.

4. The *Evening News* did not publish the police retractions of their original statement (in one of which the police actually said they had never made the statement to the media in the first place).

5. After the verdict, the *Evening News* now says the murder was not racist. The *Evening News* quotes no proof for this. It seems the *Evening News* doesn't mind pre-judging aspects of the independent inquiry now being set up (even though it says it welcomes the inquiry).

6. We leave it to readers to judge who is being racist. And perhaps if the *Evening News* is so convinced of its own perfect behaviour, it will support the independent monitoring of its coverage of the last 12 months, as suggested by the council.

If the *Evening News* is so sure it's right, what has it to be afraid of?"

Michael Unger, the Editor, replied, saying:

"Dear Councillor Nicholson,

Thank you for the letter you and your colleagues sent to me concerning the murder at Burnage High School.

I will answer each of your paragraphs individually and factually.

Paragraph One: This is true and if the City Council, Bangladeshi community or indeed anyone else had issued a statement about the killing that day, this, too, would have been published.

Two: This is also true: we did not publish the statement because by then a boy was charged with murder and under both the Contempt of Court Act and the Children's and Young Persons' Act any newspaper is severely restricted in what it can publish.

Three: The white boy's solicitor's statement was read out in open court which gives me the legal right to publish it. This statement was totally supported in court by the prosecuting solicitor and privately by the solicitor hired by the Bangladeshi community. I was not asked to publish any denials of this statement; and I can hardly apologise for a statement read out in court which was accurately reported.

Four: This refers to a letter that Chief Superintendent Anthony Merricks, head of the community relations department, wrote to Mr A.T.M. Chowdhury, of Greater Manchester Bangladeshi Association. Mr Merricks said: "It is highly unlikely that this statement (by Chief Superintendent Ray Sherratt that the murder was not racist) emanated from a police source. However, I dissociate the Greater Manchester Police from the statement."

On seeing this letter I immediately wrote to the Chief Constable asking for a retraction because the Merricks letter was wrong. On October 24, Mr Anderton replied apologising for Mr Merricks' letter saying that the initial view expressed by Mr Sherratt was accurate; that Mr Anderton supported this view and that the *Evening News* accurately reported the statement as issued by Mr Sherratt on the day of the murder.

Five: You say that I gave no proof that the murder was not racist. My conclusions were based on personally listening to the evidence in court, and also by talking to members of the Bangladeshi community, before, during and after the trial. I also discussed the case at length over many weeks with the solicitor hired to represent the interests of the Bangladeshi community.

Six: We have not said that we would not support an inquiry. What I did say is that I doubted the value of such an inquiry and that I wouldn't fund the inquiry. I did, however, as you know, suggest that the post-graduate students at Lancaster University might be interested in doing the survey. Hardly a lack of support."

The trial was to decide who killed Ahmed Ullah, but the public wanted to know why he had died. This was why the Macdonald Inquiry was set up. Our task was to try and find some of the anwers to some of the questions.

The idea of an inquiry came from the Greater Manchester Bangladeshi Association, who raised the question of an inquiry soon after the murder of Ahmed Iqbal Ullah. The idea was quickly taken up by the City Council. At a meeting of the Schools Sub-Committee held on September 25th, 1986, it was announced that the City Council intended to set up an independent inquiry into the circumstances of the school, following the tragic death. The statement promised consultation on the terms of reference and composition of the Inquiry with the community, school governors and other interested parties.

In early October, Ian Macdonald, a barrister and leading authority on race and immigration matters was approached to chair it. He accepted.

There was then a lengthy delay during the period when Darren Coulburn was awaiting trial and during the trial itself. This followed a formal request by solicitors acting on behalf of the accused, asking for a postponement of the Inquiry. During this period some work was done on the terms of reference but consultations with the community and other organisations were held over until the end of the trial.

There then began a lengthy process of consultations with as many interested groups from the school, from trade unions, from the community, and from the Education Department, as was possible. Ahmed Ullah's family was also seen. A panel was eventually chosen by the Chairman from names that had been submitted. The terms of reference were discussed with the various interested parties and a final draft was settled. Although the Council were closely consulted at all times, the final choice of panel and terms of reference was the Chairman's, not the Council's. This was felt by all parties to be important, in order to ensure the Inquiry's independence from the City Council.

It soon became clear that if the Inquiry sat in public, many of the potential witnesses – professional and non-professional, White, Asian and Afro-Caribbean – would be afraid to come forward. The message that Ian Macdonald received from the unions, from community groups and from parents and students was identical: if the Inquiry was held in public, with the full glare of media attention, witnesses would not come forward. It was thus decided that the Inquiry would sit in private. Hopefully people could come forward without fear.

The City Council provided two clerks to the Inquiry from their staff, Moira Suringer and Martin Lugsdin, and appointed Yasmin Masood to cope with the secretarial work of the Inquiry. Marguerite Russell was chosen as Counsel and an experienced local solicitor, Jack Thornley, as solicitor. An important feature of both counsel and the solicitor was that they were independent of the City Council, even though they had been chosen by them.

The terms of reference were set:

Terms of Reference
The purpose is to receive evidence, examine, report on and make recommendations in respect of:
1. The extent to which there was a racial aspect to the circumstances and events leading up to and surrounding the death of Ahmed Iqbal Ullah at Burnage High School in September 1986.

2. The extent to which there are racial aspects to the problems of violence and discipline in Burnage High School and other Manchester schools.

3. What can be done to eliminate or reduce racial harassment, racial violence and racialism in schools.

After Counsel and solicitor had consulted with various interested parties, including the teaching trade unions, procedures were agreed on. These procedures were handed to everyone who gave evidence to the Inquiry and were also widely publicised.

Procedural Rules of the Macdonald Inquiry

1. The Inquiry will usually sit in private.

2. In order to hear evidence the Inquiry will be prepared to travel to places where students or parents will feel less intimidated.

3. Where evidence is taken from a student or parent about any incident, the witness will be asked (a) whether the incident was reported to anyone in the school and (b) if so to whom.

4. If it is known that a teacher intends to make an allegation against another named teacher the Code of Practice applied by teacher unions will operate and that teacher will be expected to inform the other teacher in accordance with the Code.

5. If any statement received contains an allegation against a named person, that named person will so far as is practicable be informed of the nature of the allegation to enable them to have the opportunity of giving evidence to the Inquiry.

6. If as a result of a statement given by a named person, the Inquiry will be inviting that person to give evidence, then the person against whom any allegation is made will be notified in advance of the date time and place at which such evidence is going to be given, and thereafter will be entitled to attend at that session accompanied if they so wish by a friend or representative of their choice.

7. Any persons who are attending a session as representatives or as unrepresented individuals should, if they wish to ask questions of any witness, submit such questions in written form during the session to either Counsel or Solicitors for the Inquiry who on consideration will either ask the question themselves or pass it onto the Inquiry Panel for their consideration.

8. The Inquiry reserves the right to vary all procedures, having regard to the interests of natural justice for all concerned.

9. At any session of the Inquiry the Inquiry Panel on advice from Counsel or Solicitors to the Inquiry shall determine who may be present at such a session.

10. An allegation against an identifiable person will not be pursued unless the Inquiry is in a position to give the name of the person making the allegation to the person against whom the allegation is made.

The Inquiry was launched on Tuesday, May 5th, 1987, in its rooms at the Longsight Library, Manchester. The press attended, with a lot of attention focussed on the composition of the panel. Questions were raised. Why was only one member of the Panel white? Was the Inquiry to be a witchhunt? Had the police not already investigated and ruled out any racism?

The organisation of the Inquiry presented many problems. One of the panel members – Nigel de Noronha – could not serve, because his LEA would not release him for duty on the Inquiry.

He had to choose between the risk of losing his job and sitting on the Inquiry Panel. Not surprisingly, in an area with high unemployment like Manchester he felt no alternative but to resign. This decision was regretted publicly by the other panel members and the chair.

Immediately after the Inquiry began on May 5th, the small firm of Jack Thornley received an abusive death threat on its answering machine. In addition they had to deal with a potentially vast amount of information, and to interview potential witnesses. The pressures of work from the Inquiry were enormous, and must have conflicted with the pressures of the firm's other work. On June 12th, Jack Thornley resigned. The firm of Robert Lizar was then appointed. Forewarned of the enormities of the task, he appointed three talented interviewers, Airinne Ryan, Carol Micah, and Hilary Somerlad, with secretarial assistance from Margaret Irving.

The Inquiry identified witnesses in a variety of ways: placing advertisements in newspapers, having unions contact their members, and writing to individuals. The solicitor's interviewers took statements from potential witnesses. These statements were then considered by Counsel and Solicitor to the Inquiry, and witnesses were called to give live evidence at the formal sessions. The Inquiry also commissioned independent research from Elinor Kelly, of the Extra Mural Department at Manchester University, and Nigel de Noronha and Salma Ahmed, in order to present as large a picture as possible of the overall situation in Manchester schools.

The Inquiry usually sat for an average of three days a week between the

21st of May and the end of July, and from the 7th to 30th of September 1987. All in all, the Inquiry met for 38 days. In these 38 days, we heard evidence in formal session from the 165 witnesses, which produced numerous pages of transcripted evidence. The record that was produced also included background information and statements from an even larger number of witnesses.

The range of witnesses included City Councillors, the Chief Education Officer, school students, head teachers, union officials, press reporters, teachers, governors, youth workers, parents, relatives, and community representatives. In addition, the Panel met in informal sessions with community groups, groups of school students, groups of teachers, and union groups, visited over a dozen schools, and attended a joint schools production of a play about racism and sexism, put on by students with the Frontline Theatre Group. We were provided with a vast quantity of documentary material from the City Council and its departments, including its report on anti-racist education, and the report from the Council's Race Unit. We also reviewed documentary evidence provided by the Schools Psychological & Child Guidance Service, the Inspectorate, the National Union of Teachers, the Governors of Burnage School, and various other schools.

The Inquiry had no power to order any one to give evidence. We could not summon witnesses to attend. We had to rely on the goodwill of those involved in education in Manchester and on the goodwill of the ordinary people of Manchester. Many of those who did come forward did so in great fear for their jobs and safety. Many of the witnesses showed personal courage in their contributions, and many of the witnesses shared their grief and suffering with the Inquiry. Without this great mobilisation of school staff, students, parents, relatives, inspectors, youth workers, town hall officials and other people concerned about the issues of education and race in Manchester and the country as a whole, our Inquiry would have been a dismal failure. By their contributions we hope that we are able to make some sense of the events we have been looking at.

Despite this support and co-operation, which produced a mountain of material, there were still areas of evidence that the Panel would have liked to have developed further. The input from governors of Manchester schools, other than Burnage, was disappointing. Despite apparent and repeated requests to the unions, and despite union assurances of co-operation with the Inquiry, the input from teachers was also disappointing. Parents and students who attended the Inquiry made valuable contributions, but we felt that many parents and students were nevertheless still intimidated by the quasi-legal format. In addition to these there were certain areas where no evidence at all was forthcoming, or there was a lack of co-operation.

For example, the police refusal to give evidence was particularly disappointing. In an exchange of letters the solicitors to the Inquiry asked for police information, but were told, initially, that the City Council did not have the legal authority to conduct such an Inquiry, and, later, that the police officers who attended at the school were not to give statements (see below for the text of this correspondence). Secondly the Roman Catholic schools did not consider their experience to be at all relevant to the Inquiry, and so it was only through the testimony of some teachers, parents and students at these schools that insight into this sector was gained. Some members of the larger community, including the Pakistani Workers' Association, who had been actively involved in the Ahmed Ullah Memorial Committee, refused to co-operate, for a variety of reasons.

The Chief Constable of Manchester was written to on May 22nd 1986. There then followed a series of letters, four of which we reproduce:

C. James Anderton CBE, C St J, QPM, CBIM. Chief Constable

Your ref: JT/KM/16079/87/84   12 June 1897

Dr Mr Thornley,
            The Macdonald Inquiry into Racial Violence
                    in Manchester Schools

Your letter of 22nd May in the above matter was received at this office on 27th May.

It is the first intimation I have had that police assistance is required or desired in connection with the Inquiry.

There has not, hitherto, been any suggestion of this, and I find it surprising that the intentions of Mr Macdonald, which must have been known from the beginning, were not made clear at the outset.

Furthermore, your letter does not refer to the several telephone messages left with staff at your office between 8th and 22nd May, none of which have been answered. The purpose of the calls was to obtain from you the precise authority under which the Macdonald Inquiry has been established, since your reference to Section 172 of the Local Government Act 1972, contained in your letter of 7th May, would appear to be totally incorrect. I am not aware that any other section of that Act specifically provides for an Inquiry of the kind in question.

Perhaps, therefore, you would be good enough to enlighten me on this before I decide whether or not to respond to your requests.

Yours sincerely,
Chief Constable

Mr. J. Thornley
Jack Thornley
Solicitors
Deansgate Court
244 Deansgate
MANCHESTER M3 4BQ

C. James Anderton CBE, C St J, QPM, CBIM. Chief Constable
24th July, 1987

Dear Sir,

Macdonald Inquiry

I refer to your recent letter concerning your inquiry into Racial Violence in Manchester Schools and the specific points raised therein.

With reference to your first specific question, officers, at the request of the Deputy Head, did attend at Burnage School. The Constables were familiar with the school and its students and with the Deputy Head thought it would have the effect of quietening what the school interpreted as a certain amount of student disruption.

Subsequently the police were asked to periodically call at the school, primarily when students passed between the upper and lower schools between lessons. This was done for a limited time.

It should also be noted that officers have visited the school as part of their routine duties for some time, both prior to and following the unfortunate incident in September 1986.

The second point, that pertaining to a meeting held at Bagladeshi House on the 18th September 1986, which officers attended. The officers concerned responded to a request regarding the release of the unfortunate boy's body and arrangements were made with the Coroner to meet that request. In addition, the officers gave the family advice and whatever assistance they could regarding the funeral arrangements.

On the same question in your letter, it is true that a senior officer attended the school on the day of the murder of Ahmed Iqbal Ullah and his purpose there was to co-ordinate the police enquiry and he had no dealings with any subsequent event.

Referring to your third point, that of the Education (No.2) Act of 1986, of which I am fully aware, I can say that I am at the moment formulating a policy in regard to the recommendations of Sections 17, 18, 19 and 30, throughout the Greater Manchester Police area. You will obviously be aware that in any discussion concerning this particular subject there are numerous schools which fall within the control of a number of Education Authorities and therefore considerable consultation may be required.

Yours faithfully,
Chief Constable

Robert Lizar, Esq., (Solicitor),
2 Woodcock Square,
Manchester.
M15 6DJ

MACDONALD INQUIRY TEL: 061–225–4204   RL.
Mr. C. James Anderton,
Chief Constable, P.O. Box 22 (S. West PDO),
Chester House,
Boyer Street,
Manchester M16 0RE

                                                    11th August 1987
Dear Sir,

                        Macdonald Inquiry

Thank you for your letter of the 24th July 1987 which is most helpful.

The Inquiry Panel would be most interested to hear evidence from the officers concerned who attended at the school on the day of the murder and periodically thereafter, and also from officers at the meeting at Bangladeshi House on 18th September 1986 and those who gave the family advice and assistance regarding funeral arrangement.

Would you agree to supply the names and present station of the officers concerned, particularly those in leading roles, with a view to

them submitting statements to the Inquiry or alternatively, so that I could arrange to interview them and take statements.
Thank you for your assistance.

Yours faithfully,
ROBERT LIZAR.

Your reference RL
Our refernce DW/LMF
Date 12th August, 1987

Dear Sir,

Macdonald Inquiry

I refer to your letter of 11th August, 1987.

The information supplied to you in our letter of 24th July contains all the relevant information and covers the salient points you had requested be addressed.

I am sure that members of staff at the school and members of family and the community have confirmed those details or could do so.

There does not appear to me anything further that could assist you within the terms of your Inquiry by police officers submitting statements or being interviewed and I must therefore decline your request.

Yours faithfully,
Deputy Chief Constable

Robert Lizar, Esq., (Solicitor),
2 Woodcock Square,
Manchester.
M15 6DJ

CHAPTER 11

Storm in a Dinner Queue

By February, 1987, Darren Coulburn's trial was over and he had been convicted of murder. The Chairman of the Inquiry had begun consultations on the composition of the panel and the terms of reference. Ahmed's family still mourned Ahmed and were seeking permission for Selina to go into the school and speak to the students.

In February 1987, another incident took place at Burnage School, this time in a dinner queue and this time at the Upper School.

When hungry boys queue up and have to wait for dinner there are often incidents of pushing and shoving. When angry boys queue up for dinner these incidents can become explosive.

After the murder, Burnage reacted differently to the discussion of the murder and its implications. Discussion was usually initiated by the students, and while some teachers would talk about it with students, some would not talk about it at all. Some white students felt that the incidents that then occurred at Burnage in February and March of 1987 would not have happened if "both groups had sat down and talked about it". Students told us that after the killing, the white boys and the Asian boys had moved into different camps, and friendships between white and Asian students were affected.

These groupings were not without a history. Following the announcement of Ahmed's death, it was noticeable to some students that Asian students had sat grouped together and that white students had done the same. Some white students told us that because they were white they felt that they had something to do with Ahmed's death. They felt guilty in some vague undefined way. Ahmed's white friends mourned him, and some white students simply felt that Darren Coulburn should be put away. A few white students saw Darren Coulburn as some kind of hero.

By February, the students were aware of a drifting apart. It was obvious to some students that tensions were building up, and that the Asian students felt that they had to retaliate. The tension needed a little spark.

When hungry boys queue up and have to wait for dinner there are often incidents of pushing and shoving. When angry boys queue up for dinner, these incidents can become explosive.

91

On February 24th 1987, a white boy (call him "J") pushed an Asian boy (call him "A") in a dinner queue at Burnage Upper School. There was a scuffle. The Asian student later collected some friends together with the intention of retaliating. Jack Hewitt, the Deputy Head of Upper School, got to hear about the scuffle, and called both boys in to interview them. Of particular concern to Mr Hewitt was the way that A had collected friends together to retaliate. A's family were called in and told about it. After a discussion, it was agreed that in future A should make any complaint to staff. This was not reported as a racist incident via the Education Department reporting system, and it was not considered to have any connection with Ahmed's death.

Ahmed Ullah had died in a chain of events that had begun with a white boy bullying an Asian student. One white student at Burnage said that "The teacher should have known there was pressure building up and that any little thing could spark off trouble. The J and A confrontation was just treated like a normal little thing even though it wasn't."

Two or three days after this, Mr Hewitt had a meeting with a group of Asian boys who told him they were concerned that white boys were forming gangs. Mr Hewitt explained to this group that their own group might look like a gang, and that they themselves therefore might be adding to the problem. In our view this was clearly a missed opportunity to understand the Asian students' concerns, explore them further, and to deal with the growing tension. It is true that Mr Hewitt later addressed separate 4th and 5th year student assemblies. He told them not to gather in gangs, and that any students who had complaints should go to a member of staff. That is exactly what the gang of Asian boys had done. Their only redress was to be told that they too looked like a gang. The message must have come over loud and clear; telling a member of staff solved nothing; far better to organise and deal with the situation themselves.

To students at the school, definite groups were building up: "it was getting so bad that we used to stand in the playground and watch the goings on every lunch and dinner time". As the situation got worse, some white students felt that some of the Asian students would not talk to them because they were afraid of what the other Asian students would do to them. Later, we heard, white and Asian boys, who were friends, shunned and avoided each other in school, but kept up their contact through secret phone calls at night.

The racial lines were being drawn. Polarisation was taking place. "All links were sort of broken in school".

When the school later prepared a report on the incidents that had taken place at Burnage in February and March of 1987, it stated that there were no major incidents in the next few weeks or so after the talk to the 4th and 5th year assemblies about gangs. It would appear that the school was unaware of the tensions that were about to explode. About two days before that explosion finally came, according to one white student, an Asian student (call him "M") came into the classroom and challenged him: "You think you are hard, you and all your white mates. Come outside". After the next lesson, there was further taunting: "You said us Paki's are all mouth and no action. . .'

Monday 23rd March

Burnage is an all boys school. Boys learn how to fight. On March, 23rd 1987, the Asian student M paid the price for his taunts when he and a white student (call him "G") fought. M's nose was injured.

After school that afternoon, A, the Asian student who had been involved in the dinner queue incident in February, was attacked by two white students (later to be convicted of this assault) D and E. A's nose was broken in this attack, and later D and E were convicted of this assault. At this time Mr Hewitt was in charge as Dr Gough was absent from school through illness.

Tuesday 23th March

On March 24th D was excluded from school. Then A's older brother came into school to express his anger and concern about D and E's attack on his brother. As he and A were on their way to see the school management, A saw another boy (call him "B") who had been involved with D and E in the attacks and said "there's one of them". Incensed by the attack on A, his older brother grabbed B and put him against the corridor wall, and head-butted him, saying "don't touch my brother again".

During the early part of the morning, rumours began to circulate that the Asian boys were going to retaliate; that they had prepared a "hit list".

A group of about twelve white students had been singled out by the Asian students. Why, or on what basis, is not entirely clear. Some had been involved in the bus stop incident or hung around with those boys. On the 24th of March they became identifiable targets and were then isolated in the gym for their own protection during the morning of the 24th. They were locked in there by staff for two periods for their own "protection". During the third period, they were let out and advised by staff: "don't go out of school at lunchtime".

Burnage is an all boys school. Boys learn how to fight. The Asian students were forming into large groups, and were preparing for retaliation. About 150 to 200 of them were in the grounds of the school. As the dozen or so white boys who had been locked in the gym tried to go into the dining hall, they were confronted with a large group of Asian students. A member of staff refused to let the white students enter the dining hall. The white boys then ran to the Year Head's office and the Year Head escorted them into the dining hall for lunch.

Once they were in the dining hall they sat down at a table. The dining hall doors were locked, just as the gym doors had been previously. A group of Asian students, including T, who had complained to Mr Hewitt about white gangs forming, then gathered outside the dining room shouting, "get together for protection". As the group grew in numbers, they were joined by youths who were *not* students at the school.

There are two sets of doors to the dining room. The now terrified group of white students saw Asian students at both doors, trying to kick in the glass, and throwing chairs. The dinner women came to the rescue. Some of the dinner women ran to make sure that the doors were shut. One woman noticed the terrified white group jump over the serving hatch into the kitchen area in a panic shouting "let's get out of here; they are going to attack us". She realised that the only other exit was locked, and quickly herded the terrified white boys into a small storeroom leading off the kitchen and locked them in for their own protection. This was the third time that day that this group of white boys were locked up in the school for their own protection.

Meanwhile Mr Smolka, a member of staff, tried to intervene and calm the Asian students. Other staff arrived and began to disperse the Asian students. Mr Smolka then spoke to the white boys in the storeroom to reassure them. Mr Hewitt met with representatives of the Asian students in the hope that the white boys would be able to return to class. The white boys themselves were apprehensive about this; instead, one of them phoned his father.

For this parent, the first he knew of the matter was when he received a telephone call from the school. He spoke both to his son and to Mr Smolka. His son asked him to "come and get me". Mr Smolka said there had been an eruption in the school, and asked the parent to help by coming down to school and taking some of the lads out. The parent got into his transit van and drove to the school. He had been given no idea of what to expect when he arrived at the school. He had merely been advised by Mr Smolka to come into the school via the back gates to the kitchen area. So, as he arrived, he was surprised to see a lot of Asian students outside school, near the entrance to the school where the kitchens are.

When the parent arrived, Mr Smolka asked him to reverse the van as close as possible to the door of the kitchen. When the parent asked Mr Smolka "what was going on", Mr Smolka's only reply was "if you don't mind I'd rather get the lads out". What happened next was, in the words of this parent, "unbelievable". The door was opened and boys ran out: "they were that frightened that they dived in". According to parent and students alike, it was "like a scene out of a film".

In his meeting with the Asian students, Mr Hewitt found out that they were convinced that the original incident between J and A in the dining queue had been instigated by a group of white boys, who were then, in fact, "on a hit list". Asian students were apparently assigned to each of the white students on the list.

A dinner queue incident had become a battleground. The battleground now spilled out into the street.

Staff at lower school were told that there had been some sort of incident, and they were asked to see boys safely off the premises at 3.25. One member of staff accordingly walked down Briarfield Road to Kingsway, near Mauldeth Road. About half way between two bus stops she saw a crowd of about twenty to thirty 4th and 5th year boys streaming across Kingsway. They were mainly Afro-Caribbean. But a few white and Asian boys were with them. She went and spoke to some of them. The group stood at the bus stop for a few minutes and then set off towards Birchfield Road. Following the group, she saw the boys running across Kingsway, ignoring the traffic. The next thing she remembered was an Asian boy (call him "J") on the ground. She ran to him. As she did so, a few of the large group watched her and then regrouped outside a row of shops. When the teacher helped J to his feet, she saw that his nose was bleeding and that he had been kicked in the face. He was dishevelled and dirty. He described the boy who had kicked him down, but he was unable to say who had kicked him in the face. On the way back to lower school with that student, the teacher spoke to two police officers. At the school, the incident was brought to the attention of management, and the member of staff drove the boy home in her car. On the way, they saw another Asian student (call him "K"), who had also been injured. The teacher stopped the car and picked up K. He then told her about his assault, and that when he had

95

reported it to the police, they had advised him to "tell his parents". K gave the teacher the names of the boys who had assaulted him, but begged her not to tell anyone because he was terrified of them. K told the teacher that he had also reported the assault to a member of senior management, who had told him that "there was nothing anyone could do". K went on to say that "nobody can do anything; we are all frightened and nobody cares".

A third Asian boy had been assaulted even more seriously than J or K, but K refused to name him until he had spoken to him, because the third student was also terrified. K refused to let the member of staff drive him all the way home, but he did promise to tell his parents about the incident.

The member of staff then drove on to J's home, but finding that J's mother was still not at home, she took J to the Manchester Royal Infirmary. J's nose was not broken, but it was very swollen and was likely to cause him headaches for some days. He also had a very badly bruised elbow.

On the way back from the hospital, J told the member of staff that "there had been a lot of trouble", that there had been a fight in school the day before, and that he was also frightened of two Asian students. He begged the staff member not to tell anyone else about this.

When the member of staff who had helped J and K went home, she wrote out a report for the school management, in which she named both the boys from the large group that had been recognized and the injured boys. We were shown a copy of this report.

CHAPTER 12

Battleground Burnage

Ahmed Ullah and Darren Coulburn had both been at Burnage Lower School. The students at the Upper School, however, had moved from silence to violence.

By the end of Tuesday March 24th at least five Asian students had been assaulted. By the end of that day, a group of white students had found themselves powerless, locked up and forced to retreat from the school, hidden in the back of a closed van. By the end of that day Asian students had discovered that self activity and retaliation meant power – the power to roam free out of class, and the power to make demands. By the end of that day, staff and police had been involved in several incidents and students had to be escorted on their way home.

The question arises: were the March events related in some way to the murder of Ahmed Ullah in September or the trial of Darren Coulburn in February? On the face of it there appears to be no relationship at all. The March events concerned fourth and fifth year students in the upper school rather than third year ones in the lower school. However, we believe the links are clear. The March events are directly linked to the incident in the dining room in February. This followed quite soon after the end of the trial. On the evidence given to us it is quite clear that many Asian students had gained strength and confidence from involvement in the demonstrations and pickets organised around the aftermath of Ahmed's death and the trial of Darren Coulburn. They also took strength from the conviction of Darren Coulburn. For the Asian students it seemed easy to trace a direct link from the beginning of self organisation in September 1986 to the events of March 1987. Quite apart from the involvement in the demonstrations and pickets, there was also a small number of upper school students who felt the need to protect younger brothers and others in the lower school.

For white students the links are more tenuous. Other than hanging around together in groups or gangs and getting up to a certain amount of mischief, usually at the expense of Asian students, there is little evidence of any organisation among the white students. Racist groups from outside the school may have been around and may have dropped leaflets in the school, but they played no significant part at all, so far as

97

we could discover. Seating patterns during dinner time had usually been along racial lines. Asian boys sat together and the white and Afro-Caribbeans grouped together. The polarisation of the white students was nothing to do with any active organisation on their part. Rather, they were left to their own devices, as the Asian students talked, discussed, and took common action together. However, there are indications in the evidence that white students were somehow made to feel guilty for Ahmed Ullah's death. The school view of the murder as racist, and as an escalation of racist name calling, put them all more or less in the same camp as Darren Coulburn. All this happened within the racist culture of the school, in which all the Asian students became "Paki" and which in turn was fed by the racists operating in the neighbourhoods where the students lived. Because the school had never dealt with the aftermath of Ahmed's murder in a positive or realistic manner, starting from the experiences and grievances of the whole school community, black and white, there was a certain inevitability about the confrontation that took place in March.

Apart from spreading out to the neighbouring girls' school at Levenshulme on one particular day (which we discuss below) the confrontation at Burnage did not happen in any other school in Manchester. In that sense it was a peculiarly Burnage event. It was not a city wide or even district event. In these circumstances, it seems to us that the March events can only be explained by reference to the particular history of Burnage. Ahmed Ullah is dead. Darren Coulburn was detained at Her Majesty's pleasure. But the ripples of their fatal meeting in September spread out from the lower to the upper school from September to March.

By the end of Tuesday, March 24th a worried group of white parents wanted to learn what their sons' positions at Burnage were going to be, their sons having been forced to flee from the school.

The pattern of non-communication and lack of managerial responsibility which had characterised the response to Ahmed's murder again emerged. According to Mr Hewitt, he telephoned the parents of the boys who had left school in the van on the Tuesday night. According to more than one of their parents the contact was the other way round. The school never thanked the parent who had rescued the boys in his van and delivered them safely to their homes. According to the parents who gave evidence to us, they had to contact the school to find out what was going on. One mother and father, whose younger son had been a close friend of Ahmed, and whom they had had to console over a period of weeks because of the terrible impact Ahmed's death had had on him, now had to face the situation that their older son could not go to school because Asian students thought of him as a white racist.

Another student had been telephoned by the school on March 24th and told not to come back for the rest of the week. His family was told that the school would ring them when they had to go back. The following day, his parents went to the Lower School with their son and had a meeting with Mr Hewitt. According to the student and his parents, they were told that the students were being kept out of school for their own safety. According to Mr Hewitt, the parents were asking for guarantees of complete safety that he felt he could not give. He responded to the parents as he always did: we will do everything we possibly can to keep students safe but cannot guarantee anyone's safety. Mr Hewitt felt he had been honest with them, because even in normal times he could not guarantee that one student will not hit another deliberately. According to the parents, one of the fathers asked for reassurance that the school could guarantee the safety of the children and Mr Hewitt replied that he couldn't "guarantee their safety under normal circumstances".

When the parent who had rescued the boys in his van, attended the Lower School with his son for the appointment with Mr Hewitt on March 25th he too was told that the boys were being kept out of school for their own safety. When asked about the exams his son was preparing to take, Mr Hewitt allegedly replied: "it might be a case of doing the exams or having no son." He told us that Mr Hewitt couldn't be sure of his son's safety at any time during school.

It is not clear exactly how many white students were off, but a group of some sixteen white students remained out of Burnage not only for the rest of March but, with one exception, for ever. None of them was excluded formally; none was the subject of any disciplinary inquiry; and none was ever asked by the school about their part, if any, in the events of March. We will return to them later.

Wednesday 25th March

During the day of March 25th there were no major incidents at Burnage. However, rumours of hit lists persisted, white boys were seen gathering outside the school, and the school had contacted specialist youth workers as extra assistance to work with the Asian and white students.

The member of staff who had helped the assaulted Asian students, J and K, on the previous day suggested on March 25th that staff should go out on the streets and be at bus stops after school that day. One member of senior management felt that this might be construed as inflammatory. Others agreed with the proposal or had themselves decided this sort of measure was necessary. So after school, a number of Burnage teachers came out of school to patrol the surrounding area.

Teachers were not the only people outside the school on that afternoon. Asian families who were concerned for the safety of their children also came in their cars. A large group of Asian boys congregated on the far side of Kingsway, standing in silence. Despite attempts by teachers to stop them, they moved off after a white boy who had apparently been involved in the canteen incident. The police were there.

The Asian boys then formed a march. There were three older Asians with them. The march proceeded down Kingsway towards lower school. When they reached a local garage near the school, some of the white garage workers who saw the group picked up weapons and shouted out racist taunts. The teachers were watching from a car. They saw a fight start. It was not in any way provoked by the Asian boys. One teacher got out of the car just as the police arrived. The teacher tried to persuade a man who looked like he was in charge at the garage to get his workers to go back in.

The police then arrested two young Asians. They made no attempt to arrest any of the white youths from the garage. One of the teachers went and remonstrated with the police about the arrests, telling the police officer the only assaults she had seen were committed by a white youth hitting Asians. The police response was "they're banged up, and will stay banged up".

The rest of the Asian boys were incensed at the arrests, and it was with some difficulty that the adults persuaded them to form up again and proceed to the library. To the members of staff who saw the incident, two things resulted: an admiration for the way in which the three older Asians had calmed the situation after the police had made their arrests, and the determination to inform the school that one of them certainly would give evidence on behalf of the arrested Asian youths, who had done nothing to justify being arrested.

Three local Councillors, Byrne, Strath and Khan Moghul went to Longsight police station after being telephoned by the parents of the arrested youths. According to one of the councillors, the senior police offcer said that everything possible was being done to calm the situation, and that he would not tolerate attempts to breach law and order. The officer went on to say that he was ready to meet community people who came to see him. It was the understanding of the councillors that the two young Asians had been released without being charged, but that they had been formally cautioned by the police.

Nevertheless, by the end of the day two Asian boys had been arrested by police, and two white students had also been suspended from school. The number of white students out of school for their "own protection" was between 11 and 16.

Thursday 26th March

On Thursday, March 26th 1987 two very experienced youth workers were asked by Adge Warm of the Inspectorate to go into Burnage to work with the white and Asian students. The youth workers were Geoff Turner and Mukhtar Khares.

When they arrived at the school, Mr Hewitt briefed them on the school's version of events. However, even as this meeting was going on, it was interrupted by a group of Asian fifth formers who wished to invite the youth workers to a meeting in the main hall. The speed of the Burnage students grapevine in discovering that the youth workers had arrived in the school was extraordinary.

Geoff Turner and Mukhtar Khares went to the hall. There were about three hundred students there. The atmosphere was excited. It appeared to Geoff Turner that there were two groups established in the hall. One was the group on the stage, who wanted to calm the situation down and talk things through with the other young people. The other group was more excited, saying: "The teachers can't do anything. We are running the place. We can deal with the situation."

Geoff Turner felt that the tensions in the room were quite strong. At one point, a white student interrupted the meeting to argue with the Asian students about a fight. During this argument, many of the Asian students in the meeting turned aggressively towards the white student. Geoff Turner and Mukhtar Khares had to use all their skills to arbitrate the argument. After the worst of the tension was eased, Geoff Turner attempted to have a further conversation with the white student, on the involvement of outside gangs of white racists. Geoff Turner had had considerable experience in working with such young people, and arranged to meet with the white student later. The meeting never took place because a teacher would not release the boy from class. He learned nothing more about the involvement of white racists in the March events.

As Geoff Turner and Mukhtar Khares walked around the school that day they were surprised not to be challenged by any of the adults as to who they were. The building seemed barren and cold. They met with Mr Hewitt, the Chief Inspector John Taylor, and Ethel Milroy. They also spoke to the canteen women. The only person who ever asked Geoff Turner who he was when he arrived or walked round the school was the community police officer who was patrolling outside the main entrance.

Geoff Turner had understood from his briefing by the school that he was going to be involved with a group of "very racist white youths." Both the school briefings and the newspaper coverage had prepared him to meet a group of louts, the thuggish element of society. Instead, he met with an intelligent and neatly dressed group of boys who in all respects mirrored the Asian students who had put them on a hit list. He constantly checked and tested, and finally satisfied himself that none of them had any connection with racist organisatons.

Geoff Turner felt shocked that the situation had developed to a point that these boys were out of school. Eventually Mukhtar Khares, who was working with the Asian boys, and Geoff Turner, who was working with the white boys, managed to get each group to consider each other's perspectives. Despite all this work, there was still an element within the school that did not come into this reasonable discussion. Nobody could say what could happen if the white students came back. No guarantees. The white boys in the end had the feeling that it did not matter enough to anyone. They did not want to go back to school.

Looking back on his first day at the school Geoff Turner felt that the presence of the police vans around the school had exacerbated the situation. The first time he had seen boys leave the school, there were two special patrol vehicles as well as other police vans around the school. When the Asian boys came out of the school, the police and senior management shepherded them through the streets to Kingsway, where Ethel Milroy and John Taylor of the Inspectorate were watching. Geoff Turner felt that this performance, which was repeated on his second day at the school, exacerbated the tension. He would have preferred the school to have arranged special buses to take the students from school to home, even though the students had rejected that idea at a meeting on Friday, the 27th of March.

Shortly thereafter, the large police presence was removed and patrolling was done by community police officers.

CHAPTER 13

Meeting Ground Burnage

After the murder, there had been too much silence. After the silence, there had been anger. After the anger, there had been violence. People needed to talk.

Communications at Burnage seems to have been a continuing problem. A number of teachers felt that senior management had not communicated with them adequately. A number of students felt that teachers had not communicated with them adequately.

Geoff Turner, the youth worker, felt that the communication problems at Burnage were clearly demonstrated on the morning of Friday, March 27th, when he and Mukhtar Khares attempted to establish communication with teachers and students at the Lower School. They both thought that there might be staff, who commuted between the schools, and students, who might wish to speak with them.

Accordingly Geoff Turner and Mukhtar Khares entered the Lower School. When they asked a male teacher where the staff room was, all the man did was to point up the stairs. They entered the staff room at breaktime. The staff room was crowded and buzzing with conversation. When Geoff Turner introduced himself and Mukhtar as youth workers, they were met with stony silence. People put their heads down or looked away.

Geoff Turner felt incredibly embarrassed. He tried to lighten the situation by saying: "If you really force me, I'll have a cup of coffee." He was met by more silence. He then said: "What do you have to do round here – do you have to sing and dance before you get a cup of coffee." Nobody would look at him. A woman teacher finally got up and said: "You can have a spoonful of coffee from my jar." Just then the bell went and the teachers left very quickly. Geoff Turner and Mukhtar Khares were left feeling very confused.

In the following week, this pattern of non-communication continued. On one occasion, Geoff Turner found himself effectively accused of stealing the wallet of a male member of staff. On another occasion, he was approached by an Afro-Caribbean student who asked him whether he would take some homework to one of the excluded white students.

When Geoff Turner said he would, the Afro-Caribbean student then turned toward a male teacher who had been standing behind him. The male teacher then walked over to Geoff Turner and silently handed him a file. The teacher never spoke to Geoff Turner.

Communication at Burnage was not easy. On the night of March 25th someone had written "Death to Pakis" on one of the school walls. A caretaker cleaned it off before school started.

Communication about the situation at Burnage was not easy. On Friday, March 27th, there was a meeting at the Central Mosque. Community leaders – including Mr Jamal of the school governors – felt strongly that students should be bussed home after school, but the Burnage students unanimously rejected the suggestion. They said that they "wanted normality." Some of their elders – including Mr Jamal – felt that their attitude was actually confrontational, but communication between the older members of the community and the young people was so difficult that this difference could not be resolved.

Within a day or so of the incidents of March 24th, the students set up a student council. The members of this council were not elected. After they constituted the council, they then issued an appeal to other students to join them. The composition of the student council raised some concerns: one of the students on it was an Afro-Caribbean boy who had alllegedly attacked an Asian student. When a member of staff who had some knowledge of those who had participated in the attacks suggested that such a student should not be on the student council, the teacher was given two reasons why no further action could be taken: firstly, that there had been a misunderstanding about the report of the incident, and secondly, that the balance of power at the school was so delicate that to exclude that student in any way would excite the situation because he was very popular with the students.

No one at the school seemed to consider that there was anything wrong with letting this boy remain on the student council. No one seemed to wonder how it would affect other students to learn that one of the students who had allegedly been directly involved in a violent attack on a smaller Asian boy was not only immune from punishment, but was also a representative on the student council.

Communication at Burnage was not easy. And, as time passed, it became apparent that few members of the Burnage community had any idea of how to deal effectively with those communication problems. This was illustrated graphically by the events that took place during the week of March 30.

On March 27th, the Chief Education Officer for Manchester had sent a letter to all Burnage parents in which he had announced meetings to be held with students and parents about the events of February and March. In his letter, he announced that staff would meet with the students at a special assembly on March 31st, and that there would also be information meetings for parents that evening.

The special assembly seemed to create more problems that it solved. Part of the difficulty seemed to lie in the fact that the youth workers, Geoff Turner and Mukhtar Khares, were excluded from the entire process. Part of the difficulty seemed to lie in the fact that the school education officials who conducted the meeting insisted on taking a patronizing and "top down" approach to communicating with the students in the school. And part of the problem seemed also to have been caused by the ill-considered intervention of a community worker who involved a group of students in a process that was made to look like they were being heard, when in fact they were actually being kept occupied.

These difficulties began to develop on the Monday morning before the special assembly was to be held. Geoff Turner and Mukhtar Khares learned that there was going to be a meeting just before the special assembly on Tuesday morning. They understood that the meeting was to be planned and conducted by Richard Leese, the Chair of Education, the Chair of Governors, the police, the inspectorate, and senior management. When Geoff Turner and Mukhtar Khares asked Ethel Milroy, the senior secondary stage inspector, whether the meeting would require assistance from them, Ethel Milroy seemed to be genuinely surprised at the idea.

At this time, Geoff Turner and Mukhtar Khares were the only links between the white students who were out of school and the Asian students in school.

Since no one from senior management had asked either of them for any kind of review of the situation, and since they felt that their opinions might in fact be useful in the planning meeting, Geoff Turner and Mukhtar Khares decided to go to school very early on the morning of the 31st to be available if they were in fact needed.

When they got to the school that morning, they sat on a bench in the entrance hall so that those who were attending the meeting could see them clearly. Almost everyone who attended the planning meeting noticed that they were there (DC Davies, Gordon Hainsworth's Deputy, Councillor Ken Strath, people from the Multi-Cultural Working Party and the Equal Opportunities Group, the chair and deputy chair of Governors, Ethel Milroy, Dr Gough, Peter Moors, Jack Hewitt, and senior uniformed police officers), but none of them suggested that they could or should actually attend the meeting.

Even when put in the best possible light, the special assembly was a disaster. Everyone who had attended the planning meeting in the Head's study filed onto the stage in front of the assembled boys. Richard Leese, the chair of education, addressed them in strong terms, the general line of which was: "What is going on in the school is intolerable and it is not going to be tolerated." Richard Leese read from a prepared statement, which was later published in the press.

During the assembly, an altercation broke out at the meeting between a student and one of the police officers. The officer, who had become involved in an exchange with the student, apparently said something to the effect of: "I already told you at the police station." Since the student he was talking to had been denying that he had ever been at the police station, the student he was talking to and some of the other students became angry and resentful at the officer's insistence, as well as at his apparent mistaken identification. Even Richard Leese later admitted that the way the special assembly had been handled had been a complete disaster. But it took the efforts of the Burnage students to begin to take steps to salvage the situation.

After the assembly, a community relations worker, from Manchester Council for Community Relations, met with a group of Afro-Caribbean, Asian, and white students, allegedly to make an attempt to figure out what could be done about the atmosphere and the violence at the school. These students had not been elected by their peers, nor had they been selected by management or teachers to do this work; they were simply students who had been recruited by the community relations worker.

Working with the community relations officer, the students drew up a list of steps that they thought should be taken, and an appeal to other students to take constructive steps. The community relations worker then approached Geoff Turner after school and asked him to assist them. Specifically, they had worked out four points that they thought would "solve" the current situation, and they asked Geoff Turner to go with them to a meeting with those in authority at 4 o'clock that afternoon. The meeting was to be attended by DC Davies, Richard Leese, the superintendent of police, Ethel Milroy, the head, and two deputy heads. The four points were:

1. Mr Moors should be based at Upper School because he is better in situations like we are in today. Those situations are most likely to occur at Upper School.

106

2. Dr Gough should be taking a more active role in school.

3. Staff should be more aware or involved in situations at school.

4. There should be a meeting with the police.

The boys were euphoric, and seemed to feel that they were on the verge of making a real contribution to the situation. They went with Geoff Turner to the meeting at four o'clock and presented the four points to those in attendance. They left the meeting with the clear impression that they had been helpful, and that their four points – and an appeal to all students that they had yet to draft – would be circulated the next day to all the students.

When Geoff Turner went down the hall to photocopy the four points for distribution, however, he was called into the head's office where he was asked not to duplicate the document. Even though the boys had been given the clear impression that their views would be considered and that they would be allowed to hold a meeting at lunchtime the following day, it was made clear to Geoff Turner then, that "We have had enough of that really now. We are going to start curtailing those sorts of meetings."

Geoff Turner was told that the document could not contain any reference to specific individuals. Geoff Turner indicated that he was reluctant to change the document without discussion with the students, but he did agree to try to prepare an alternative document when he met with the boys the next morning.

The document that was eventually distributed raised the following points:

1. The students who are out of school should return.

2. Teachers should work at improving communication.

3. The head teacher should be more involved in the upper school.

4. Students should suggest representatives and structures for fourth and fifth year councils.

5. The head teacher should consider and look at the roles and placement of senior staff within the school.

These suggestions were accompanied by an appeal to all students:

"We ask all students to help calm the situation in school. If people still feel there is any further issue, please get in touch with student council representatives."

Meanwhile, the process that the school management had devised to deal with the situation was also unfolding in a less than satisfactory fashion. Not all parents had actually received the letter informing them of the two community meetings that night. In particular, some of the parents of the excluded group of white students had heard about the meetings only from the newspaper reports. Geoff Turner had not been requested to attend. However, he decided to go because he knew many of the students and parents who were involved.

The first meeting, which was held at Burnage Upper School at 6.30 that night, was attended by approximately 150 people. Three quarters of those in attendance were white and the rest were mainly Asian. Only a few Afro-Caribbeans attended. The meeting was also attended by Burnage students and representatives from the education department, including DC Davies and Richard Leese.

The parents of the boys who had been involved in the dining room incident felt that it took a long time at the meeting before the school and the Education Department officials actually brought up what they wanted to know. A lot of parents were still unclear about eaxactly what had happened, but when they asked Dr Gough for more information, he rather unhelpfully pointed out that he had not been in the school at the time. When parents became angry and frustrated with this attitude, they were met with cutting responses: "Some students at this school are better behaved than their parents." This response came from a City Councillor. When both Asians and whites expressed fear about the incidents and asked what the school planned to do, those in authority responded with general phrases and made general comments about what was expected of a school.

The second meeting was not as emotional as the first one had been, but both of them failed to come to grips with the central issues. Most of the people who attended the meetings were afraid – they knew that a boy had been murdered at the school earlier in the year, and now they were reading newspaper reports of gang warfare. Most of the parents who had attended the meeting had left without having spoken personally to anyone connected with the school, and no concrete suggestions had been made at all, other than the suggestion by DC Davies that parents could write to the Education Department to raise any issues that worried them. Some parents even felt that their sons were being made responsible for everything that had happened in the school – that they were being made scapegoats. Even the multiracial group of students who had met with management earlier that day had been able to take more constructive steps than had those who conducted the community meetings.

Communication at Burnage was not easy. The students who had been excluded from school after the dining room incident suffered in their own way from the communication problems. These students entered a kind of limbo. Due to do exams, procedures were set up for them to attend at examinations at Shawgrove. The school sent letters instructing them where to attend for their examinations. Letters concerning examinations to be written on April 2nd were not mailed until April 1, and letters requesting teachers to make special arrangements for the excluded students were not sent until April 9.

Burnage High School

Ref.   DRGG/SME
         1st April 1987

Dear
I would like to confirm the arrangements which have been made for you to take examinations before Easter. The examination venue will be Shawgrove School, Cavendish Road, (map enclosed). Naturally we are not announcing this venue other than to those concerned.

German Oral. Thursday 2nd April 12.20 p.m. (Mr Pugh)
Maths Oral. Thursday 2nd April 1.45 p.m. (Mr Poritt)
Art. 12 hour supervised session is being arranged for three days next week and I will confirm this and venue for you as soon as possible.

Please try to do your very best in your examination in these difficult circumstances.
My best wishes,

Yours sincerely,
Headmaster

TO HEADS OF DEPARTMENT
FROM JACK HEWITT
         Dept: 2

The following boys were out of school and are not returning. Alternative arrangements are being made for examinations.

(List of 16 boys names)

NAME   WORK   DEADLINE

PLEASE LIST (and enclose where possible) ANY WORK WHICH THE BOYS CAN BE DOING IN PREPARATION FOR EXAMS:

NAME   WORK

A STUDY CENTRE IS BEING ARRANGED FOR AFTER EASTER. THIS WILL BE STAFFED FULL-TIME BUT I WOULD BE GRATEFUL IF SOME SCHOOL STAFF COULD VISIT TO HELP WITH PARTICULAR PROBLEMS.

PLEASE GIVE A SUITABLE TIME FOR THE MEMBER OF STAFF
   NAME   DAY   TIME

I understand the pressures of time upon staff, but it would be most helpful if all this could be tied up during the Easter holiday. I would, therefore be grateful if this form could be returned by the end of Friday or dropped into school early next week.

THANK YOU all for your help.
             signed Jack Hewitt

The excluded students felt, naturally enough, that these arrangements were unfair and unsatisfactory. They felt that they had been treated badly, and that they – the ones who had been locked up and threatened – were the ones who had lost two or three months schooling. Some of them were told that there would be a place for them to go to study, but it was only made available to them a few days before examinations – or, in some cases, after the examinations had actually occurred. None of their teachers ever visited them.

One of the Burnage students summed up the events of February and March of 1987 with bitter accuracy: "That's the tragedy of it. Something could have been done earlier on, because it was sort of a little problem that grew."

We would go further. It is clear from the evidence given to us that there was a high degree of organisation and self discipline among the Asian youth. Grievances were first raised with staff at the upper school, and it was only when these were ignored or brushed off that further action was taken. Then, as we saw, a "hit list" was drawn up. It may have been unfairly and inaccurately drawn up. The evidence given to us suggests that it clearly was. Some white students on that list might have been racist, but this was not the impression formed by Geoff Turner or any of those who had to work with them, or who had known them as a group in the school. Some of them gave evidence to us and made a very good impression. They were not the racists that the hit list suggested, not in any way. Nor were their parents, who accompanied them.

110

Whatever the rights and wrongs of the hit list it was clear that those on it were regarded by the Asian students as legitimate targets, and seemingly all others were to be left alone.

The staff involved at the time of the March events were always able to move freely amongst the Asian students, however many of them were gathered together. No one was threatened and no hostility was shown. So far as we could discover, there was no display of hostility to any member of staff by the Asian students at the time of these events.

Outside on the street, as the garage incident shows, the Asian youth displayed great self discipline in the face of obvious provocation. The capitulation of the school authorities to their demands for exclusion of the boys on the hit list clearly gave them a taste for power and a measure of confidence they had not previously experienced.

This contrasts sharply with the white side of the student population. They had no similar positive incentive to organise, and this showed. They were surprised and bewildered by the extent of the Asian boys' organisation, but had no means of matching it. Those targetted by the Asian students were very frightened and eventually had nowhere to go.

Their fate was sealed by the ineptitude of the authorities. The Asian hit list and the hurried withdrawal of the boys from the upper school kitchen was allowed to substitute itself for any attempt by the school to deal with the Asian students' grievances. In our view what happened to the white students is a disgrace and a scandal. At this stage we make five points:

1. The school failed to recognise or deal adequately with the grievances of the Asian students when they were put to members of staff shortly before the eruptions of March.
2. If the school had dealt effectively and adequately with these grievances, there probably would not have been any hit list or any forced withdrawal of students from the school population at Burnage.
3. It is clear that once the school discovered the existence of the hit list they did nothing effective about it, and were unable to discover those who had compiled it or to make it clear that hit lists as such were unacceptable, but finding a remedy for the grievances behind them was not.
4. Mukhtar Khares and Geoff Turner were put into the school as part of a fire brigade operation, but no attempt was made by the school to draw on their experience or have any kind of debriefing with them. For example, no contact was made between either of these two and the head of fifth year, who would continue to have responsibility for the students concerned, Asian and white, until the end of the Summer term.

111

5. The white students who were taken out of the school in an emergency were effectively left to rot, and the school showed scant regard thereafter for their welfare or education.

We were astonished at the response of a number of witnesses. including Dr Gough, to the fate of these boys. Even more astonishing was that all these witnesses, almost without exception, were strong supporters of Dr Gough's stand on anti-racist policies. For each of us on the Panel, anti-racism involves a respect for the integrity of all persons, black and white, irrespective of their colour, race or ethnic origin. We have no doubt at all that if it had been a group of Asian or Afro-Caribbean boys who had been forcibly withdrawn from the school because their safety was threatened by a large group of white boys who had congregated around the dining area, there would have been an almighty uproar. To have continued to keep them out of the school would have become a cause celebre – a national scandal. To dismiss the fate of these boys, because they are white, is to us both racist and offensive.

At several stages of our inquiry, we were told that racism in school derives from the racism in the wider community. Indeed some told us that until the racism in the wider community was dealt with, nothing effective could be done about the racism in the schools. Yet here we have an example of action taken by senior management which pays great lip service to the cause of anti-racism acting in an obviously discriminatory manner in its treatment of a small group of white students. It is one of the greatest recipes for the spread of racism from inside the school out into the community. Some of the parents and some of the boys affected came to give us their evidence. We were greatly impressed by their moderation and restraint. But they were justifiably angry and resentful at the treatment that they had received. If those parents had been in any way actively racist, they would have had a field day. In our view it is a matter of great fortune that the handling of these events by the school management at Burnage did not lead to far more widespread eruptions of communal violence outside in the community.

All these matters were put to Dr Gough when he gave evidence, and this is what he told us:

Ms Bhavnani:
"You refer to Mr Hewitt's report, which you are kindly going to present to the panel, on the incidents. You did say that the white boys had remained out of school because of choice, and you said that they

112

were afraid to come back. Did you take any steps to relieve their fears in any way?

A. I personally, no. We had a youth worker working with them, and going between, and it was a matter of assessing their feelings and trying to assess the feelings of the boys in the school and the sort of reaction they might get if they did come back, and then taking that back to them, and so on. The youth worker was the principal agent in that.

Q. You felt that it was the youth worker's responsibility?

A. Not so much his responsibility, but he would be in the best position to do the job, in that he was not associated with us or the hierarchy of the school or whatever; he was neutral, as the other youth worker was.

The CHAIRMAN: We are talking about Geoff Turner? A. Yes.

Q. His position was that he was not – and he made it quite clear – in any way an agent for the school. He was acting as a quite independent person in relation to those young people?

A. Yes

Q. So far as any relationship of those people to the school was concerned, that could not be conducted, if that is right, through Geoff Turner, could it?

A. No. But before I, or anyone on my behalf said to those students, "You must come back", we would need to know how they felt and what their reception would be, and the way we should manage whatever their reception would be, and Geoff was working with the boys on that sort of basis. The strategy we opted for in the end was to provide off-site education, and off-site provision for examinations for the boys.

Q. Were any of them taking examinations?

A. Yes.

Q. How many?

A. I can't recall how many, but in this schedule I have it tells you everything we did in terms of arranging examinations. You have got letters that went from school about this, and if I can read you –

Q. I think we can save time, Dr Gough, and look at it later. We have had some indication of this already.

A. They did take examinations. Some did not in the end, but I think most of them did.

Q. The reason why it was suggested that they should not come to school was because the school could not guarantee their safety?

A. I do not know whether anybody suggested that. I think they took the decision that they would not come.

Q. You say you think?

A. I was asked by a parent on one occasion whether or not I could guarantee, and the short answer is that I cannot guarantee anything when you are talking about human behaviour.

Q. You just left it there, did you?

A. In what sense do you mean?

Q. You were asked by a parent at a meeting, and you say that you cannot guarantee anything in human behaviour. Is that where the matter rested?

A. One cannot give guarantees; all one can do is indicate that there is a high probability that things will be okay, but –

Q. What had you done to ensure that it would be okay?

A. What was done was largely done through that students' group, and the influence of students in that group on their peers in terms of what the effect would be if the boys came back –

Q. Was there a hit list that you knew of?

A. I have heard talk of a hit list.

Q. What attempts did you make to find out about that talk you heard of the hit list?

A. I have heard talk of a hit list. The existence of a hit list is denied by the Asian students. There is no such thing. But white students say that there was a hit list, and that is part of it. I don't know whether it is just wild rumour and speculation, and the sort of thing that goes around.

Q. Did you take steps to identify the particular leaders of the Asian boys at the time, and have them in to speak to them?

A. They denied entirely that there was a hit list.

Q. You actually interviewed them?

A. Mr Hewitt interviewed them, and at times I mentioned it casually in the corridor to the boys and there was always disagreement – there is no such thing as a hit list; it is just stupid speculation.

Q. Did you see fit at any stage to have into the school the parents of the white boys who were out of school as a result of the canteen incident and speak to them personally?

A. Mr Hewitt met with them on Wednesday 25th March.

Q. That is two days afterwards. Any subsequent meeting with them?

A. I had not met the parents, except parents who have approached me at some of the various meetings we have had, and we have talked then.

Q. Did you not think it was important to have those parents in to discuss the situation with them vis-a-vis their children and the continuing education of their children, either individually or as a group?

A. That is something I did not do.

Q. Do you think, looking with hindsight, it is something you ought to have done?

A. It may well have helped. Others were in contact with the parents quite regularly. Mr Hewitt was in contact with them also.

Q. During your career as a teacher or as a head have you ever been in the situation where there are nine or ten boys – or thirteen or whatever the particular number is – who cannot come into school because it is feared that if they did so it might either spark off a riot or their safety could not be guaranteed? This is the first time you have faced that situation, is it?

A. Yes.

Q. If any boys cannot come into your school because of fears for their safety, that in itself is quite an indictment, is it not, of the situation in the school?

A. No, I would not go along with that.

Q. You would not?

A. No, I would not indict the boys in the school.

Q. I am not talking about indicting the boys. I am saying that it is an indictment of the school?

A. Unfortunately most people do indict them. When feelings and passions run as high as they have amongst people those last twelve months, I do not know that any system copes as well as we would wish.

Q. But Dr Gough, you told us that you have the fifth form consultative group and the other strategies you put in which you thought had worked well, so that although passions may still have been high when Mr Hewitt saw those parents on the 25th by the beginning of the next term, as we understand it, things had died down to a moderate degree, had they not?

A. Yes.

Q. Would it not have been not only a wise and useful thing but, we would suggest, an essential thing that you as head should at least call in those parents and discuss with them the future of their children at the school?

A. By that time arrangements I think had been set in hand for them to continue their studies outside school.

Q. Maybe that is so, but would it not have been right and proper, and we would say essential, for you as headmaster to have those parents in so that you could discuss with them face to face at first hand what was going to happen and what arrangements were being made for the continued education of their children? Is not that the least you could have done in the circumstances?

A. It is something I could have done, and probably should have done, yes."

Some of the parents and some of the boys affected came to give us their evidence. We were greatly impressed by their moderation and restraint. But they were justifiably angry and resentful at the treatment they had received. We were told by them that some of the students had decided not to go on to college to pursue further education because they feared they would meet up with the Asian students, and the colleges would then become the arena in which those scores would finally be settled. We also spoke to some of the Asian students, who were unequivocal in their condemnation of the school's failure to help the student body deal with the problems. But they also expressed anxieties about what might happen if those groups of Asian and white students met up in the colleges. Far from seeing the exclusion of the white students as a complete triumph, therefore, those Asian students realised that a problem which ought to have been dealt with in Burnage had been left to fester and grow elsewhere.

We heard this evidence towards the end of the Summer term in July 1987. Such was our concern about what we were hearing, that we felt it necessary to take the unusual step, as a panel of Inquiry, to contact the Education Department and explore the possibility of Geoff Turner and Mukhtar Khares working with both groups of students, white and Asian and also their parents, together with others whom the students chose to involve, and do that work in whatever setting they considered to be appropriate. In our view it was essential that both groups of students had the opportunity to thrash out the problems that had arisen, to explore their origins, and to work out the collective responsibilities of each group and of the school management. With the summer vacation fast approaching, however, and the unavailability of a number of the key students concerned, it proved difficult to take this initiative any further than the exploratory stage.

We nevertheless remain convinced that if those white parents had been in any way actively racist, they would have had a field day in June and July of 1987. In our view it is a matter of good fortune that the handling of these events by the school management at Burnage did not lead to far more widespread eruptions of communal violence outside in the community.

In July 1987, before our summer recess, we heard evidence that one of the boys, allegedly on the hit list, was spotted at a bus stop by a group of Asian students. He was with some of his friends. He was recognised and the two groups began to square up to each other. What was disturbing was that, almost immediately, an unknown group of white youths and men began to emerge from betting shops and nearby public houses to lend a hand. Some were openly racist. They were not known to the white boys in question. Fortunately the Asian boys had the good sense to disperse. However, it is easy to imagine a situation where they go off to collect greater forces. An equal gathering of forces then takes place on the white side and before long there is open racial fighting out on the streets of Manchester.

The failure to deal with the hit list and the failure to deal with the withdrawal of the white boys from the school had within it the seeds of a far greater confrontation and polarisation. It would not have been an import of racism into the school from the community but an export of it from the school to the community. In our view an adherence to some kind of cosmetic anti-racism, which carries with it a failure to deal with the real racism experienced by the black community is a very dangerous thing.

Our conclusion is that there is very little chance of racism being eliminated from Burnage High School under the existing management structure. Our condemnation of Dr Gough's style of management stems in part from our view that he has proved himself unable to tackle racism effectively in his school, and, in his position as Headteacher, to work to eliminate it from amongst the wider school community, including the white parents. We feel that the man has become so obsessed with the ideology of anti-racism that he has become unable to see what was needed and what had to be done. For us, it is sad to see a man, who is so committed to principles that we would hold dear, being responsible for one of the most obvious acts of discrimination we have come across in the course of this Inquiry. His failure to see the link between the way the school treated those white students and the potential for racial conflict in the neighbourhood outside the school is in our view unforgivable. The fact that the school would have had no control over the course of those events once racial conflict had spread outwards makes Dr Gough's responsibility as Head even more obvious.

CHAPTER 14

Levenshulme: A Second Front

A school is part of the community, and when incidents such as those that occurred in the week of March 23rd, 1987 occur, the community hears about them – whether through its newspapers or through rumour, gossip, or scaremongering.

Levenshulme is a girl's school. It is not far from Burnage, the boys' school. Some girls who attended Levenshulme had brothers who attended Burnage. Some girls who attended Levenshulme had friends who attended Burnage. There are white, Afro-Caribbean, and Asian students at Burnage. There are white, Afro-Caribbean, and Asian students at Levenshulme. There were rumours at Levenshulme: "Burnage boys are coming round to beat the girls up." "They'll be coming at lunchtime." "Whites who had started on Asians at Burnage are going round to Levenshulme." Despite the fact that fights were not common in Levenshulme, Asian girls were saying that "Because Asians in Burnage had beaten up whites, they could as well." The students at Levenshulme began to form groups just like those at Burnage.

One Levenshulme student was warned by a fourth year friend: "Watch how you go home tonight, there's going to be trouble." The student was scared. Another student heard the rumours. Teachers had also heard them and advised students: "Take a different way home; go through the main roads." There were rumours of boys coming down. The police were at the main gates.

Four Asian students took the advice to take different routes home, and walked along Ernwood Road. But on the way home, they saw a group of eight or nine white girls, followed by a few Afro-Caribbean girls. The white girls in the large group shouted after the Asian girls: "Get that one, get that one there."

One of the Asian girls ("F") did not even have time to look around at the group of girls behind her before she was hit on the head with something hard. She went down on the ground in a puddle and then her hair was pulled and she was kicked. No one said anything, but she heard a bottle smash and she was terrified. As the result of this attack, some of her hair was pulled out, and she was bruised.

119

The attack on F ended only when a white man who lived in a house nearby came out of his house and intervened. After the attackers ran off, the white man helped F and another friend who had also been attacked into his house. He and his wife helped the girls by letting them clean up and make phone calls. The other Asian girls had managed to run away from the attackers. When the police investigated the attacks, they made no attempt to interview the man or his wife as potential witnesses.

Later on, one of the students who had been attacked was further frightened when other students came asking for her and asking questions about her. Eventually those students even came to her classroom to look for her. Her classmates – white and Asian alike – sheltered her by denying she was there and by denying that they knew who she was. When one of her teachers was told about the incident, she did not seem at all shocked; her only reaction was to say that "these types of incidents do happen." The teacher's reaction made the girl who had been beaten up feel as if that was part of normal everyday life.

According to Dr Kirby, the Head Teacher at Levenshulme, the rumours around the school panicked parents as well as girls. He spoke to a number of parents on the telephone. The attacks on the girls caused a real shift in the atmosphere around the school. During the last week of March, he had observed that girls of all races seemed to exhibit roughly the same amount of fear. On Friday, March 27th, the day the attacks occurred, he felt that a subtle change took place round about lunchtime. Instead of seeming to be frightened of something from outside, the girls seemed to have internalized fear and anger. This fear and anger polarised the students along racial lines, and it became Asian girls against white and Afro-Caribbean girls.

Dr Kirby first found out about the attacks on Friday night when Chief Education Officer Gordon Hainsworth telephoned him with the information. Dr Kirby was appalled by the attacks, and decided that Levenshulme should make a high profile institutional response. Although the girls who were attacked did not recollect that any classroom time was devoted to discussing what had happened, the institutional response was firm. When twenty Asian parents came to see him on Monday morning, Dr Kirby opened the school to them, showed them around personally, and reassured them while talking with them. He discussed the attacks directly in assemblies with the students. Seven or eight girls who had directly participated in the attack or who were involved by way of encouragement were sent home, their parents were contacted, and the girls were eventually readmitted.

120

Dr Kirby also met the girls who had been attacked, spoke with the members of their families, asked them if they had recognized their attackers, and told them he would suspend the culprits if they could be identified.

CHAPTER 15

What Are Little Boys Made Of?

> *What are little girls made of*
> *Sugar and spice and all things nice*
> *What are little boys made of*
> *Slugs and snails and puppy dogs tails*

The old rhyme was echoed in the remarks made to the Inquiry by one Manchester head who, when writing a paper on good comprehensive schools, was told by a number of other head teachers anecdotally:

"We were founded from 2 schools, a boys secondary modern and a girls secondary modern, and it was said in the area that the girls secondary modern turned out young ladies who were a credit to the institution, but the boys school was a blackboard jungle. Fortunately we joined them together and now we have a successful comprehensive school."

When the same Manchester head had pointed out to him in questioning that, although mixed sex schools might civilise the boys, some educationalists were aware that mixed sex schools reduced the quality of schooling for the girls. The response to this was "It depends what you consider to be the purposes of education."

Manchester City Council has an anti-sexist anti-racist policy. Manchester City Council has an Equal Opportunities Group.

To Morgan Morrison, the Principal Educational Psychologist and head of the Schools Psychological and Child Guidance Service in Manchester, to which service the most "disturbed" children are referred, problems of violence can be identified as stemming from so called "male" attitudes. "It is not just that this is a view within the service. I think that our society is a violent one; I think that our schools are – our institutions are, and that includes our schools to some extent, more or less. Yes. They both generate and perpetuate it; yes. One aspect of our schools being violent is the extent to which what they are about is determined by our notion and image of what people are

123

about, and that means the male model and the male image, and that means *dominance, aggressiveness, playing down of feeling, competitiveness rather than co-operativeness, heterosexuality, innate dominance* and so on. So I think those are some elements of what I call a racist society, but also our racist institutions are, I am saying, dominated by those ideologies as well as dominated – and that certainly goes for high schools, by a specimen of that product, namely men. Our high schools particularly are male dominated, so we are products of and perpetuators of that very observation that I make. Yes, it is a judgment; it is a view. I think that violence – *some of those things I have talked about give rise to violence.* Let me give you another example not of boys' schools per se, but mixed schools, and again this is a view of mine based on evidence to some extent that is coming out quite recently, which is that violence – and it does not have to be physical violence – but certainly a dominance of, in the dis-interests of girls and in the interests of boys in terms of what goes on in mixed classrooms, and the extent of which, for example, boys have two-thirds of teachers' time, they take two-thirds of the space, they interrupt significantly predominantly. Those are just ways in which research has shown that in this sense it is a sort of violence; it is a domination that is in the interests of one party and in the dis-interest of the other, and the girls, even if they are given the chance to express – and by and large they are not – find that nothing is done. Those to me are non-physical aspects of what I would call violence."

Pauline Collier, aware of the disproportionate number of boys referred to the Service for violence, feels that "the potential violence which moves in and concerns all male groups is well overdue for attention," and "that serious problems are caused in schools by violent male behaviour and boys damaged by the imposition of 'masculinity'."

To Morgan Morrison the "male" structure of schools is a good meeting ground for racism and violence.

Students at Burnage, bullied by their peers, and subjected on occasions to physical and verbal violence by teachers, are living the "male ethos" daily, although it is not as reliant on physical abuse of children as previously. Although there has been an increase in the number of female teachers, the evidence given to us suggest that an appreciable number of staff still feel that Burnage was "better" at a time when boys were punished physically or disciplined, that Burnage was "better" when the Grammar School ethos of success and failure predominated, that Burnage was "better" when the staff was almost entirely male, and that at some time in the past there existed a "proper education system", a "proper school" and an "English Education" in which violence and indiscipline and racism did not exist, and in which all children flourished.

This group does not seem to have reflected significantly on the changes that have occurred inside schools and in society outside, such as the increase in violent material in the media, the increase in unemployment, the widespread existence of racism in the society, black people's organisation to deal with racism, the financial cutbacks in education, or the teachers' industrial action as all affecting the education of the country's children. In particular this view ignores the evidence that in an all boys' school, like Burnage, there is likely to be greater aggressiveness and a greater propensity to solve problems through force and violence. This derives not just from the male culture of such a school, but also springs from the "golden age" of "English education" when the authority of teachers and the "proper" hierarchy of the school depended on corporal punishment as the ultimate sanction.

CHAPTER 16

Violence at Burnage

The tendency to violence and aggression is known to be greater in all-boys schools than in mixed schools or all-girls schools. Burnage is an all boys school. Is this true of Burnage? Or is it different? And if a culture of violence and aggression flourishes and the school is also divided into different racial groups, will there inevitably be racism and will that violence and aggression take on a racial form? All our evidence suggests that it will.

First the atmosphere of violence.

When the governors made their investigation of the school in 1985 they appended some quotes from teachers and management. These included:

1. "There's an awful lot of shouting going on in this school."
2. "For the first time, I as a teacher feel very vulnerable, I feel if I have a *confrontation* with a child I will be seen as the instigator of the trouble."
3. "I've taught in tough schools but this lot knocked me for six. It is a *confrontation* situation."
4. "This place needs to become teacher-centered for a time."

Violence in schools is normally perceived in terms of student to student. Is there another level of violence that exists, that is rarely recognised, that between teacher and student?

Teachers exercise considerable power over students. Until 1982 they were allowed to use corporal punishment at Burnage. That in itself creates a certain ethos. If force dominates the way teachers and students relate to each other, it is highly likely that it will also become the prevalent tone in relationships between students, particularly if it is an all boys school.

Ending corporal punishment does not automatically lead to a change in attitude or suddenly subvert a whole male culture. Nor does the introduction of child centred in place of didactic teacher methods necessarily lead to any great reversal of power relations, or reduction in

127

the authority of teachers, though many teachers think it does. Given the need to assert their authority and given the dominant male culture in an all boys school, there is every likelihood that, despite the ending of corporal punishment, there will be teacher violence against students at a school like Burnage. And so it was, as the following incidents show.

On July 14th 1982 a mother complained to Burnage school because her son allegedly had his clothes damaged and a bump on his head caused by 2 teachers, one of whom dragged him out of a line of boys outside a classroom, the other of whom threw a roll of paper across the classroom.

In 1984 a member of staff called students "spineless turds", in class, and threw his keys across the room, where they hit a boy a glancing blow to the head. Grabbing another student who laughed, he put him into a storeroom, allegedly telling the student "I'll kick the shit out of you". This was later denied by the teacher, but he did admit calling the students "dickheads", "shit heads" and "stupid bastards".

Late in the year 1984 the same teacher admitted grabbing a student by the scruff of his neck and pushing him against a wall.

In January 1985 a teacher got drunk in front of the students, while escorting them on a visit to London.

In February 1986, a teacher found some students mucking about and throwing aquarium gravel around and threw an old dining room tray at one of them causing the following injuries: a broken nose, and a deep hole adjacent to the nose which bled.

In January 1986 a member of staff, who had previously thrown a blackboard rubber at a student, admitted that he had hit a student in the chest with his foot and that the student had fallen as a result.

Are these isolated incidents or are they part of a pattern? All occurred at a time when corporal punishment had been abolished.

What about student violence? How is that perceived, how is that acted on?

In January 1983 the following memo was in the possession of the Education Department:

Burnage High School and
Whalley Range High School

S1/CT/AS   6.1.83

Two students currently suspended from Burnage High School, F and M, are to appear in court 21 January 1983 on charges of robbery i.e. obtaining money with threats of violence to fellow students.

The Probation Officer Miss G who has been supervising M reports that according to him, there are gangs of Pakistani boys, groups of blacks and gangs of white boys at Burnage. When Miss G expressed her concern he replied "everybody is doing it". He says it is normal practice for boys to "beg borrow or steal" money.

Miss G says she believes the Headteacher is trying to stamp out this behaviour.

I bring this to your attention because of your concern last year that the Acting Headteacher at Burnage did not appear to grasp the possible racial significance of the attack on MSH in 1982.

Miss G further reports that there have been incidents at Whalley Range High School of attacks on Pakistani girls by both whites and blacks.

On February 11th 1983 Dr Gough responded to the Chief Education Officer, and in that letter made the following observation:

"In general, in all schools, groups are demanding money from other boys. There is a pecking order of groups – White/West Indians etc with Pakistanis at the bottom of the pile."

It is my policy that when witnesses come forward and report criminality such as this, a prosecution shall ensue. I look for support for this policy from the police, which I have, from the probation service, which I have, and from officers in Crown Square. In the latter cases there seems to be some doubt".

According to one parent, there would also appear to be some doubt as to whether Dr Gough's policy is in fact carried out at Burnage. In June 1986 this parent (a white parent with boys at the school) was driving past the Lower school with his wife, when he saw 4 or 5 boys beating up a Sikh student. They had the Sikh boy against the railings and were going through his pockets demanding money. The parent jumped out of his car, grabbed the biggest of the attackers and marched him into the Year Head's office. He told the Year Head what he had seen and left the boy with him. He was never contacted by the police for a witness statement so presumably there was no prosecution, nor was he contacted by the school after this incident either to be thanked for intervening or to be told what action the school had taken.

After Darren Coulburn's trial, a statement was attributed to Dr Gough that Burnage was "not a violent school". One teacher was so alarmed by this that he decided to keep a record of violent incidents that came to his knowledge over a 3 week period.

129

1. On February 6th 1987
A boy was found in school with a knife. Apparently this boy was suspended.

2. On February 9th 1987
Two white boys intruded into an Asian Teacher's class and ignored requests that they should leave. They were abusive, and the teacher grabbed them and made them leave the class. The teacher was asked to apologise because the parents of the white boys complained and were threatening prosecution. We come back to this incident in a later chapter in more detail.

3. On February 11th 1987
A boy was held over a stairwell by 3 or 4 other boys. According to hearsay accounts the reaction of a member of Senior Management was: "What was the drop?" and "were any Asian boys involved?" Although the boys were meant to have been suspended, one boy was back in school within two days before there had been discussion with his parents.

4. On February 11th 1987
There was a fight in a classroom at Lower School as a result of which a boy had to attend hospital.

5. On February 11th 1987
A female teacher was assaulted by a student who had been suspended a few days earlier for fighting with another student.

6. On February 12th 1987
A student was argumentative and offensive to an Asian female member of staff. This boy had previously been found in possession of school keys in suspicious circumstances.

7. On February 27th 1987
A number of Stanley knives were removed from a woodwork class. Another knife was found on one of the boys who was being searched for these. The boy claimed he had brought it into school for modelling.

This member of staff felt that these incidents indicated that there was rather a violent situation, that behaviour was going on that really was dangerous and unacceptable, and that a consistent pattern of response was required from senior management at the school. According to certain members of staff, this consistency was lacking.

One teacher told us that when she inquired of Dr Gough in February 1987 (less than six months after Ahmed's murder) about an allegation that a boy had had a knife in school, the reaction of Dr Gough was to take a dinner table knife out of his drawer and place it against his stomach saying that "they're making mountains out of molehills. This, (referring to the knife) couldn't do any damage". We come back to this later.

Burnage is an all boys' school and there is certainly evidence of greater aggressiveness and a greater propensity to solve problems through force and violence. It is part of a male culture. While Burnage remained a school in which corporal punishment was used there is no doubt that these tendencies would be validated and reinforced.

Despite the removal of corporal punishment as a sanction there is still evidence of teachers imposing their authority from time to time through acts of violence towards students, as we have seen in this chapter.

It is not altogether surprising that violence is widespread among students, given that Burnage is an all boys' school and given that an important section of the staff still think of force as the ultimate sanction for imposing teachers' authority. From evidence given to us this view is also quite widely held among students. The evidence set out in this and other chapters suggests that there is an atmosphere of aggression at the school, and that violence, aggression and the use of force is very much part of the culture of the school.

Burnage, however, is a school which has been very much under the spotlight. Since 1982 not very much has happened quietly and unobtrusively, as at most other schools in Manchester or the UK. It is, therefore, very difficult to judge whether Burnage is any different from any other all boys' school in an Inner City area in respect of the culture of violence and aggression. We suspect not. So in our view it would be wrong and quite unfair to single Burnage out as anything special as regards an atmosphere of aggression or a culture of violence.

However, the evidence given to us does suggest that if there was any return to the sanction of corporal punishment, there would be a probable escalation of violence at all levels in the school. A different strategy for dealing with violence is needed. During the course of the Inquiry, therefore, we asked for assistance on this question and received a detailed and considered paper from three of the Education Psychologists. We return to their suggestions in a later chapter.

CHAPTER 17

Racism at Burnage

Burnage is not just an all boys' school. It is not just a school where the majority of the staff are male, many of whom feel it was a mistake to get rid of corporal punishment.

It is also a school where all but a tiny handful of the teaching staff are white and of Christian upbringing, but over 35% of the students are black – Afro-Caribbean or Asian. Most of the Asian students are from Muslim homes.

Issues of race and religion and cultural practices have to be added to issues of male violence and teacher authority. In any school population we would expect to find examples of racial intolerance and bigotry on much the same scale as exists outside in the community. Teachers and students are no more immune to these social forces than other sections of the population. And so it was at Burnage.

We look first at life on the outside, then at teachers, and then at students.

Part 1: Life on the Outside

What is it like to be an Asian living in the community outside Burnage?

"I still don't feel safe, I don't live in a very good area. If I go to the local park with my son often there are gangs of white boys aged about thirteen or fourteen who throw stones at us and call us names."

"I think Afro-Caribbeans are more acceptable to whites because they appear to fight back."

"Most of the parents in my area are not happy about children playing in the street, because of racial attacks."

"Often if I go out I get racial abuse from groups of white boys aged about twelve to fourteen."

"White boys call us Paki F-----s in the street."

"We have had stones thrown at our house.'

"I have had stones thrown at my house on many occasions."

"I have been called names like Paki B------."

133

"When I picked up my younger brother from St James School in Longsight, older white boys aged eleven to fourteen used to call me names 'Paki' or 'Nigger'. Once a white boy attacked me, called me names and tried to take my bus fare, he pulled my hair and hit me. None of the white passersby helped my little brother and me. I never go out alone. I am scared stiff. How can we grow up and look forward to adulthood in Manchester, because all our experiences have been painful – very sad and painful."

"The white boys tell me they can run faster than me because they are white and I am 'chocolate face'."

"One day my son aged fourteen came home with a 'black eye' he had been called 'Paki' 'Swot' – and asked how he could be in the top form when he was a Paki."

"If I go on a bus upstairs after 7.00 pm at night the kids create problems. I have been spat at."

"I could not come to the city centre at night."

"There are a lot of gangs in our area, which is a poor housing area. I don't think this is racist it is just to do with it being a poor area."

"When I worked on the buses there was spitting and abuse."

"I was very sentimental when I came here. I feel hardened by my experience."

"I live in Longsight, in the area there is sometimes graffiti 'Paki go home.' This does not get removed."

"I have been frightened for my children's safety in school and on the roads for many years because of the racial abuse and hatred that happens."

What is it like to be African/Caribbean in the community outside Burnage?

"The worst incidents of racialism happen outside the school, the neighbours ignoring my children as if they were invisible. It was here that they realised that they were Black. One night my daughters were in the bath and I found the two of them in the bath scrubbing themselves to make themselves white and trying to take the curls out of their hair."

"he's called names like 'you Black African shit'."

"I didn't see myself as Black, I used to call myself half caste, I had a feeling of superiority to all Black people and a feeling of inferiority to whites."

"I remember as a child I used to run home from school and scrub myself – I want to be white."

"My nickname was 'chalky'."

"When you are a Black child in a white area people sort of pat you on the head."

"When blackboard got mentioned everyone would look at me and go Ha Ha Ha."

"If Robertson's jam got mentioned, people go Ha Ha Ha, if anything got mentioned that had to do with black, even black pens or black ink – it's a joke."

"People used to talk about the National Front and all that, I used to say that I was in the National Front for a joke when I was younger. If I said that I wasn't in it, then I'd get beat up, or whatever, so there had to be a way of handling it."

"Words like 'nigger' were used, racial abuse was an everyday thing."

"He was being called 'Nigger' 'Black Bastard'."

"They used to cut my washing down during the night and put rubbish through the letter box."

'We got a lot of 'go back to where you belong'."

"Gangs – that's what frightened me, my children were very small aged four and five; gangs of youths aged fourteen, fifteen, sixteen would just come and hassle them and push them around."

"They did get beaten up outside school, after a month or two they just simply did not play outside."

What is it like being white in the community outside Burnage?

"The area is deprived."

"There is low income, poor housing and scant community facilities."

"Parents have hopes for their children, they want them to get out of the neighbourhood and resent anything they think will affect their children's education.

"They look to the schools as a way of their children getting on."

"I asked if racism doesn't work two ways."

"I thought am I in England."

"I feel that this enforced focus on multi-culturalism produces prejudices."

"I feel that the best way to bring about avoidance of racial hostility would be to ignore people's ethnic origins and racial characteristics."

"I am thus advocating that non-Christian people in this country including white and Asian become united, as it were, by becoming Christian."

"I am aware that two Asian ladies visit these classes and I believe that they teach Urdu to everyone, especially to the white children."

"My older daughter does in fact, have a particular Asian friend and we do not object to this."

"I get teased because I'm Irish. Some of them are joking, but some really mean it."

"When they call me names like 'honky' I feel sick."

"I have been called white shit and it feels terrible to learn that someone does not like you because of your colour, race, or creed."

Concern was expressed at the drift of children from white families into other schools. Parents do not wish children to be educated alongside Asian children, accompanied by reports of behaviour which can be interpreted as racist; and related matters.

"Some people think that only white people can be prejudiced, but anyone can be prejudiced."

"It's thought that only we are racist but they are as well, the Asians call us white bastards, they think because they are Black they can't be racist."

"Soon it'll just be all Asian, they get in more and more."

"The teachers are scared, they're frightened to take the white side in case they are accused of being racist."

"My son had more West Indian friends than English."

"My children walk around with their eyes closed so they don't see any different, they are not taught any different."

What's it like to be black in Council housing?

This leaflet was put through the door of Asian families:

PATRIOTS

(Anti-Paki Division)

WARNING = FUCK OFF
NO PAKIS HERE
SAY ME AND MY FRIENDS –
MY NEIGHBOURS IN THIS STREET
THIS SO FAR IS ABOUT THE ONLY AVENUE ROUND HERE
WITHOUT PAKIS SO WE DON'T WANT YOU FUCKING
BASTARDS
BUD BUD

The following incidents are from reports recorded by the Housing Department of Manchester City Council. They indicate the level of harassment in Manchester as a whole rather than in Longsight or Burnage.

Stabbing of tenant; recorded at Collyhurst Police Station. Car attacked, windscreen shattered; report to Plant Hill Police Station.

Verbal abuse; handbag snatched; constant harassment; spat upon; milk stolen once or twice a week.

Racist abuse; spat upon; missiles thrown; windows smashed constantly; burgled; tenant under sedation by GP.

Human excrement deposited outside and daubed on front; slogan NF etched in paintwork. Post Office refuse to deliver mail. Verbal abuse while in local shops; air rifle fired.

Harassment of boy aged 12 years.

Vandalism of home; windows of car and house smashed; lighted tapers through letter box.

Home burgled, turned over, furniture destroyed; obscene racist graffiti sprayed on every wall; bathroom and kitchen flooded. Report of attack to CID.

A useful account of the extent of racial harassment in Manchester is given in the Manchester Council for Community Relations publication: "Racial Harrassment in Manchester and the Response of the Police, 1980–85." (MCCR, Elliot House, 3 Jackson's Row, Manchester, M2 5WD).

Who Are The Racists?

When the Macdonald Inquiry sat, no one came forward and described themselves as "racist". No one came forward and described themselves as fascist. Yet is was a common theme that outside groups, outside extremists were involved at Burnage.

Anti-Fascist Action is a group formed about two years ago to try and co-ordinate in a national way, as well as on a local basis, anti-racist and anti-fascist work. It was specifically set up in response to organised racist attacks and to combat the growth of fascist groups that was occurring. In Manchester there has always been a fairly strong anti-fascist movement and some distinction has to be drawn between anti-fascist work and anti-racist work. AFA has been particularly strong on anti-fascist work and not quite as strong on anti-racist matters.

137

However, fascist gangs for a lot of reasons, including the traditional strength of the anti-fascist movement, have not been able to operate openly in Manchester for some time. AFA basically sees its work in Manchester to monitor what is going on in terms of the sharp end of racism, the current of racist attacks and serious racist harrassment. In general terms, the problems in Manchester that have been perceived have been characterised by mainly young racist gangs harrassing people on estates, Asian families, black families, whatever. Shops particularly have been the focus for this and, in the last few months, AFA have been involved in countering a series of incidents in Burnage which were around a group of shops. The problem here basically is young people between the age of 14 – 22, meeting around the shops, principally because they have no where else to go, and causing trouble, partly through boredom. AFA think it is probably also due to some racist input, although they have not managed to isolate that so far. AFA think it is a very difficult problem to deal with because in a lot of cases these incidents are exacerbated by the fact that the kids do not in fact have anything else to do or any where else to go, but at the same time it is an extremely serious problem for the people involved. The kind of problem that AFA have encountered in the Burnage area has been smashed windows, wrecked cars, systematic insults in the shops, people running in and causing trouble and generally terrorising the families. It is a serious problem, which is quite difficult to counter. The Police have been involved and AFA have found them to be less than helpful.

Another case that AFA have had concerns the Anson Estate in Longsight, where again a racist gang with no obvious organised fascist links was systematically harassing families on the estate. AFA response was first of all to find out who the people involved were and work at how best to isolate them. AFA have leafleted the estate, they have been in touch with the Residents' Association and, over a period of time, the people involved have been basically isolated by their own community, for which AFA don't really take a lot of credit. It is in AFA's view the people in the areas themselves that are basically the people that fight this sort of thing. Again the Police were less than useful in that case. It's a situation that exists across South Manchester. AFA know of incidents in West Point, between Longsight and Burnage, in Rusholme itself, in East Didsbury, in Fallowfield and in Hulme.

According to AFA they have not come across any significant support for the National Front, the British National Party or any other organised fascist group within schools in Manchester for quite a considerable time now.

So far as Burnage is concerned, AFA received no evidence that fascist groups have moved in and tried to capitalise on the problems that are existent in Burnage, either at the time of Ahmed's murder or during the later incidents in February and March of 1987. Although individuals might have been influenced to do so by fascist groups on the outside, AFA have no evidence of it.

To AFA, the state of the fascist organised gangs in Manchester is such that they have not had the resources to put into the Burnage problem. In numerical terms, there exist the National Front flag group and the National Front, the so called official National Front. In terms of paid up members there are probably about 30 in Manchester and in the case of the British National Party even less than that – about 15. But a quite considerable number, possibly a couple of hundred of racist activists, a group organised around the National Front, can be added to the paid up members.

AFA did not attach too much significance to the finding of fascist materials in Burnage as that is something that happens in a very large number of schools and AFA have not found systematic leafletting of schools for some time.

AFA are in contact with Manchester Council for Community Relations (MCCR), who also monitor racial harassment.

Their approach, though, seems to be significantly different.

In identifying the attacks on the Asian-owned shops in the Burnage district, AFA see them as mainly the work of young people, who are bored and have nowhere to go. AFA accept the fact that the targetting of Asian shops and Asian property generally suggests that those attacks are racially motivated, but nevertheless place a great deal of emphasis on the fact that those young people do not have anything better to do or anywhere else to go.

Clearly there has to be a reason why this destructive activity is directed at Asian families in a way that is calculated to hurt, to injure, to deprive and to humiliate. Such activity could hardly be put in the same category as destroying the local bus shelter or telephone kiosk. As MCCR put it, in their 1986 Report on Racial Harassment in Manchester and the Response of the Police:

"Racial harassment is not 'vandalism', though vandalism is involved; neither is it 'hooliganism', although that too is sometimes present. It is not 'neighbourhood disputes', even though its perpetrators usually live nearby or even next door. Itis racist intimidation, with the message 'Get out, or else!', aimed at people from an ethnic minority and motivated wholly or partly by racial hatred in its crude, pure form, occasioning fear and stress for the victims.''

"Tackling racial harassment is not an optional extra for anyone; it is one of the great social challenges of our time.'

"Racial harassment happens because racism is deeply impregnated into British society and the challenge has to come from all parts of that society. A range of voluntary and statutory groups need to address themselves to the question – what can we do about racial harassment?'

The example of AFA working with the residents on the Anson Estate to identify the "racist gang systematically harassing families on the estate" and to make sure they were isolated "by their own community" is an encouraging one.

The picture of racial violence, harassment and abuse endured by the Asian and Afro-Caribbean population in the areas surrounding Burnage High School is unfortunately nothing new. Such evidence repeats itself all over Britain in any area where there is a black population, as is indicated by any examination of the growing literature on racial harassment and racial violence.

Part 2: Racism in the Staff

How does Burnage High School staff reflect the racism that its student and parent community experience on the outside?

"I believe they should all be sent back to Pakistan."
– teacher commenting to Headteacher.
"I don't like them, they smell."
– teacher commenting to Headteacher.
"A member of staff was grabbed by colleagues and had his face blacked with shoe polish at a party because he was known to support the multi-cultural and anti-racist policies."
"Students, told by teacher during cricket match: It's us English against the Paki's."
Anonymous racist mail was sent to Section 11 staff by other staff."
"A teacher knocked the turban off the head of a Sikh student."
"A teacher who showed an interest in Asian culture was asked by a colleague, 'why don't you wear Indian dress?' and was greeted by a mock Indian prayer movement every time she passed this colleague in the corridor.'

"A Section 11 teacher who was wearing a hair slide was asked if it was a West Indian hair slide she was wearing. She replied: 'no, it's just a hair slide', and was told 'why don't you take the bone out and wear it through your nose?'"

"Objections by staff to pictures of buildings from non-European cultures being displayed. Strong objections to notices in languages other than English."

"The wearing of pig badges by a large group of staff, many of whom were members of middle management, after the Deputy Head, Peter Moors, had suggested that pork was less suitable than turkey for the school's Christmas dinner, since it prevented Muslim boys from taking part. Pork scratching packets were pinned to his notice board and he was and still is referred to as 'Porky'."

Also, following that suggestion:

"In the year head's office – they all operated out of one office – there appeared, and in fact covered one wall, pictures of pigs – lots and lots of them."

"It was the last lesson in the morning on Friday morning, and the students had been behaving not too well in the lesson. The teacher had reprimanded them. The Muslim boys wanted to leave a little early to go straight to Friday prayers, and in fact the Muslim boys were kept behind and the white boys allowed to leave. Comments were made such as: 'you are like a cart load of monkeys; you are not fit to pray; in my country and my culture people respect women."

"Some women staff didn't see why they should 'pander to that religion' by covering their heads at Ahmed's funeral."

"Many staff have expressed resentment at being expected to attend the funeral."

"When an English person who speaks Urdu was speaking in that language to the Urdu teacher, two other teachers started speaking in German."

"Some individual staff made blatant racist statements – most common was referral to Asian boys as 'Paki's' – sometimes directly to students."

One teacher, who has since left, told us that the general atmosphere at the school was very hostile, that it was very unwelcoming to students and their families, and that there was open hostility to work on racism. This teacher complained to senior management about a remark made by a staff member, that to get a Scale 4 (i.e. senior) teaching position in the school you had to be a Muslim. In reponse to the reporting of this incident, some other members of staff set up a 'Censor Free Notice Board' so that they could make racist or sexist remarks without censorship so-called, and thereafter there were pointed remarks about "moles" and "tell tales", made loudly and frequently in an intimidating manner in the staffroom.

Add to all these anecdotes the experience of black teachers at Burnage, which we document in a separate chapter and it is clear that there have been teachers there who have behaved in a blatantly racist manner to both students and colleagues and have been guilty of racial bigotry at times.

There is, however, no evidence to suggest that this sort of racism is rampant or widespread or dominates the behaviour of the staff. That would be a complete distortion of the evidence given to us or our own perceptions of the many teachers whom we met and who gave evidence to us. Secondly there is nothing to suggest that the attitudes which produce the behaviour depicted are so entrenched and rigid that they have become unchangeable, nor indeed that the people concerned have not themselves already changed.

Individual behaviour of this kind is almost inevitable in a school which must reflect to a great extent the racism which permeates the whole society.

Three things, however, are in our view unforgiveable:- (1) not to acknowledge or recognise such attitudes. Usually this is based on some sort of fear of undermining the authority of the teaching body. The racism of teachers therefore remains unspoken and is not dealt with. (2) to regard such attitudes as beyond the pale and irredeemable. The assumption here is that individual racism is some sort of fixed category, an ineradicable part of the individual personality, and that people do not change. (3) to assume that because a person exhibits racist attitudes and behaviour it means that social relations between that person and black people must at all times and in all places be dominated by racism and that there can be no positive give or take to the relationship because of this. Racism undoubtedly distorts human relationship but it is also a matter of degree.

Part 3: Racism against students

How do black students, and Asian students in particular, experience the atmosphere at Burnage High? To what extent did that atmosphere contribute to Ahmed's death.

Did Ahmed Ullah die at the cross-roads where the power of masculinity, male dominance, violence and racism intersect? And if so, what are the lessons for the future? Here we look at the evidence, formal and informal, given to us by students at the school.

One Asian student complained to staff on more than one occasion that he had been called "Paki" but the only action taken was to tell the offender not to do it again. A white student overheard a teacher call a 13 year old boy "nigger" in a dinner queue incident, but when other students reported the incident to a form teacher, they were not believed. At dinner-time, we were told boys tend to sit in separate groups, Asian boys on one side, white and Afro-Caribbean on the other side.

Members of the 6th form consultative groups told us of racism at different levels in the school:

"During the first three years there are things like name calling but there is quite a lot of mixing between the groups." They felt that primary school experiences often did not prepare students for a different environment. White students often came to Burnage with no direct experience of people from other groups and had not learned anything in their primary schools to prepare them for a multi-racial environment. Pakistani boys from primary schools with a high proportion of black and Asian students found it difficult at first to be in a predominantly white environment.

By the 4th and 5th years, we were told, there is a marked development of racial groupings. The sense of rivalry between the groups hardens and it is difficult to break down the barriers. One of the white boys in the 6th form group had wanted to take Urdu. He was told he was an idiot by the Pakistani boys and was called a "Paki lover" by the white boys. The responses of the staff were not encouraging. The 6th form group felt that some aspects of the school organisation reinforced the racial grouping in the 4th and 5th years – for example football is seen as not for Asians and cricket as being exclusively Asian. It is very difficult to step outside of these expectations without the support of parents and teachers, which is not always there.

A Pakistani student, who was determined enough to break the mould, experienced considerable isolation and embarrassment; for example, after a football game the only sandwiches available were ham sandwiches.

To white students perceptions of racism or anti-racism are often confused, and nothing is ever explained:

"It's thought that only we are racialist but they are as well. The Asians call us white bastards, etc. They think because they are black they can't be racist. You can't say anything to the teachers, not even the 365 teachers – they don't want to know. Even before March, if we got done, we'd get really done – but they don't.

"The teachers and the police were taking the Asians side. You can't blame them or you'll get accused of being racialist. We can't win. They are scared of saying to Asians it's their fault or they'll be accused of being racist. Some of the teachers tried to get us together, but others didn't, we were called the trouble causers.

"When we were picking our options they brought Urdu in, but they know none of us would do it. Taking Urdu is like making us move towards them. They'll think we've got one less lesson – now we'll get another. Everyone should be equal but we're not – like now they've got an Urdu lesson they've got one up. They will think if they get one assembly that now they've got that. Like with food, we've got all the Asians' foods but not much normal food – why don't we just have normal food? Why do we have to have their food? They have their own Christmases and ours as well – we have only one. We can't celebrate theirs because what can one person do on their own. It would be alright to learn about Asians in primary school, but now it's too late. At primary school eveyone was on the same level.

"With the black lads – we don't bother them they don't bother us. We feel the teachers favour the Asians – perhaps because they don't mess about. You get some Asians who don't like other Asians. They don't get done, when they do mess about. Soon it'll just be all Asian, they get in more and more.

"I think more trouble will happen when we go back for the Autumn Term. It's like a war – you can't stop it. The teachers should stop it but they can't – they should treat everyone equal.

"I would like to see a change in the teachers because they're the ones who really started it. They call us scum etc. They say there's a class over there wanting to learn – you are just scum. They don't help you. One teacher said to me 'just go to the back of the class and go to sleep.' Or if they ask you to do something and you refuse, 'I don't care because I'm still getting paid.' Teachers think they can hit you, provoke you and you can do nothing. They think you're on another level."

The above evidence of Burnage students was taken in the form of formal statements in the official setting of Longsight Library. We were acutely aware, however, of the fact that there is much about the informal and submerged culture of a school which most teachers are not party to, and which students would not be inclined to reveal to a panel of inquiry in a semi-legal format.

One member of our panel, Gus John, lived locally, and therefore had numerous requests from groups of students to meet with them in the places where they pursued their leisure activities, in youth clubs, parks, or in their homes. Certain meetings were also made possible by the youth workers at the Greater Manchester Bangladeshi Association headquarters and at the Longsight Youth Club.

As we mentioned in Chapter 10, Nigel de Noronha and Salma Ahmad were commissioned to conduct a series of interviews with students from Burnage and other Central/South Manchester schools on behalf of the Inquiry.

Both Gus John and Nigel de Noronha supplied evidence gathered from students at Burnage as well as from other schools. Many students were reluctant to talk openly because of fear of reprisals. They had had the experience of students being assaulted for their part in the Bandung File programme on Channel 4 after the murder. Those assaults had taken place both within their communities and at Burnage High School. The students were particularly concerned that they should not be identified from their descriptions of events and so we have tried to disguise their identities. Their stories, which we re-produce here, describe what life is like for most Asian students in Burnage.

1 X is a first year student at Burnage High School who previously attended St John's Primary School. He said there was no teaching about racism or Bangladesh at school and he felt there should be.

   He had been called racist names at least once every week – in the class, playground and on the bus.

   He was involved in an argument in the class about one of these name-calling incidents, and was made to go outside with the other boy and shake hands.

   He was playing football in the playground when an older boy took his ball. He reported it to a teacher who wanted to know the name and form of the older boy. No action was taken and he did not get his ball back.

   Another Asian boy had his money taken in the playground by two white boys. He was crying and a teacher lent him the bus fare. The teacher asked the two boys about the incident, but they denied it and nothing further happened.

2　X is a second year student at Burnage High School who previously attended St Agnes Primary School. He regards himself as a Bangladeshi though people other than close friends consider him to be an Asian.

　　Name calling was a common occurrence on the bus, in the classroom and on the playground. It happened several times a week.

　　During the first year, he was thrown off the bus by the driver about ten times though he felt he had not been doing anything wrong.

　　He was often called "Paki" in the street and threatened for money. He tended to stay together in a group. There were a group of older white kids, where he lived, who picked on smaller children – particularly Asians.

　　Around Easter his jacket was smeared with dog excrement at school. He reported it to a teacher, but nothing further happened.

3　A is a fourth year student at Burnage High School. He is of Asian origin, but had recently come from Falkirk, Scotland, where he attended primary school.

　　In the school he felt different teachers acted quite differently – some were kind, some did not seem to care. His decision about subject choices had been well supported, but often the City and Guilds 365 (Foundation course used as an alternative curriculum) was selected for Asians because of language problems.

　　If his parents needed to see the school about him (or vice-versa), it was necessary to make an appointment. General events, such as parents evenings, are publicised by letters through the students.

　　A speaks English at school, but sometimes translates between Bengali and English for friends whose English is not that good.

　　He has never seen the National Front – but heard about the "Anson mob" coming to school and did not go in that day. There was a period when there were policemen in the playground and at bus stops.

　　He had a feeling of fear, not wanting to report any incident or the aggressors would attack him again.

　　Regular name-calling occurred in the third year (twice a week) at bus stops and in the playground.

　　He came to England in his 1st year and was pushed around because of his Scottish accent. The teachers ignored what was going on unless something serious happened.

　　He was beaten up with a friend at going home time by a group of whites from Upper School when in third year. There was no reason – just a random racist attack on some Pakis.

He was punched in the face by a white boy from Upper School. He pretended to his parents that he had hurt himself playing football to avoid repercussions.

4 Z is a third year student at Burnage High School and knew Ahmed Ullah. He was a member of the Ahmed Iqbal Ullah Memorial Committee and was unwilling to be interviewed formally. The notes reproduced are therefore not in the same structure as other interviews.

He knew Ahmed because of some trouble he had had in the second year from a fellow student and his older brother and friends from Upper School who used to regularly bully him and demand money from him. *Before that he had only had a couple of friends, both English, who had become scared and stopped seeing him once the trouble started.*

For about a term he was pushed around, spat on and beaten up a couple of times. On the second incident in a local park, Ahmed intervened and his attackers ran away.

Since then he had admired Ahmed a lot and had not had much trouble at school. He mixed only with Asians and when the fight with Darren Coulburn started brewing, he thought Ahmed would win easily.

He was in the playground at the time of the murder and was extremely upset when he described what he saw (he cried for about five minutes). He described Darren sticking the knife in Ahmed and saying "Do you want it again Paki", then running off.

He joined the Memorial Committee as soon as it was set up, having seen some of the people involved at a previous meeting at the Greater Manchester Bangladeshi Association building.

He attended all of the events organised by the Committee, and a number of planning meetings. He was also involved in distributing leaflets and publicising the events.

He felt disappointed that the Memorial Committee had not continued and was unable to get involved in doing things at the school. He enquired a lot about other members of the Committee with whom he had established a close relationship and said he would like to get involved with a more general anti-racist/self defence organisation if anyone would set one up.

5 D is a fourth year student at Burnage High School and had previously attended St Agnes Primary School. The school was strict on discipline – no messing around in the corridors or shouting/talking in class. Most of this discipline was fair – sometimes the

teachers tried to find out what had happened and judge who was in the wrong.

The treatment of students was not the same – Asians were ignored more by the teachers and were more likely to be bullied. There used to be a lot of open racism, in fact it seemed to go up and down in cycles.

If parents wanted to see your teachers they must make an appointment. If the teachers wished to see them, they sent a letter or telephoned. There was a tendency to suspend students for petty offences.

At home he was regarded as Bengali, at school as Argentinian (he is a very keen footballer) and either as an Asian or an individual by teachers.

He had only two friends – one English, one Bangladeshi. He described himself as a loner at school – he sometimes speaks in Bengali.

He felt that teachers understood nothing about his home background or culture, but that they should do to be able to deal with personal problems that arose.

He is not aware of any National Front type activities at school and was unaware of the existence of any anti-racist organisations.

He was playing football when some fifth years came to push him off the field and one started hitting him. He felt it was probably because he was Asian. This type of incident was very frequent when he was in the first and second year.

The boys on the Alternative Curriculum Studies (CG 365) say that they are from the NF and regularly threaten people – mainly Asians. He had never reported it.

He remembered Ahmed as someone who was very kind to everybody.

He felt he was popular because of playing football. He never caused any trouble. He did respond though if he felt he was being pushed around.

6 X is a fourth year student at Burnage High School who was one of the main organisers of the Ahmed Iqbal Ullah Memorial Committee. He did not wish to be interviewed or named and these notes are based on recollections of a long conversation with him.

He had been a friend and classmate of Ahmed's and after the murder, attended the first meetings at the Greater Manchester

Bangladeshi Association. He had been very annoyed with the way they attempted to exclude young people from the discussions about what to do and empathised closely with the group who went on to form the Memorial Committee. He joined in and encouraged other Asian students to boycott the school in response to the call from a group of parents. He attended the nightly meetings immediately after the funeral to organise the demonstration and first public meeting. He agreed to be the main student speaker and prepared a speech which he delivered at the rally following the demonstration.

He spent most of those weeks trying to mobilise people from school to attend the meeting and demonstration – distributing leaflets and talking to people.

The elder people from the mosque and GMBA visited his parents and warned them about their son's involvement – asking them to prevent him taking part and organising activities.

Eventually he gave in to his parents' pressure and stopped being actively involved though he has kept in touch with the activities of the people who stayed in the Committee.

At the time of the murder S was a very bright, articulate spokesperson for the disaffected Asian youth within the school.

His contributions made very clear the level of shock and anger felt throughout the school, not only at the murder, but at the attempts by the school's administration to cover up what had happened and their petty refusal to allow white or Afro-Caribbean friends of Ahmed to attend the funeral.

From meeting him, it was clear he had given up at school, and was in a deep depression about his own future. It is possible that he was taking drugs, but our interviewer was more inclined to believe his state of mind was caused by the events of which he was a part.

His family are taking him to Bangladesh in the near future for a few months – presumably in the hope of restoring him to his bright, easy-going personality which events have stolen from him.

He talked fondly of the days of activity – but rather in the style of a weary World War veteran who had been completely burnt out by his experience – though still remembering it as the one time in his life he was alive.

In his introduction to his report, Nigel de Noronha states:

"The level of incidents reported in the interview are so far in excess of the number reported under the City Council's procedure for notification of incidents of racial harassment/violence as to make any comparison meaningless."

This was also the view of Gus John from his interview with Burnage students and their parents.

The failure to report incidents to teachers and, often, to parents, is to be contrasted to the position with youth workers. It was clear that the students shared many of their experiences with the youth workers at their clubs, and looked to them for support.

Nigel de Noronha comments:

"The support and involvement of the youth workers in encouraging youths to talk about what had happened, together with discussions with them, made the work conducted possible. Their commitment to supporting the youths seems to have received little recognition or support from the local authority."

In general terms, Nigel de Noronha and Salma Ahmad found that:

"The major cause for complaint was the unfairness of common practices. The treatment for individuals fighting was apparently even-handed but caused resentment because the teachers did not generally try to find out who was in the wrong.

There were also complaints about different types of punishment being thought appropriate for different races.

In the reported incidents there were a number of cases in which no effective action was taken against people involved with racial harassment and this had resulted in many students no longer reporting such incidents.

In the first two clubs described, the youths had an apparently strong relationship with the youth workers and in both the youth workers had been told about a number of incidents that had occurred at school and in the community. They did not act on this information – primarily because they were employed as part-timers and did not feel themselves to be part of any structure which could provide the kind of support they felt the youths needed.

Amongst the boys at Burnage, there seemed to be general agreement that racism was cyclical – an atmosphere would build up in the school over a particular incident and there would then be an explosion of racist violence directed indiscriminately at Asians within the school.

The effect of racism in Burnage seemed to be a polarisation of the students within schools into racial groupings and a marked reluctance on the part of these students to be seen to be fraternising with other races.

Reports of violent incidents in the interviews confirm that most of the victims and their friendss perceive racism as a major factor in the attacks. The effect of this perception is in many cases a fear – leading to lack of confidence in many playground and outside situations.

Very few of the respondents seemed to be satisfied with the effectiveness of reporting procedures or with any action taken when they did report incidents.

This outline of student-incidents indicates that in the minds of the victims, at least, racism is a major factor in the harassment and/or violence to which they are subjected. There was little evidence of confidence in the existing system of reporting such incidents, and little evidence of the effectiveness of such a system.

In our view it is crucial that any policy on reporting, monitoring and dealing with perceived racist incidents has the confidence of the victims of such attacks. It seems likely that the only way in which this can be achieved is to involve the youths in developing appropriate procedures – a devolution of power in at least one vital area of education policy.

Among the students a picture emerges of Asian students, in particular, being subjected to a daily or weekly dose of racist name calling and other petty acts of racism. There is a strong feeling that many are picked on because of race. A strong sense of racial identity emerges from the evidence, for both black and white students, and at dinner time there had tended to be a separation of Asian from white and Afro-Caribbean students.

The elements for the sort of conflict that led to Ahmed Ullah's murder have been in the school for a long time. So have the elements that led to the racial polarisation in March 1987. We were, therefore, very interested to see what lessons, if any, the school and education authority had learned from an incident in 1982, when the son of the Bangladeshi Deputy High Commissioner was badly beaten up. That incident contained a similar mix of violence and racism.

CHAPTER 18

Learning Lessons at Burnage High School – An Incident in 1982

Burnage is an all boys school. Was what happened in 1986 unforeseeable, extraordinary, or have incidents of violence happened before? Have these incidents involved racist violence? If they have, what lessons have been learnt?

In January 1982, Burnage School was under the Acting Headship of Mr Walmsley. Dr Gough was not yet appointed. There was still corporal punishment. Multi-racial approaches were in their infancy, anti-racist policies not yet adopted. This was an era with which, according to all accounts, staff at Burnage felt most comfortable.

Darren Coulburn and Ahmed Ullah were at Primary school.

On Thursday, January 21st, an Asian student at Burnage attended the Withington Hospital. His injuries included a fractured cheek bone:

On January 25th 1982, his father wrote to the Chief Education Officer Dr David Jones as follows:

Dear Sir,

My son MSH is a student of Burnage High School (Upper), Manchester in 5th year (Form 5N). On January 21, 1982, he was in school as usual. At 1.30 P.M. during the lunch break he, along with a class mate and friend – JB, was in the Careers Library in the school building and was consulting books for his appointment for career selection interview. All of a sudden, a group of 5 youngsters and fellow students of the same school got into the Careers Library. Having seen my son and his friend J alone in the room, one of the group went out and called in others. Then one of the gang turned the light off and the room was also locked from inside. They started hitting both JB and my son in a cruel manner. My son was kicked upon his face and got grievous injury with fractured cheek bone.

Needless to mention that the Careers Library where the incident took place is situated just next the Headmaster's and Teachers' room;. It is stated to be a small room without any window and light ventilation. The incident appears to be racially motivated as the gang attacked them in an organised manner without any provocation.

After being hit severely on the face, my son screamed out and his friend J somehow managed to run out and called the teachers for help. One of the teachers came in, saw my son, the victim of the cruel attack and asked all the boys to vacate. He heard my son and his friend JB and then asked some member of the office staff to inform the parents and arrange sending my son to hospital. Mrs H called and told me that my son had met with an accident and got bruises and cut on his face. I wanted to know about the seriousness of the injury and as to which hospital my son was going to be sent and if anybody was accompanying him. I enquired categorically if any teacher were going with him and she replied in the negative.

I however rushed to the hospital with my wife and a member of my office staff. On arrival there I found my son and his friend JB, the two victims of the dastardly attack, sitting in the casualty department of the Withington Hospital. Doctors examined my son and gave stitches to his cut injury. He was subsequently admitted to hospital after detection of fracture on his cheek bone.

Several police officers subsequently visited the hospital and tried to obtain statement from my son and his friend JB. A statement was made by JB naming the attackers in my presence immediately. But my son was unable to make any statement until the following afternoon.

My son has been still in the hospital in Ward 4B. He was operated upon yesterday for repairs of his bone fractures. I was given to understand by the Surgeon that my son would possibly need another two operations, one after three weeks and the other sometime later.

Meanwhile on Friday January 22, 1982, I contacted the Headmaster of the Burnage High School over phone and inquired as to how such a dastardly incident could take place within the premises of the school and particularly in the Careers Library which is next to the Headmaster's and the staff rooms. The Headmaster expressed his total ignorance of the matter. He then passed me on to Mr Hewitt who let me know that the incident had been within their knowledge and the police had been to him in the school.

It remains a great shock and surprise to me as to how my son while reading in the Careers Library Room, adjacent to the Headmaster's and staff rooms could be attacked by an organised gang of school boys and injured grievously during school hours. I believe it is the responsibility of the school administration to ensure protection of the students within the school premises during the working hours.

Furthermore, it is also shocking to me that my son was sent to hospital with such a grievous injury without being accompanied by a responsible person from the school. It is again unfortunate that no body from the school had so far visited my son in the hospital, nor did anybody inquire about his welfare.

It is under the dictates of conscience as the unfortunate parents of the ill-fated victim of the organised attack that I am constrained to bring the fact to your kind notice. I am not however sure if any measure is possible to be taken against those responsible for the incident and also to put things right in the school ensuring an academic atmosphere in the interest of helpless parents like me who send their wards to school for education.

Yours sincerely,
AKNNH"

A NOTE TO FILE IN THE EDUCATION OFFICE
dated 25/1/82 reads as follows:
Assault upon MSH (pupil of Burnage High School)
1 A written report of the incident is in preparation by Mr Hewitt. It will be posted this evening. In the meantime the following verbal report by Mr Hewitt will serve as a guide.
2 On Thursday 21 January 1982 MS was alone in the Careers Library at Burnage High School. (The room is left open at lunchtime for the use by fifth and sixth form pupils). Six boys entered the room, one turned out the lights and two of the boys (C and C) assaulted MSH.
3 Immediately following the assault another boy of Asian origin entered the room and consoled his friend. A teacher reported to Mr Hewitt that an assault had taken place and that MSH was injured.
4 Mr Hewitt went to the room where he found MSH to have bruising and a cut to his face. An ambulance was called, the boy's father informed and the Police advised to meet the father at the hospital.
5 The six boys involved were told that the Police had been called. Initially all six denied knowledge of how MS came to be injured.
    Later two of the boys came to Mr Hewitt and named C and C as the assailants.
6 The following morning (Friday 22 January 1982) five of the six boys were again seen by Mr Hewitt and C and C admitted the offence. The Police were informed and in the afternoon the two boys were formally charged.
Note 1. Mr Hewitt does not consider the incident to have racial undertones. He says he has no reason to believe that any of the

six boys are in any way connected with the National Front. He believes that the incident would have taken place irrespective of the ethnic origin of the assaulted pupil i.e. whichever pupil of the school had been alone in the Careers Library at the time would have been assaulted.

Before speaking to Mr Hewitt I spoke with Mr Walmsley. He was surprised that there should be any suggestions that the attack had a racial motive and that the assailants had National Front connections.

Note 2. When I spoke to Mr Walmsley he was not as familiar with the detail of the case as one would expect with an assault of such severity. He said he would get Mr Hewitt to speak with me as he knew the details.

Note 3. I have a gut feeling that something is amiss in this case. I have, of course, no evidence to disbelieve Mr Walmsley and Mr Hewitt's insistence that the assault had no racial bias. What worries me is that they seem to have not considered that it might.

In 1982, then, random violence was apparently a more acceptable concept than violence with racial undertones. By January 28th, 1982, the following internal memorandum was circulated in the Education department:

INTERNAL MEMORANDUM

FROM		TO	
SUBJECT	YOUR REF.	OUR REF.	DATE
			227
Assault on MSH			28.1.82

I have gone through, with Mr Walmsley, the list of questions you gave me concerning the assault on MSH. A more detailed response will be sent later, but the following points are relevant:

1 Mr Walmsley and I met Mr H at the Bagladeshi High Commission in Princess Street at 1.30 p.m. on 27th January. The meeting was a cordial one and we were able to discuss the incident in a very reasonable manner. Mr H's concern was expressed in two areas: as a parent he felt that the steps the school had taken were inadequate in certain respects, and as a representative of the Bangladeshi community he was concerned that the community should feel that the incident had been dealt with firmly by the school.

2 Full consideration is now being given to the two boys who were assaulted and their parents. Arrangements are being made for MSH to have school academic work sent to him.

There is no doubt that certain procedures in the school for informing parents and in follow-up at hospital, when serious injury occurs, need to be revised immediately. The school is dealing with this.

3 The school is taking appropriate action against the 6 boys who were involved in the assault, and I am sure this will be fair and firm.

4 The longer term implications to staff, pupils, relations with ethnic minorities, etc., will be given prompt consideration by the school.

On the day this memo was circulated MSH left hospital but had to return two weeks later for a further operation to remove a pad from his cheek and have stitches removed. He would also need a further operation in a years time to remove a steel pin.

On February 17th, 1982 the following File Note was made by the Senior Assistant Education Officer (Schools) David Jones.

Note for File: Assault on MSH and JB

1 I spent nearly two hours with Mr H at his office on 11 February 1982. I found him to be a most reasonable and charming man who obviously is keen not to over-react to the position, even though it is also fair to say that he is particularly sensitive about the affair, the general safety of his son, and the racist attitudes which he perceives in this country.

2 He did not receive our earlier letter, of 29 January 1982, and I carried a copy with me for him. His response to our letter of 8 February 1982 was entirely positive.

3 His son has to go to hospital on 24 February to remove a pad from his cheek. He had had an intital checkup on 9 February 1982 and all seems to be as well as can be expected, though he continues to have a lack of sensation in the side of his face that was affected. Mr H makes it quite plain that his son believes that the damage was occasioned by a kick and not by any contact with the furniture of the so-called careers library. The hospital will keep him under observation and may at some future stage need to operate again. He may come back to school during the second week in March. In the meantime he is keen to work and I have the impression that the work set for him by the school is not fully meeting his requirements (I subsequently checked with Mr Walmsley who indicates that MSH is not managing to complete the work set.) Furthermore it seems clear that our

arrangements for home tuition have not yet extended so far as providing someone to be with him (I subsequently spoke to Mr Parsons who is personally sorting it out).

4 Mr H would be willing to accept his son's return to Burnage if assurances could be given as to his safety, and he would not suggest that further punishment be meted out to the six boys, providing the headteacher can guarantee that they will conduct themselves properly. He feels that Mr Walmsley should be able to get such assurances from the boys and their families. Mr Walmsley had an appointment with Mr H on 12 February 1982 and when I telephoned Mr Walmsley in the afternoon of 11 February he said that he would be able, the following day, to give Mr H those assurances. Mr H felt that the police investigation should be allowed to take its course; we spent a fair amount of time talking about the action taken in respect of the six boys which seemed to satisfy Mr H in part, though not completely, because he cannot quite understand why the police action has been, should we say, less vigorous than we would have expected.

D Jones

On February 18th, 1982 there was a meeting at Eileen Grove Mosque. The subject was racial attacks in Manchester Education Committee Schools. Amongst those groups present at the meeting were the West Indian Organisations Co-ordinating Committee, the Greater Manchester Bangladeshi Association, Manchester Muslim Association, The Sikh Temple Committee, Jewish Representation Council, the Multi-cultural Development Services and an MCCR observer.

At the meeting there were repeated expressions of concern by those present about why the meeting had been called, why community representatives were being consulted rather than representatives of parents with sons at the school, and the motives of the Manchester Education Committee (MEC) on this issue. After lengthy discussions a list of questions for the senior staff of Burnage High School was drawn up for discussion at a proposed meeting on the 2nd of March 1982 with senior staff at Burnage High School. It was agreed that the list of questions be sent to the school before the meeting. The list of questions was as follows:

Questions proposed by minority community representatives as a basis for consultation on understanding racial violence, its content and what must be done about it.

1 What happened in this particular incident?
2 How was it handled by the school?
3 What approach has been made since to all the pupils?
4 Is this a solitary incident? If there have been others, what has been done to address this problem?
5 In what ways can the minority communities assist the school in addressing this problem?
6 Who is behind this? Is it organised or supported from within or outside the school?
7 What is known about the boys who committed the attack, their attitudes and those of their families?
8 In the light of previous information (most recently in the form of the Home Office report on racial attacks) has the problem been discussed with staff?
9 In the light of MEC's policy statement on education for a multi-cultural society, what is the school doing?

These questions were asked in 1982. Had any of them been answered by 1986? Was Ahmed Ullah murdered simply as a result of a disturbed boy's action? By February 26th, 1982, the Education Department was sending out the following letter:

"Dear
Meeting on Racial violence and its implications for Schools
I am writing to say that I believe that the reasons for the meeting called for on 2 March 1982, which was to involve senior staff of Burnage High School and Ethnic Minority Leaders seems to have been misunderstood. If this is so, it is of course entirely the fault of the Education Department. The intention was to discuss ways in which Burnage High School could be better enabled to tackle their approach to promoting a greater appreciation of our multi-cultural and multi-racial society and to heighten their awareness of problems and issues. It was not the intention to discuss in detail any particular incident. I now appreciate that you may feel that a particular incident, and the request for help from Ethnic Minority Leaders, were connected in the way which the questions drafted at your meeting on 18 February 1982 demonstrate.

There is no question of the meeting on 2 March 1982 being called off, as far as we are concerned, I believe that a meeting with senior staff from Burnage High School should be delayed and therefore Dr Jones (Senior Assistant Education Officer Schools) will be with

159

you on 2 March 1982 to discuss the issues further. The venue and the time of the meeting remains the same.

Yours sincerely

D. Fiske
Chief Education Officer"

This letter was replied to on 19th March 1982 by the Manchester Council for Community Relations in the following terms:

"Dear Mr Fiske

Thank you very much for your letter dated the 3rd of March 1982, which was presented to the Executive Committee of MCCR at its meeting on Tuesday 16 March 1982.

I have discussed the meeting on 2nd March with Mr Kabir Ahmed who informs me that from his point of view the meeting was disappointing in that it did not deal sufficiently or in any detail with the incident of the 21st January. Neither did it give any indication as to what steps, if any, was going to be taken to prevent any further occurrence of a similar nature.

Consequently, my Executive Committee are anxious to know from you that steps have been taken to deal with the incident of the 21st January and what further action has been proposed to prevent incidents of a similar nature.

We hope you will treat this matter urgently.

Yours sincerely
Chairman"

Urgency is a matter of degree; the schools response to what was described as an intolerable level of violence was contained in a Report on the Incident in 1982. These were the responses:

ACTION III   A planned response to the intolerable level of violence in the school.

The overall aim of this programme is to create for all pupils a pleasant and co-operative atmosphere in the school in which the school's objectives may be realised as outlined in the brochure.

The following areas have received attention:

1. The leadership of the Headmaster is crucial.
2. Corporal punishment is being phased out and has not been used in this academic year.
3. Through meetings and daily instructions the Head and his Deputies have underlined their support for staff.
4. In dealing with all pupil misdemeanours, parents are increasingly involved and their support requested.
5. Violence is the concern of all staff and not just those with pastoral responsibilities.

   The staff have recognised that although violence may have many causes, and that the way the school deals with pupils in the early years is a significant contributory factor in the level of violence. This suggests a long term strategy, the initial stages of which are outlined below:
6. The staff have identified and agreed a set of social objectives. Ways in which these might be achieved in the classroom have been and will continue to be discussed with departments.
7. Work in the form periods has been put on a more formal basis using the Lancashire Active Tutorial as the initial framework.
8. The content of assemblies is now planned to relate to work in other areas of the school.
9. It is intended to increase the amount of time given to personal and social education in the Upper School, and to introduce this in a systematic way to the whole of the Lower School.
10. In September 1981, Year Councils were introduced for every year in the school.
11. The staff tutor has a very important role along with other senior staff in helping to create a much more positive relationship between staff and pupils.
12. A pilot scheme to give pupils a say in their own assessment is to be started.
13. The Withdrawal Unit is being used to attempt to modify pupil behaviour before it presents a major problem.
14. A number of approaches such as reward schemes, curriculum appraisal, continue to be used.

Let us examine in more detail the responses to that particular incident.

Firstly, the boy's parents.

The incident took place on Thursday. On Friday the boy's father contacted the Headteacher and asked how such a serious incident could

161

have taken place next to the Headteacher's room. "The Headmaster expressed his total ignorance of the matter." Mr Hewitt then informed the father that the school was aware of the incident and had involved the police. The father's letter goes on:

> "It remains a great shock and surprise to me as to how my son while reading in the Careers Library Room, adjacent to the Headmaster's and staff rooms could be attacked by an organised gang of school boys and injured grievously during school hours. I believe it is the responsibility of the school administration to ensure protection of the students within the school premises during the working hours.
>
> Furthermore, it is also shocking to me that my son was sent to hospital with such a grievous injury without being accompanied by a responsible person from the school. It is again unfortunate that nobody from the school had so far visited my son in the hospital. nor did anybody inquire about his welfare."

So, the Headteacher was still unaware 24 hours later of a most serious assault which took place next door to his office, resulting in a boy being taken to hospital. And there were no representatives from the school for the parents to talk to, when they eventually got to the casualty department at the hospital.

Sixteen days later, on February 11th, 1982, the Senior Assistant Education Officer saw the boy's father and described him as

> "... a most reasonable and charming man who, obviously is keen not to over-react to the position, even though it is fair to say that he is particularly sensitive about the affair, the general safety of his son, and the racist attitudes which he perceives in this country."

Mr. AKMMH was not just a parent. He was a black parent with a black son. Moreover, as the Deputy High Commissioner for Bangladesh, his conern about "the racist attitudes which he perceives in this country" would have arisen from his experience of the racism suffered by Bangladeshi citizens whom he represented, and more generally by black people in Britain. Despite what David Jones perceives as his keenness not to over-react, Mr. AKMMH was clearly making a link between what happened to his son and the racist attitudes he perceived in this country.

The school, however, steadfastly refused to make that link. The Headteacher was "surprised that there should be any suggestions that the attack had a racial motive". Mr Hewitt "has no reason to believe ...", not unlike the police. All of this was taking place at a time when the Home Office report on racial attacks was receiving maximum publicity, and black people, especially those from the sub-continent, were publicly asking how many deaths and maiming of innocent black people it would take before the Home Office took the issue of racial attacks seriously.

When "minority community representatives" responded to the seriousness of the attack on that student and decided to focus attention on racial violence in Burnage and posed some searching questions for the school to answer, Dudley Fiske, the then Chief Education Officer, arrogantly reminded them that it was he and the Education Department who were setting the agenda. That agenda deflects the concerns of the minority community representatives and substitutes the concerns of the Education Department.

The purpose of the meeting was not to discuss what was paramount for those communities, i.e. ensuring the safety of their children from racial attacks in Burnage High School, but "to discuss ways in which Burnage High School could be better enabled to tackle their approach to promoting a greater appreciation of our multi-cultural and multi-racial society and to heighten their awareness of problems and issues." In other words, having already decided that the attack could not be racially motivated, the authorities made sure the school was not drawn into a discussion of racial violence within its community.

When, eventually, the school and the Education Department came to deal with the issue of the attack, they formulated "A planned response to the intolerable level of violence in the school".

Throughout their 14 point plan, no mention is ever made of racism, racial attack, racial violence or racial name-calling. The casual observer would not have the slightest inkling that there were black children in that school, or that the school attracts students, black and white, who live in areas where racism flourishes, and whose experiences of racist behaviour, both as perpetrators and victims, are reproduced in the school.

By denying the existence of racial violence the school is, in this classic instance, doing a number of very dangerous things:

1 It is signalling to white students (and by implication to white staff) who indulge their racism that their indiscriminate attacks on black students would simply be viewed as "misdemeanours". In doing so, it encourages them to de-value and abuse black students, and have a go at "Pakis" under the guise of "just bullying" or just "being violent".
2 It absolves itself from the responsibility of dealing with the felt discrimination and personal hurt of black students, and making the

issue of power and its abuse by white staff and students one which the whole school community needs to confront.

3 It is saying to black students and their parents: "what you experience and feel as racism is something else. We don't accept your definition of your reality. We will continue to call it something else which fits our view of how life should be, regardless of what it really is for you".

4 In doing so it is not simply using its power to re-define the situation, it is also endorsing racist practices and endangering the lives of black people. At the same time it is underlining the power which white students feel racism bestows upon them.

5 It is acting in the most blatantly insulting way to black people by displacing their anxieties and concerns with platitudes and empty rhetoric about "promoting a greater appreciation of our multi-cultural and multi-racial society".

The slavish hankering after consensus which is implied in that last quotation could be seen over and over again as a typical establishment response whenever black people call for action in response to the racial oppression they experience.

Point 4 of the 14 point plan states:

> "In dealing with all pupil misdemeanours, parents are increasingly involved and their support requested".

Is it to be assumed that this is done purely on the school's terms? Is it done simply in relation to the definition of the situation that the school presents to the parents? Are parents there simply to go along with the solution cobbled together by the school, based on its definition of the situation?

In this particular instance, the school, aided and abetted by the Education Department, tried to manage the incident by manipulating "minority community representatives". There was no organisation amongst the Asian students in the school. Many ordinary Asian parents concluded that the matter was managed internally and hushed up. Some feared for the safety of their sons and moved them from Burnage. The general sentiment amongst them at the time seemed to be: "if this terrible thing could happen to the son of the Deputy High Commissioner, who provoked no-one and wasn't even involved in a fight, what hope is there for my son?" – as one parent put it to us.

But the problem did not go away, simply because some parents relieved their anxieties by removing their sons, any more than it did by the school denying the racial aspect of the attack and concentrating on the multi-cultural nature of the society instead.

164

There is no evidence that white parents were encouraged to understand the basis of the attack let alone the seriousness of it. Three facial operations were required. It was an experience that was to leave that student marred for life.

There is no evidence that the school attempted to answer the questions posed by the "minority community representatives":

1 What happened in this particular incident?
2 How was it handled by the school?
3 What approach has been made since to all the pupils?
4 Is this a solitary incident? If there have been others, what has been done to address this problem?
5 What is known about the boys who committed the attack, their attitudes and those of their families?

All of those are questions which any self-respecting management that was not wilfully seeking to present a nice, tolerant image of its school would have asked itself and demanded of its staff.

In not dealing with the questions posed for it by concerned and interested communities, it not only denied them and their students answers, it denied the whole school community a critical opportunity to wrestle with those issues and work to transform the racist culture of the school.

If that racist culture refused to be willed away by the school and the Education Department, how did it continue to manifest itself? How did Asian students continue to exprience it? Do "intolerable level(s) of violence" in a school like Burnage leave racism alone, or does racism and racialist attitudes provide the backcloth for acts of violence as perpetrated by and against specific sections of the school population?

Also we must ask what lessons the school learned from this incident and how might they have affected the events that resulted in Ahmed's murder in 1986.

We saw no evidence that the school focused on the 1982 incident and explored the issues surrounding it. Having decided that it was not a racist incident, no further investigation seems to have been made as to why it was that the student attacked was Asian. On what basis could the school have concluded that had a white boy been in the library at the time he would have been similarly attacked?

In a school environment where racist name-calling, for example 'smelly Paki', reflects the way in which Asian people are oppressed and made vulnerable to attack within their communities, the notion of 'Pakibashing' will not be unknown to most of those doing the name-

165

calling. It does not require a great leap to move from name calling to racial violence or for boys who are looking for a target for their aggression to target on those who are the subject of racial name-calling. They become an obvious and appropriate target. The connection between violence and racial violence is one to which a school has to be alert. It should always be prepared to investigate the racial dimension when an Asian or Afro-Caribbean student becomes a victim of an otherwise senseless and unprovoked attack.

'Baiting wogs', 'nigger hunting' and 'Paki-bashing' are all part of the culture of racism in Britain in which all children are brought up. No school can afford to ignore that culture or the effect it may have in schools. No school, therefore, should tolerate the use of the term 'Paki' by students, teachers or parents, black or white. The crass ignorance which certain teachers displayed to us when they claimed to see nothing wrong with the word 'Paki' because it is simply a shorter way of saying 'Pakistani' is unforgiveable. Teachers who are prepared to condone such name-calling on that basis put all Asian students at risk and fail in their duty to those who call Asians 'Pakis'.

We heard evidence from Burnage students and teachers that the word 'Paki' is frequently used at Burnage. We also heard that Asian boys are picked upon because they tend to be smaller in build and are frequently not expected to react as Afro-Caribbean boys would.

We received no evidence to suggest that the issues raised in this chapter were discussed amongst staff and students following the 1982 incident. If one gave the school the benefit of the doubt and accepted their view that the attack was just a violent attack of which anyone could have been the victim, the issue of violence amongst students or violence by staff against students was not dealt with in any meaningful and sustained way. Between 1982 and 1986 teachers continued to assault students, in some cases causing grievous bodily harm, and students continued to settle differences by violence. 'I'll have you a fight' seems to have been a password at Burnage. Students talked to us about fighting and about staff being abusive and violent towards them in a way, as if such conduct was natural and commonplace.

The dust settled on the 1982 incident, the school affirmed its commitment to 'promoting a greater appreciation of our multi-cultural and multi-racial society', and business proceeded as usual. Smaller Asian boys continued to be picked upon and humiliated and physically attacked, boys and teachers continued to refer to Asians as 'Pakis', and the fights and the intolerable level of violence persisted.

The makings of a 1986 were there in 1982 and continued to be there and to take a foothold right up to September 1986. Ahmed Ullah was big and tall for his age. He found himself having to fight, literally, against the intolerable level of racial violence he witnessed in order to protect smaller Asian boys. Teachers may not always have known of those fights, but they ought to have done.

We take the view that a more vigorous approach to the issue of violence and of racial abuse and racial violence on the part of the management at Burnage High School would have made both teachers and students much more alert to the situation that Ahmed Ullah found himself confronting in September 1986.

We believe it would at least have created a climate in which Asian students would have felt more secure in the knowledge that the school recognised the constant harasssment and threat they were under and were actively doing something about it.

While there can be no guarantee that such an approach in the aftermath of 1982 would have deterred Darren Coulburn from harassing and physically attacking smaller Asian boys in a manner that was to bring him and Ahmed into fatal combat, we nevertheless feel that the school failed in its duty to its students, and particularly its Asian students, by taking such a complacent approach to an unprovoked and potentially fatal attack on an Asian student. That it was not fatal was purely a matter of luck. Given the severity of the facial injuries the student sustained, it is not too difficult to imagine what might have resulted if he had been kicked in the temples with equal ferocity.

Throughout the Inquiry we were told of the disruptive effects of the teachers' action in 1985–1986. Since 1982, and throughout the teachers' action the school has continued to provide as near normal a curriculum as possible. The nature of the 'unofficial' culture of the school, i.e. what students do away from teachers, what happens in corridors and playgrounds, what students suffer silently or have feuds about without reporting to teachers, in other words, that culture within which racism thrives, does not seem to have been considered at all within the formal curriculum. When discovered, those things became a matter for disciplinary action, quite properly, but that's as far as the school's response went.

Meanwhile, the soft underbelly of multi-culturalism, Indian music, Eid festivals, multi-faith assemblies, and Section 11 continued to give Burnage High School its image of a school implementing the local authority's policies on race. The fact that the education department endorsed the school's response to the 1982 incident rather than encouraging them to raise and deal with the issues outlined here, gives some indication as to why the school went so far up the blind alley of doctrinaire and dogmatic multi-culturalism and anti-racism.

What, then, has changed in 1986/87?

The evidence we received does not suggest that the school or the education department has learnt many lessons since the 1982 incident. Asian students and parents lived with the knowledge and the meaning of 1982 right up until Ahmed's murder. Given their collective experiences it was inevitable that they would see the stabbing as racist. In publicly acknowledging that fact, unlike their response in 1982, the school and the education department were dealing with only one aspect of the situation, and very clumsily at that, as we have seen. The matter of an Asian student being stabbed by a white student, and the particular background to the stabbing incident still have not been dealt with by the school as far as the students are concerned. The division into black and white 'camps' that arose after the murder, and the school's failure to deal with that division contained within itself the potential for furhter serious conflict and violence.

Both the 1982 and the 1986 incidents are in our view examples of how common-sense and judgement which a school such as Burnage might well exercise in relation to other matters, get displaced by the confusion and lack of logic which the application of a dogmatic multi-culturalism/ anti-racism engenders. How then has this multi-culturalism and anti-racism developed at Burnage? To this we now turn.

CHAPTER 19

Managing Burnage: Part 1

Anti-Racism at Burnage

A school is an institution that has to be managed. The structure is pyramidical, with the Head at the top. Within the education system the Head exercises considerable power.

Dr Gough's appointment and initiatives need to be seen against the background we have already described in Chapter 1. He immediately tried to co-operate with the policies of Manchester Education Department and abolished corporal punishment, having arrived at the school in the middle of a prosecution taken out by a parent against a member of staff for hitting her son. He found the extent of corporal punishment much bigger than he had imagined. "Unofficial corporal punishment" also existed, with members of staff keeping slippers for the purpose.

One of the problems that Dr Gough faced on arriving at the school, was that much was done by tradition and the "this is what usually happens" approach, rather than through written procedures. Some staff still looked back to the "golden age" of Burnage. Low morale in the profession, an uncertain future, poor facilities in the school and inadequate resources, made it difficult for some teachers to accept that parents, children, and the LEA have different expectations, and some might be seeking a different relationship from teachers. Ways of resolving problems with students had to be looked at other than by having recourse to the strap.

According to Mr Moors, the Deputy Head, staff reaction was hostile and there was pressure on Dr Gough to reintroduce corporal punishment. Criticisms were also made about the new child centred approach compared with the more traditional methods of teaching, and silence in classrooms was still equated with good classroom behaviour. Children were regarded as receptacles for knowledge that the teacher dispensed, and consequently there was little attempt to involve children in their own learning.

There were clearly some areas of good practice in the school, and, according to Dr Gough, the staff were an extremely hard working group. However, because of the split site, there was an upper versus

169

lower school divide to some extent. Dr Gough was told that one of the previous Heads, who retired in 1977, had been unable to unite the two staffs. Some staff refused to teach in the Upper School, and in the Lower School, tensions were caused by the larger class sizes which result from this.

The Head of Lower School and the Deputy Head of Upper School were all appointed at approximately the same time as Dr Gough. They were all in favour of the policy changes. The management team, however, was smaller than the teams employed in equivalent schools of that size in the area. Dr Gough told us that in his first year the senior management group consisted of himself and two deputies, assisted by a senior teacher who was a union officer who spend a lot of time out of school on union duties. Compared to reorganised schools of the same size this was a very small team – similar size schools had management teams going up to seven, excluding the Head. For example, Levenshulme, which was smaller in size, had a management team of five apart from the Head.

In the last five years, the Education Department has allowed a gradual build up of the management team at Burnage. A head of Lower School, a head of curriculum development, and latterly a head of school community development, and a head of Upper School are four additions since the beginning. At Lower School, there is a Deputy Head, Head of Lower School and two senior teachers. Middle management consists of year heads and departmental heads. It is also notable that during Dr Gough's tenure, there has been an increase in the number of women staff employed. There have also been a number of Section 11 appointments, as we shall see.

Multi-Cultural and Anti-Racist Policies

We have already referred to racist attitudes and reactions among staff at Burnage. It is also true that in the early days of Dr Gough's headship a great many staff saw no need for multi-cultural education. The attitude seemed to be, "They are over here, and must accept our culture; eventually they will be assimilated". Others were overtly racist. One member of staff allegedly told Dr Gough regarding the anti-racist/multi-cultural policy, "I believe they should all be sent back to Pakistan" while another said, "I don't like them – they smell". Others said it was not necessary to implement anti-racist policies, and the monitoring of books for racist content was seen as fascist. Mr Moors was told by one staff member that he must be in constant contact with Cuba, and appeared to receive his instructions from them.

In the early days of Dr Gough's headship, we were told racism "permeated the whole school". Racist jokes were acceptable, racist comments were made in the corridors and the introduction of anti-racist policies within the school was necessary and important. This was echoed by the Governors who also saw the need for anti-racist policies, as Dr Ben Glaisner, Vice-Chairman of the Governors, explained to us:

"Although the reasons for these views were never consciously stated I believe it was because the persons concerned, teachers, held to the view that is the common one. That view is that people from other countries that come to live in Britain should become assimilated into our culture. They held the view that multi-cultural education was obtrusive and 'left wing'." Those people naturally would not be receptive to a multi-cultural and multi-racial approach. There were regular meetings held for teachers by Peter Moors, the senior deputy head, so that the approach could be explained. However, on the two occasions or so that I attended there were never more than a dozen teachers there. I think this was significant of the reluctance or unwillingness to co-operate fully with the Governors' policy."

Mr Jamal is one of three Asian Governors of the school and also a parent. He found that there was a marked difference between his elder son's time in 1976 and his younger son's time which started in 1983.

"During my elder son's time the staff and higher management were unapproachable. Racism in a real sense was rampant at that time, when teachers used to call the Asian boys 'Pakis.' There used to be fights and scuffles which when reported went unattended or uncared for. The whole atmosphere of the school then was 'that the Asian boys were there only because they were admitted.' Neither the staff nor the management were concerned for any of their special requirements. Unlike now, the fights and the quarrels were first of all not reported and if they were they went unattended."

"Since the time Mr Moors and Dr Gough took over the atmosphere started changing slowly. Until I became a governor I wasn't in a position to see from the inside, but I could see the leaflets and other information had started coming in Asian languages. Urdu language teaching and Jumma prayers were introduced and that was a recognition by higher management that due to the large Muslim Asian studentage there is a need for these extra curricular activities."

171

Drafting the Policies

In 1982 a working party of staff was set up to produce a draft policy document on multi-cultural education and racism. A document was prepared in Spring 1983 and distributed to all staff for comment:

"Policy Statement on Racism – for discussion."

Preamble

1. Our aim at Burnage is to ensure that every student is in receipt of an education which will enable him to realise himself socially, emotionally, intellectually. Our students are from widely different cultural, social and racial backgrounds. They, therefore, require support from us which is variable in nature and degree if they are eventually to contribute effectively to society they join on leaving school. Support for boys from ethnic minorities should, therefore, be seen as a part of our overall educational and pastoral strategies.

   Racial discrimination in the community at large is a fact of life and Burnage as a concerned and supportive school must play its part in the promotion of a multi-cultural society and, through schooling, help reduce and eradicate this discrimination.

2. At Burnage overt racism is not apparent to any significant extent. This lends support to those who dismiss or seek to minimise the problem. Covert racism is more subtle and in the long term more damaging. Staff need to be much clearer about their multi-cultural responsibilities and more sensitive to both overt and covert manifestations of racial discriminations.

   Irrespective of the level of racism in school and the community outside, the lack of a positive policy on racism condones it.

3. A school policy on Racism will help ensure that staff are aware of the need to constantly review:

   i teaching and learning strategies in the classroom,
   ii teaching resources,
   iii student behaviour, and
   iv their own attitudes and beliefs.

   in the context of racial problems.

   Tolerance and understanding will be more effectively and more quickly achieved if planned for than by accident."

172

As a result of consultations this draft was modified or "toned down" and the revised version was distributed to staff in Summer 1983. This is how the preamble to the revised document reads:

"Policy Statement on Racism

Preamble

1. Burnage has a long and honourable record of fostering good race relationships amongst its students. It is generally to the credit of both past and present staff that they have engendered a harmonious atmosphere in which all boys have been encouraged to develop their full educational potential and the ability to realise themselves socially, emotionally and intellectually.

    Burnage, however, is not complacent. It realises that there is racial discrimination within the community outside the school. As a concerned and supportive school it must continue to play an increasing part in promoting the aims and ideals of a multi-cultural society and thus help to reduce and eventually eliminate discrimination.

2. Burnage as an integral part of the community has to take a positive approach to combat racism whether it be overt or covert. Staff have already begun to re-examine their multi-cultural responsibilities and the need to be more sensitive to both overt and covert manifestations of racial discrimination. Irrespective of the level of racism the lack of a positive policy on the part of the school would appear to condone it.

3. Pupils at Burnage come from widely differing cultural, social, religious and racial backgrounds. All our students require support from us which is variable in nature and degrees so that they may contribute effectively to society. Support for boys from ethnic minorities should be seen as a part of our overall educational strategy.

4. A school policy on Racism will ensure that staff are aware of the need to constantly review:

    i   teaching and learning strategies in the classroom,
    ii teaching resources,
    iii student behaviour,
    iv their own attitudes and beliefs in the context of racial problems.

    Tolerance and understanding will be more effectively and more quickly achieved if planned for than by accident."

It is interesting that Paragraph 1 of the modified version defends Burnage School against charges of racism. Paragraph 2 speaks of staff as having begun to *re-examine* their multi-cultural responsibilities. They no longer need to be *clearer* about them, as in Paragraph 2 of the original draft. The revised document also contains a *blueprint* for the future. Its later part has detailed recommendations for action in the areas of staffing policy, in-service training, curriculum development, resources, community languages and links with outside agencies.

It was in 1985, in accordance with local authority policy, that racist incident log books were placed in both Upper and Lower Schools for the recording of "incidents likely to lead to an increase in racial tension". Further guidelines on the identification of racist incidents and proposals for a more efficient system of recording were distributed to staff and black parents for discussion in Autumn 1986. These were being revised in January 1987.

By the Summer of 1985, increased awareness amongst some staff led to feelings of dissatisfaction with the earlier document which no longer appeared to meet the needs of the school. The guidelines for action were too general and only referred to the 1983–1984 period. Furthermore, they failed to deal with a number of important issues, such as pastoral care, home school liaison, teaching English as a second language, and institutional racism in the school's own practices and procedures (for example, in areas such as assessment, selection, and option choices). In particular, the lack of involvement of black students and parents in the formulation of the initial policy document was considered a cause for concern.

It was proposed, therefore, that a new policy document be prepared. The process by which this document would be drawn up and the mechanisms by which the policy would be monitored, evaluated and developed in future years were felt to be of crucial importance.

A number of factors influenced the direction of this document. These included the need for involvement of black parents, the need for participation of all groups making up the school community, the need for preparatory training programmes appropriate to the needs of each group, and the need for effective monitoring and evaluation.

Establishing a dialogue with black parents was considered important, since by 1985, no direct avenue of communication existed. An Ethnic Minority Advisory Group (EMAG) was set up. (Details of how these groups were set up and our comments are given below.)

In Autumn 1986, proposals for the production of a new school policy were drawn up and presented to black parents for discussion. *White parents were not involved.* A number of parents, students and staff agreed to draft an initial discussion document for Spring/Summer 1987. The final document is targeted for Spring 1988.

The involvement of students in their school and education would appear to be an afterthought following Ahmed's murder and the March disturbances. The 5th form consultative group and the 6th form anti-racist strategies groups are of very recent origin, and it is too soon to say whether their experiences will be used and will make an impact on the operation of the anti-racist policies.

Staff Appointments

It has been the policy of the school in recent years to appoint staff who are in sympathy with the school's multi-cultural/anti-racist policies. Prospective applicants for teaching posts are advised of the school's philosophy prior to their application through the school's "Guidance to Candidates" and in job specification, all of which contain the statement:

"The school is actively pursuing on-going, anti-racist strategies within all aspects of the institution. The appointee would be expected effectively to support and contribute to the continuing development of these strategies."

Questions related to the candidates attitude towards multi-cultural/anti-racist education are always raised at interview. This is clearly an important recruitment strategy but it does not necessarily lead to the sort of creative education which values all students and parents – a point which emerges later.

Burnage School also recognises the need for more black teachers and has sought to appoint black staff whenever possible. Currently employed at the school, as we have seen, are two full-time teachers of Drama and Physics and one full-time reprographics technician. Part-time staff include two peripatetic teachers of Urdu, two peripatetic teachers of music, one library assistant and one school meals supervisor.

The development and promotion of the school's multi-cultural education policy and the introduction of suitable anti racist strategies are two of the first responsibilities listed in the job description of the Deputy Head (Curriculum).

Section 11 Staff

In order to achieve success in Burnage's anti-racist policies, great use has been made of Section 11 funding.

Section 11 of the Local Government Act 1966, under which all Section 11 funding is made, reads, so far as relevant, as follows:

"11 Grants for certain expenditure due to immigrant population

(1) Subject to the provisions of this section the Secretary of State may pay, to local authorities who in his opinion are required to make special provision in the exercise of any of their functions in consequence of the presence within their areas of substantial numbers of immigrants from the Commonwealth whose language or customs differ from those of the community, grants of such amounts as he may with the consent of the Treasury determine on account of expenditure of such descriptions (being expenditure in respect of the employment of staff) as he may so determine."

Extra staffing for multi-cultural/anti-racist development was introduced to Burnage School using Section 11 funding. Prior to 1983 one Section 11 teacher of English as a second language was attached to the school on a full-time basis from the Multi-cultural Development Service. In September 1983 two further members of staff were appointed to take responsibility for multi-cultural curriculum development in English and Humanities. These were both scale 1 posts. In 1984 two further staff were appointed with similar responsibilities in Art, Craft Design and Technology (CDT), and Science. Again they were scale 1 posts. The present Head of Community Education, Ms Aisthorpe, also came to the school in September 1984 on a head of department scale (scale 3), with responsibility for ethnic music, community liaison and in-service training.

To one Section 11 member of staff, who has since left Burnage, the rest of the staff were not very clear as to why Section 11 teachers were at Burnage or what their role was. We found it difficult to find out whether this attitude of the staff to Section 11 teachers came from a real lack of knowledge or was a deliberate choosing to be unaware. The impression given to this Section 11 teacher by staff was that the Section 11 staff had to "prove themselves" as teachers. They were seen as people who had come in on a "bandwagon". To many staff they had been imposed on the School from above without prior consultation or discussion. They were people who had no assigned work or classes. After one of the Section 11 staff had reported a racist remark in the staff room and the "mole remarks" started, a number of Section 11 staff and their sympathisers withdrew more and more from the staff room, because they felt that the atmosphere was so unpleasant.

Ethnic Minority Advisory Groups (EMAG's)

There is no doubt that there has been some antagonism towards Section 11 staff, but it is difficult to resolve whether it arose from the way in which multi-cultural and anti-racist initiatives were introduced into the school, from the staff's resistance to change, or from a combination of both. One thing is certain. In about 1985 the Home Office, who give out Section 11 money, required local authorities to consult in the community before making Section 11 appointments. In Burnage the response was the setting up of Afro Caribbean and Asian parents groups which came to be known as the Ethnic Minority Advisory Group (EMAG). There is no doubt that these caused concern and hostility. Rightly so, in our view.

In 1985, Lesley Aisthorpe drafted a letter, which was sent to a number of schools and colleges working with anti-racist initiatives. It proposed the setting up of an EMAG at Burnage, and asked for advice. One of the responses, from the Head of Tulse Hill School, a large comprehensive in London, was as follows:

9th December, 1985

Dr G Gough,
Burnage High School,
Burnage Lane,
Manchester,
M19 1BU

Your Ref. Dr G/PM/SP

Dear Dr Gough,

Thank you for your inquiry concerning parental involvement in the life of our school.

Nationally this has been a problem for many schools especially in working class areas. The problem becomes even greater where there are large minority groups in the community.

We do have a reasonably small faithful group of parents who regularly attend our Tulse Hill School Association meeting. This Association is made up of Parents, Staff and friends of Tulse Hill. It meets about once a month.

I would *strongly* advise that you do *not* set up a separate ethnic system for minority groups. Two or three schools have tried it in the London area and it has been a fiasco. It is divisive, creates suspicion and can lead to unnecessary squabbles with indigenous white parents who often feel that they are being pushed aside. (Our emphasis).

What I would suggest is that you throw some sort of social function initially e.g. a variety concert, and ask all parents including those from the various ethnic groups to help in providing the entertainment and food. Hold a preliminary meeting and inform them of your intention to develop strong parental ties with the school and that you see this as a start to the way forward. We held such a function and it was a resounding success.

Where there are open discussions with all groups, the veil of suspicion is removed. If you do set up separate parental groups, free discussion and exchange of views will not take place, and you would have created an atmosphere of division.

The teaching staff should be represented on any such organisation so that they may give some impact to the group and in turn be receptive to some of the views expressed by parents.

You may find it difficult to follow my advice since your letter indicates a commitment on your part to set up an EMAG.

I can only repeat that in doing so you will be creating a multi headed monster which could turn into separate pressure groups, and the result would be to defeat your original purpose and create embarrassing problems for you.

Best wishes.

Yours sincerely,

signed
Ken Noble.

Despite this advice an Ethnic Minority Advisory Group (EMAG) was set up for parents in the spring of 1986. In his evidence to us Dr Gough agreed that as a result of setting up EMAGs some boys would get letters in class to give to their parents but other boys would not. But he did not believe this would be necessarily divisive. To Dr Gough a prerequisite for the whole community getting together – its long term aim – is the empowerment of black parents. Black parents, be it noted. Not white and black parents. But only black parents. He sees white parents entirely negatively, just wanting a piece of the action, being resistant to anti-racism, being the possible cause of their own alienation, being suspicious and being adequately consulted through monthly meetings of the Parents' Society. Since these issues are particularly important to black parents it is obvious that they should be consulted, as he told us, but he did not feel that there should always be joint meetings, in which white parents could take part, and he was totally resistant to any suggestion that the EMAG's in Burnage might have been a mistake.

Lesly Aisthorpe took the same line. She told us that the consultation with "ethnic minorities" regarding submissions by the school under Section 11 had to be set up in a rather rushed way. She had informal meetings with those who were interested, some from established organisations, and some individual parents, who did not belong to any organisations. The parents were all non-white. They gave conflicting advice. Some were for groups on a separate basis with one group for Afro-Caribbean and one group for Asian parents. Others were against this. She then decided to go ahead with the separate groups. She saw no room for amalgamating the Parents' Society or any of the area consultative groups, which contained white parents, with the EMAG's because those organisations consisted of middle class parents, who are not representative or elected. It is clear, however, that the black parents may also not be "representative" and they are certainly not elected.

Lesley Aisthorpe agreed with Dr Gough that EMAGs were not necessarily divisive. If the situation had been explained sensitively, then the division would not arise. She says:

"I was a form tutor at the time and I explained to my form what it was all about. I explained that there was a group of parents who met with staff at the school, particularly to discuss those matters that were of importance to them. Also when I was asked by children, 'Why do they have a meeting and we don't?', I reminded them of the meetings that we held for all parents and hoped their parents would attend those meetings."

A different perspective is given by a black teacher:

"I get very embarrassed when I get letters that we have to send out to Asian and Afro-Caribbean parents, because I have two boys in my class . . . it took me a year and six months to realise that (one of them) was Afro-Caribbean, because he is white, and it was only his brother saying: 'Doesn't Matthew look like one of the boys in our class – one of the Arabic boys?' and I said, 'He does, doesn't he?' and that is when he said, 'Don't you realise, Miss, my grandfather is black'. And all the time I had been giving out letters and missing him out."

She also indicates how it affects white students:

"I remember on one occasion calling the register, and as the boys were coming out for the letters, one of the white boys came, and I said, 'I'm very sorry, there is not a letter for you' and he said, 'Why not Miss?', and I said, 'Because these meetings are only for the Asian and black students', and then it suddenly clicked that the only time our white parents are invited into school are parents' evenings, careers evenings or presentation evenings; no other times are they communicated with in terms of what is happening in the school, and what the school has to offer their children, and what the school is doing as a community."

This same teacher relates how she was taken aside by Section II staff, when she first started at the school, and told that the other staff were racist. She also claimed that she has never been consulted about her experiences as a black teacher in the school, even though she would clearly have a major contribution to make. She gave an example of the time when the school was setting up a course for Creole speaking, she was not consulted at all, and only found out about it at the last moment, to her great embarrassment.

At a meeting of the EMAGs on November 8th 1987, a white teacher arrived at the meeting and met Lesley Aisthorpe, who asked him to leave. He was told that if he was allowed to stay then "teachers would be coming in droves" to future meetings. One agenda item covered the Christmas Social, in which another staff member wanted to be involved. There was an indication from senior management that she would also not be welcome. On 'phoning two of the parents, however, she was told, "interest from teachers would be good and helpful in fostering good relationships."

When EMAGs started, letters were sent out in Bengali, Urdu and Punjabi and it was also made clear that interpreters would be present at the meetings. Twenty four Asian parents attended the first meeting. Initially the Afro-Caribbean parents met in a separate group. However, towards the end of 1986, the decision was taken that the two groups should join together. One of the parents thought that this joining together of the two groups was a good idea and that the relationships had been harmonious since then. The same parent felt that there would be greater harmony if white parents had also been involved in the process.

Shortly after the appointment of Lesley Aisthorpe as Head of Community Education all Section 11I staff were grouped together as the Community Education Department.

The redesignated Head of Community Education was then able to join the school consultative committee alongside Heads of Year and Heads of subject departments. The upgrading of the post of Head of Community Education to Curriculum Co-ordinator status in 1986 enabled the postholder to join the policy committee, and so increase the influence of Section 11 staff within the school. Other staff viewed Miss Aisthorpe's meteoric rise with suspicion and mistrust, an attitude which inevitably moved from the person herself to the issues she was seen to represent.

There is certainly evidence that anti-racism and the policies related to it at Burnage have met with resistance from staff and some have felt these policies have been "imposed" on them as part of a package of new policies on discipline and teaching methods. Because senior management are seen to be "imposing" rather than "managing", existing staff polarisation has probably hardened and become fixed and unyielding, as we shall see when we deal with the management style in a later chapter.

But that is not the only peculiarity of the implementation of anti-racist and multi-cultural policies at Burnage.

We also find it strange that a Community Education department ends up being a co-ordinating unit for Section II work. It is even more strange because the anti-racist and multi-cultural thrust of that department was concerned almost exclusively with Afro-Caribbean and Asian issues. The notion of 'community' as necessarily embracing the white community, and multi-cultural as including the culture of white working class people appears to have been ignored by the staff in that department. Nor did we hear any evidence to suggest that the issues arising in the community had any influence on the organisation and delivery of the curriculum by the Community Education Department.

In our view using Section 11 to "graft on" anti-racist policies has its dangers. It can easily marginalise the issues and take them out of mainstream education. At the same time it shuffles off onto Section 11 staff the responsibility which should belong to all staff at the school for anti-racist education. At Burnage these dangers were compounded by the setting up of the EMAGs.

Apart from Dr Gough, Mr Moors and Lesley Aisthorpe, the overwhelming weight of evidence suggests that the EMAGs were divisive and counter-productive. They divided students in the classroom and created resentment among white students. They led in at least one case to a difficult problem of racial identification by a teacher who was obviously sensitive to this sort of thing. They were also divisive of parents, initially creating a separate group of Asian, Afro-Caribbean and white parents. They make it appear that white parents have no business in the development of anti-racist education, a notion which we reject. Also we do not accept Dr Gough's view that white parents were adequately consulted through the Parents' Society. The advice of Ken Noble, the Head of Tulse Hill School, was trenchant and apposite and should have been followed.

CHAPTER 20

Managing Burnage – Part 2

Investigation and Inspection

The main responsibility for the day to day running of the school rests with the Head, but he or she is also answerable to the Governors of the school and may rely heavily on the Inspectorate employed by the local education authority.

Since Dr Gough's appointment as Head of Burnage in 1982, the school has been the subject of two major internal inquiries, both in 1985:

The Governors' Investigation
The Manchester Education Department's Inspection

The Governors' inquiry has provoked considerable controversy and speculation, mainly because of the first draft of the report, which was later edited extensively and has remained secret until now.

How did it come into being? Different accounts have been given by Dr Gough, by Joe Lowry of the NAS/UWT, by Diana Kealey the Chair of Governors, and by Audrey Jones, one of the Governors. Dr Gough claims the credit for initiating the investigation. The unions say the investigation was set up to head off a staff revolt against Dr Gough. The Chair and Vice-Chair of Governors got the impression that the inquiry resulted from an approach to governors by Dr Gough.

According to Dr Gough he would have liked Inspectorate involvement in the school in his first year. By November of 1984 there were further meetings to discuss Inspectorate involvement in the school. Although some Inspectors did visit, the report which resulted was not a complete picture of Burnage. Dr Gough states that two union representatives expressed the view to him in 1985 that child centred teaching methods had become the worst form of appeasement, and complained that management refused to adopt a punitive approach to some students. Dr Gough says he informed the Governors of this and asked them to intervene and consult with staff and make recommendations.

A different account is given by Joe Lowry the General Secretary of NAS/UWT in Manchester. His account begins in 1984 with off the record discussions with the Head over staff concerns about discipline and staff morale. Afterwards, working parties were set up but they did not achieve much. By July of 1985, staff were expressing grave concern about the situation in the school.

On several occasions Joe Lowry was approached by the press wanting to know what was going on at Burnage, and he had several discussions with union representatives on the school staff. Eventually reports reaching him were so serious that Joe Lowry arranged to meet the Chief Education Officer to discuss the matter. He took Alan Hill (Secretary of AMMA) and Brenda Judge (NUT) to the meeting with him. He warned the Chief Education Officer that staff morale at Burnage was very low and if something was not done pretty soon "the lid would blow off the place". It appeared that the Chief Education Officer was aware of problems within the school. As a result arrangements were made to contact the Governors and to offer support to the school through the Inspectorate. A Governors' Inquiry was then set up and the governors spoke to all staff who wanted to express their concerns. The Governors eventually produced a report that went to the Education Committee.

The current Chair of Governors, Diana Kealey, recalls that it was in May or June of 1985 that Dr Gough told the Board of Governors that he felt there were problems in the school amongst the staff. There were grievances and disagreements about particular educational approaches, which he was not going to be able to resolve by himself. He suggested that it would be very helpful if the Governors became involved. Out of this came the idea for a sub-committee of governors which would investigate the problems and present their findings to the rest of the Governing body.

Another Governor, Audrey Jones, who served on the sub-committee, was under the impression that there was unrest in the school and that it was staff pressure through the unions that caused the problems of the School to be looked at. She agreed that the Head had made the request for a sub-committee to tackle the problem, but she felt that this was in response to the pressure that the Head was under.

(A)   *The Secret Report*

The Governors Sub-Committee was set up on July 8th 1985 and met some eighteen times between July 16th and August 9th 1985. They interviewed some eighty-five staff out of a total of approximately one

184

hundred. The sub-committee started off with seven governors, but ended up with five, since two were unable to take part. Dr Ben Glaisner was the co-ordinator. He and the other four Governors, which included the present Chair of Governors, prepared a draft report for presentation to the other governors. This is the report which became the subject of further controversy. It summarised its findings in the following way:

"There are, and have been for some time, serious problems within the School which have resulted in an ever-widening breach between the teaching staff and the Senior Management.

The non-teaching staff are affected to a lesser degree by the problems but have expressed their concern.

The consequences of the problems are:

"Very low morale among the majority of the staff."

"A significant lack of confidence of the majority of the staff in senior Management."

A factionalisation of the staff.

An atmosphere of mistrust, allegation and innuendo.

A significant number of teachers actively seeking new positions elsewhere.

An alleged deterioration in the behaviour of the boys.

The problems are exacerbated by the industrial disputes. The problems are worse in Lower School.

Criticism of the senior management team by the staff is directed almost entirely to the Headmaster, Dr Gough, and the Deputy Headmaster, Mr Moors. Some other members of the team are in fact praised.

There are members of the staff who are content but they are greatly outnumbered by the discontented.

The problems stem from the transition over the past eight years from a rather autocratic, traditional and stable regime to one encompassing the more progressive requirements of central and local government and of educationalists. The requirements of the local authority were urgent and the time, resources and money available were inadequate. The changes were therefore too rapid and too intense for some members of the staff, particularly those who were basically unreceptive to change, and the seeds of a division between traditional and progressive methods were sown."

Imposed on that situation was a period of changes in the management team. Mr Marshall introduced the first of the changes but only remained in office for two years. Mr Walmsley, acting as caretaker Head, accepted the status quo for one year. The main changes of the reorganisation of 1982, the abolition of corporal punishment and the directives toward anti-racism, multi-cultural education, and Section 11, etc, fell to Dr Gough for implementation.

The staff had therefore experienced a period of some years of basic changes, changes in the direction and management of those basic changes, and changes in philosophy. They required leadership, guidance and an agreed policy. They required to be consulted in the formulation of that policy, to have their opinion sought and respected, and to be supported in their endeavours by the Senior Management.

Dr Gough introduced measures to implement the mandatory requirements placed upon him, together with measures which he himself wished to incorporate, and these were accepted by some members of the staff with enthusiasm. To the majority they were not acceptable in the manner in which they were presented. The pace of the changes aggravated matters.

Some members of the staff are fulsome in their praise of senior management and examples are quoted of their sympathetic and caring attitude in private and personal matters.

On the basis of this analysis, the members of the sub-committee reached a number of wide-ranging conclusions:

(1) They concluded that there were serious problems at the school, and that urgent action was required to resolve them.

(2) Senior management was charged with "a large share of responsibility for the present situaton" as well as for resolving it.

(3) Senior management (Dr Gough and Mr Moors) must change their attitudes, even if it was traumatic and required a great deal of support from other senior staff.

(4) Obstructive and intransigent attitudes by staff members had also been a problem and had resulted in over-reaction, over-sensitivity and pettiness toward senior management.

(5) Management of the school should be democratised, intransigent attitudes should be left behind, and processes of changes should be presented "in a manner which shows due consideration of their (the intransigents) opinions, endeavours and achievements".

(6) The entire staff should spend a week in consultation on policy formulation including communication, discipline, conduct codes and philosophies.

186

(7) The physical plant, equipment and teaching supplies required "major refurbishment".

(8) Section II and other management staffing should be increased at the senior level.

(9) Governors should remain in close contact with the school and a programme of annual reviews should be adopted, but it should be expected that the "healing" process and adaptation to change will require a long term view.

The members of the sub-committee expressed unqualified confidence in senior management and staff, concluding that they "have the ability to make the healing process a success".

(B)   *The Edited Report*

There is a conflict as to whether the secret report was a report in final form that was intended to be published, or whether it was merely intended as a draft, to be circulated and amended before submission in final form to the full governing body. According to Audrey Jones, Dr Gough and Mr Moors reacted strongly to their findings, challenging the accuracy and truthfulness of some of them. As a result, she told us, the management section was rewritten "so that it would not be necessary for anyone to resign; so that no one would feel the need to resign". The Governors wanted the school to continue to function. They hoped that they could build on their findings in order to change things. As a result, according to Audrey Jones, the original report was shortened. The edited version was dated the 9th of September 1985.

The secret Report ran to twenty-eight pages. The edited report ran to ten pages. The summary was deleted and alterations were made to the conclusions. Comparisons of the two reports made it clear that: whatever the reasons for the changes, they were intended to soften criticism and divert attention from the very negative picture painted in the secret report. Most importantly, the emphasis on senior management was taken out completely (item 3 in the list in the previous section), as was the discussion of staff obstruction and intransigence, and over-sensitivity (item 4). The overall effect of the changes was to take out the most critical observations relating to staff (resignations, "seeds of division", unreceptivity to change), while leaving a fairly heavy burden of responsibility on senior management. One key addition to the edited report was that "senior management should examine its style and methods to see what changes are necessary". This positive injunction replaces the much more negative conclusions reached in the secret report. Although the edited report remains critical of the senior management "style", it is somewhat less critical of staff attitudes than had been proposed in the first report. Some of the concrete recommendations made in the first report were also softened. The recommendation that Section II staffing be increased at the senior level was dropped, as was the recommendation that all staff – line and management – spent a week in consultation on communicaton and policies. Recommendations on increased Governors' participation were also condensed and softened.

The full text of the two reports is to be found in the Appendices A and B.

(C) *Impact of the Goveror's Report*

Although the types of changes are evident from a comparison of the two versions, it is more difficult to deduce the precise motives for those changes.

Diana Kealey, the chair of Governors, and Ben Glaisner the vice-chair, felt that the reason for the shorter report was that the sub-committee wanted to be positive and constructive. They argued that the longer report was never intended to be published to staff unless the Governors had adopted it. They also felt that it would have been very difficult for Dr Gough and Peter Moors to function if a shorter, less critical report had not been produced. The last thing the Governors wanted to do was to push Dr Gough and Peter Moors into resigning. On the one hand, they wanted the report to be helpful to the school; on the other hand, they did not want the staff to feel that they had not listened to them. In the end, according to Diana Kealy the final report seems to have been somewhat suppressed (Audrey Jones said that she never received a copy), and it "did not please anybody". Despite the care evidently taken in the entire process of carrying out the investigation and then revising the report so substantially, Diana Kealey felt that the Governors were concerned about the situation at Burnage by the end of the entire process. They felt that Dr Gough's response to criticism of his style of management, especially when combined with the subsequent suppression (by the Governors) of both versions of the report, were not likely to increase staff confidence or to set the tone for a more open discussion which would take into account the endeavours and opinions of the staff. They felt that those whose opinions were "entrenched" might possibly become even more entrenched and that reports that were shrouded in secrecy might further alienate staff, who were already losing confidence in senior management.

Even more seriously, the entire process especially the content of the first report, seems to have made it clear that there was actually a serious schism between staff and senior management. Looking to the later events at Burnage, and particularly at the difficulties that have been encountered in implementing multi-cultural, anti-racist, and other progressive policies at Burnage, the question now becomes what could have been done then – and what should still be done now – to eliminate that schism.

And events were to try staff and management at Burnage further. As we have seen by November 1985, Darren Coulburn was in his second year at Burnage High School. In the summer holiday of 1985, in August just before the September 9th Report was produced, he and another boy were involved in setting fire to the new Lower School Art Block. By November 5th 1985, two days after the formal inspection finished, Darren Coulburn pleaded guilty to arson.

Inspectors' Report

The Inspectorate entered Burnage Lower School on November 6th 1985 and they concluded their inspection on November 13th 1985. They produced a Report from the Chief Inspector, which ran to some twenty-eight pages.

They also produced thirteen Supplementary Reports which addressed departmental issues. Full copies of these documents are available from the Education Department.

General

In general the Inspectors' report discussed the changes in the school in the last few years in the context of limited physical resources and prolonged industrial action. The Inspectors felt that the fact that Burnage had not been reorganised in 1982, together with a lack of curriculum reviews, had produced "strains of mismatch" at the school.

The Inspectors felt that these changes had clearly brought about "turbulence" in the Lower School. They stressed that both teachers and students seemed to be talented, but that some staff seemed to want a "return to a stable past". Overall they reported that the management team as well as the governors appeared to be supportive, and that "together with the quality of staff there is potential to develop a fine school". We summarise the most relevant findings:

(A) *Discipline and Pastoral Care*

The Inspectors felt that order seemed to be sometimes maintained in a repressive, inconsistent and overly punitive fashion. Students were being sent out of the classroom for a range of behaviour, from "not listening" in class to "taking part in scuffles". Students who were sent outside might leave the premises altogether. This was seen to be totally unacceptable, and to place unfair constraining behaviour on senior management.

They reported that the overall impression on the corridors was of aggression released, petty violence, and the ignoring of adults, all of which generated an institutionalised and regimental atmosphere in which the fittest survived.

The Inspectorate did note that some staff got respect through supportive relationships with students, but urged other staff not to give way to cynical sarcasm and lack of praise of students. They concluded that the predominant mode of teaching in Lower School was of teachers talking and students listening or copying off the blackboard.

The Inspectorate commented particularly on the use of memos on student behaviour. They concluded that the duplicate memo incident or referral system seemed to be working well as a logging device, and would in due course enable the school management to make a detailed analysis of events, so that appropriate intervention could be planned. We have already seen that Darren Coulburn featured in a number of behaviour memos, prior to September 17th 1986. Yet none of these memos was produced at the Governors' meeting on December 3rd 1985, or was subject to the sort of analysis envisaged in the Inspectorate Report. Appropriate intervention, as we have seen, did not, therefore take place.

The Inspectors noted that there was seen to be a small number of students who presented significant management problems for staff. It was hoped that the establishment of a support resource would assist in developing effective strategies for the resolution of particular social or emotional difficulties, and the construction of suitable individual programmes to re-engage these students in learning activities.

As far as Darren Coulburn was concerned, this proposal never progressed beyond the realm of wishful thinking. As we have seen, the school was not aware of a supervision order, imposed on him in November 1985, until February of 1986. In the month of February 1986, he was involved in three separate incidents, one of which involved setting off the fire alarm and another involved throwing stones at an annex window. Yet no effective strategy was developed to deal with his obvious behaviour difficulties.

(B) *"Ethnic Minority" Students*

Given national concern about the suspension of black students the Inspectors specifically reviewed Burnage's record against the background of ethnic monitoring by the City Council. Based on the following figures, the Inspectors decided that disciplinary action in relation to black students was not an issue at Burnage.

Time Period	Total disciplinary actions	Ethnic minitories	% ethnic minorities
June 1983 to June 1985	32 suspensions	2	6.24
January 1984 to November 1985	59 exclusions	13	22
September to November 1985	246 detentions	73	30

These figures are not as clear cut as they might first appear to be. The only basis for determining whether a student was black was by the student's recorded name. This method could be useful to identify students from the Indian sub continent, but it totally ignores Afro-Caribbean students. If the local authority does make a commitment to ethnic monitoring, exercises such as this will need to become more meaningful and precise. Until such changes have been made, these figures can only be viewed as an initial and crude attempt to analyse a contentious issue.

191

(C) *Parents*

In a sub-report on pastoral care, the Inspectors felt that the school's relationships with parents needed attention. They pointed out that even though the school sent very few letters, they were negative in tone and tended to summon parents rather than invite them to school. More positive interaction with parents was needed. The entire section on parents in the report implies that there is a distinct lack of understanding and communication between parents and the school. Even at the time of the inspection, this was clearly an area in which little progress had been made, notwithstanding Dr Gough's initial concerns about the lack of contact between parents and the school. In addition the Inspectors felt Section II staff could assist, particularly with "ethnic minority" students. They suggested greater encouragement should be given to home visits by form tutors. Had this recommendation been followed up, a form tutor might have learned from the Ullah family of the bullying and fights that Ahmed experienced at Burnage. A form tutor might also have discovered that Mrs Ullah spoke English fluently and articulately. The panic and insensitivity over providing "interpreters" on the day that Ahmed was stabbed might thus have been avoided.

(D) *Follow up to Inspection*

The Inspectors followed up the inspection with a visit to the school in June 1986, and with a report to the Schools' Sub-Committee in July 1987. Individual inspectors have been into school to monitor developments in departments at various times throughout the year. A residential conference for senior management was held in November 1986, and a school sub-committee received a follow up report on July 16th 1987.

Burnage staff had co-operated with the Governors' inquiry; they had co-operated with the inspection. Burnage parents were not involved in either. Burnage students continued as usual. On both occasions the fundamental crisis in the school was identified in more or less clear terms, but the opportunity to do something about it was missed. By the time our Inquiry sat nothing had been resolved, but resentment, distrust, fear and misgiving had become very much the order of the day, as we found when we tried to obtain evidence from the staff at Burnage school.

CHAPTER 21

Managing Burnage: Part 3

The Management Style

It took a long time before teaching and support staff at Burnage felt confident enough to come and give evidence to the Inquiry. At first we surmised that because the murder had occurred in their school, the staff were nervous about having to share what happened and how they saw their responsibilities in relation to it. Gradually, however, it became clear that the majority of the staff were concerned whether or not the Inquiry was going to look at Burnage in depth and genuinely listen to what the teachers had to say or whether we had already received signals, from whatever source, about who and what to target.

Fear and Mistrust

As teachers started to come, however, it was evident that there were distinct "camps" within the staff, and some individuals were anxious that it should not be known that they had given evidence to us.

This sometimes led to some amusing scenes, as staff leaving the Inquiry rooms went to astonishing lengths to avoid being seen by those who were still waiting to give their evidence.

Teachers gave examples time and again of the management style of the Head and Deputy Head, which they felt was responsible for a good deal of the mistrust and polarisation in the school. One teacher felt there was a conspiracy of secrecy, as well as widespread mistrust:

"It is an awful thing to say, but whenever you are talking to somebody, you are always looking over your shoulder, and that is not a very nice thing."

The feeling of mistrust was also mixed with fear. A large number of witnesses commented that they were no longer seeking promotion and could, therefore, be straight and candid about what they wished to say to the Inquiry. Others were fearful, because they were young and were committed to a career in teaching and to working at Burnage. They agonised between wanting to assist the Inquiry and improve the situation in the school and not wishing to be victimised because of their co-operation or the nature of their evidence.

One person put it like this:

"There are still a lot of staff who are very loathe to come here, and if they do, they will be very guarded as to what they say. I do not think they would tell the truth. They would not tell lies, but they would not tell the whole truth because they feel that if they did and they were found out the consequences could be quite difficult to cope with later on.

Q. So that is not an atmosphere in which there is a sort of free spirit of constructive criticism?
A. No, that is quite right.
Q. Does that fear, so far as you are aware, run across all sections of the staff?
A. So far as I can say, 90%, 95% of the staff, I would think. I know I will be quite frightened if Mr X is still there after the Inquiry and after the results have been published. I feel that he will go through the evidence that has been given, or the report, or the questions he is going to be asked, with a very fine toothcomb, and I feel that I am going to be in some quite deep water, I would have thought, and possibly other people might be. So I feel under pressure, I must admit, at the moment.
Q. But nevertheless, despite all these fears, you have overcome them in order to come and give your evidence?
A. Yes, I have to tell the truth. I think that is important.

Another member of staff became very worried and had quite a struggle with her conscience because she "got a very clear message from Mr. X as to whether or not she should co-operate with the Inquiry". The message was to "keep out of it and keep a low profile". That member of staff felt that her interest in the students and her anxieties about what was going on in the school were such that she could not fail to respond to the Inquiry's call for co-operation from all staff. In the end she consulted other staff colleagues and was given support in overcoming her fears and coming to the Inquiry.

Witness after witness made reference to the management style of senior management and how that management style in their view undermined staff attempts to make the school function cohesively.

The one issue which staff raised over and over again was the lack of value placed upon what they actually did to create a healthy school environment and help students learn. Two problems were identified in this respect. The first was the perceptions Dr Gough had of the staff he inherited and their perceptions of him.

One body of staff felt that prior to Dr Gough's arrival they had coped with the upheaval of having no solid sustained management leadership, and had succeeded in keeping the school together.

A teacher with years of service at Burnage told us:

"We had a 12 month period when everybody was acting. You needed to be a member of the actors' union, more or less. We had an acting headmaster; we had an acting head of lower school/deputy head; similar at Upper School; and we had two acting year heads as well. We had gone through four or five years of rather whirlwind change, which dragged us away from what was a very traditional set-up, and brought us more or less into the modern era, so to speak."

The CHAIRMAN:

Q. You think that Mr Marshall was instrumental in bringing that about before he left?

A. Yes, oh, very much so.

Q. From your point of view in a beneficial way?

A. Yes . . . from my point of view, (and) from the point of view of the school as a whole. There were inevitable hiccups, but nothing that we couldn't and didn't in actual fact cope with. Put in terms of attendance, participation, and school activities, put in terms of results at the end of the academic year publicly and within school, nothing untoward manifested itself at all. Then with the arrival of Dr Gough, as I said, more change was instituted in line with the policies that the Education Committee and the City Council were in favour of."

Resistance to Change

There is no doubt that Dr Gough's attempts to push forward the various policies met with resistance amongst the staff groups. There is no doubt either that, given the history of Burnage High School, its grammar school ethos, the length of time many of the teachers had served there, their traditional approaches to discipline and what they saw as the role of discipline in shaping an "academic" environment, such resistance could and should have been expected. Part of the management function in such a situation is to evaluate the contribution made to the well-being of the school as a whole by all the staff, including those who resist change, and seek to create a culture within which one appeals to the sense of professionalism and a commitment to teaching which most staff would claim. An effective management style could succeed in isolating those staff who insist that violence is an inevitable part of the culture of a boys school or who are openly and unapologetically racist; isolation not so much by management but by their peers.

The evidence we have suggests that the staff saw Dr Gough as wading in with a pocket full of policies and not entering into sufficient debate about the practice and staff morale implications of those policies. Some staff seem to have resisted out of cussedness and in protest against Dr Gough's style as much as against the policies themselves:

"One of the great difficulties in teaching is getting teachers to do things which they perceive as being articulated or formulated by administrators and people who are remote from classroom experience, and don't actually have to come and do the dirty work in getting it across to students. Yes, I accept the cynicism. I think the cynicism and rejection of management initiatives, probably reached a peak in the first round of anti-racist developments when the atmosphere in the school was almost electric. Because, staff would say that the intiatives were presented in a way that assumed everybody was racist, and that everybody would have to change. Whatever you say about whether people as professionals have a right to feel that way or not, that I felt was a fact. I think that people were very opposed to initiatives being taken because nobody on the staff wanted to be called a racist. If somebody is called a racist, they take that as being deeply offensive. That was the message that was being, in my opinion, very obviously transmitted.

But over the years, I would say actually over the last four years, I think staff have changed. I think people in the lower school now, I would speak with a greater degree of confidence about their commitment to change in all sorts of way. . . . I would attribute quite a lot of that to the influence of . . . (the) senior teachers there, . . . who worked very, very closely with the staff always, because we felt that this was what was needed; that people needed to be reassured about what they were doing; needed to be set an example; needed to be in close contact with management. We would often meet and talk about this, and we would do this."

Portrait of Ahmed Ullah, in the family album.

Ian Macdonald, Q.C., Chairing the Inquiry.

Courtesy of Manchester Evening News

The Inquiry Panel and staff at press launch. From left to right: Moira Suringar, Martin Lugsdin, Reena Bhavnani, Ian Macdonald, Lily Khan, Gus John, Marguerite Russell.

Ian Macdonald answering questions at Press Conference.

Burnage High School.
Courtesy of Manchester Evening News

Burnage High School Governors.
Left to right: Vice-Chair, Chair, Parent Governor.
Courtesy of Manchester Evening News

Burnage High School (Lower School).
Courtesy of Manchester Evening News

Corridors at Burnage High School.
Courtesy of Manchester Evening News

Arriving at School.

Courtesy of Manchester Evening News

Asian students 'on the march' against racism in schools.

Courtesy of Manchester Evening News

School students picket the Education Department at Crown Square.
Courtesy of Manchester Evening News

Police on guard at the gates of Burnage High School (Upper School) in
March 1987.
Courtesy of Manchester Evening News

The picture that emerges is that the majority of the staff "gave up" on Dr Gough, and felt he had done the same on them. His strategy then seemed to be to invest in a number of advocates of multi-culturalism/anti-racism, especially through Section 11 appointments, and to appoint new staff with an obvious or assumed commitment to taking those policies forward. We will return to the pivotal role of that front line group of staff presently.

Remote and Aloof

The second main issue had to do with Dr Gough's profile in the school, both in relation to the staff and to the student body. He is seen as being highly intelligent, incisive and quick, but rather aloof and retiring. A valued senior teacher who did a great deal to re-build the school community after Ahmed's murder had this to say:

> "The whole basis within a school depends on relationships. It depends on the tenor of relationships and mutual respect for a start, and also with involvement. Unless you were an absolutely brilliant bureaucrat with people who you can delegate to wonderfully, effectively, you cannot afford to distance yourself from the people with whom you work. That is where the whole relationship thing comes in. I think you have to be prepared to take criticism and to be shown to try the things you are advocating."

Dr Gough is seen as a remote figure who does not lead from the front. Staff, therefore, feel rightly or wrongly that a leadership vacuum has been created, but when the most competent and professional middle management staff step in to fill that vacuum, their efforts are not appreciated by senior management.

For example, the Head of First Year acts as an "ambassador" for Burnage to the feeder schools. We heard glowing reports from students, parents and Heads of feeder schools on the work that he has developed with them over the years. Two years ago he became permanent Head of First Year and ended the practice of following a year's intake through to the fifth year and then beginning at the first again. This new role enables him to assist primary teachers in understanding the first year work at Burnage, and in working with him to smooth the students' transition from primary to secondary. He teaches in the junior schools, and has meetings with parents both at the juniors and at Burnage. Burnage is very dependent on that member of staff because of its numbers, and in the period after Ahmed's murder his role became crucial. He needed to work overtime to counteract the bad press Burnage was receiving, and to allay the many fears and anxieties of parents of intending students. He deals with the annual intake of students:

"We were 240 at one time, and then 210. Last year we had around about 200, I think, and this year we have gone right down to 125.
Q. That is a fairly dramatic drop?
A. Yes. Actually, we did not expect as many as 125, but I worked very hard this year and spent an awful lot of time in junior schools and I was quite pleased in a way, if you want to put it like that, that we got as many as 125.

Despite this important work at a critical time for Burnage High, the Head of Year felt he had reason to be dissatisfied with the level of support he received from the Head and Deputy Head. The situation seems to be little different from a normal year. Meetings between Burnage and Heads of feeder schools are convened, but there is no prior briefing between Dr Gough and his "ambassador", and the Head of Year finds it:

"Quite embarrassing sometimes, not knowing what is on the agenda until the agenda is put in front of you, and sometimes being asked to speak on a certain subject not knowing that you are going to have to speak."

Discipline and Support for staff by senior management

Many staff talked to us of discipline at Burnage. However, it is clear that this issue relates to different teachers' expectations about education and learning, and how that links with sanctions. One staff member told us why he did not feel there was a discipline problem at Burnage:

"In working with ACS students, what other people would perceive as a discipline problem, perhaps I wouldn't, or people that I would work with wouldn't. I think it's obviously to do with different people's expectations, and it's also to do with how different people react to students. I'm sure that if people walked into my lesson some time, they would feel that I have got one hell of a discipline problem, because of the style that some my lessons might appear to outsiders to go along."

198

On the other hand, a teacher who has recently left feels that Burnage is a violent school, and standards of discipline have eroded. He mentions 10–20 fights which could take place in any one week.

A recurring theme in the evidence we received was the inconsistency in sanctions or the lack of sanctions. One member of staff responsible for supervising students at dinner time gave us descriptions of boys standing in front of staff, dropping their dinner trays full of crockery on the floor, pouring salt and pepper into other boys' drinks, and then taunting the staff about not being able to exclude them. That member of staff felt totally unsupported by the lack of a clear statement from management about the sanctions staff on lunch time duty could apply.

One further source of irritation was the fact that Mr X was seen as showing "preference" for Asian boys as opposed to Afro-Caribbean boys or white boys, by shaking hands with the former, and not with the two latter groups. The response of the Afro-Caribbean boys was not to bother, but the white boys would say:

"What have we got, Miss, that's catching?" You say 'Look, son don't worry about it.' Some of the boys then were saying "Is it because of the boy that was stabbed at this school?'"

Lack of communication and feed back about the students and general lack of communication is a recurring theme amongst staff who gave us evidence. This is particularly marked between Lower School and Upper School.

A senior teacher at Lower School, Jackie Hill, wholeheartedly supports the policy initiatives but feels also that there has been a lack of openness within the school as a whole:

"many staff complain that they are not fully informed of what is happening and I agree to some extent, because often I feel uninformed about events and plans. There is little opportunity for staff to express their views and feelings about the running of the school. Discipline is a key area where staff have previously complained of a lack of consistency and firmness. This was generally perceived as being the result of lack of direction/leadership from the Head."

Some staff perceive the failure to share information with them about students – done supposedly in the interests of the students – as undermining staff functions and responsibilities. Staff are concerned that far from helping to protect students, this practice may place the students at risk and could result in situations which staff find difficult to handle because they lack background knowledge. The following cases help to illustrate this and other points of criticism about Dr Gough's style of management.

(a) *Witnesses at Darren's trial*

Heads of Year told the inquiry that they had no knowledge of the names of the boys who were either going to give evidence at Darren Coulburn's trial or (after the trial) who had given evidence.

One Head of Year told us:

"I think it would have been quite crucial (to know the names), yes, because if I had known that some of them had to go to Court to give evidence, then I think form teachers should have known as well, and staff who taught them, because we would just like to have known because things like that can do strange things to 11-year-old boys."

The CHAIRMAN:

Q. You would want to know them in what capacity?

A. From my pastoral point of view.

Q. Do you think that all Year Heads should have known these boys, or just the Year Heads of the boys concerned?

A. Just the Year Heads of the boys concerned would have been quite sufficient.

Q. Although you were not told who the boys were, were you given any information by the senior staff at the school about arrangements made for those students to have any kind of counselling or support of any sort?

A. If that was taking place, I did not know anything about it, and a boy actually who was in my year, his parents came to see me towards the end of this last year asking me, 'could he go to another school because he was unhappy', and it was at that time that I found out that he had given evidence in Court, . . . that he was having nightmares, and that he hated coming to Burnage. I was totally unaware of that and, obviously, if I had been aware of that maybe at an earlier stage I could have helped and supported him . . . It was a good three to four months after the trial . . .

. . . In fact, on this occasion I think I actually made the first contact with the parents because this particular boy was causing problems. He was being naughty; he was being silly. He was not behaving in class; he was not doing his work.

It was not until the parents came in and said, 'Actually, he was involved in giving evidence, he has been having nightmares about it,

200

he does hate the place. That may give you some indication as to why he has been behaving unusually'.

Q. It may well have been that could have been sorted out very much earlier?

A. I would have thought so."

(b) *Informing other staff of Darren's conviction for arson*

The second incident, referred to in Chapter 2, concerned a memorandum sent by Darren's Head of Year informing his form teacher of the result of Darren Coulburn's trial for setting fire to the Art Block. At a Heads of Year meeting, Dr Gough suddenly announced that that information should have remained private, and suggested that staff should not pass on this sort of information to each other. Staff, however, felt that it was desirable to have this information so that Darren could be given some support, particularly if he became the subject of ridicule or teasing by other students. In any event, staff with pastoral responsibilities would wish to know this sort of thing.

(c) *An incident with a stanley knife*

The third incident concerned a boy who had stabbed another in the neck with a 'Stanley' knife. The injured boy needed to go to hospital and have two stitches to the wound. Staff understood that the boy who used the knife was going to be allowed back into school after a two-day suspension. The form teacher or Head of Year went to see the governors and expressed concern that the re-admission of that boy might lead to an escalation of the conflict, and possibly unpredictable consequences. At least one governor and two other teachers went to see Mr Moors to express their views, and eventually the boy was transferred to another school. One of the governors told us:

"I am sure that the other two people involved would agree that they had gone to see Mr Moors and tried to persuade him. There was no way I could prove that Mr Moors changed his mind on account of our protest.

Q. But either way, what that means is on a stabbing incident, where a student has stabbed another student . . . the initial impression that the staff got was that a decision had already been taken which they had to modify, rather than a special meeting being called? Do you see what I mean?

A. Yes.

Q. For example, on a serious incident like that, one might have anticipated that there would be an immediate special meeting with the year head, the form teacher, union representative and maybe even the Governors to discuss what action the school was going to take?

A. Yes.

Q. Obviously, there was no specific meeting like that set up?

A. No, . . . the only thing that I can say . . . is that I was worried enough that he might be let in and I thought that would be a bad move, and I went to see Mr Moors as soon as possible as a union representative."

(d) *Dealing with knives in school*

One incident which disturbed a number of teachers, concerns the Head's handling of the case of a boy found with a knife in school.

It was the middle of February 1987. Ahmed had been dead five months, and Darren had just been convicted of his murder by stabbing. A teacher was taking a fourth year lesson for an absent colleague when two students asked whether he knew that student X

"had been suspended because he'd brought a knife into school and was threatening somebody with it."

Since the teacher did not know student X he wrote his name down and told the two lads that he knew nothing about it.

At the end of the lesson he asked the Year Head whether the information he had was true. Her reaction rather surprised him. For instead of answering she simply looked at him. He concluded that she did not wish to talk about the matter, and so, not wanting to press it, he simply said:

"'I don't want you to say anything that you should not say. I have got this name on a piece of paper. Can you confirm that this boy brought a knife into school?'

and she just nodded . . . She was clearly shocked that I knew about it, and did not want to get involved in talking about it."

This teacher was concerned about the seriousness of the matter, about the Year Head's reaction and went to see a teacher governor. The teacher governor had not heard of the incident, but had taught the boy concerned for three years. She therefore went to see the year tutor about it. The year tutor confirmed the story without giving too many details. The teacher governor advised her, in her own interests, to make a report as quickly as possible, and also asked for a copy of the report.

202

A few days later, the Chair of governors 'phoned the teacher governor to say that she was "out of line asking for such a report (and) was putting the Head in a very difficult position".

Shortly afterwards, a meeting was called after school, involving Dr Gough, Mr Moors, the Chair and Deputy of Governors, two teacher governors and the teacher whom the fourth year boys had told. At that meeting, that teacher inquired about the boy who had been found with the knife. His recollection is that either Dr Gough or the Chair of Governors responded by asking how he knew about the incident. Eventually, the meeting was told that Mr Jamal was dealing with the matter in his capacity as governor.

The fourth year student concerned was Asian.

The teacher governor who had contacted the year tutor told us:

"As time went on I kept asking the year tutor what had happened to this boy, and she said that she did not know, and that she had repeatedly asked staff senior to her, and there was no satisfactory answer. During June, . . . I was at a meeting with the Chair of Governors, and I mentioned it to her again, and she appeared to have forgotten about it. On the Monday after half term a meeting was arranged between the parents of this boy and other boys who were concerned to meet . . . From February to June, this boy had no tuition, the staff did not know about it, and the governors were not told."

We heard evidence later that the boy had been readmitted to school round about September 14th, 1987. No one seemed to know how he came to be away from school between February and the middle of September, nor precisely what was meant by Mr Jamal 'dealing with it'. As far as the teacher governors, year tutor, and governors were concerned, the boy had not been officially suspended because the matter had not been dealt with at a governors' meeting, and they had had no notification from Dr Gough or any of the deputies concerning this boy's suspension.

One teacher govenor recalls that it was in July 1987 at the last governors meeting before the summer vacation that this matter was raised with governors for the first time, but, not raised by the Head or a member of senior management. The teacher governor told us:

"At the end of each meeting, in . . . the confidential part, information is usually given about boys who are suspended, and information was given about one or two boys, and then I asked about this particular boy, and I think the answer (that came from Dr Gough) was, 'Oh yes, I forgot'.".

Dr Gough then gave evidence to the meeting to the effect that a meeting had been held with the boy's parent and that his sister had had a lot to do with him. Governors were therefore given information only after a teacher governor, with inside knowledge had asked about the boy.

The following extract from the transcript further illustrates the strange way in which Dr Gough dealt with this matter.

Q. Once you raised the matter and the Head responded, was there any further discussion by other members present apart from yourself?

A. I think somebody must have asked, 'What is this about' and I said that I was rather concerned that this boy had had no tuition from February, and this was the July meeting.

Teacher governor B: I confirm that one other governor did ask why he had been out of school so long, and that was the first that she had heard of it.

Q. Did the meeting ask for any fuller report on the matter; from the Head or anybody else?

A. We got the impression that it was being dealt with.

Exempt from Causing Harm

If Dr Gough's failure to inform staff and Governors about the incident was perceived as a serious matter by teachers and governors, his attitude to their concern about knife carrying is seen as being even more bizarre.

The teacher governor told us that in addition to talking with the year tutor after she had been told about the incident, she also went to see Dr Gough. On mentioning the incident to him, she alleges that Dr Gough went into another room and came back with what looked like a table knife, he poked it into his stomach and said, "Look, they are just making mountains out of molehills, and this just could not do any damage at all". She was not told and had no way of knowing whether the knife whose 'harmlessness' Dr Gough was demonstrating was the same knife that student X had brought into school.

She found Dr Gough's reaction unbelievable, and wondered why, "if it was such a simple incident", the boy had not been in school.

The year tutor later reported to her that in answer to numerous requests from the fourth year boys to be told what was happening to student X, she had eventually sent two boys to Dr Gough. They had reported back to the year tutor alleging that Dr Gough had shown them the knife, and poked it into his stomach to show that it would not do any damage.

Dr Gough was present when these allegations were made, and did not then or subsequently deny that they were correct.

It seems extraordinary to us, therefore, that a group of students who clearly understood that one of their year had brought a knife into school to threaten violence, could be told by their headteacher that that was not a serious matter because the knife was incapable of doing damage.

In the light of Ahmed's murder, Darren's conviction and sentence, and the March events at Burnage High School, we consider Dr Gough to have acted with an insensitivity that ill-becomes someone in his position at that time.

Report at Your Peril

The teacher governor, perfectly legitimately in our opinion, had suggested to the year tutor that she should do a report of the incident. When, two or three days later she had asked for a copy, the year tutor informed her that she could not have one because when Dr Gough had seen the report, he had asked for all copies of it. As far as the teacher governor knew, no other members of staff had seen the report except perhaps senior management. The teacher governor understood from the year tutor that Dr Gough was so furious that she had written the report that she (the year tutor) refused to have any meetings with him unless her union representative was with her.

At the end of the teacher governor's meeting with Dr Gough about the incident, he had requested her to go and see the year tutor, to say that he was not angry with her, and that it was quite all right for her to go to see him on the normal everyday school business.

Apart from her concern at Dr Gough seeking to involve her in this way rather than dealing with the year tutor directly, the teacher governor was also concerned that Dr Gough had chosen to enlist the support of the Chair of Governors without sharing information openly with the staff and the rest of the governing body. The Chair of Governor's message to her was "you have no right making this your business. You're undermining the Head." The teacher governor was not told what Dr Gough had said to the Chair of Governors. He spoke to her, to the year tutor and to the Chair of Governors separately, and then asked each to pass messages to the other. There was no open discussion of any issue in any group, and no sharing of information, not even with the governors. There are clear parallels between Dr Gough's handling of this particular incident, and the aftermath of Darren's trial for arson to the Art Block.

The Governors' View

It is obvious to the Chair and Deputy Chair of Governors that there is something consistent about Dr Gough's method of management. The Chair of Governors, commenting on staff complaints that Dr Gough created antagonisms and polarisation, had this to say:

> ". . . To say that he actually adopted this policy and he had thought it through . . . I think will not be justified. I think it is his style, to be perfectly honest though. He deals very much like that, in my experience of him over a period of time. There is no reason in some ways why you shouldn't, but at Burnage it can exacerbate things at times . . . He deals on a one to one basis, and people go away thinking one thing as a result, and then he will see somebody else. He won't necessarily say something that is not true, but I think that nobody knows what has been said in a group. I think in Burnage, most importantly, would be this need to have the right number of people there when a particular issue arises so that they know what has been said and agreed as opposed to, 'I will talk to this one and talk to that one' and so on. It keeps them in control of the situation. It makes others feel insecure, and to a certain extent this is true of the management team itself, and it is something (the Deputy Chair) and I have persistently tried to persuade him to do differently; he should use his senior management team more than he does, and as a team."

Dr Glaisner:

> "On this business of being manipulative, it seemed to be an instinct with him . . . If I have been at a meeting with (the Chair of Governors) and he knows about it . . . he would get on the 'phone at home and bend my ear for half an hour or an hour talking about it. You find towards the end of the period you are coming back to the questions he started with that you thought you had deflected him on, and he knows you have not given him the right answers. He would go round and round . . . He is really very skilful."

Diana Keeley:

"As you get to know him you know what he is doing. I will give you a small example . . . The Asian boy who broke into the Art Block with Darren, transferred at his parents' request to 'Walmer'. In about June or July Gerry (Gough) sent me a letter saying that (the boy's) parents had asked if he could be re-admitted to Burnage because he had not settled at 'Walmer', and could I give this matter my consideration. My immediate response was to feel, 'No, I do not think we can re-admit him. In different times of course we could, but at the moment that would be adding something additional that we really don't need'. This is one of the problems with Gerry, you know. At a time when it would be most sensible to keep Burnage on a lower profile he won't. He will keep it at a high profile because he feels you must go on as you would in any case. Anyway, I saw him . . . and said to him, 'Look, I really have reservations about this but we will discuss it'. He said, 'Oh, I couldn't get you on the 'phone at the time I wrote that letter but I spoke to Ben (Glaisner) about it, and Ben is quite supportive of him coming back.' I said to him, 'Gerry, don't do this to me. I know what you are at. If Ben supports then all right, but I don't. Obviously we will discuss it at the Governors' meeting.' "

Divide to Rule

We heard a good deal of evidence about "moles" and about "spy rings", and about deep-seated mistrust. Various witnesses suggested that what cripples relationships and obstructs staff cohesiveness at Burnage, above all else, is the manipulation practised by the Head-teacher. This manipulation, we are told, leads to certain staff being favoured more than others, and to inter-staff rivalries and antagonisms.

Burnage staff indicated to us that they have lived with this situation for some years, and have given evidence to external assessors on both the Governors' investigation and the school inspection, and after each review their situation deteriorates.

One of the reasons for the persistence of the bad odour in the school is given as Dr Gough's lack of directness:

"I know, it happened to me. He would talk to a person as though, 'you are the one person I can really talk to', and then try and talk about other people and set colleagues against each other. This works, particularly on younger, more impressionable people because he can make people feel very important and that their opinions are very important."

A senior teacher described the nature and extent of the manipulation as follows:

"It became apparent that the staff felt that . . . that some people were going to the Head and telling tales. One of the ways that it affected multi-cultural initiatives was that many staff certainly felt that some of the Section 11 teachers were being used improperly . . . to find out what was said in the staff room and what was said in the confidence of meetings and put it back to the Head. It was not that we were anti-racist, but they were nick-named M15, and some of them were really good and enormously helpful and had skills that we did not have. But one thing we stated was that there were a group of staff, perhaps only eight or ten, but it had a very corrosive effect and a very divisive effect, and that stopped the staff working together to attack the problems on a whole school basis.

"Similarly with multi-cultural meetings, which I and a lot of the staff went to. A lot of people became a bit disenchanted with them because after meetings, or even towards the end of meetings, there would be talk about other colleagues that was verging on the unprofessional, verging on tittle-tattle, and you just heard that some of them had gone to the pub afterwards and talked about staff who were not there. It seemed to establish a small clique. There had been persistent criticism of the Head's management style, and he had established a small clique, who claimed to have special access and perhaps a special social relationship, and this produced the feeling that people were not treated in an even-handed way, and that is really the staff feeling I am trying to convey. Certainly it has been expressed in meetings."

It is clear that at the time of the governors' review, the review group felt they would be examining the conflict caused by resistance to Dr Gough's policies. The governors, nevertheless, found that staff criticisms of the management style of Dr Gough and Mr Moors was based on genuinely held sentiments.

Some of the difficulties the governors identified were that Dr Gough does not involve himself sufficiently with the staff and in the life of the school. The governors also commented on the tendency of Mr Moors to write notes and leave them for staff rather than speaking to them personally.

The way the senior management functions would suggest that they see the conflicts and the existence of the various camps within the staff as fixed. The three senior teachers at Lower School told us they felt they needed to take some action to unify the school and get it functioning. No lead was given by senior management, and Mr Moors was effectively spending most of his time at Upper School during that period.

In fact Alan Hill, at Lower School, strongly feels that Lower School almost functions on its own as an independent organisation:

"Mrs Hill and I have said, "Look, we have got to get this place running". We hold regular staff meetings with the senior staff – not including the Head or Mr Moors. We set up – in many ways it is quite amazing because we say set up, the rules for the children; we set up the rules for the staff; we set up the systems for the misdemeanours; we set up the system for duties for all the supervision; we talk to the staff about what we want of their behaviour and of the behaviour of students in classrooms. We do this almost completely independently of anybody else. We do it because we simply feel that it has to be done."

Resolving this divide amongst schools, amongst staff would not be easy according to Alan Hill:

"I think I feel the antagonisms at the moment to be greater than they have ever been, and I feel that these mutually hostile groups have to be in some way broken up, moved around, either by moving staff into other schools, or by moving administrators. I would say that the divisions are pretty well irreconcilable.

The governors were concerned that the Head seemed to be unaware of the role he needed to play in breaking down those antagonisms."

"We know there are people opposed to the policies themselves, and they disguise their opposition and use their personal differences between the Head and themselves as the main plank. We thought we would perceive that, and we did, but we also saw that there was justification as well. You don't insult people if you want them on your side. If they are in error and you are in a managerial position you explain and you persuade, and you are not rude to them, and so on. That is the kind of thing we discovered, and that is what lies behind much of what is there. I think it rather shook him that we actually saw these other things, and we just didn't see the stars that he pointed out to us."

The General Secretary of the NAS/UWT for the whole of Manchester felt that he had an overview of all the schools in Manchester. He believes that the policies and ethos of Burnage school are fine in theory, but the staff felt that they do not actually work; that they are not actually put into practice, or if they are, there is not sufficient communication between staff involved, so that everybody knows that they work. In fact he goes further on management style:

> "I believe the situation at Burnage to be unique. I have never before experienced the deep rooted mistrust, almost to the extent of fear, amongst members of staff. I have never before experienced the lack of confidence in management. I have had dealings in schools where there have been disputes with management, or between different members of staff, but never in any other case has there been the long lasting effect."

A senior teacher at Lower School echoes these sentiments in relation to staff reactions to every initiative:

> "Unless there is a means for resolving these antagonisms, the ability of the school to move forward will remain severely impaired."

Where do Section 11 staff come in all this? In Chapter 19 we described how they have become marginalised within the school in terms of status and of ability to influence the content of the school curriculum. Now they found themselves caught up in the cross-fire between Dr Gough and the section of the staff who were out of sympathy with his style of management.

What has been their experience?

One member of the Section 11 staff, who had been instrumental in developing work directly with students and across departments, talked about being treated as unimportant by subject heads, usually based at Upper School:

> "Even when in my second year more staff joined Section 11, and one brought her Scale 3 post across schools to promote us as a department, I was still told that it would be better if I did not attend a music meeting, and for the Scale 3 to go instead, as it might offend the Head of Music if a Scale 1 was present from the Section 11 staff."

Section 11 staff were particularly vulnerable to the attitudes and stances of other staff towards senior management. New Section 11 teachers met a hostile atmosphere, and needed to learn pretty quickly about the various "camps" within the staff group and what they represented.

"On joining the school it was clear that there was a divide – some staff identified multi-cultural, anti-racist and "child centred" education as being the focal point of that division. It appeared that staff new to the school were instantly aligned with one group or another, arguably on the basis of a philosphical disagreement. Lower school staff room I found very unfriendly. A few weeks into my first term, a teacher there whom I had never previously met, asked me what I taught. I explained in a friendly manner, and silence "fell around". She said "your lot are unpopular" and closed the conversation. A few people didn't speak to me at all for 18 months.

Partly because we initially reported directly to the Deputy Head-teacher, some staff viewed us with suspicion. In view of the attitude of some of the middle management, often *junior staff needed to be and were supported by and supportive of members of the senior management. That caused resentment.* Other staff who were also committed to child centred, anti-racist policies were accused of 'sinister' collaboration." (Our emphasis).

Those experiences, especially at the hands of middle management, led certain Section 11 staff to adopt an attitude of working with a few teachers whom they found supportive, and concentrating on developing relationships with and supporting students.

"I came to identify more and more with the students who were appreciative of any interest shown in them. The black students who shared their experiences of racism with us and the white students who wanted to examine their society. They offered the possibility and allowed us to enter their youth culture, to provide an arena where racism could at least be challenged on some level. I worked for some time in the youth club attached to Burnage. This helped also. *It was the students' friendship and support which encouraged me to continue.* (Our emphasis). I wish I could have said the same for the staff.

That same member of staff was concerned about the effect of the divisions amongst the staff group on the student body. And while she and another Section 11 staff member see some changes occurring, as compared to 1984, she still feels that the staff are so caught up in their internecine struggles that they fail to encourage students to develop. Students are not seen as people with needs or having the potential to have some say and effect in regard to their own learning. This is a serious indictment of a management style which sets teacher against teacher and thereby undermines the child centred approach to education

211

and the emphasis placed on anti-racism by the management of the school.

Conclusions

1. The management style at Burnage High School, as exercised by Dr Gough and Mr Moors, would have rendered that school virtually unmanageable but for the professionalism and commitment of a large number of able and dedicated staff. We did not hear the same volume of complaint about Mr Hewitt, and he was never singled out in the same way as the other two. However, he was part of the senior management team, just as they were, and he was reponsible, so he told us, for monitoring Darren Coulburn after the art block fire, and for handling the events of March. We, therefore, take the view that he and the other two senior managers must stand or fall together.

2. We were impressed with the way many of the staff below the top level gave their evidence and with the skill and resoluteness with which they managed a number of crises. Such execution of duty is in our view all the more commendable because it was done in the absence of any involvement, lead, or support from the most senior managers of the school.

3. One of Dr Gough's most important functions as the Head and overall manager of the school and its staff is to lead, and to be seen to be leading. With heads of lower and upper schools and a number of senior teachers, who have demonstrated a high degree of competence, professionalism and management skills, as well as with two deputy heads, an astute manager would have little difficulty in utilising his or her staff and building and managing a vibrant school community.

4. The volatility that has existed at Burnage High School amongst staff and students alike results not from some invisible cosmic force, some externally generated influences or some bad hangover from the pre-Gough era, but from the way that school is managed and run.

5. In any body of staff a manager will find conservative people, progressive people, racist people, awkward people, people who have a tendency to bigotry, people who have and sustain a commitment to good practice, and people who are unabashed by mediocrity or sheer bad practice. All of those people expect a new manager to nail

her or his colours to the mast and declare what their bottom line is. The manager establishes, in other words, the parameters within which leadership is to be provided, within which a certain standard of professional conduct is to be expected, and within which decisions are to be taken about matters which affect the ability of management and staff to function effectively. In our view this was not done clearly or effectively at Burnage.

6. Leaving aside the 'bottom line' on corporal punishment, violence by staff against students, racist conduct, and the general orientation towards an anti-racist, child-centred regime in Burnage High, Dr Gough and his immediate senior management colleagues seem to have overlooked the fact that there is more to manage in any school than racism, crucial though combatting racism obviously is.

7. The categories of, on the one hand, 'old fashioned' 'conservative', 'traditional grammar school', 'change resistant', and 'racist', and on the other 'liberal', 'young', 'progressive', 'child-centred', 'mostly women', and 'anti-racist', have become fixed and static in two dominant camps, with some people floating and not resting easily in either.

8. The evidence we have is that rather than breaking up these categories and reconciling those rigid camps, Dr Gough and Mr Moors particularly have tended to view them as those who are for and those who are against, cultivating and nurturing people in one, and failing to appreciate sufficiently the skills of the people in the other.

9. The 'ambassador' Head of 1st Year, and the black teacher who had to handle a double tragedy, as we shall see, were, in our view, insufficiently supported by those senior managers. No one expects the Head and his deputies to be in everybody's pocket, particularly when there are competent senior teachers about. There are times, however, when managers have to *be there and be seen*, giving support, saying 'we value what you're doing. In what ways can we help?'

10. At many crucial stages in the events this Inquiry has been investigating, the views and advice of senior teachers, Heads of Year and form teachers have been undervalued, or disregarded by senior management, but at the same time they have had to deal with the consequences of decisions taken higher up.

    Let us recall a few of the critical ones:

    a) The aftermath of Darren's trial for burning down the art block: informing the form teacher of the sentence he received in the Juvenile Court, dealing with the school governors and obtaining

213

a decision to keep Darren in the school, and making a decision to monitor Darren's progress without informing any staff below the level of deputy head.

b) Dealing with the Stanley knife incident.

c) Dealing with the boy found with the table knife.

d) The manipulation of staff and the consequent arousal of suspicion by them, one of another.

e) The leadership vacuum created in Lower School which resulted in the senior teachers virtually declaring the Lower School independent of Upper School.

f) The question of the examinations of those students kept out of Upper School.

But the story does not end there. It has been suggested to us by a number of witnesses that the shortcomings of the management style can and should be overlooked in view of the clear and strong commitment of Dr Gough and Mr Moors to promoting child centred anti-racist and anti-sexist policies in the school. If they have to leave, the plea goes, the anti-racist teachers remaining in the school will be at the mercy of the hard-core of bigots who will then come out of their closet and destroy the modest progress achieved under Dr Gough. This argument was presented attractively and forcefully to us and we have had to consider it very carefully. In the end, however, we felt we had to reject it, because (i) it ignores the failure of the "liberal" regime to recognise or deal with the racial polarisation which took place in Burnage following Ahmed's death, (ii) it overlooks the treatment of the white students in the aftermath of the March events and the possibility of further serious racial disorder occurring and (iii) it leaves out of account the perceptions and experiences of the black teachers at Burnage. To these we now turn.

CHAPTER 22

Managing Burnage: Part 4

Black Teachers in an Anti-Racist School

We noted in Chapter 1 that 35% of Burnage's student population are black, as are two members of the full-time teaching staff, and four part-time or support staff. We have given evidence so far in this report about the extent of racism at Burnage amongst staff and students. This section of the report looks at the experience those black staff have had of Burnage, and the support they receive from the management of the school.

In the chapter on the Management of the Tragedy (chapter 8), we noted that a black teacher had asked to be moved from Burnage after Ahmed's murder, and was transferred to another school. We received no direct evidence from that teacher, and the background evidence we have points to the fact that he found the school a difficult place in terms of his experiences of management, staff and students, and was particulary distressed at the way the school handled the stabbing incident and the aftermath of the murder.

However, we did receive evidence from other black teachers at Burnage, and, in the light of all the issues raised so far in this report, we find that evidence sufficiently disturbing to warrant a separate section. In each case we have disguised the names of the teachers by using false names or initials. In a school with a majority of white staff, a few black teachers stand out. In a school with a minority of black students and a majority of white staff, black and white students come to have expectations of black staff, and display a wide range of attitudes towards them. In a school with a clear commitment to multi-culturalism and anti-racism, the way in which black staff experience the school is an important yardstick by which to measure the relevance and effectiveness of the anti-racist or multi-cultural policy.

What do the experiences of the black staff at Burnage tell us?

1. *Ms A K's Story*

Ms A K has taught for many years in schools in and around Manchester. Among those schools have been "difficult schools where racism has been a problem inside the school". She was deeply affected by Ahmed's murder, and told us that after the initial shock she found herself becoming more and more disturbed by the authorities' handling of the situation, and concerned for the continuing safety of other boys in the school. After the court case she made it her business to go and visit the Ullah family. She told us that "sharing their grief made me determined to ensure that what happened to Ahmed does not happen to any other child in this school".

Ms A K expressed concern about the adverse publicity the school was receiving, which in her view was not being countered forcefully enough. Consequently, "the staff and other students at this school are being branded as callous racists. This is a slander which goes against my three years experience at this school". Part of her concern was that Dr Gough had not done enough at the time to refute those claims. Her statement to us claimed that in answer to a question by a parent asking him to counter the newspaper reports that were rife at the time, Dr Gough publicly stated that the facts surrounding the murder were still sub-judice because of the Macdonald Inquiry. The anguish that staff suffered and the difficulties they had coping with Ahmed's murder were accentuated in her view by the minimal information given to staff and the strict imposition of the sub judice rule, which "meant that more than one of my colleagues thought that it had happened outside school right up to the day of Darren's trial, and . . . were shocked when the trial revealed that it had taken place inside the school".

"Nobody spoke of the incident, there was deep confusion, staff felt very bitter, but were not organised in any way to respond independently of the Head and the Governors. The morale in the school was extremely low – police continued to patrol outside the school in uniform, when asked why by teachers who were concerned about the effect of this on children, they said they were there in case there was a race riot!"

Ms A K suggests that with the very irresponsible press reports and the inevitable response from the community, "the children (were) under a very great pressure to actually be divided along racial lines".

She concludes:

"The situation was one where there were very great dangers of the people being divided, either on racial lines, or staff against parents or students against staff. The action of the City Council, and the Headteacher at this point exacerbated this situation, it was only the maturity and cool headedness of staff, students and parents that upheld the unity of the people involved".

As a concerned teacher, sorely distressed at Ahmed's death and sharing his family's agony, Ms A K felt that she was not assisted by the management of the school in understanding the tragedy, its background, and what the school itself needed to do. As someone with experience of racism in schools and in the community, she was appalled at the way every other concern seemed to have been displaced by the school's preoccupation with the 'racist' nature of the incident.

Although the school management's handling of the murder and its aftermath affected Ms A K in an intensely personal way, she was not directly constrained by their actions during her time at Burnage High School in the way the next witness was.

2. Mr Gill's Story

Mr Gill is a teacher of music within Manchester's Ethnic Music Department. He visits a large number of junior and secondary schools around Manchester and teaches Indian music.

Mr Gill can spend anything from half an hour to half a day in any one school. On being allocated a school, he would normally be introduced to the staff by the Head or Deputy Head, and staff would know that he is a part-time staff member or visiting tutor. He would expect to work closely with the Head of the Music department, and to teach Indian music in the context of the overall work of that department. As a teacher he had a general criticism to make about the schools' approach to Indian music. In India, he argues, music is not about playing instruments. The creation of the music is linked to what the music is an expression of, and the playing of the instruments has something to do with the social context in which the musical activity arises. In the schools he visits, however, no attempt is made, in the majority of cases, to give the students an appreciation of the country, the social customs, and the background to the development of the music. Rather than music departments working in this way, his experience is that some schools are " . . . not welcoming at all – I was left to find my own rooms, carpets, chalk etc. I found that in some schools not being allowed to attend the music classes is used as a punishment . . . for some of the children".

When he first started at Burnage he got a lot of support and "people were very helpful". And then he discovered that he was being sent

Bengali-speaking students whose command of English was poor: "These boys were in fact channelled to me", he told us "because the teachers just didn't want to have them in their lessons because the teachers couldn't cope. The boys would end up at the back of the class".

Before the music department at Burnage was re-organised, the head of department was responsible for music in the whole school. Now he is assisted by a Scale I teacher. But their time-table is such that Mr Gill and they never meet and never speak to one another:

"It was interesting because about four weeks before the end of the term the head of music made a point of coming to see me to see if it was possible to organise some kind of music for one of the Eid parties that they were going to have at the end of the term, which I felt was rather insensitive . . . I had not seen that fellow the whole of the year . . . it was just – well, what could I say? . . . It is just another blatant example of ignorant tokenism.

Q. So you left him none the wiser about the relationship between Eid and Indian music?
A. No, No".

If the work that teacher did was not integrated within the work of the music department, how did he find students and staff reacting to him as a person coming into the school for half a day a week?

Mr Gill told us his position in the school is marginal and low status and he finds the atmosphere there to be "very hostile":

" . . . Even in taking the key (to my classroom) out of the office the action is as if you in effect can be caught out . . . the only time I was spoken to by the office staff was when they had actually thought I had walked out of the office without signing the little book for the keys.

"J . . . another music teacher, and I were walking around the school looking for various members of staff to chat to. Whilst we were walking round other members of staff were walking round and still, you know, they wouldn't acknowledge that we were there. No 'good morning', nothing. You know, we could walk straight past people and not be acknowledged. 'I would go into the office, collect my key, and disappear to my room . . . the prefabricated little room in the corner of the playground. I would spend the whole morning there. The first group (of students) would be waiting for me, but other groups would then turn up throughout the day . . . The atmosphere is so bad that I never go into Burnage for a break. I prefer to have the boys right through. In fact I do it on many occasions. They play music right through the break".

In relation to Ahmed's murder, Mr Gill told us that he was shocked by the whole affair. The first time he went into the school after the murder he felt he needed to talk to someone about it. It was the Monday after the killing, but no one said anything to him about it, how the school was dealing with it, how it was affecting the students he was going to be teaching, or anything. He did not receive any of the bits of paper that had been passed to full time staff in the interim, because he does not have a pigeon hole in the school, and in any event he does not go into the staff room.

Q. "So, do you not get any communication about what is happening?"
A. "Nothing; absolutely nothing. I mean, if I spend half a day in a school, I would like to know what is happening in that school".

That Monday morning he could not concentrate on his work. He felt as though the school was trying to pretend the murder had not taken place. He could not even find the Section II staff he would normally talk to.

"The boys had actually mentioned it themselves; my own group of boys. I quizzed them actually; I tried to find out what had happened that day, and they said, 'Really we are not supposed to tell you; we have been told not to tell you; we have been told not to discuss it with anybody'."

Mr Gill left the school at the end of his session that day, and was driving away when he felt so disturbed at the apparent normality in the place, less than one week after the murder, that he turned arund and went back to the school. He walked around until he met two teachers with whom he shared his feelings.

As a peripatetic teacher, Mr Gill suffers constantly from racial abuse by students. He told us he has been regularly spat upon by students from floors above ground level when he has been walking around the school. He has been called names, pelted with conkers, and with snowballs by menacing groups of students, and been generally subjected to humiliation.

Students are reluctant to help him carry his musical instruments through the school because they are ridiculed when doing so.

For Mr Gill himself, the most distressing incident at Burnage was when he had been "walking through the school with the sitar case, and there was a group of boys in the door. One had said to the other, 'Oh, that 's a fucking big vibrator', and the other boy in reply said, 'yes, his wife must have a big cunt'."

The boys concerned were 12–13 years old. This incident occurred when the Poundswick issue was still not resolved, and Burnage teachers were giving support to their Poundswick colleagues. Mr Gill complained to a Senior Member of staff, and the way the incident was dealt with led Mr Gill to think that: " . . . if that [Poundswick] situation was looked at in a similar light to my treatment by this boy at Burnage, similar things would have happened because it was quite strong and quite abusive, the language that that boy used".

For taking the trouble to complain, Mr Gill, "got a pathetic written apology; a two line apology", given in the presence of two senior members of staff.

> Q. "What was the wording of the apology?
> A. It was to the effect that he was sorry that he had said it and it wouldn't, happen again.
> Q. Did any senior member of staff talk to you about the incident and about your feelings in relation to such conduct?
> A. Not really; it was just a very apologetic excuse really for this boy's behaviour.

The Chairman:
> Q. What would you have liked to have happend?
> A. I would have liked to have gone into great discussion, great detail, with his parents as to what he had said.
> Q. Do you know if his parents were informed at all?
> A. They were informed by letter. Now, as to whether they were informed as to what the boy had said, I don't know.
> Q. Were they brought into the school?
> A. That again I don't know.
> Q. So you were not told?
> A. I wasn't told. There was no follow-up from that.
> Q. Was that boy ever part of your music classes?
> A. No, not before or after."

A general problem Mr Gill sees is that:
> "teachers – children in schools really see [him and other peripatetic music staff] as visitors and not, sort of, having definite links with the schools, and so they think they can get away with it. It is a horrible situation because we never really feel that we fit in.
> Q. Presumably if the students saw the staff identifying more with you, or could identify you as part of the staff group . . .

A. That would change the attitudes . . . [their attitudes would alter] I am sure; of course they would.

As a means of changing attitudes, Mr Gill has suggested to Burnage that he be incorporated in to the preparation of an assembly, so that he and the students he teaches could actually contribute to an assembly. This is something he has done successfully in other schools.

" . . . I have been working with small groups of children in schools and they have got to a . . . particular playing standard where they can . . . do a little performance. I feel it is important that I can go along and perhaps do a little chat about the instruments, about the music, the background of the music, and present this particular group who are proficient in playing, which I am sure is more approachable to children rather than adults coming in and performing".

Mr Gill's evidence was that he had made that suggestion two years ago to Lesley Aisthorpe, the Section 11 department head, who told him it was a good idea but would need time to organise. Nothing materialised. He repeated the suggestion the following year, but still nothing had come of it.

3   Mr Sharif's Story

Mr Sharif is a peripatetic Urdu teacher and has taught, part-time, at Burnage High School for some years. He is one of a group of eight part-time and full-time staff who make up the community languages team of the Equal Opportunity/Ethnic Minorities Team. Although the Inspector of Modern Languages within the Manchester Schools' Inspectorate includes Urdu among the modern languages, it is not taught as a modern language in most Manchester schools. Like the peripatetic ethnic music team, the Urdu teachers 'float in and out' of schools and conduct classes in varying kinds of accommodation, and then move on. They are not part of the Modern Languages Department and are not identified with it either by students or staff.

Because the Urdu class is seen as a strange activity that takes place outside main-stream teaching, something 'for them', the status of the language, the class, the teacher and the students is very low in most people's eyes.

Mr Sharif reported the incident as follows:

"Before I opened the door of room 52, I asked the boys to stand in a line. I went in first and the boys entered one by one while I was standing near the door. I noticed that three boys, who were not members of that class and had never attended my lessons before, entered the room with their heads lowered down. I asked them, 'who are you?' They did not respond and sat at the tables at the back. I saw them giggling. One of them covered his face with the front portion of his coat and the other two put their arms across their faces. It was clear that they were full of mischief and wanted to disrupt the lesson. I asked them to stand up, but they kept sitting. I went to them, I caught two of them from the collars of their coats behind their necks and forced them to stand up and leave the room. I said, 'Why have you come here? You will find me a different teacher from what you think'. I left their collars. Now they started to swear at me and two of them threatened me and said, 'we will get you'. When they went out of the room I asked the class if anybody knew these boys. Just then I noticed that another member of staff (Mr X) was coming towards the door, who had seen the three boys and perhaps the incident also. He said that he knew these boys and wrote the names of the boys on a piece of paper for me. He also asked if he should report it to (the Head of Year), and ask him to come to me. I said, 'Not during the lesson, I will go to him at the end of the lesson'. After some time Mr Moors came to me. I briefed him about the incident. He asked me if I was alright. I told him that I was breathless at the time, but now I was alright. I realised that the case had been reported to Mr Moors and that I need not go to (the Head of Year) after that".

The case had indeed been reported to Mr Moors, the Deputy Head, not by the Head of Year or any other member of staff, but by the boys themselves. This is what they told Mr Moors:

Boy 'A'
"W and S invited us to go into the classroom. We were about to sit down ('B', 'C' and myself) when the teacher came over to us. He didn't say anything he just got hold of us by the neck and collar. He swung me around and broke this chain round my neck. 'C' got away and I got hold of a desk and knocked it over so that the teacher could not follow me. Then we went into the park between the two French annexes. I ought to have been in French. Then I came here to tell you".

Boy 'B'
"We went into the classroom to tell Irfan something. We sat down at the back of the class to tell him. The teacher just came up to us and

pulled us up by the collar/neck. See the scratch I have on the side of my neck. The teacher didn't say anything to us before it happened. I didn't shout at him, well I might have shouted after the incident had happened. Then we went into the park and came to tell you".

Boy 'C'
"K.C. waved to us so we went in and went over to his desk. The Urdu teacher said, 'What are you doing here?' He came over and just kicked and punched them ('A' and 'B') and really battered them. He pulled a chair over as he went on kicking them. I got away without him touching me and went with the others into the park. The other two were crying. 'B' said, 'I'm going home. I'm not having a teacher hitting me'. Then we came to see you".

All three boys were white. They clearly had no business in that class, and one of them even admits that he 'ought to have been in French'. Their accounts of what happened, especially that of 'C', are as malicious as their original purpose in joining the class.

Mr Sharif was well known in the school as a highly respected person within his community, an Imam at the Mosque, and a quiet and dignified teacher. This came over, when he gave evidence to the Inquiry. The senior management of the school would regard as totally absurd the suggestion that he was prone to violence or that he was inclined to manhandle students now and then.

Given that background and those accounts of the event, how did the senior management of the school respond?

Mr Moors interviewed each student separately and their statements were recorded. One boy showed Mr Moors a necklace which he claimed he wore around his neck and which, according to him, Mr Sharif had broken in the scuffle. Another boy showed Mr Moors scratch marks on his neck which he claimed had been caused by Mr Sharif in the scuffle.

As soon as he had taken the boys' accounts Mr Moors went to see Mr Sharif who told him what happened. Mr Moors asked him to come and see him at the end of the lesson. Mr Sharif did not go.

The following day, Tuesday February 10th, the mothers of two of the boys went to the school. A note in the Education Department's file describes their visit as follows:

"They were very irate. They spoke of prosecuting Mr Sharif for assault and they also made remarks such as 'if any of ours had done it, it would be different'. This Mr Moors took to be an indication that they felt he was protecting Mr Sharif because he was Asian".

223

Mr Moors arranged a meeting with the parents hoping that Mr Sharif would be present at it. He also spoke to Mr Sharif about his interview with the students, and suggested that Mr Sharif met the parents and explained what had happened in the class. If that were done it was felt that the parents would be reluctant to take out a prosecution. Mr Moors also suggested that Mr Sharif contact his union. Then Mr Moors met Mr Hewitt, and they decided that Mr Hewitt should handle the interview with the parents and Mr Sharif because he had known 'A''s mother for a long time.

In fact, Mr Sharif did not meet Mr Hewitt or the parents as had been agreed, as Mr Moors was later to explain in a note to Roy Jobson, the Senior Assistant Education Officer.

"I met with Mr Sharif on Friday February 13th just before he was due to meet with the parents. The purpose of the meeting was to stress my confidence in him and to make it clear that in any expression of regret he might make to the parent, he should not apologise since the parents were intending prosecution and this might prejudice his position.

Mr Sharif asked me whether I could guarantee that he would not be prosecuted if he did meet with the parents. I explained that I could give no guarantee but I had a reasonable expectation that all matters would be resolved at such a meeting.

I explained to Mr Sharif that I felt it important that the parents did not prosecute even though I was sure he would leave the court without a stain on his character. The problem was the way the local press would report the matter. This would cause him considerable distress whatever the outcome.

I went on to report to Mr Sharif the substance of a telephone call I had received from his son earlier that morning which was that his son could bring 30 Shi'ites from the Mosque that afternoon to 'sort Burnage out', I explained that whilst I was certain that such a statement was an expression of love and concern by a son for his father and that I was sure this action would not take place, however, within this whole situation there was the recipe for racial conflict. It was therefore better in my view if matters could be resolved amicably with parents and in a way which would allow us to deal with the boys concerned.

Subsequently, on the advice of his union, Mr Sharif declined to meet with parents."

During the whole of this saga, no-one within the senior management of the school gave Mr Sharif any indication that the school intended to deal with the conduct of the three boys who had disrupted his class, quite maliciously. Instead, Mr Sharif was placed on the defensive and pressurised into meeting the parents of the boys in order to stave off some vague and probably empty threat of prosecution. Yet no-one could give him any guarantee that by taking this action and even apologising to the parents they would automatically desist from prosecuting.

The matter dragged on. Nothing was resolved and Mr Sharif was given no reason why a student who, by his own admission, should have been in a French lesson ended up disrupting his class. No explanation was forthcoming either as to why these three students came to report to Mr Moors rather than to their form teacher or Head of Year. None of that, or the possibility of racial overtones to the disruption of the Urdu class or the obvious humiliation of Mr Sharif received any attention from the senior management of the school. Their total focus was on the threat of prosecution by the parents of the boys.

A note to Roy Jobson dated April 6th 1987 from one of the Inspectors indicates a similar attitude to the incident:

"This incident was originally brought to my attention by Mr Moors on 4 March.

I was of the opinion that the Disciplinary Procedure should not be invoked but that I should arrange to see the teacher after the school had finished its internal discussions. The purpose of my meeting with the teacher was to stress that 'rough handling' can result in a charge being laid in the Civil Court for battery and to explore alternatives open to a teacher faced with a similar situation. I arranged with Mr Moors to see the teacher on 20 March. I was then contacted by Mr Moors to say that the school had not yet finished its discussions and could I postpone the meeting.

On 25 March I happened to meet Mr Sharif at the Greenheys Centre. He asked if we could talk about the classroom incident that happened at Burnage H S on 9 February. His account was much the same as what has been written. He acknowledges that he should not have used physical force to ensure that the three boys left his class. I promised to arrange a meeting at school to include Dr Gough, himself and his union rep to seek a solution. The meeting took place at 10.00 o'clock the next day. It was agreed that the teacher and the union representative would prepare a written statement and that

Mr Hewitt could communicate to parents. The statement would not be an apology, which was not appropriate, but rather would express the teacher's regrets that he had been forced by the actions of their children to take a course of action which was less than ideal and that he regretted this.

I indicated my opinion that a meeting with parents and teacher as originally suggested by the Senior Management Team could have been used to counsel the parents on their children's behaviour.

Here again the emphasis is on appeasing the parents and the admonition of Mr Sharif.

The Chair and Deputy Chair of the governing body took a different view. They only learned of the incident later. The Chair of Governors told us:

"Now, actually the way it was handled I think was quite disastrous in some ways, but it started off for the best of reasons . . . Mr Sharif was in a very difficult situation because he was between his union and senior management trying to deal with it; senior management dealt with it in a way that was not helpful to him I think. He felt the parents might go to solicitors, and so on, and I think for that to be implied to him by senior management at some stage was not sensible. It was clear to me that the parents had not a leg to stand on when they went to solicitors, and they weren't going to take it to Court. To pretend that this was going to happen, and that was why it should be continued to be dealt with in this informal way by Jack Hewitt, was not helpful".

Because of the support he received from his union (and somewhat later in the day, from the governing body) Mr Sharif was not required to explain himself to nor apologise to the group of parents. On the other hand, we received no evidence that either the boys or their parents were required to apologise to Mr Sharif for the humiliation and personal distress they caused him.

The school's apparent insensitivity to the fact that all of this was happening during and in the wake of Darren's trial and conviction, and that, therefore, the incident was likely to have had a profound effect on the Asian students in the Urdu class, is yet another example of the clumsiness and lack of sensitivity that characterises so much of the Burnage management style.

Another black teacher was to experience yet more of this style of management. We now turn to her story.

226

4 Ms X's Story

Ms X's 'welcome' to Burnage went something like this:

"When I got there my first introduction to Burnage was to be taken into the library by a member of Section II, and sat down and given a cup of coffee, and told that it would be better if I did not go into the staff room because most of the staff in the staff room were racist . . . to which I said:

'I know only one member of staff in this school; I have known her since I was 17 years old, and if you are going to tell me that she is racist, seeing as she goes into the staff room, then that is where the problems are going to start', and at that I just went. After that, conversations with certain sections of Section II were very superficial."

Within her very first week, then, Ms X was being sought after by at least one camp that expected her to be an easy recruit because she is black. No doubt, she adopted an attitude towards them as a result and they to her.

It was not going to be plain sailing with regard to the students either:

"At first when I went it was very difficult. Certain members of staff had prepared certain sectors of the students – namely the black students – to expect a certain type of teacher. A black woman is coming, and this black woman is going to be a, b, c, d; she is going to basically let you do what you want. So my first major problem came from disciplining Asian and black boys who felt that 'Perhaps this woman will overlook what I am doing!' That was my first problem that I had to encounter."

Ms X soon found that in addition to that particular attitude which she had to challenge, students were also "playing off the senior members of senior management against teachers, knowing that their side would be heard first and taken as the truth." She also formed the impression that in relation to certain matters, different racial groups were treated differently by senior management:

"I had an incident where some third year boys called a first year boy a coon – some Asian boys called a black boy in the first year a coon. It was only one boy at first, and then others joined in. These boys were dealt with by myself, by . . . my head of department, and then put outside the main office to wait for . . . their Head of Year. These boys went to a member of senior management instead. They had already told me they were going to report me to the governors . . . They went and spoke to this member of senior management, who then sent for me and told me that I had not dealt properly with the incident, that unless I could provide proof that these boys had actually said that to this boy, he was more inclined to believe the third year boys involved, because from what he knew of them that was not likely, and from what he knew of the first year boy he was quite likely to make it up."

This was one example of the way she felt senior management undermined her position as a teacher. Her evidence was backed up by other background information we received in relation to the management of the school. We were told of a small group of boys making a serious accusation against a black teacher and telling other boys they had done so maliciously. Initially they were believed by senior management, who refused to accept the teacher's denials or those of other staff present, and only changed their opinion when the boys concerned backed down and admitted to making the whole thing up.

Apart from a note instructing the boys not to repeat the accusation, the teacher saw no written apology and received no verbal apology either from the students or from the senior management concerned.

Another incident we were told about demonstrated not only a lack of support for Ms X, but could also be construed as failure to challenge effectively the racism directed at her as a black teacher. This is what Ms X told us:

"I had been back at school for six weeks, and this boy was out of my class, and I was never told why he was out . . . So, at the end of the lesson I went to find out what was going on, why this particular boy was out – all his friends wanted to go with him. I was then told that whilst I had been off ill a letter had been sent to the school saying that they did not want me teaching their son because I was racist, and I had made racist comments about white women . . . The boy had gone home and told his parents this . . .

Q. "What did the member of senior management tell you that he had done about the letter?
A. Nothing, just that he had had the parents in and spoken to them, and that it had not been mentioned to me because I had been ill and I had not been at school.
Q. Did he say how he had spoken to them – what he had told them?

228

A. No.

Q. Did you get the impression from what he did say to you that he had been supportive of you?

A. Not particularly.

Q. He had the parents in without any kind of consultation with you as to whether this was an untrue allegation that the boy had made.

A. Yes."

The background to this particular story is that some time after Ahmed's murder, two of the white boys in Ms X's class who used to go around with Darren Coulburn "took over my lesson and used the time to make statements about people like me coming and taking their jobs. It was a very unpleasant lesson and I found it difficult to defuse the lesson."

On another occasion what started as disruptive behaviour from four white boys in Darren's old class, resulted in two boys (one white and one of mixed parents) breaking down in the lesson.

"They started shouting at me saying, 'you're ashamed of us. You don't like us. You think we're all racist and that we're all responsible for what has happened. When I said that was not the case, one of the boys . . . asked why then do the papers call us a school of shame. It was at that point that they started to talk to me about how they felt regarding Darren being in school and in their class and about the fact nobody questioned how they felt."

She had then sent for Mr Ellis to assist in giving the boys some support, but they "did not want to talk . . . and . . . went off for dinner". In that same lesson, one of the boys had "lamented Ahmed's death and said, 'what a waste of a young life. In fact, what a waste of two young lives. We have one boy dead and one who might as well be dead'."

Were senior management who dealt with the letter from a parent complaining about Ms X in a position to share this background with those parents? Did senior management give the parents and the students an opportunity to see and talk to Ms X and work out a way of dealing with that situation? Our evidence is that senior management was in no position to do the first and certainly did not do the second.

Ms X told us that part of the problem was that those 'cries for help' from the white classmates of Darren were not picked up and responded to when they should have been. She informed us that she had sent a report to Section II, but no account was given to her of the way those boys were dealt with. She had no information from any source, for example, whether any of the boys received counselling from the school pyschological service.

The Death of Asim Malik

Sadly, however, Ahmed's was not to be the ony death Ms X and her class were to encounter that term. Two months after Ahmed's death, another classmate, Asim Malik, was run over while crossing the road on his way to school. He was on a life support machine for four days before the doctors declared that he was brain dead and switched off the machine. Asim was a steadying influence in the class and had a special relationship with Ms X and with the class.

She says of him:

"You always say that you are not going to have a favourite student, but Asim was my favourite student. I have a very special relationship with his parents, especially his father, who would come to see me every single Monday morning to find out his son was getting on . . . He had a very special place within my form in that he bridged the gap between both sections of the religious communities and the racial communities within my form."

Here, then, is a teacher who had taught Ahmed, Asim and Darren and had to cope with the fears and emotions of their various classmates. She had seen Darren on the morning of the murder after he had done the stabbing, and had summoned the assistance of a colleague in getting Darren to disclose where he had disposed of the knife. She had found another boy in possession of a knife that very morning, and "it later transpired that one of Darren's friends had asked this student to bring the knife in". And, she had had to deal with the sense of anger and outrage some of her class felt at not being allowed to grieve or to share their feelings, or to pay their last respects to Ahmed at his funeral.

What support did this woman get from the senior management of the school?

Ms X told us:

"With the exception of people like Mrs Hill, Mr Hill, Mr Brown, very, very few people actually thought about (my support needs). Some of my friends thought about it, but in terms of management very few people thought about it, and nobody spoke to me about it, just like I say, Mrs Hill, Mr Hill. When Asim died because I was really upset . . . Mr Hill and Mrs Hill took it in turns to go to the hospital and see him and report back to me; they would report back to me and then I would report back to the boys."

230

The hospital turned off Asim's life support machine at the weekend. Ms X told us that Mr Hill 'phoned the supply teacher who taught with her, and with whom Ms X had a very good relationship, and told her to go and be with Ms X. He later telephoned Ms X and informed her of Asim's death. He also informed another of Ms X's friends and ensured that she was able to go and be with her.

Ms X also received much valuable support and assistance from other teachers as she dealt with her class and their bereavement. She prepared the class for grieving and enabled them to talk about Asim, about themselves in relation to his death, and to attend a memorial service in his honour. The whole class attended the service, and it is obvious that Asim's family valued enormously all that Ms X had done before and after Asim's death. There seems to be little doubt also that Ms X's way of handling that situation was instrumental in enabling that class to cope with a second tragedy even as they, with little assistance from the senior managers in the school, were attempting to deal with the horror of the killing of one of their classmates by another. But her class also helped her to cope. Ms X describes how they did it:

"On the morning of the memorial service I was sitting in the office; I had been doing the cards for the wreath because one of the parents had made a wreath from the boys, and I was doing the card for that, and I was crying. One of the Asian boys came in and said, 'Don't worry Miss, he used to come out of the classroom and he used to jump on the step and say, 'I love Miss X, I love Miss X'."

"It was very difficult; whilst I was having to comfort them they were realising they also had to comfort me, so it was something very different (to when Ahmed died). There was also a grieving process which the boys did not have for Ahmed's death

Q. What, in terms of your own support needs and assistance in dealing with that trauma, was organised for you by the school?

A. None, other than Mrs Hill coming to talk to me and having an open door for me to go in at any time, there was none. It was basically me along with Mr Ellis providing that support for the boys, but in terms of me getting any, none. In terms of other members of senior management talking to me about it, none at all. Since the incident, Mr and Mrs Malik have been to see me at the end of every single term, and when they don't come they 'phone ... What they are basically saying to me is, 'we are grateful for what you did for our son, and seeing you helps to keep this memory alive' . . . In lots of ways it is supportive."

The Aftermath of March

Come Easter, this teacher was to experience yet more frustrations caused by the senior managers of the school. As drama teacher, Ms X was involved with some of the group of students who had been bundled out of the school 'for their own safety'. She told us that the two parents whose house she went to were very keen for her to come round to their house and talk to their son and work with their son. So, as far as those parents were concerned, they certainly wished their son to return to school, even if that is contrary to what the school was claiming. That particular student with whom Ms X worked at home was eager to do his practical exam in the school. We questioned her closely about this:

> Q. "What you are saying is that the student would have been ready and willing to come in for the group practical, and that his parents would have supported his decision, but they got the distinct impression from the school that the school would not countenance that?
>
> A. That was what I was told, because it was the drama exam, and they had a practical where they had to act and be marked by a moderator and I asked Mr P what I was to do about it. I said that I had got his written work and had been to the house, but what was I to do about the practical, and he said, 'either you do a piece with him at his house, or you request a special dispensation for him'. I asked why, and he said, 'we could get him in, but if we did somebody would hear about it and we would probably have trouble on our hands.'
>
> "My head of department was also there when it was said, and that was part of the information that I had to pass on to the moderator because I had to talk to the moderator and say just why he was not there."

The Two Factions Among Staff

In her evidence, Ms X was extremely sceptical about what she described as 'the liberal faction within the school':

> Q. "Is there a kind of ideology of racism which is very powerful for those people?
>
> A. Yes. They spend a lot of time looking at South Africa, and talking about the problems of apartheid. That's where it's at

232

basically for them, but in terms of their relationship with me it leaves quite a lot to be desired."

Ms X's view is that the staff against whom she was warned on her first arrival at the school, warned to avoid because they were racist, are the very people who have acted most professionally in their relationship with her as a teacher and as a black woman. When it came to running the school in the interest of the students, and supporting her in relation to students' nccds or the need to develop an ethos of non-violence and of discipline in the school, the group of staff "considered to be old-fashioned, objectionable and even racist" have been much more supportive than the anti-racist liberal faction.

Ms X told us that the members of staff that deal specifically with ethnic problems in the school and are involved with structures such as the ethnic minority advisory groups have never been interested in her experience as a black teacher in the school, nor have they valued her skills in her own subject. She found it quite distressing when, in her own subject areas of English and Drama, they planned a course on Creole teaching and she "was not included in the course and was only asked to join in after (another teacher) complained and the outside guest speaker, . . . could not attend."

Conclusions

1. In our view the stories and experience of the black teachers at Burnage are a clear indictment of the effectiveness of anti-racist policies at Burnage High School.

2. The peripatetic music teacher and the Urdu teacher both had experiences which were humiliating and degrading. The fact that the music teacher did not feel he could look for support from either Dr Gough or Mr Moors, and appeared to get precious little help from Ms Aisthorpe leads one to wonder what quality of advice those managers are receiving from the ethnic minority advisory group, or rather how much that group knows about the way black staff are treated at Burnage.

3. Ms X's story suggests that the involvement of senior management with her at critical times in the life of the school was too little. She struck us as a teacher of enormous courage, child-centred, and concerned about parents and students, whether they were Afro-

233

Caribbean, white or Asian. Yet, in our view, her position and authority as a teacher was undermined by the senior managers of the school.

4.   As a black teacher she was welcomed by the parents of white, allegedly racist, students who had been kept away from the school. She worked with them in their homes – a professional and committed teacher concerned, as any teacher should be, with the education of their children; and achieved a good measure of success with at least one of the students. To those white parents, although she was black, she was Burnage High School; in her own eyes she was merely doing her duty to her students, although they were white. She presented the school with an opportunity to deal with the mess they had created in the aftermath of the March events and appease at least one boy by letting him come and do an exam for which she had helped him prepare. Instead of grasping the opportunity, the senior management instructed her to tell the moderator that the boy could not do his practicals because if he came back to school there might be trouble.

5.   The morale amongst the staff at the school is low to an extent that people are operating with what we were told were distressingly high stress levels. The apparent lack of a foreseeable solution to the problem at Burnage might well be a reason for certain highly able and competent members of middle/senior management looking for employment elsewhere.

6.   We consider that Burnage would be worse off for that calibre of staff leaving and creating even more space for the doctrinaire and anti-racist crusaders, who fail to see the extent to which their fixation with categories and camps alienate competent and committed teachers, black and white alike.

7.   We have no doubt that Dr Gough inherited a group of racist teachers amongst the staff at Burnage. Given the history of the school he was taking over as Head, and his own analysis of British education and British society, that was something he could have predicted, just as he could have predicted a certain culture of violence amongst male staff and students. We have no doubt that racism remains a problem to be confronted both amongst staff and students.

8. Dr Gough's style of management which, in many respects was reinforced by the management style of Mr Moors and Mr Hewitt, makes it unlikely that the various divisions amongst the staff group can be reconciled. We take the view that even if such reconciliation is possible it will not come about under the leadership of Dr Gough and his deputies.

9. We do not assume that those amongst the staff who support Dr Gough and his deputies and those who are at odds with them would automatically decide to work together and go forward in a spirit of unity under a new leadership. We take the view that some of the staff will not work happily in a school like Burnage nor in a manner that is conducive to the effective guidance and education of the whole school community.

10. The division and argument over the Gough management approach has undoubtedly deflected attention away from the bigotry and racism of some Burnage staff and directed it against Dr Gough and Peter Moors particularly. It is regrettable that they have been unable to deal effectively with what was actually taking place within the staff group, teaching and ancillary, and have attracted a good deal of unnecessary criticism, ridicule and hostility.

11. We take the view, therefore, that even if the leadership of the school were to change, one would not easily, if at all, manage to bridge the chasms that exist within the staff. For the sake of the students and their parents who welcome the opportunity to send them to a neighbourhood school, and for the sake of the many hardworking, self-critical and dedicated teachers who have a desire to make the school work, we feel that there is every reason to re-organise Burnage High School, and re-deploy some of the longer-serving staff who were not affected by the 1982 reorganisation, to give them an opportunity to exercise their skills elsewhere in a quite different environment.

12. We also take the view that in any event Burnage High School poses difficult problems of management in view of its size and its split site, and it would be better if the school could be reduced in size and put on one site. However, we also understand that there are difficulties in making either of the existing school sites into viable single school units without embarking on considerable capital expenditure on new school buildings. We, therefore, express a view but make no further recommendations.

CHAPTER 23

From Burnage to Manchester

The Community Languages Team

Mr Sharif heads a team of eight full time and part time teachers who teach in five primary schools, four secondary schools and one sixth form college. They are a peripatetic team, based at the Educational Development Service Centre. They hold a weekly team meeting there, and have a stock room for their materials.

In 1985, Manchester Education Committee issued a policy document entitled "The Language Needs of the Ethnic Minorities". In it, the Committee recognised the importance of the language children use at home, and of the children's attitude towards the proficiency in their home languages. The policy document commits the Education Authority to doing whatever they can to provide the main community languages spoken at home by school students.

The Community Languages Team feel that they should be teaching Bengali, Gujerati, Punjabi and Urdu, but, so far, all their teaching is confined to Urdu. They explain this by the fact that 80% of the South Asian population in Manchester speak Urdu, whether they originate from India, Bangladesh or Pakistan.

They are concerned, however, that they are only catering for an estimated 10% of the Urdu speakers they should be reaching. Currently, they work with some 500 out of a possible 5,000 Urdu speaking student population. In their view, this does not augur well for the Bengali, Gujerati and Punjabi speaking children who are in the minority in the schools.

More importantly, however, is the team's comment on the status in schools of Urdu as a community language, and the perceptions that headteachers, staff and students have of them as teachers of Urdu. The view is that although Manchester has designated Urdu a modern language, it does not have the same status or importance in the curriculum as French, German, Spanish or Italian.

Most students who learn these languages, they argue, do not use them in the community. They are seen as having commerical uses. Urdu, on the other hand, is a live language within communities all over Britain, and students taking Urdu as a modern language can use the language in the community. Yet, in the words of one member of the team, "(Urdu) is being seen as a sort of side-track language . . . and you can say whatever you like – the reason is racism".

The way headteachers decide to provide the teaching of Urdu was also of concern to the team. One teacher observed:

"There are many heads of primary schools and of secondary schools who have approached the Modern Languages Inspectorate at Crown Square . . . to stress that they would like to have teachers of Urdu and other languages to teach in their school, but because of, shall we say, this cold attitude of the Authority, they are not providing them or making any provision for those teachers".

Another member of the team stressed that if those heads were that keen, they would have a member of the "Urdu Team" as part of their school provision . . . "If I were a head and I wanted Urdu in my school, I would get an Urdu teacher on my school staff".

The team gave another key reason for the "side-line" status of Urdu. Headteachers, they claimed, would appoint French or German teachers as a part of their Modern Languages Department with no difficulty. But they are only interested in having Urdu teachers if Section 11 funding will pay for them. The team could think of only three schools that had appointed full time teachers to teach community languages, Burnage, Margaret Ashton and St John's Primary.

Burnage High School had had a peripatetic Urdu teacher for about five years, although its Modern Languages Department had some seven full time teachers teaching French, German, etc. Yet, as one of the team observed, "the total population of the school is 40% Asian children who would like to learn Urdu, Bengali or Punjabi". The team informed us that Burnage had now appointed a full time Urdu teacher to start work in 1988.

A number of other reasons were given for the way staff and students perceived Urdu and Urdu teachers. While students start other modern languages at first year, Urdu is done only from fourth year upwards. So, those children who learn Udru in primary school do not return to it until four years later. In some schools, students have only one Urdu lesson, i.e. forty to forty-five minutes per week. In others, the same group of students might have two or sometimes three lessons. For the team, however, a particularly contentious issue is the practice that certain teachers have of using Urdu classes as a sort of dumping ground for particular students. One Urdu teacher observed:

238

"Some children who have opted for Urdu or who have been made to opt for Urdu are those children who can't do woodwork or physics, or whatever, so the attitude is 'Right, give them Urdu'. They are sort of remedial children who, because they are Bangladeshi or Pakistani, can't do anything else; that's the sort of attitude".

But even when this system is not operating, some students still end up in Urdu classes by default. When students are given the option, at the end of the third year, of choosing subjects to do in the fourth and fifth years, they are often unable to do the subject of their choosing such as computer studies or biology and end up taking Urdu not because they choose it but as a last resort.

If the Community Languages Team are not part of the modern languages teaching staff in any one school, where do they teach? In most schools their teaching is done in the dining hall, the library, the community rooms, or in little corners in other halls. Teachers have had to take Urdu classes in the Sciences Laboratory, with science teachers and students coming in at all different times, interrupting the lesson, and asking the class to move. The Urdu teachers and their students consequently become demoralised, and the subject and its teachers acquire a very low status in the school.

Of the eight members of the Community Languages Team, the team leader is on Scale 3, one team member is part time Scale 2 and part time Scale 1, and the other six members are all on Scale 1. The team leader moved from Scale 1 to Scale 3, having acted as temporary team co-ordinator until a replacement was found for the holder of that post. He was later appointed permanently and placed on Scale 3. The part time Scale 2 had been on that Scale as part of a team teaching English as a Second Language, and retained the Scale when the Community Languages Team was formed, as well as getting a Scale 1 post as an Urdu teacher in the team. All eight members of the team are Section 11 funded.

Speaking for the team as a whole, one member told us:

"As community language teachers we have said a lot. As Asian teachers, we would say that definitely we are not getting our due rights in this Authority. The number of Asian teachers in this Authority is alarmingly low. We are suffering institutional racism in this Authority. Why do we find that other teachers in the other Authorities . . . in the North West, in the South, and in the Midlands . . . are in a much better position than we are . . . There are many

239

more Asian teachers there than we have in Manchester, where the population here is in thousands".

One teacher told us that she was qualified to teach English, biology, sociology and geography, and could also teach general subjects. Another said he was trained to teach mathematics and science, and had in fact taught science for eight years in another North West Authority. We were told that one member of the team has an M.A. in English Literature, and another a Ph.D. in Chemistry. Two of the team had had Masters degrees from Pakistan, one in Education, but only one of them had been given DES recognition. Another member of the team had come to England with a Masters degree in Education and had done a Post Graduate Certificate of Education course to qualify for DES recognition.

The problem of DES recognition of degrees awarded outside Britain and particularly in the sub-continent is now well known. Manchester, in consortium with a number of other North West Authorities and the University of Manchester, now runs a course which enables South Asian teachers to "convert" their qualifications and satisfy DES requirements.

But the Community Languages Team think it would be a mistake to see this as the main issue. The issue, as they perceive it, is not lack of qualifications amongst South Asian teachers, but a systematic blockage of opportunity even to those who have recognised qualifications in subjects other than community languages.

Manchester has a poor record of appointing Asian teachers outside the community languages area. Asian teachers have low status. According to the Community Languages Team, their marginalisation as Urdu teachers is even more damaging to the status of Asian teachers in Manchester. Commenting on their work as part of the Equal Opportunities Team, and the complex hierarchical structure of that team, one of the Urdu teachers told us:

"... We are supposed to be Equal Opportunities, but what's equal opportunities? It doesn't appear to me, because we are down below and they are all equal, we are the low caste ones, untouchables".

Despite their low status, the Community Languages Team are called upon by schools to perform a range of functions which have nothing to do with teaching Urdu classes, and for which they are not paid. They are required to provide "a social service" within the school, and on the school's behalf to the home. As one of the team put it:

240

"There are so many problems with the heads . . . The heads find problems in communicating with the parents, inside the school and out of the school, and they come to us to help them. We have gone out of our way to help them . . . we have really helped the school. We have visited the homes and we have come to the Headmaster's office to interpret and to write the letters and to translate letters for them, but they are not ready to pay for this service, for these extra activities".

The team are called upon to perform these various functions in the time allocated for their Urdu classes. They comply with the school's requests, but in their own time.

So, apart from being on Scale 1 and teaching in inadequate rooms, those teachers are being exploited further by headteachers. Schools have come to expect that they will perform those functions.

The team's view, however, is that what they do is not appreciated and that the school's attitude is that a teacher is not really doing anything in an Urdu lesson or even after the lesson, and therefore the school is not really asking a favour but is merely requiring them to do their duty.

The Community Languages Team stressed that it was the demands of the Asian community which led to teaching provision within the schools in the first place. In response to those demands, the Education Authority started to provide classes in 1979.

Originally, the classes took place after school and in "very shabby conditions". While the team now operates within the main school day, the conditions have not improved significantly in eight years.

How does the community respond now?

The team leader dealt with the pressure from parents in the community in this way:

"The parents have made demands, of course. It is because of the pressure of the parents that we are here. When they find that the Authority is not paying any heed to them, they have started their own classes . . . There is a trend in the Asian community to have their own schools and to establish their full time day schools, just because their special needs are not being met in the State schools. If their needs are met in these schools, perhaps their trend of having their own schools will disappear. The evening schools and the weekend schools are

241

called supplementary schools, I will not call them "supplementary", they are complementary schools. They are completing the job which is not being done in the school".

It is not that Manchester Education Department is unaware of how the structure and organisation of community language teaching reflect particular entrenched attitudes on the part of headteachers and language departments.

In August 1986, Chris Beswick, Modern Language Inspector for Manchester wrote a discussion paper entitled "Modern Languages and Anti-Racism".

In that paper, Beswick was inviting "modern linguists" as a particular group of teachers to ask themselves, "what am *I* doing as a member of a departmental team to help combat racism.?" He argued that racism was more than likely to be present "in the inferior status accorded to non-European languages in the curriculum".

Under a heading "What can you do about this?", Beswick recommended that the department, working in a subject context, could:

"Consider ways in which status can be accorded to teachers from ethnic minority groups in the modern languages area. In the long term, this will continue to be a national issue as there are simply nowhere near enough black teachers going into the system. Status is not accorded, however, in the initial act of appointment. Status comes from an appropriate career structure and from time-tabling/ rooming/resourcing of the language taught. If you have a teacher engaged in work in community languages in your school/college at the moment what messages are being given out to staff/students about the community language as compared to European languages?"

Here is a subject Inspector giving mild exhortation ("departments could consider") to modern language departments in the city, no doubt based upon his own perceptions of the lowly status of community languages. Nevertheless, the Community Languages Team gave no evidence of the Education Department doing anything more pro-active than that, or of intervening in combatting the racism, as defined by Chris Beswick, which they were actually experiencing. Anyone reading Beswick's paper would be left with the distinct impression that Manchester is sensitive to the whole issue of community languages, if they did not have an opportunity to learn of the experiences of the Community Languages Team. Furthermore, they would no doubt wish to conclude that that sensitivity underpins the provision that is made for the teaching of community languages. Sadly, however, in this as in other areas we have explored, the rhetoric and the reality are worlds apart.

Conclusions

The experiences of the Community Language Team echo those of the peripatetic teachers in the ethnic music department. It seems to us to be inevitable in either case that both the subject and the teachers would have low status. Given the prevailing ethos of most schools, and the ignorance and bigotry of staff and students towards Asian cultures and languages the Community Language teachers are placed in the most invidious position, having to organise their work in the manner we have described – both these need to be changed, and the issue of their pay and promotion which we deal with below needs to be seen to as a matter of priority.

We believe that the Modern Languages Inspectorate should see to it

(a) that Urdu, particularly, should be afforded the status of a modern language and located, as a subject, within the Modern Languages department of secondary schools and sixth form colleges;

(b) that attention should be given to the possibility of employing full time teachers of Urdu to do bi-lingual work in primary schools;

(c) that Urdu teachers, whether Section 11 funded or not, should have the status of "bona fide" members of the Modern Language department in schools; and

(d) that they should be able to offer students the subject in their 1st, 2nd and 3rd years, as well as in years 4 and 5.

Teachers need to be seen both by staff and students as belonging to the school community, and "not just that teacher who comes in at lunchtime and everybody who is passing by shouts and screams".

Similarly, Headteachers need to be interested and concerned about the progress students and staff are making in the subject. The Community Languages Team told us that they achieve 95% passes in "A" level and 99% passes in "O" level, but that Heads seem uninterested either in the children's achievements or whether or not those achievements are due to work done by teachers in lunch breaks, after school or in other free time.

The issue of pay and promotion for the Community Language Team is one which, in our view, causes them legitimate concern. The prospect of teaching a subject at "O" and "A" level in conditions which are conducive neither to teaching nor to learning, acting as home/school liaison teachers, letter-writers and translators, and not being able to look forward to a post above Scale 1 is not simply gloomy, it is a spectre of sheer exploitation. Moreover, the underlying assumption is that it is a sacrifice such staff should be prepared to make because it is "their" language, and "their" people in "their" community.

When such staff have little or no status, and are at the base of a pyramid, they become acutely aware of how vulnerable they are and of the power that others higher up that pyramid are able to exercise over them.

The Community Languages Team realised that by coming to give evidence to us as a team they would inevitably be making comment about the Equal Opportunities Team, the Modern Languages Inspectorate, the Education Committee and its policies, and, not least of all, the Heads and staff of the schools in which they work. They shared with us their anxiety about whether or not their evidence would result in victimisation or even worse conditions within which to operate.

We acknowledge and commend their courage in coming to us with their evidence, and trust that that evidence will encourage all those who are empowered to do so to take a hard look at things – at institutionalised forms of racism, at tokenism, and at the extent to which sound opportunities to make meaningful changes in curriculum and staffing become their opposite, and end up placing black communities at even greater disadvantage.

CHAPTER 24

The Tip of an Iceberg – Part 1

"This verdict is not a victory for us, we have lost a son. What it shows us is that we must organise to ensure that what happened to my brother, to my family, does not happen again."

– Selina Ullah

Thus spoke a courageous Selina Ullah to a rally of demonstrators outside Manchester Crown Court on the day Darren Coulburn was found guilty of Ahmed's murder.

"What it shows is that *we must organise.* . . . ."

In the course of this Inquiry the Ullah family, and Mrs Ullah in particular, stated their position to us in the following terms:

"Many people are questioning the purpose of your Inquiry and asking us why we are co-operating with it. We could take the view, like them, that it will serve no purpose: what's the point of an Inquiry now? What does it prove? Ahmed is already dead, and the authorities should have done something about that school before something as fatal as that happened.

But no! We want to co-operate. We have to find out why, and find out what can be done, because no other family must suffer the pain, the anguish, the devastation we are suffering at the waste of such a young, innocent life. Ahmed had everything to live for.

We have to make sure that it never happens again."

Making sure that it does not happen again is not just the responsibility of the Asian community and all those whom Selina called upon to organise. The majority of people who gave evidence to the Inquiry (particularly those for whom to do so was an act of immense courage) were guided by the same concern as the Ullah family.

Could it happen again? Could it have happened before? How many headteachers in Manchester and other parts of the United Kingdom on hearing about the tragedy did not have cause to look about them and say "There, but for fortune, go I."

245

In this respect, Burnage is not unique. That fact is reflected in the way the "terms of reference" of this Inquiry were couched. The third item in the terms of reference relates to racial harassment, racial violence and racism in Manchester schools.

Do other Manchester schools harbour the conditions in which the Burnage tragedy could occur?

What is the evidence?

Throughout the Inquiry, students, parents and teachers from Manchester schools other than Burnage provided evidence of racial harassment, racial violence and racism that they had experienced or had assisted others in resisting. In this chapter we provide some of that body of evidence. In the next chapter we provide evidence from the interviews conducted by Salma Ahmad with girls in schools in Central and South Manchester, and at the youth clubs and girls' projects used by Asian girls.

Thirdly, in order to gain a more accurate picture of the overall situation in Manchester schools than we assumed we would get from a number of personal testimonies, we commissioned a survey from the Extra Mural Department at Manchester University. The survey was conducted by Dr Elinor Kelly with a team of four more researchers. The report of that survey is included in chapter 26.

Fourthly, in chapter 27, we examine evidence from an incident at a North Manchester school and draw certain parallels between those happenings and the Burnage events of February/March 1987.

Finally, we look at what all of this tells us about racism and racial violence in Manchester schools.

Part I – Anecdotes From Other Manchester Schools

The following are quotes from students and parents at other Manchester schools (– the names have been disguised):

"In School A you can cut the atmosphere with a knife, inside and outside school . . . one boy, one of the very few that doesn't go around punching the girls in the back is teased like something not right. The other boys tell him his mom is a dirty whore because she is white and his father is black. In my school there are many Asian people; by many they are considered dirty, disgusting and unhygienic. In the first year there are three Asian gangs, nine times out of ten they are bullied and picked on because of their race."

"At School X it's mostly Asian girls who get bullied, some of the Afro-Caribbean girls get bullied. The bullying is mostly taking money, these attacks occur at lunchtime when there are no teachers around and if you go out of school."

School A

"Like what happened with D. We were in English and something happened between D and this other boy. D was almost killing this kid, he had him gripped up against the wall. D then pulled out a sharp pencil and stabbed the boy in the neck with it. D never got expelled for it. We students wanted to tell the press, but were told "it'll be bad publicity for the school.""

School B

"A black student – "me and X were laughing in class", the teacher called us "a pair of laughing monkeys". I don't think he would have called two white lads "laughing monkeys". Another boy called me a "nigger". After a dispute with a non teaching member of staff, "even the white kids said 'why are they picking on you. They must be racialist'.""

School C

"X is a thirteen year old Asian boy there and has suffered from bullying to such an extent that he did not go into school. He has been called names such as "Paki", and "Bud-bud". His parents went to the school when the "bullying" turned into fighting. They have been five or six times. They do not know if there is a parent/teachers association at School C."

School D

An Asian parent told him "a white boy tripped my son up and began a fight in which my son's arm was broken. The white boy was just suspended for a couple of days. The white boy called my son a "black bastard". I work near the school and I've seen boys with knives, I have reported it when I've seen boys truanting, but the school don't seem to do anything about it. Racial attacks do occur in the school. I've heard of others".

School E

A student involved in the Frontline production, aged thirteen – "Sometimes I've felt like taking a knife into school, because of the fighting, to protect myself. I've seen boys attacked because of their colour".

What about the Manchester schools as perceived by teachers:

"I have worked in three Manchester schools and I meet a lot of teachers. As an Asian I'm tolerated until I have proved myself. I feel that many teachers have attitudes towards Asian and black children that are negative."

"When I went for interviews the Head asked me how I would feel being the only West Indian teacher in the school. I said I'm not West Indian, I was born, have grown up and been educated in Britain. In some staff conversations people would say things like 'considering you've not got a fat nose, or considering you've not got fat lips'. When a boy defaced a book with the words 'wogs out', 'niggers out' he was punished for defacing the book. When another incident occurred with this boy the Deputy Head told me 'oh you've got to expect these things if you're not normal' or on being asked what was meant by that the Deputy Head continued 'being black is like being disabled or having a squint'. The same Deputy Head asked me 'have you ever thought of teaching in a black area with your own people'."

"I heard two other members of staff at School F, joking about incidents in class – one where a black child got up to the blackboard and was called 'Black Adder' in front of the class. The teacher involved said 'he's a great kid, he laughs at that'. The other joke story was about a black child wanting to be on the sports team, and a teacher replying 'oh yes we need someone to chalk the score up on'. When I remonstrated with the other members of staff why they found these stories funny the response I got was 'it's people like you who cause racial problems'. There are no black teachers at the school. The school has an anti-racist policy. I looked into it, but have never seen it. The communication in the school is very poor. The staff have little respect for management. There is little communication between parents and the school. The children say things like 'I don't mind blacks but we don't like Asians'. They misquote articles from the Sun about white children not being *allowed* to count in English, having to eat curry etc. They say things like 'we have to eat everything which comes into the canteen, but if I was a paki I could eat anything I asked for'."

The school has one white boy who is very close to a Sikh boy. I have heard other children making fun of this white boy for playing with this Asian kid. The two boys are very close but when "teased" by the other white boys about having a "paki friend" the white lad claim that he is not really friends with the Asian kid. He feels so intimidated by it.

In fact today whilst I was in school I heard children telling a joke and the punch line was something about "petrol bombing Paki's and getting 10 to the gallon".

Evidence of a Senior Teacher:

Some examples of racist incidents in schools:

a. *Teacher:* "I hate coming to school in the morning on this bus route – it's always full of those smelly black people". This same teacher always chose black children to do the most menial and unpopular tasks in the classroom.

b. *Teacher* (to mother who has several children of mixed race) "you are a monster and ought to be sterilised".

c. *Police road safety officer* said to school staff room: "I don't know how you get on with this lot from the jungle". (This P.C. is now a high ranking liaison officer).

d. *Head Teacher:* A West Indian family came to our school for admission, they had been refused at another school because according to the Head, there was no room. The parents felt that the Head had refused them because of their colour. This school which was near to ours (in the same multi cultural community) had only two black students but had often denied it was racist. One of our teachers (white) went to the school on the same day and stated that she had two children (in the same age group as the West Indian children) and that her husband had just started lecturing at the university and she was looking for a place for her children at the school. She was offered immediate admission for her children.

e. *Parent:* "I don't want my child to come out of the school with 'this lot'" – pointing to a group of Pakistani children. The Head allowed the child to remain behind in the classroom every day until all the other children had gone and then the parent collected

249

her. Although all the staff objected to this discrimination he refused to alter the situation.

f. *Teacher:* This head had been appointed because of his awareness of "cultural diversity". He allowed T.V. cameramen to come into the school playground and photograph Asian boys and girls kissing one another.

g. *Member of the public* (seeing me take a school football team to a match): "Good misus, what . . . are you doing letting him (a white boy) play with them black bastards".

These are only a few examples of racism encountered in the school situation, but no day went by without some instances of racial abuse, especially verbal abuse by children to one another, and *this was in a school that had a good reputation for being anti racist!*

A Teacher at School A:

"In my opinion School A in theory has a commitment to multi-culturalism and anti-racist studies. They have a strong policy commit-ment to these types of things but in practice this wasn't so. One 4th year girl actually said to a member of senior management in front of me that she has suffered racism from the staff. This was a really bright girl who was talking. We asked her why she hadn't told the teachers about the racism she had suffered. She said "there was no point because nothing would be done and her days in school would be made even worse". They actually had a fear of reporting things because of any retaliation which might occur.

"Some of the teachers' attitudes to the kids and to teaching is terrible. The teachers just want to get through the day as quickly and as smoothly as possible. One incident I remember vividly was when I was running around trying to organise work some of the children had done for an exhibition. One of the teachers walked up to me and said "Don't bother, they're not worth it". That was terrible because these children were really enthusiastic and had worked really hard for this exhibition. The kids hated the school, they said the atmosphere in the school was hostile towards them."

"Some of the teachers were so racist they believed the racist myths such as 'Asians come here to try and get all the money and build their businesses and bleed the country dry' etc. The racial divides amongst the children wasn't challenged at all but just allowed to grow. I heard

250

black kids calling other black kids because they were of a darker skin than them etc., and the teachers would just laugh about it later in the staff room."

"After Ahmed's murder, (School A) did not even speak about it in the school. The other Asian children in the school did not even know about it until some articles were brought in about it to tell them what was going on. Basically, the staff did not see it as their problem, the attitudes being 'there is no racial tension in our school so we're alright Jack'. But basically where there is racialism there is a possibility of racial tension.

"The communication between the school and home was very very bad. The teachers speak to parents in such a way as to make them feel inferior, so parents don't come into school and so very few parents actually question the staff."

Another School A Teacher:

"There has been a lot of innovative thought at the school but this has been met with resistance from the more established members of staff who preceded the present Head's arrival, and secondly the new strategies which have been implemented without adequate planning, exacerbate staff resentment."

"The local community feel that the school is failing their children because of the bad exam results and because it is too easy for them to leave the premises – that is, they don't like the lack of discipline. Also I feel that if you live in an area you are frustrated with, you generally try to send your children out of this same area in the hope that they will make connections which will perhaps help them later in life."

"There is not actually any overt racism expressed amongst the staff at (School A), at least not amongst the colleagues I choose to circulate amongst. There is however a general depressed air of frustration about the place. Staff do feel they are not given the best support and there is also a clash of ideologies. Many of the staff are quite traditional in outlook and find it diffiuclt to go along with some of the new ideas.

"I feel that what happened at Burnage could have happened at any Manchester secondary school; it could certainly have happened here at our school because of the level of aggression amongst the students albeit sometimes in jest. The school did observe a minute's silence (following MEC guidelines) after the murder and I talked about the matter at length with my class."

251

CHAPTER 25

The Tip of the Iceberg – Part 2

Salma Ahmad's Interviews

Salma Ahmad interviewed eighteen girls of Asian and Afro-Caribbean origin during September 1987 in an exercise equivalent to that of Nigel de Noronha and Gus John. In keeping with the undertakings given to students who co-operated with the research, neither the girls' real names nor those of their schools are given in this account of interview extracts.

"Perveen" who is of Pakistani origin was concerned about the level of violence at her school. She thought that there were more fights at her present school compared with her primary school although they were not always between different ethnic groups. Most fights, she reported, were between girls from different years and only a few involved "white" against Asian or Afro-Caribbean pupils. "Perveen" summed up the situation as follows: ". . . some English and Africans are friends with the Pakistanis, you know good friends, and they don't fight a lot with them. It's only sometimes". When I asked her how the teachers responded to the violence she told me that some of the fights were reported to the headteacher who either warned or suspended the girls concerned.

With regard to the fights between different ethnic groups, "Perveen" recalled that an Asian girl in her class was beaten up by seven or eight English and Afro-Carbbean girls from the fourth year. The Asian girl claimed that they threw bricks, kicked and pushed her into the road when a car was coming. She fell, grazed and cut her face and was taken to hospital. "Perveen" was unable to recall exactly why the incident had happened but offered two explanations. She thought that "English people are always causing trouble with us (Pakistanis)" and the "English and the West Indians. . . were battering up the Pakistani girls". And she also thought that the incident was related to Ahmed's stabbing at Burnage High School because it happened shortly after he was murdered.

"Rohina" is of Pakistani origin. She mainly talked about a major outbreak of violence between different ethnic groups which occurred at her school on or two weeks after Ahmed was killed at Burnage. In this incident (the first of its kind to have taken place at the school) "white" pupils were fighting Asians. Around fifty or sixty fourth-years and a few fifth and third formers joined in the fight but, apart from one or two girls, the Afro-Caribbeans at the school did not become involved. 'Rohina" was not sure what had led to the violence. She thought that some boys from Burnage High School had said something to the "white" girls at her school when they were going home and, as a consequence, the "white" girls said that they were going to "get" the sisters of the Asian boys. the "white" girls at her school told "Rohina" that they were not going to "get" their Asian friends (people like her), but only the younger Asian girls because they wouldn't fight back. At first, they said they would only pick on girls with brothers at Burnage but then changed their minds after finding only a few at the school.

"Rohina" thought that these "white" girls planned their attack well in advance. After school they went to the gates at the front of the school, but after finding teachers and parents waiting there, they went to the gates at the back of the school where they found some Asian girls and "beat them up". "Rohina" didn't actually see the incident and was unable to say how badly the girls were hurt. But she felt powerless because she could not prevent the situation from occurring especially as some of the girls involved included her white friends. After the event "Rohina" told her "white" friends that she disapproved of their actions but they were defensive and said that it was up to them to decide how to behave.

When I asked "Rohina" for more information about how the teachers responded to the incident she told me that rumours of the imminent attack were reported to the headteacher beforehand by Asian girls who were beginning to panic. The teachers responded by standing at the gates at the front of the school to ensure that there was no trouble. The father of an Asian girl offered to take some of the pupils home but a teacher refused to give him permission. "Rohina" disapproved of this decision and was critical of the teacher's behaviour. She thought that the teachers should have allowed the Asian girls to go home earlier. She said that after the fight had taken place a lot of the Asian girls were frightened and some "white" girls disapproved of the violence.

"Zarina" is in the second year at School Y and is of Pakistani origin. Her best friends are mainly Asian girls, although she has some white and Afro-Caribbean friends. "Zarina" was worried about the level of discipline at her school. She thought that teachers were unable to control some girls and didn't notice when they smoked or bullied others. She also thought that there was a lot of bullying in her school. When I asked her for more information about the bullying "Zarina" claimed that groups of three or four older "white" girls (third year upwards) tended to verbally or physically abuse the younger Asian girls. The Afro-Caribbean girls were occasionally harrassed although sometimes two or three of them joined forces with the gangs of bullies. She elaborated that Asian girls in her class sometimes asked one of the Afro-Caribbean girls to tell the "white" girls off if they were being bullied because they were "big and strong".

"Zarina" thought that most of the bullying happened during the lunch and other breaks in the basement corridors near the toilets. She had never been picked on but her friends had. She thought that the English girls left her alone because they regarded her as a "special" person. The bullying involved calling her friends "rude words" and pushing them around. "Zarina" said that these incidents were not reported to the teachers because they feared that the "...other girls would get into a gang and beat them up, or something like that". "Zarina" was also unhappy with the way some teachers responded to incidents of racist name-calling. On one occasion when name-calling was reported the teacher said "Oh, no I don't think she said that". "Zarina" thought that the teachers probably responded in this way because they couldn't do anything about racism and even if they told the girls off it wouldn't make much difference. She added pessimistically: "The badness is still going to carry on".

"Zarina" also discussed specific incidents that involved racism. For example, she reported:

"There's a girl in our class, she's English. She's not racist to our class. She's really good to our class. But the people going into the dining room. There she's always punching them or something like that. She's always joking, but she knows that it upsets them. She calls the girls Paki and things like that. She sometimes apologises a few days later, depending on her mood".

"Nasreen" was born in Britain and is of Pakistani origin in the fifth-form at school Y. She was also unhappy with the general level of discipline at the school and thought that the teachers had problems with controlling the girls' bad behaviour. "Nasreen" was very upset that day because she had been bullied by some English fifth formers and an Afro-Caribbean girl who had recently been suspended for beating up another Pakistani girl. The girls had called her "Paki", they pushed her, took her shoes off and threw them away. This had happened in the basement. She had gone there to do some work in the common room. When she cried they told her to get out and they tried to push her face in water with detergent in it. This was not the first time that "Nasreen" had been pushed around but it had been a particularly bad day for her. Afterwards, she told a teacher about the incident who said that she would speak to her later but left the school without seeing her. The teacher also said that she would talk to the parents of the girls involved in the bullying. "Nasreen" told some of her English friends in her class and her sister about the incident but was reluctant to tell her parents because they might worry. She was going to ask the teacher if she could be transferred from her science group because it included some of the girls that had bullied her. "Nasreen" knew that the girls generally picked on people they thought were stupid or weak and these were not always Asians.

"Nasreen" was extremely disturbed by the racism in her school. She told me that some time ago on a Friday she heard that English and Afro-Caribbean girls were threatening to stab all the Asian girls "with [white] skirts". She was frightened and stayed away from school on the following Monday although her parents tried to persuade her to go. When she eventually went back to school her parents said "God bless you". She thought that this particular incident was not reported to the teachers.

"Pratima" was born in Britain and her parents are from Kashmir. She attributed most of the violence at her school to a couple of small gangs comprising seven or eight "white" and Afro-Caribbean girls who picked on others quite regularly. She wasn't sure which years they were from but thought they included some of the yonger girls. She said that they were not particularly racist because they didn't just pick on the Asian and "black girls". For example, she said, ". . .they call you 'tramp' if you walk past and if you look back they say 'what are you looking at'". They had caused fights in the past and were involved in the major incident following Ahmed's stabbing. On that day "Pratima" was in school and heard that:

". . .the Asian and black boys from Burnage were going to come up and beat up the English girls. But they didn't turn up. That night loads of girls went outside school, English, and afterwards – there's two entrances – we went out of the back entrance where there were about eight or nine girls beating up some Asian girls. I think one girl was beaten up quite a bit. She was on the floor and she had blood coming out of her, I think, of her face. . .She had a little scar there. You could tell she had been beaten up".

When "Pratima" saw the incident she said:

". . .we just ran, we couldn't actually do anything about it. They were all big as well. It came all of a sudden, we never knew that anything was going to happen. . .They just came towards us and we just ran. There's usually a big crowd going past. They were mainly third, fourth and fifth years because they were generally big. . .The girl on the floor was getting a bit trampled on as the girls ran past. . .We came back to see if she was O.K. but she had gone in an ambulance. . .I told my dad and he came back with me".

This incident took place at the back of the school when there were no teachers around. She told me that it was reported to the teachers and on the following day they stood on guard at the back entrance.

"Rucksana" is of Pakistani origin and born in Britain. She claimed that the Asian girls were sometimes teased about their colour but not about the way they dressed. She thought that the Asian girls were teased more frequently than the Afro-Caribbean girls and the latter sometimes ganged up with the English girls against the Asians. However, some of the Afro-Caribbean girls were friendly with the Asian girls and were against the "white" girls. On fighting at the school "Rucksana" commented: "It's mainly English girls hitting the Paki girls". She had a fight once with a white girl in her class who kept on slapping her and telling her to ". . .go back to your own country". The "white" girl also said: "Why do you come around to our country? We don't go around to your country". The "white" girl had recently left school. "Rucksana" complained bitterly that ". . .most English girls do not know how it feels when yoau get bullied". She had not reported the incident to the teachers or her parents because ". . .there's a whole racist gang of them. Even the one's that are not that racist were saying "go on, go on, box her head in'."

"Rita" is of East African Asian origin. She had been called "Paki" at school by "white" girls usually during the break-times. She estimated that she was called racist names at least once a week. Sometimes if she was near a group of "white" girls they would push past her and say ". . .get out of the way you stupid Paki". She usually ignored them, especially if they were in a large group, but at other times she answered them back or refused to move.

Sarah's parents are of British and Asian origin. She thought that racist incidents were reported once every two weeks, but they occurred more frequently than that. Her friend "Korsa", of East African Asian origin, thought that under-reporting occurred because the Asian girls were frightened of being "beaten up" by the bullies. "Sarah" said that sometimes teachers saw incidents and did not do anything about them because it ". . .was only a lot of paper work for them". She also said that the Afro-Caribbean girls at her school ". . .didn't know what they were doing". If there was a racist incident ". . .they would go on anybody's side". Sometimes they were also called racist names but the Asian girls bore the brunt of the abuse from the "white" girls.

In one of Salma Ahmad's interviews we hear of English girls who ". . .kicked and pushed her into the road when a car was coming". It does not need an over-active imagination to see the possible consequences of such violence. This body of evidence suggests a pattern which is as obvious as it is dangerous. The perpetrators of such acts of racial violence pounce on their targets in areas of the school or the school grounds where they least expect to be interrupted by teachers.

"This had happened in the basement. She had gone there to do some work in the common room."

The similarities between this act of violence and the 1982 incident at Burnage High School (Chapter 18) are strikingly obvious. Another interview pinpoints "most of the bullying" as happening during the dinner times and breaks, often in the basement corridors near the toilets.

This evidence suggests that for Asian students, girls no less than boys, schooling takes place in an atmosphere of constant intimidation. The attacks come apparently from nowhere, and the severity of the physical damage done to the individuals targetted seems to depend completely on luck. The extent of the psychological damage done to students concerned, as individuals and in terms of their collective identity is no doubt immeasurable.

The failure of those schools to guarantee the safety of black students (and particularly the Asian students) as they compulsorily attend those corridors of terror is one of the biggest indictments of the English schooling system. Students are entrusted to schools for twelve years, from the age of 5 through to 16. The secondary system picks them up at the age of 11. By then they have already worked out where they are on the racial divide, with the racial language and conduct to underpin their position. Could one expect, or should one not expect, that with 3 to 4 years, in secondary education, fourth year students would be assisted in unlearning their racism and in dealing with the oppression that they themselves face?

Elinor Kelly and her team of researchers attempted to look at this very issue by doing a "trawl" of a cross-section of Manchester schools and gathering information from 1st and 4th year students. We present their report in full, and trust that the schools concerned and the City of Manchester would wish to own and take responsibility for these findings as a useful if somewhat disturbing, window into the nature and extent of racial harrassment, racial violence, and racism in Manchester schools.

CHAPTER 26

The Tip of an Iceberg – Part 3
Elinor Kelly's Survey and Report

Students, Racial Groups and Behaviour in School
Working Paper No. 3, Report of a Survey by
Elinor Kelly, December 1987

Elinor Kelly wishes to thank many people who have helped her during this research study but especially her research team – Cathy Stopes, Sitara Shaikh, Nyrmla Singh, Alison Kelly and Eva-Lotta Carnestedt – and to the teachers and students in the three schools. "We" refers to the survey team and not the Macdonald Inquiry.

A. Introduction

The Macdonald Inquiry commissioned a research study from Manchester University in which students were to be asked about their views of and attitudes to racial violence in school. This study was carried out between July and October 1987. A questionnaire suitable for use with all students, white and black, was designed and administered to 902 students in three Manchester secondary schools. Fieldwork was carried out in the classrooms with first year and fourth year students; the teachers were present and students were encouraged to enagage in discussion with the research team once they had completed the questionnaires. The findings of the survey are being communicated to the students and teachers who took part.

The identities of the three schools have been obscured throughout this report and only the details essential for the analysis are included. This precaution is one which readers are asked to respect so that the anonymity of the schools, their teachers and students can be retained.

The schools which were selected for the survey represent a cross-section of schools across the city and the region in a number of ways, but especially because of the fact that one in five of their students is Afro-Caribbean, Asian and Chinese. This proportion is lower than is to be found in inner city schools but is common among many other schools in the towns and cities of the north of England. One of the schools selected is a boys school, the other two are mixed. The inclusion of the boys school was considered particularly important because it enabled us to compare the responses of boys in a boys only setting with boys in mixed schools, and with girls in those schools.

The first year students were selected in order to take advantage of the fact that they had just arrived in their new schools and would be applying what they had learnt in the cultures of primary schools to a different, large-scale situation. The fourth year students were selected for similar reasons, they had just moved into the upper school, an environment of greater pressures with its emphasis on academic achievement and study options. Comparing the responses of students aged 11 with those aged 14 would enable us to assess their different experiences and viewpoints, and would also show how young students develop a range of ideas and beliefs, especially in relation to racial issues.

The students were questioned in two ways in the questionnaire. Firstly they were asked about their personal experiences – of teasing and bullying in school, especially name-calling and fighting. This approach gave all students an equal opportunity to take part in the survey and its findings, whatever their racial group, because they were being invited to comment on everyday issues in the mainstream of school life. But secondly the students were asked questions about racial names they had heard and racial fights they had seen, in the hope that valuable information about the views and attitudes of a full cross-section of individuals would be obtained. We gave no explanation of the term "racial" and we encouraged those students who did not understand the term or who became confused, to answer "don't know" or "don't understand".

The students were not asked to define what they understood about the different forms of behaviour and the research team did not interview students. This is unsatisfactory, but it was decided that, given the present state of knowledge of racial issues in schools and the speed at which the survey needed to be completed if the results were to be of use to the Macdonald Inquiry, this limitation should be accepted. Readers of this report should view the survey as being a substantial "trawl" out of which indicators and patterns have emerged and which the Inquiry, the teachers and the students may put to good use.

The usual class teacher was present on every occasion when we administered the questionnaire and we expect that their presence had an off-putting effect on some students. However, it was felt that teachers and parents would be best reassured about the content and purpose of the survey if the research team was observed in action. Racial issues are known to cause acute anxiety and tension among adults and we had to balance the dangers of the survey being misrepresented against the expected loss of information. As it turned out, many of the students took the opportunity to state their views openly, in their written responses and in the classroom discussions with the research team, but we cannot estimate the effect on those who kept quiet.

This report gives a summary of the main findings of the survey in relation to students and teachers and to name-calling and fighting. All the results have been analysed and cross-checked with reference to school, year, gender and racial group and these details are highlighted as and when relevant. Other material collected in the survey has been put aside and will be analysed and presented on other occasions and in different forums.

B Schools and Cultures

In a survey such as this, it was self-evident that some form of racial/ethnic categories should be developed. Manchester City Council recently finalised a standard form for all parents to complete to enable them to put together a record from all schools of students' ethnic origins. This form and the categories it contains were designed for use by adults and not by students aged 11 and 14, so it needed to be adapted if we were to expect students to complete questionnaires without close guidance. The Council's questions on language and religion were revised and another concerning 'community' was added. Students were then asked to tick which language, religion, community applied to them from the lists which were given in the first pages of the questionnaire.

Having coded their responses to these questions, students were each assigned to one or other 'racial group' by using the computer to tabulate language x religion x community. Those who ticked Gaelic or Welsh Languages, or Irish, Scottish or Welsh communities were assigned to the 'Celtic' group. Those who ticked a European language (including Turkish, Hebrew or Yiddish) or the Jewish religion or Polish or other European communities were assigned to the 'European' group.

Those who ticked Caribbean English or Creole, or Rastafarian religion, or African or Caribbean communities were assigned to the 'Afro-Caribbean' group. Those who ticked Cantonese, Hakka or Vietnamese languages, or Buddhist religion or Chinese or Vietnamese communities were assigned to the 'Far Eastern' group which was renamed the 'Chinese' group once it was clear that all the students in it were indeed Chinese, whether of Hong Kong or Vietnamese origin. Those who ticked Arabic, Bengali, Gujarati, Hindi, Pashto, Punjabi or

263

Urdu, or Hindu, Muslim or Sikh religion, or Bangladeshi, Indian or Pakistani communities were assigned to the 'Asian' group.

And the 'English'? It is an interesting commentary on the current state of racial and ethnic adjustments in Manchester, and Britain as a whole, that the single most difficult racial/ethnic category to define constructively is 'English'. It is far easier to count the English as being the ones who are not anything else, and the students were aware of this. Several of the first years became anxious because they had no other language than English and they tried to find some language association in their family which would, as it were, earn them ethnic credentials.

It was also revealing to note how many students, especially first years, did not recognise the word 'Christian'. They thought of themselves as Protestant or Catholic or Methodist etc., not as 'Christian' even when the list contained references to Buddhist, Hindu etc. In addition, when it came to the matter of 'community' many had obviously not discussed at all the possibility of 'being English' in the way implied in the survey, nor had they discussed the other kinds of community identity which could be theirs, eg class and neighbourhood.

The 'English' in our study became those students who ticked on English language, Christian/Humanist/Atheist/None for religion and English for community and who did not indicate, by tick or in writing, details in any section which would draw them into one of the other five categories.

Once this work of assigning students to racial groups was complete, the racial breakdown of the students in the three schools could be summarised as in the table below:

Summary of the Racial Groups of the Pupils in the Survey

	Afro-Carib	Chinese	Asian	Celtic	European	English	TOTAL
School A	16.5	4.3	7.0	14.3	4.8	53.0	230
School B	2.1	2.1	6.3	12.4	9.1	68.0	331
School C	6.2	0.9	18.5	17.9	6.7	50.0	341
TOTAL	66	20	100	135	64	517	902

It is clear that the racial and cultural contexts of these students vary. In School A, 53% of the students in the survey were English, 17% Afro-Caribbean, 14% Celtic, 7% Asian, 5% European and 4% were Chinese. The number of Afro-Caribbean students was higher and of European students lower than in the other schools. We learnt that many of the

Afro-Caribbean and numbers of other pupils come from outside the catchment area because their families have chosen to send their daughters and sons to this school which has specialist traditions. Nonetheless, the neighbourhood of the school is significant in shaping the cultures of the school. The council housing estates which border onto the school were described by some of the students in graphic terms as rough and tough. 69% of the local population rent council housing, much of which is in the form of high-density blocks of flats and the local rate of unemployment stands currently at 43%. The housing estates are also predominantly white (in 1981 only 8% of local households were New Commonwealth or Pakistani) and poor working class – only 11% of the local workforce are in non-manual occupations, compared with the city average of 24%, and 14% of the local population are unskilled manual workers – almost double the city average of 8%.

In School B – the boys school – more than two thirds of the students are English, 13% are Celtic and 11% are from the black/asian groups. The catchment area for the school is overwhelmingly white (only 2% New Commonwealth and Pakistani households) but it is not as poor as that of School A – for instance the local rate of unemployment is 18%. Social class differences are more marked in this area – 23% of local residents are in non-manual occupations and while 46% of local households live in council rented housing, another 44% of residents live in owner-occupied housing. Moreover, relatively little of the local housing is high-density, instead terraced family housing and semi-detached houses with gardens border the school grounds with only one tower block to be seen in the vicinity.

The students in School C are divided between 50% English and the other groups – most notably, 19% Asian, 18% Celtic, and 6% Afro-Caribbean. These statistics do not tally with the 1981 Census data in which, for instance, only 6% of local households are New Commonwealth or Pakistani. However, this discrepancy may be accounted for by the fact that this school's neighbourhood has a high rate of mobility in its local population, indicated by a remarkably high rate of privately rented housing (31%) and correspondingly low rate of council rented housing (26%). The local wards are not poor – much of the local housing is terraced and semi-detached family housing and many of the large 19th century houses have been sufficiently well-maintained to be desirable housing even today. The 1987 rates of unemployment stand at 20%, but that is spread unevenly, for 32% of the local population are in non-manual occupations.

Discussion

These three schools are not in the inner city, they do not have large populations of black/asian pupils, but they are still multi-racial situations. One of our tasks in the survey was to explore whether the particular racial mix in each school and neighbourhood traditions had any noticeable effect on the students and on their behaviour.

C: Behaviour in School: Name-calling and Fighting

Any caring adult has clear memories of the teasing and bullying that went on at their own school, whether they experienced it themselves or witnessed the mistreatment of other students. Parents dealing with an anxious or frightened child explain that they themselves went through similar experiences and had to learn how to deal with it. Adults also have memories of the impact of seeing or hearing what the teachers did to sort out such problems; they can remember which children were left to fend for themselves, which children took matters into their own hands, which children were immediately and consistently backed by school staff.

Teachers' responses to pupils' complaints about teasing and bullying can become an effective commentary on the school ethos – who is valued and supported, who is taken seriously, who is regarded as a nuisance and troublemaker. Any parent who wants to make enquiries about the school to which their child is to be entrusted is certain to think, and ask, not just about a school's educational achievements but also about the reputation of its teachers in dealing with conflict among students. Often parents have no choice and they have to send their children to a school which they do not feel they can trust; but that does not mean that they accept the situation. They will do all they can to support and back their children if they become the targets of serious teasing or bullying. In such situations the extent to which they can protect their children will depend a great deal on what they are told and on their relations with the teachers.

In spite of this generalised concern, little is known about the ways in which teasing and bullying in school are patterned and structured – most people have tended to assume that they are so widespread and frequent a feature of school life that there is nothing to say. 'It's a fact of life, isn't it?' is a common response. If questions are asked about who become the victims and why, the answers are often given in terms of circumstances which are individual and extraordinary, not in terms of group and hierarchical processes which could have been developing for some time and which would require different responses from adults if they are to be effective in stopping the mistreatment of children by others.

And yet, students themselves are very alert to groups and hierarchies in school and to the part which teachers play in the tensions and conflicts which arise among themselves. They are learning all the time, not just through what they are taught in lessons, but also through what they can observe and absorb about behaviour and response. It is for this reason that we consider there could be much to learn from students themselves when it came to a study of inter-racial behaviour in schools. We also felt they would have much of value to say not only about their own experience, but also about what they had heard and seen in relation to others.

The two aspects of teasing and bullying on which we concentrated were name-calling and fighting. Name-calling is usually regarded as a trivial, harmless form of behaviour but it is known that it can also become extremely serious if the target/s of the name-calling become distressed, angry or aggressive in response. It is also known that the name-caller can be calculating and deliberate in her/his intent to hurt and provoke, sometimes goading a victim to the point where she/he erupts into violence and then gets into trouble with the teachers. It is therefore important to distinguish the trivial from the serious in name-calling and to identify both intent and effect – we have given attention to these points.

Fighting, on the other hand, is a form of behaviour which is taken more seriously by students and teachers and which is far more likely to lead to someone being disciplined. But again there is a question to be asked. When is a fight a fight and not just 'messing about'? And who is to decide, and how, which student has picked the fight and should be disciplined? We attempted to assess the relative seriousness of fights by means similar to those we employed in relation to name-calling and we gave particular attention to the connection between racial name-calling and fighting.

One of the first things which we learnt from the survey is that being teased and bullied is a common experience; at least two thirds of the students in each school, both years, boys and girls stated that they had been teased or bullied at school. Only one third of students consistently and repeatedly stated that they had 'never' been teased or bullied. This third was spread across the three schools (31–40%), and included numbers of students from each of the racial groups; however, rather more girls (42%) claimed they had never been teased or bullied than did boys 36%).

When questioned about the forms of teasing and bullying which they experienced, the students picked out name-calling as the single most significant – 66% had been called names which made them angry or miserable. More boys (55%) recorded name-calling than did girls (50%) and more students in the three black/asian groups (76%) recorded name-calling than did the students in the white groups (64%). Gender and racial differences were noticeable in the analysis of the data even at this early stage and they were to persist as we delved into more detailed questions about both name-calling and fighting.

Name-calling

It is important to distinguish between the trivial and the serious when it comes to name-calling and we asked a number of questions which were intended to find out how seriously it was taken by the students themselves. For a start we emphasised 'names which have made you angry or miserable', then we looked at who had done the name-calling.

66% of students recorded having been called names which made them 'angry or miserable' – 67% of boys and 63% of girls. There were no marked differences between the schools or between the years in rates of name-calling but there were differences between the racial group. 71–80% of the students in the black/asian groups had been called names, compared with 64–65% of students in the white groups.

Who called these names? We asked the students to indicate whether they had been called names by 'other students' and/or by 'friends'. 53% recorded being called names by other students. Again, there were no differences between schools or boys and girls on this point. However, there were marked differences between the racial groups. 66% of the Asian students recorded name-calling by other students, compared with 56% of Celtic, 55% of Chinese, and 50–52% of European, Afro-Caribbean and English. It would seem as if the Asian students in particular suffer from name-calling by students – 13% above the average for all.

Less than a quarter of the students (23%) recorded name-calling by friends. The racial groups in which the highest rates of such name-calling were recorded were the Celtic (28%) and the Afro-Caribbean (27%). This could suggest that within these groups are numbers of students who enjoy name-calling as a form of joking among friends. Thinking of the figures this way isolates the Asian students further because not only are more of them called by other students, fewer of them (17%) are called by friends.

Names which make me Angry or Miserable

First Year			Fourth Year		
			—	—	—
Tiny toddler	—	—	—	—	—
—	—	—	White bitch	You boot	Daft S***
Knob head	Fatty	Sweaty	None	—	—
Wally	Dive	Dickhead	Paki	—	—
Nigger	Slag	Tramp			
Titch	Gay	Slag	Cow	Bitch	Silly names
Fat pig	Fat bitch	Stupid cow	—	—	—
Bastard	Smelly	Dickhead	Slag	Dirty	—
Goofy	Idiot	Prat	—	—	—
Racist names	Fish	Dog	—	—	—
Nob head	Shit head	Dickhead	Paki	—	—
Big head	Skinny				
	Dumplin		Fart head	Fart breath	Fart features
B word	Stinks of pro	Nob head	Your mum is a fat bitch	Dad's a tramp	-
Smelly, Dickhead, your parents are dead			Pakis	Swearing	—
—	—	—	—	—	—
Bastard	—	—	Personal remarks	—	—
Skid	—	—	Personal remarks	Lies	—
Pig	Skinny	Bitch			
Nothing has made me miserable			Bitch	Cow	Slag
Dickhead, Your mum's dead, Knob head		Bitch	Cow, slag	Fish, dog
Dickhead	Nobhead	Your mum	—	—	—
			—	—	—

These figures still tell us little in themselves about the impact of the name-calling and we felt that it is important also to know the content of what is called. To this end the students were asked to list three names in response to the question 'Which names make you angry or miserable?' and then these names were then classified according to their content, as summarised below and in the list above which is taken from one of the sheets on which we recorded their responses.

It can be seen that between the two age-groups there are differences in the range of words; anal + sexual references such as 'dickhead' and 'smelly' and physical references such as 'specky four eyes' and 'fat slob' are prominent in first year vocabulary – appearing 316 times. While still the largest single category in fourth year vocabulary, it is noticeably smaller (124). In fact the fourth year vocabulary is more varied; 397 words do not lend themselves to rapid classification and have had to be grouped together as 'miscellaneous' for the time being.

There were certain points of similarity, nonetheless. When questioned by the research team in the classroom discussions, students in both years agreed that the single worst form of name-calling was 'family' – e.g. 'Your Mum's dead'. They thought that family name-calling was always meant to hurt and expected it to cause trouble. Also, much of the name-calling was individualised – to do with details of personality and physical appearance rather than origin or neighbourhood.

The one exception was what we have called racial name-calling – words such as 'Yid', 'Nigger', 'Chink' and White honkey' which imply notions of group or community, and not in terms of praise but of dislike and offensiveness.

Discussion

Racial differentiation has emerged strongly in this account of name-calling. More of the black/asian students report being called names than do the white students. In particular, two thirds of the Asians report being called names by other students and only 17% by friends – statistics which we interpret as indicating tension about the name-calling. In addition, although we expressed no interest in racial names as such, they came up as the third most recurrent in type. Moreover, they proved to be the names which locate students most firmly into stereotypes and depersonalised categories.

Fighting

What then about fighting – the other aspect of school behaviour which was investigated? Pupils were asked a series of questions very similar to those in the section on name-calling and, again, the results were analysed by school, gender, year and racial group.

59% of students stated that someone had picked a fight with them in school; as one would expect, this was more true of boys (64%) than girls (43%). However, there were also differences between the racial groups; more Afro-Caribbean boys (79%) reported fights being picked than did any other racial/gender group, than all Asians (70%) and the Celtic, European and English boys (61–63%). Of girls only the Asians had a rate equivalent to that of boys (7 out of 10).

How seriously do the students take these fights? Only 16% reported that friends had picked fights, 7% less than in the case of name-calling, whereas 49% reported other students picking fights. Differences between the racial groups were again evident. 52–56% of the Asian, Afro-Caribbean and Celtic students reported fights picked by other students, compared with 44–47% of English and European and only 35% of Chinese.

Discussion

Name-calling is a common phenomenon in schools, fighting also, but we do not know much about how students distinguish joke-name-calling or toy-fighting from 'the real thing' and there are dangers in taking the discussion in this report beyond what can be substantiated by the data.

However, details of the racial differences in the schools are beginning to emerge. Pupils in the Celtic and Chinese groups felt themselves to be particular targets of name-calling. Disproportionate numbers of Afro-Caribbean boys reported fights being picked. Significant numbers of students in the Asian group felt that they are the targets not only of name-calling but also of fights being picked. It would seem that even before considering issues which are overtly racial we can detect racial inequalities and discrimination in students' experience of school.

D: Racial Issues

To what extent do the students themselves perceive 'racial' content in name-calling and fights and what do they understand as being 'racial'? Because this survey was carried out among all students the questions we asked about racial issues – eg 'what racial names have you heard?' and 'have you seen any racial fights?' invited comment and observation rather than reporting of individual experience. The questions were designed this way so that all students could have an equal part in the analysis. We also avoided the use of any racial vocabulary in the questionnaire, other than using the word 'racial' itself, and 'racist' with the fourth year students.

Racial names:

We began by summarising the data about racial names. Each question-naire contained the questions 'have you heard anyone being called racial names in school?' 77% of students claimed that they had heard racial names in school, 72% of first year and 84% of fourth year students.

Such a response, however, would have little significance if there were signs that the students just did not understand 'racial' at all and were only answering out of a misguided sense of obligation to their teachers and the research team. We therefore listed and analysed their responses to the question – 'Which are the racial names you have heard most in school?'

'Which Names make you Angry or Miserable?'

	First Year	Fourth Year	Total
Physical	117	52	169
Family	66	64	130
Animal	45	13	58
Anal + Sexual	316	124	440
Racial	75	79	154
Miscell	257	397	654
No response	429	654	1083
Query	12	6	18
Total	1316	1389	2706

* The totals sum to three times the number of students because each student could list up to three names.

We list overleaf a selection of the names they wrote and in the table above we display a summary of the major categories.

For this exercise a strict system of counting was maintained. We preferred to undercount at this stage and excluded all words which did contain a term as explicit as 'Paki' or 'Nigger' for instance. Terms such as 'Bud-bud' which we know applies to Asians, and 'Ice-cream' which applies to whites, have been left in Miscellaneous for the time being.

There are signs that some of the first year students were confused about 'racial' – almost 50% of their available spaces were left blank, and in 129 instances, they wrote down names which had no obvious racial connotations. Nonetheless, many of them proved to be well aware of racial vocabulary, repeatedly noting the same words as the fourth year students.

With the fourth years, what is noticeable is that more of the students paid attention to this topic than to our general questioning – a sign of greater interest? By listing their words, they revealed that their vocabulary is harder and more compact than that of the first years. 'Paki', 'Nigger' and 'Black' – appear even more frequently than with the first years.

Which are the Racial Names
You have heard in School?

	First Year	Fourth Year	TOTAL
Paki	172	306	478
Nigger	102	185	287
Black	67	105	172
Chink	24	47	71
White	14	27	41
Yid	8	26	34
Anal + Sexual	129	17	146
Miscell	152	123	275
No response	644	551	1195
Query	5	2	7
Total	1317	1389	2706

Discussion

In relation to racial name-calling, the differences between first and fourth year students are prominent and this is true for both girls and boys and across the racial groups. At this stage of analysis it is not possible to correlate and quantify much of the names data, but it would appear that the first year students are divided among themselves. Some are familiar with the same vocabulary as the older students, but there are others whose grasp of 'racial' is uncertain as yet. By the time they are fourteen, the students recognise the term and apply it far more accurately.

Racial fights

The students were asked 'Have you seen any racial fights in the school'? 48% claimed they had seen racial fights – 43% of first years and 49% of fourth years. How do they know the fights are racial? We asked the students this question and there was a deal of consensus about their answers, some of which are listed below in the form of statements which we asked them to write in this section of the questionnaire. The words are the students' own.

'Because there is a lad at school who has a plait in his hair and everybody hits him and fights with him (including 2nd years and 3rd years and he is only a 1st year)'

'Once a white boy went up to an Indian and called him names then battered him'

'I have been in one against the Paki'

'You hear people calling someone and then a fight'

'Because it is dead rough and lots of people crowding round'

'Because they said bad things like tramp, whitey, blacky'

'People that pick on other people for no reason'

'Because of the words they said like 'get back to your own country''

'Because I know the lads who were doing it and they were shouting "Kick the Paki bastard's head in' "'

'Because someone called him a fuckin stupid bud'

'Because they call them racial names and start fighting. And news goes around'

'Because there was a Paki and me a white'

The students judge whether a fight is 'racial' by looking at, or hearing about, who is involved and by the names which are called. They are not, it seems, so concerned about the specific issues which might be in dispute.

We asked the students 'Who is to blame for starting these fights?' and some sharp differences emerged, as can be seen in the extracts below:

'We get the blame'

'It is always the white person'
'Racial boys'
'The people who start calling names'
'The person who is picking on a person from another country'
'White people mainly because they tend to be racist in their own community'
'Mostly the coloured, they think they own the place'
'They should not be in this country'
'I am not racialist so I cannot say who is to blame'
'Pakis, because they think all white people are against them'
'The person who calls the name'
'The people who think they are hard in front of their friends'
The fourth year students were asked if they thought other students are racist. 70% said that some were and 23% stated that they thought many were. When asked how they knew if someone was racist, they gave some revealing answers about the low-level hostility and aggression which can be sustained in schools:

'They give you dirty looks, never polite to you, when they are to someone of their own colour'
'You can tell when they look at you in a bad way or even write notes about your colour'
'They won't let any black or Indian kids play with them'
'If they call people racist names, if they pick on them only, if everyone is messing about, they get told off'
'Because they won't talk to the other colour. If they see them or they push beside them, then the remarks come out'
'Because they call the person names and some people don't go near someone who they are racist against'

Discussion

The approach we adopted in this part of our enquiry is one which has revealed that attitudes to racially discriminatory behaviour are not the monopoly of any one group in these schools and that each racial group is itself differentiated in terms of students' experiences and responses. A number of the black/asian students revealed that they are not particularly aware of, or concerned about racial issues, a number of the white students wrote quite explicitly about feeling that racial discrimination is wrong.

Our data about racial name-calling has proved to be revealing about differences between 11 and 14 year olds as well as pointing us towards the prominence of certain vocabulary in both age-groups. Given what we know already about the exposure of the Asian students to general name-calling and fighting, the fact that 'Paki' is called to such an extent in school suggests that they are being picked out and picked on to a disturbing extent.

Boys and Girls: Responses to Questions about Racial Issues

	BOYS %		GIRLS %
	School B	Schools A + C	Schools A + C
Been called names	69	69	66
Hear racial names	84	76	78
Fights picked	64	65	43
Seen fights	97	95	96
Seen racial fights	56	49	38

The data about racial fights did nothing to alter the impressions we were gaining about the Asians, as a group, or about the Afro-Caribbean boys who had also been picked out in our earlier analysis. The selection of extracts about racial fights reveals resentment, cruelty and victimisation as well as competitiveness. It also reveals how difficult it is for students from different racial groups to argue, fall out, scrap or compete with each other because their encounters will be viewed as 'racial' by other students.

Girls and Boys

As a final check on our results, we analysed the numerical data about racial name-calling and racial fights with reference to school and gender. There were no significant differences between girls and boys when it came to having heard racial names in school – 77–78% for both. But when it came to fights, there were marked differences between the two – 37% of girls recorded seeing fights as compared with 51% of boys. These findings were consistent with the figures recorded for boys and girls in relation to the general questions about fights in school.

It was only when we included the three schools in the gender analysis and asked questions about the boys in the boys school that some important statistics were revealed – as summarised in the table below.

Racial Names Heard in School

First Year			Fourth Year		
—	—	—	Paki	—	—
—	—	—	Paki	—	—
—	—	—	Paki Basher	Grease head	—
—	—	—	Black bastard	—	Paki
Tramp	Idit	Specy	Paki	Bud-bud ding-ding	—
Nigger	White honky	—	—	—	—
Piss off	Cow	Fat	—	—	—
Cow	Slag	Pig	Paki	White trash	Black bastard
Slag	Pig	Cow	—	—	—
Paki bastard	—	—	—	—	—
			Wogs	Paki	—
—	—	—	—	—	—
Scraff, dickhead, dirty names, shithead, tramp, sipo, fuck off			Go back to Pakis	Chinkier	Paki barbers
Dickhead twat	Poony	Crap face	—	—	—
—	—	—	Black bastard	—	Paki
—	—	—	Nigger	Skid	—
—	—	Paki	Skid, Paki	Nigger	Chink
Silly cow	Stupid bitch	Dickhead	Bud-bud	—	—
Stupid cow	Dickhead	Stupid bitch	We don't want black people in our country	—	Get lost you black currant
Tramp	Dickhead	Shitbag	—	—	—
Tramp	Dickhead	Shitbags	—	—	—

The boys in School B responded very similarly to the boys in the other schools over the general questions about behaviour – been called names, fights picked and seen fights etc. The reader will recall that it was gender and racial differences which dominated the analysis of those statistics in Section C of this report.

In relation to the racial issues, the school B boys stand out, not just from girls, but also from the other boys. 84% of them have heard racial names, compared with 76% for all other boys and 56% state that they have seen racial fights, as compared with 49% of all other boys.

Discussion

Given the context in which this report is being written – the enquiry into racial events at another all boys school – these findings are important. They reveal that there is no marked difference between the behaviour of the boys in the two mixed schools and the boys in the all boys school – until we look at racial issues. How can one explain this finding?

School B stands out in the comparative analysis of racial groups as the one which is apparently most homogeneous – more English, fewer black/asian and Celtic students; more Europeans than the other schools. In this detail may lie a clue because this is the only school in which references to Jews were included in the name-calling vocabularies. Students told us about some of the inter-communal strife which has taken place in the school's catchment area. Jews, East Europeans, Irish and Chinese have been subjected to abuse and harassment on local estates in spite of, perhaps because of, their relative stability and prosperity. Racial name-calling and racial fights have neither begun nor ended with the arrival of black/asian people into the locality. It would seem as if a number of the boys who spoke to the research team were well-versed in an 'indigenous' hostility to aliens, both white and black.

It also known and expected that boy culture in school is typically more ebullient and rumbustious than that of girls – there is more physical jostling and messing about, the names called are more explicit. It is possible therefore that a boys only school has a multiplier effect on gender differences and that inter-group and inter-personal relations and hierarchies are more openly displayed. It was mainly among the boys, for instance, that we learned about the 'myths of terror', to do with 'sprogs being bashed' on Friday 13th and with 'egging' on birthdays – just two of the ways in which the juniors are socialised into student hierarchies in which senior students will dominate.

But still the same question remains – why should it be the racial issues which picked out this boys school, rather than the other aspects of behaviour which we compared?

E: Racial Groups in Schools

In the table below we summarise the responses of the students in answer to our question 'Are your friends at school from different racial groups?'

278

Friends in Other Racial Groups

	BOYS %		GIRLS %
	School B	Schools A + C	Schools A + C
Often	12	27	28
Sometimes	50	46	49
Never	35	24	21
Don't Know	4	4	2

These figures show that only one in four students claim that their friends at school have never included someone from a different racial group and that the majority of students have had such friends either often or sometimes. However, there are two points on which the boys in school B differ. For a start 10% more of these boys state that they have never had such friends, and only 12% have often had such friends.

Whether as a result of neighbourhood traditions or the current racial mix in the school, it would seem that these boys do not have the same degree of friendly relations across racial groups as do the other students. Their distinctive responses on racial issues may well be related to that fact. It is possible that it is the additional 10% of students who have never had friends from other racial groups who have swung the statistics of school B in the direction we have noted in the discussion above.

Nonetheless, 62% of the students in school B and 73–77% of students in the other schools have had friends in other racial groups and the scale of this involvement is reflected in their responses concerning the best things and worst things about racial groups in school. Many of the students proved to be perceptive about the interplay between positive and negative aspects – people sticking up for each other and learning about each other versus feeling excluded and resentful, and fearing that fights will break out more frequently:

'That you have other people the same as you'
'They stick together and try to help others'

'That you can understand how other people live'

279

'That it helps people adjust to mixing with other races'

'That they give you a chance to learn about other races and not become racist'
'You always have somebody to stick up for you if you get called something'

'That there is more fight and I don't think that when you call someone a name no matter what name it is, means you are racist'
'That when arguments begin, name-calling by colour or creed is quite common'

'They think they can have the corridors otherwise you are being racist'
'It can cause fights or name calling'

'If two people call one which are different colours they usually make racial remarks at each other'
'Racial groups tend to stick together instead of mixing'

These extracts have been selected from all three schools – girls and boys, different racial groups and both age groups – in order to demonstrate the complexities of the relationships between social position, individual personality and racial attitudes and perceptions. The students whose written responses are displayed above have captured the positive and negative aspects of relations among racial groups in ways which we find very evocative and illuminating.

Discussion

During our fieldwork in the schools, a full range of responses was displayed in front of us and we realised how much there is to learn about what many of the students almost took for granted – major differences of opinion among themselves. On the one hand we were congratulated for bringing such an important and serious issue out into the open. On the other hand, we were treated to open displays of suspicion and contempt.

It was disturbing to encounter open hostility on the parts of some students and also to read some of the accounts which were not just antagonistic to the idea of their being anything good about racial groups but which were full of foul abuse. We had to learn how to take such responses in our stride and to place them in their overall context. Then they became less disturbing because in many instances they were encountered by other students who openly opposed them.

Nonetheless, the students, whether positive or negative in their views, are actually underlining the point we have made already – how difficult it is for students in different racial groups to be individuals in these schools. With some notable exceptions, it seems that encounters between black/asian and white students are viewed as group encounters and that many of the students talk and think in stereotypical ways which their friendships have not penetrated.

F: Teachers

In the questionnaire students were asked whether they complained to teachers about name-calling and fighting and they were also asked about the responses of teachers.

Surprisingly few students had complained to teachers about name-calling – just 11%. Given that 66% had recorded being called names which made them angry or miserable, this disparity is quite remarkable. It is true that the racial groups differed in the extent to which they had complained – three of the groups most affected did complain to teachers more than the rest – 20% of the Asian, 18% of the Afro-Caribbean and 15% of the Celtic students had complained to teachers, compared with 5–9% of the other groups. But even so the gap between incidence and complaints does seem to be very wide. What explanation can there be for this?

In general, whatever the policies and practices of the schools may be, the students did not seem to be aware of teachers responding either to incidents or complaints. For the most part, the students reported, the teachers told them to ignore the name-callers and to carry on as usual. Only occasionally would they take action:

'They told the boy off'
'They did nothing and then after a while they told the students concerned off'
'She told me to calm down and ignore them'

Also, the teachers are not seen as entirely blameless – 17 students (9 black/asian and 8 white) stated that they had been called names by teachers and 34 students (17 black/asian, 17 white) stated that they had heard teachers call racial names.

What then is the pattern in relation to complaints about fights? 12% of all students complained to teachers about having fights picked with them, and the Asian and Celtic students again were outstanding among the racial groups (rates of 19% and 15% respectively, as compared with 5–10% for all other racial groups). Again the gap between incidence and complaint is extremely large because 59% of all students stated they had had fights picked with them.

When the students do complain about fights, the teachers respond more strongly:

'Move the person who I fought with to another class'
'Sorted it out there and then'
· 'They saw the students concerned'

But then 16 students (5 black/asian and 11 white) stated that fights had been picked with them by teachers. And when we asked the fourth year students 'do you think that people in your school are racist?', 180 replied that they thought that about a few teachers, 48 about some and 19 about many. They also gave us examples of what they considered to be racist behaviour:

'The way they carry on at you, telling you to do this and that, looking at you like dirt, giving you the wrong grades, telling you your work's like sh.. when it's perfectly alright'
'They are nice to the white groups of people and then if the black people say anything, they get sent out or get into trouble'

'If they call people racist names, if they pick on them only, if everyone is messing about, they get told off'
'By when the teacher called my friend as he was walking past'

'You can tell because of what they say and the way they don't involve them in things much. Teachers don't often ask them to do anything in class, like answering questions'
'They talk to the other kids in a kind way and when we say something they talk to us as if we are idiots'

These statements were written for us by a cross-section of students in both black/asian and white racial groups in the three schools. Taken together they suggest that a number of students, despite the classroom conditions in which they completed our questionnaire are prepared to criticise teachers and to suggest that teachers contribute to the racial inequalities in the schools.

Discussion

The responses outlined above have revealed that very few students have complained about name-calling or fighting, of whatever kind and however serious, to their teachers and that, when they do, they are seldom aware of positive and effective response. Whatever explanation is given for this gap between incidents, complaints and response, it points towards a disturbing element in the schools. It suggests that communication between students and teachers is not good when it comes to these forms of behaviour.

It also suggests that the teachers themselves are in difficulties when it comes to dealing with students in the racial groups which are most subjected to name-calling and fighting, firstly because they are being deprived of the information which could give them more insight into inter-racial tensions, secondly because a sizeable proportion of the students believe that they are racist. Neither of these conditions is conducive to good relations between racial groups.

G: Conclusions

The survey of students undertaken in the three Manchester schools should be viewed as a 'trawl by questionnaire' which has thrown up indicators and clues which need to be pursued if students, teachers and parents are to clarify the ways in which racial differences are filtering their way through schools. A basic premise in our work has been that racial issues do not start or end with overtly discriminatory attitudes and behaviour, but that they are meshed in with the mainstream of what goes on in schools.

By looking at name-calling and fighting we have studied only one small piece of a mosaic, but, we would argue, the insights developed in the analysis of those aspects of behaviour complement and substantiate those which are explicitly racial. For instance, who would have thought that 'specky-four-eyes' as a name which makes a first year pupil miserable, could have any connection with racial fights? The answer is that it should not and need not – it is a term of personal abuse which is hurtful, and while it may provoke wounded response it is not expected to stimulate group tensions. But, as we have seen, it is part of the same vocabulary, and less frequently used, than words such as 'Paki' and 'Nigger' which are not only personally insulting, but which can also be used to excite racial tensions. Until and unless students and teachers draw some lines of demarcation between the two kinds of name-calling, the vocabulary of racial names will continue to be prominent in schools and will feed into the dynamics of relations between the racial groups.

The students' reports suggest that the three schools need to be

283

vigilant because there is rumbling discontent and disquiet, not just among black/asian students but also among whites – most notably the Celtic group which has appeared several times in positions akin to those of the black/asians. These groups have reported in a way which suggests they perceive the schools – students and teachers – as being unjustly discriminatory. Their disquiet seems to be shared also by two other sets of students, both of whom have been observing the treatment of students other than themselves and who have conflicting views about what they have seen. On the one side there are the bitter comments of the students who resent the black/asians and who see teachers in collusion with them; on the other side there are the sad and tentative remarks of the students who think that students and teachers have been unfair to black/asian students. Either way, they are not commenting on individual and inter-personal behaviour in isolation, they are talking about relations and incidents which have the potential or actuality of group formations which could flare into inter-racial conflicts.

Students in these schools have shown themselves to be very alert and perceptive when it comes to racial issues. In thinking about the individuals who may become either 'victims' or 'aggressors' we are, it seems, talking about a small minority. But in terms of the conditions which allow racial victimisation to develop or persist, we are talking about what we can learn from the majority of school students. No racial group has a total monopoly on attitudes or experience; social class and other factors do not stop functioning simply because a school contains different racial groups.

Good teachers, who can be trusted with students, are dealing all the time with injustice and discrimination and must deal in an even-haned way with all kinds of teasing and bullying. It does not seem unreasonable or unreal to expect them to learn how to interpret the racial dimension which is feeding its way into existing inequalities and discriminations. Quite how they will be able to do that while so many students report a gap in the lines of communications is uncertain. We hope that our survey will be seen as one small step on the way towards greater insight and more effective response.

CHAPTER 27

The Tip of an Iceberg – Part 4
Plant Hill – 1984

"Last month he was attacked by a group of boys from Upper School who said he should go back to where he came from. They said they were the Young National Front and were going to sort out all the Paki's in the school.

"'X' thought all schools should have anti-racist organisations where Asian students could get together and sort out how to deal with the things that happened – name calling and physical abuse. He said that at home, he always went round with a gang of friends who looked after each other, but when they had tried to do the same at school, teachers often tried to break them up, and accused them of starting a race war."

Extracts from an interview with Burnage student.

On March 15th 1984, David Jones, the then Senior Assistant Education Officer, received the following internal memorandum from one of his staff:

Plant Hill High School – Invasion and Damage

1. Mr Speller rang to report that on Tuesday afternoon 30+ black youths between the ages of 15–17 arrived at the school; broke into three classrooms causing damage; two teachers who sought to intervene were attacked; one sustained a kick in the groin, the other's glasses were broken. The youths were carrying baseball bats and sticks. Mr Speller further reports that prior to this incident the youths had been the cause of a similar one at Higher Blackley Youth Club.

2. The Police were called to the school and later some 18 youths were arrested in the Blackley area. Since this incident Mr Speller has asked that the police maintain a high profile surveillance of the school and they are doing that. There are rumours that there will be a similar incident to that above tonight. Mr Speller has advised the police.

3. The reasons for the incident are not known nor is it certain where the youths came from. But it is thought that some may be unemployed and that others are from North Manchester Boys and

Moston Brook. Mr Speller has been in touch with the Heads of
those schools.

4. As you may know, there is a deal of National Front activity in the
   Blackley area. Mr Speller suggests that the incidents above may be
   used to encourage that. It is conceivable there may thus be a
   backlash.
5. Mr Speller phoned in order that we might note events. He will be
   writing in more detail later. I believe his union will seek compensation for the injured teacher.
6. For obvious reasons I shall copy this note to Mr Sterne, Mr Sharp,
   Mrs Underhill and Mr Warm.

Ian Hughes, 15.3.84

On March 14th 1984, Hugh Speller, Head of Plant Hill High, sent the
following letter to parents of students at his school and at the Plant Hill
feeder schools:

PLANT HILL HIGH SCHOOL

Headmaster: H. E. Speller B.A.   Plant Hill Road,
Telephone: 061 740 1831/3   Blackley,
HES/MT   Manchester M19 2WP

14th March, 1984.

TO ALL PARENTS

Dear Parent,

You may have heard from your child that yesterday afternoon we had
some problems in school. A group of youths not connected with the
school came on the premises and caused damage and frightened a
number of our students. Two members of staff dealing with the
situation were slightly hurt but there were no serious injuries. The same
group of youths had already caused serious damage at Higher Blackley
Youth Club. Eighteen youths were later arrested and have been
charged. I can understand parents' concern about this matter and I
would like to reassure you on the following points:

1. Pupils in the school reacted very sensibly which helped to ease the situation;

2. The school is taking every precaution possible to ensure that there should be no similar incidents but I am sure you will appreciate the size and layout of the school poses enormous problems.

I have reminded all students of the following:

1. If they have school meals they should remain on the premises throughout the lunch break thus avoiding any possibility of problems on the streets;

2. That they should go home directly from school at the end of the day and not congregate in groups;

3. That they should inform the school or their parents if they are aware of any particular problems;

4. That they should not go on the premises of other schools.

Hopefully the situation will soon cool down but I think it is essential that we are all vigilant.

Yours sincerely

H. E. Speller
Headmaster

This was followed up by a "Report to the Chief Education Officer on Problems Experienced at Plant Hill High School on Tuesday – 13th March 1984".

The full text in the report detailing the incident is presented in Appendix D. It fills in the details of the note to David Jones, but adds, quite significantly:

"The exact cause of the attack by intruders are not known but it does appear that they could result from a fight between a student at this school and a black youth from Our Lady's High School on Friday 9th March.

One of my concerns has been the racial overtones of the incident as all the intruders were of West Indian or Pakistani origin but *in dealing with this matter with our own pupils we have been at great pains to ensure that it should be seen as a criminal act not as a racial act.* (Our emphasis).

I am sending copies of this document to all members of the Governing Body, to the Heads of the feeder primary schools and the Secretaries of the professional associations who have asked for it."

Time passed; the Education Department accepted the Head's view that it was a criminal act, and that the police had got the matter in hand.

On April 2nd 1984, the Head of Our Lady's R.C. High School, sent his version of the events of March 9th to the Education Department:

Friday 9th March

Just after 3.30 p.m. a fight occurred in the park off Cooper Lane between David McCorkle and W ... M ... (Plant Hill). The fight was broken up by Mr Riordan and Mr Alston. A second fight involving Mr Fitzpatrick, a friend of David McCorkle's, was also broken up. In this second incident, Mr Riordan and Mr Alston were attacked, neither was injured but Mr Riordan's anorak was torn beyond repair. Both boys were sent back to school, David was very shocked and abusive to everyone, eventually Mr Moran calmed him down. Michael Fitzpatrick had a split lip, this was cleaned up and both boys were taken home by Mr Moran. Both boys were shocked and upset but neither appeared to have serious injury.

Thursday 15th March

David McCorkle came into school just before lunchtime, he was immediately sent to see me. He explained that he had come to school to get something done about the fight last Friday, 9.3.84. I informed the police and they came to see him in the afternoon.

When asked about the fight on 9.3.84, David volunteered the information that he was attacked again on Cooper Lane on Monday, 12.3.84 by three youths. He hit one and then decided to run away, something was thrown at him which hit him on the head, however, he continued running along Victoria Avenue and eventually caught a bus home.

The youths were unknown to David. He said, at this time, that he was frightened to come to school in Blackley and that he wanted a transfer. I informed him that if this was the case then his mother should come and see me so that we could discuss the matter.

The police asked David a number of questions, in my presence, and explained as carefully as they could why they were unable to prosecute. They told him that he could take out a private prosecution but it was likely that Wayne Ward would make similar allegations against him.

David also admitted that he had been at the Abraham Moss Youth Centre on the morning of 13.3.84 and that he knew some of the boys who invaded Blackley Youth Centre and Plant Hill High School on that day. However, he said that he knew nothing about the boys coming to Blackley and was not involved.

There has been no approach by Mrs McCorkle as far as a transfer of school. David's attendance, punctuality and behaviour are similar to what they were before the incident.

Time passed.

Seventeen black people had been charged with affray and other serious charges. Yet, despite the reference to racial acts and National Front activities, etc., the Education Department did not investigate the reasons for 24 to 30 black youths descending on a YTS project and then on an unsuspecting school.

Meanwhile, the youth's only support was coming from the staff at the Abraham Moss Youth Club, with whom they already had a relationship. One of them told the Inquiry:

"When I heard the background to his involvement and the involvement of other young black people in the affray, I contacted the local District Inspector who was Adge Warm. I should say that charges had already been made on 18 young men at that time.

The CHAIRMAN: That is charges of affray and other offences?
A. That is right.
Q. They having been arrested by the police?
A. That is right. There was also one young white person, who was also arrested with the group of young black people, who was not charged and was released. There was a lot of discussion between the group of young black people about this particular member of the group, and why he had not been charged.

Mr LIZAR: What was the feeling about that amongst the ones who had been charged?

A. They just saw it as part of the police's racist behaviour, that his parents apparently had attended Collyhurst Police Station, where the whole of the group was being held, and after discussions privately with the police and the parents of this young white person, he was released without being charged."

Discussions between that team of youth workers and a senior officer from the Education Department led to certain questions being asked about how much of that background the department did in fact know.

Another memorandum in the Education Department states:

"Given the questions raised by Mr Hughes, and the leads given in Mr Speller's report, especially the fact that eighteen youths had been charged with causing an affray, we need to isolate the various ways in which the system at Crown Square is so fundamentally flawed that neither Our Lady's nor Plant Hill itself was thoroughly investigated. Taking into account defending solicitors' view that the prosecution would have been prepared to drop the matter had the education department intervened and put the background facts to them in the weeks immediately following the incident I feel the lack of prompt and sustained action is regrettable, to say the least, and certainly speaks volumes about our prioritising."

That memo went to Dr Jones and was copied to six people. Could someone not have checked progress even if only occasionally?

On the 29th November 1984, the Chief Education Officer, Gordon Hainsworth, received the following memo from the officer who was by now working very closely with the youth workers at Abraham Moss.

Plant Hill Incident

Following our meeting earlier today about the above, I feel I ought to draw your attention to the report sent to these offices by the Head of Plant Hill High School on March 26th 1984, for the attention of Mr Ian Hughes, and also Mr Hughes' memorandum to Dr Jones of March 29th 1984.

For convenience, I have numbered the paragraphs of Mr Speller's report, as attached. The salient points I wish to isolate are as follows:

Para. 2 –   It is clearly stated that 18 youths were arrested and charged with causing an affray.

Para. 3 – The extensive involvement of school staff and students in putting together the Crown's case is equally clear from this account.

Para's – "There was a heavy police presence in the area",
4 & 5 understandably. But, there is no indication that the Head alerted the Area Principal of Community Education or any youth workers to see whether they knew anything about the background to the incident or the origin of the information the school received. In other words, the police are asked to have a high profile, it was obvious that youths at Higher Blackley were implicated in some way, and yet there is no consultation with youth work staff.

Para. 6 – This statement and the next are perhaps the most critical in the report. The Head has reasons to believe that the "attack" was not just unmotivated, mindless violence against school property, staff and students, and that it may well have had a precipitating cause. He makes specific mention of a "black youth" from Our Lady's High School, in a fight with "a student" from his school. Nothing is said about whether he took the trouble subsequently to ascertain from staff at Our Lady's whether they knew about that fight and its background, or about the racial origin of the student from his school, or anything else for that matter.

Para. 7 – Yet, in the very next sentence, he expresses concern about the racial overtones of the incident because of the origin of the intruders, and emphasises how painstakingly the school sought to ensure that students viewed the incident as a "criminal" rather than a "racial" act. Presumably, he quite rightly could see no reason why thirty black youths should want to attack a predominantly white school just for the fun of it. Since it perhaps did not occur to him that his school might be harbouring racists and National Front members and sympathisers, and that they may well have made some of those black youths their victims, he was prepared to "flag" racial harmony at all costs, with or without facts, and despite the intelligence about the fight, and project the black youths as "criminals".

Para. 8 – I feel very strongly that without seeking to condone the

291

manner in which those youths took it upon themselves to deal with the matter, that headmaster owes it to them no less than to his staff, students and their parents to take equal pains to correct the record and give the youths' reasons for entering the school and moving from classroom to classroom.

Para. 9 – Much as I appreciate the logistical reasons for the Head's plea for the introduction of "high tech", I feel that this is perhaps the first step to calling for security guards to solve a staffing and procedural problem. The fact that any such measure would be linked inevitably to "the day the blacks invaded" would no doubt stamp "race problem", "blacks/criminals giving rise to siege conditions" indelibly on the minds of staff, students and parents alike, while the school blissfully fails to confront "the enemy within".

Para. 10 – You will see that the Head has distributed this report to his governors and to other key persons. Begging your indulgence, I should like the part of this memorandum that deals with that report to go to all those people to whom the report was sent. I would go further and suggest that a day of in-service training be organised for the school staff and all the recipients of that report, other heads in the North Manchester area, and community education staff, to focus on that incident and the institutional response to it, to examine and seek to develop strategies for dealing with the widespread experience of racism in educatonal establishments in North Manchester, in the context of the imperative given to all of us by the Committee's anti-racist education policy.

It seems to me that whatever lessons Plant Hill School may have learnt from the incident, there are a hell of a lot more for them, the other educational establishments in the area, and the Education Department to draw out of it. I trust these comments have indicated some of those lessons, and not least of all the fact that institutional racism is not some indiscernible abstraction that oozes out of the ventilation system in our institutions, but is embodied in the assumptions, decisions and actions of well-intentioned, competent, often well-paid, powerful, professional men and women."

Following a series of departmental meetings, Gordon Hainsworth wrote to the Governing Bodies of Our Lady's R.C., Plant Hill High, and Abraham Moss High Schools.

He stated that:

1. Following the incident at Plant Hill High School on the afternoon of Tuesday 13th March 1984, eighteen youths were arrested and charged. Charges were dropped against the one white youth involved and seventeen black youths are due to come before the Crown courts on a charge of affray. I write to inform your governing bodies that solicitors for the defence intend to raise the issue of mitigating circumstances and with information now at my disposal, it is the Committee's wish and my intention to assist defence counsel in their efforts to establish support for such a plea.

2. Concern in these offices over incidents of a racial character was reflected in the letter sent to Heads of Schools and Colleges on 14 May 1982. A list of 16 reported incidents involving schools and/or young people in the North of the City has been compiled and a copy is enclosed. A separate report of like incidents recorded by the Housing Department is also attached. Counsel for the defence will therefore now be seeking to set the events of 13 March 1984 in the overall context of racist activity in the north of the City.

3. More particularly, the events of 13 March 1984 will be set in the perspective of the sequence of events reported by witnesses directly involved. Evidence, for example, already submitted by X, a student of Our Lady's, constitutes a summary version of events culminating in the Plant Hill incident.

4. Discussions with youth workers, the group of young people themselves and their parents have revealed that apart from incidents of a racial nature in and around schools, some of these young people and their parents have been subjected to physical and verbal abuse by white young people and adults, many of whom are thought to have connections with the National Front. Apart from feeling that X had been wronged, many of those involved in the incidents at Higher Blackley and Plant Hill agree that because of their experience in the community round about, to do nothing about the attack experienced by X was to leave the

way open for further attacks, to which any members of the group may have been subject.

5. My purpose in writing to you is not to comment on matters which may shortly be sub-judice but to advise Governors and Schools of the Committee's intention to afford the department's resources to assist Counsel for the defence of the youths in establishing the context of racial harassment and provocation in which the incident at Plant Hill School arose.

Yours sincerely

G. Hainsworth

The letter also lists, for the first time, McCorkle's version of events. (Appendix).

The Head of Our Lady's R.C. responded by taking issue with that version, as follows:

a. Page 2, para 1 and particularly the last sentence –
    " . . . The teachers took "X" back to school; "X" asked to phone the police but was not allowed to do so . . ."
    The Head states that the fight reported in this paragraph was in effect two fights, during the second of which "X's mate, "Y" was seriously hurt. When the boys were back in school the main concern was with dealing with the injury which "Y" had suffered. No request was received for a telephone call to the police; the question did not arise.

b. Page 2, last paragraph, last three lines –
    " . . . "X" has not attended school for 4 to 6 weeks because WW and his friends kept coming back to his school . . ."
    The Head reports that "X" had a poor attendance record and this was cause for concern both to his parents and staff, as a result of which the Education Welfare Officer was working with "X" and a place was in the process of being negotiated for "X" to attend a DISS Centre at Abraham Moss.

David McCorkle's evidence on the issue of involving the police and of the seriousness with which the school was prepared to view the incident is emphatic:

"We got taken back to school and I wanted to phone the police, but the headmaster wouldn't let me. I started arguing with him but he still wouldn't let me. The two teachers told the Head that they'd got beaten up as well. I told the Head I wanted to phone my brother and he wouldn't let me do that either. The Head didn't get in touch with my mum but the Art Teacher Mr Moran did. He gave me and Michael a lift home. When we got there, my brother who is 19 was at home, my mum was not. She was at work. The teacher told him what had happened. He didn't tell him what the school intended to do about it.

When the Head wouldn't let me ring the police I started going mad. I even swore at him, he told me he wouldn't have that sort of conduct and I should go home and cool down. I was never told to go home and think over the matter of involving the police."

– Witness Statement of D. McCorkle.

Somebody was clearly "being economical with the truth".

The Head's reaction was not the only one provoked by Gordon Hainsworth's letter.

On Tuesday, February 15th 1985, the Governors of Plant Hill High School met. Adge Warm, District Inspector, represented the Education Department at the meeting. A note to the Chief Education Officer gives a flavour of the Goveror's reaction to his letter:

"At that meeting, (and here I reproduce the notes Adge provided), the Governors were all very much against the CEO's letter. They argued very strongly that the issues of racism and the affray should be kept entirely separate one from the other, for in no way did the one relate to the other.

Strong resentment was expressed about the fact that, as they saw it, teachers were not thanked by the LEA for preventing the affray escalating.

Strong resentment also that teachers did not receive compensation for damage suffered during the affray, eg., smashed spectacles.

Strong feelings expressed about lack of LEA support for teachers at the school over this incident.

Teachers have now adopted the attitude that if such an incident were to occur again they would not try and intervene.

The headteacher has referred the matter of the CEO's and Adge's intervention to his Union, and has been advised to instruct a solicitor.

295

The teachers concerned have also referred the matter to their Union. From what Adge could gather, it appears that the Union have in turn referred the matter to their National Executive.

In Adge's words, he 'received a right hammering' and he had to face it alone. His argument to the meeting that the Committee has an anti-racist education policy and that the perspective of the black youths concerned must be taken into account simply provoked more resentment.

No one seemed to want to hear about racism or about the street experiences the young people have had. The general impression given was that the CEO's intervention was an affront to the teachers and the school, and an example of 'bending over backwards' to support black youths whose story lacked credibility anyway, while, at the same time, ignoring teachers and failing to support them."

Within a couple of weeks of this meeting, Gordon Hainsworth had received letters from both the Professional Association of Teachers (PAT) and the Natonal Association of Headteachers (NAHT).

PAT argued:

"It is surely a function of the Education Committee to be supportive of the staff, Headteacher and the school and not to undermine the good work being achieved, particularly in a Community school. To involve the school in racial incidents totally outside its jurisdiction can only lead to unwarranted publicity which will greatly impair relationships in the future. We would be grateful for your assurance that no action will be taken which will prejudice the position of the school and its staff."

What does "to involve the school in racial incidents outside its jurisdiction" mean? It is surely reasonable to expect the school to take an interest in the possibility that it is harbouring racist gangs or members of the National Front who engage in racist attacks and then retreat to the relative safety of the classroom. Whatever one might think of their method, it was not the group of black youths that involved the school. It is those whom they hoped to find in the school. The police took no action against them, and there is nothing in the Education Department's records that we have to suggest that the school did take some action in relation to them.

NAHT, like PAT, saw it as a question of taking sides, and not exposing employees of the Authority:

"The decision taken by your Committee means that it will be providing assistance to the Defence in a situation where employees of your Authority could well become vulnerable to "attack" by the Defence, bearing in mind that at least 5 members of staff are due to appear as police witnesses.

The Governing Body have already criticised the action of your Department and the clear implication that the staff of the school are not being fully supported by their employers.

The above issues are relevant not only in this case, but also to schools at large in Manchester."

This case demonstrates, yet again, how difficult it is for young black students to look to established structures for action in confronting the racism they experience within their communities. A school takes no action in relation to a serious assault. Even if the school did not itself feel it would be productive to involve the police in the first instance, it could have given some indication to the aggrieved student as to how it was going to handle the situation.

Instead, however, the focus shifts to McCorkle himself. His non-attendance cannot have anything to do with his fear of racist attacks from gangs of white youths. He has been a regular non-attender before anyway, and therefore the fact that he was set upon twice by the same groups of people cannot be considered a legitimate excuse for his non-attendance.

The Education Department accepts his view that he was baited with name-calling: "coon", "nigger". In his statement he says that the girl W . . . W . . . used to go out with, and whom he describes as his "friend" told him that W . . . calls him nasty things.

Is this just a fight over a girl who ditched one guy for another, or is it some conflict being played out in the area of race, or race and sexuality, the sexuality of the black male?

Be that as it may, the disturbing thing in all this has got to be the speed with which those in authority satisfy themselves that there is no racial aspect to the two attacks on McCorkle, attacks in which he was clearly outnumbered.

The gulf between the lived experience of racism of young black people and those in authority whose over-riding concern seems to be to outlaw that experience is one that breeds a violent response to racial violence. Young black students experience not only the violence of the racist attack, but also the violence of the might and power of the system which highlights the criminal response of the black students but does nothing about the earlier racism and violence which provokes that response and thus effectivey condones those earlier racist attacks.

The failure of those in authority concerned to heed the very clear messages coming through from the evidence in this chapter must inevitably lead to groups of black or asian youths organising themselves for self-defence and getting themselves involved in the sort of confrontation that characterised both the Plant Hill affair in 1984 and the Burnage affair three years later.

Making those links, under our terms of reference, has been the responsibility of this Inquiry.

CHAPTER 28

Manchester City Council
Anti-Racist Policies: How are they made and who makes them

In March 1978, the Chairman of Manchester Education Committee issued a brief statement of intent concerning multi-cultural education, defining the general aim of such education as the development of "harmonious race and community relations". In the years since 1978, there has been a succession of reports concerning multi-cultural education in Manchester, principally stemming from the Chief Education Officer and directed to three Manchester Education Committee sub-committees: Policy and Estimates, Schools, and Continuing Education. By June 1980 the then Chief Education Officer reported on the existing 'initiatives' covering a wide range of topics e.g.:

> "the employment of specialist teaching and non-teaching staff; the work of Curriculum Development Leaders; mother-tongue teaching; the Support Service; issues of social education; the Summer Language Project; work with parents; ethnic music; welfare and counselling services; teacher and student foreign exchanges; teacher training and in-service education; the Youth Service and youth worker training; careers advice; work with the unemployed; post-school education; the Industrial Language Training Unit; the support of Vietnamese refugees; 'ethnic minority' community groups."

The first basic approach to multi-cultural education was that black children had "special needs". This report did not mention racism.

The second basic approach to multi-cultural education was to focus on cultural exchanges designed to promote positive racial attitudes: this approach was summarised in a report dated 5.11.81.

> "The key to multi-cultural education lies in the teacher's attitudes and their willingness to become aware of the cultural background of their students and members of society at large and to take account of this in their teaching."

The more cynical comment on this approach is 'Saris, Somosas and Steel Bands'. Racism, however, is not a result just of cultural misunderstandings, it is an operation of power relationships, and whilst it is important to make space in the school curriculum for various forms

299

of cultural expression and experience, this will not be as adequate as anti-racism.

As the Intitute of Race Relations has said:

"Just to learn about other people's cultures, though, is not to learn about the racism of one's own. To learn about the racism of one's own culture, on the other hand, is to approach other cultures objectively."

(IRR, Statement to the Rampton Committee, RACE AND CLASS, 22, Summer 1980, p. 82).

Racism itself was not openly acknowledged in Manchester until a report in 1982 following the disorders in Moss Side in 1981. This report called for all educational institutions in the city to produce individual policies on racism, and provided examples of such policies produced by schools in the ILEA. Other than the definitions of racism in these ILEA statements, however, the MEC document did not define racism, nor provide guidelines as to anti-racist strategies, nor describe any means of implementation and monitoring of institutional policies to be established.

Reporting incidents of racial tension

In 1982 the Education Department sent the following letter to all Head Teachers and Principals of Educational Establishments.

14th Mary, 1982

Dear Headteacher/Principal,

RACIAL TENSION

1. The specific knowledge which we have in the Education Department about the extent of racial tension within, and impacting on, educational establishments is limited. I intend to monitor its occurrence.
2. Any serious instances indicative of racial tension should now be reported to me; please address any letters to the Chief Education Officer, marked for the attention of Mrs B Luckham, Services Branch. We should like to know about instances such as the scrawling of graffiti, the distribution of racist literature, threats to or actual disruption of social events, physical attacks upon individual students or staff (teaching and non-teaching) or groups where an

explanatory factor may be the ethnic origins of the parties involved, and racial abuse directed by students or students towards staff or vice versa. I appreciate that some people may feel that the monitoring of such events may contribute to their happening; I do not share that view and anticipate that headteachers, principals, and others will ensure that it is not the case.

3. In some instances you will obviously decide, in addition to letting me know about them, to involve the police or other agencies or individuals as appropriate. There have been discussions between officers of the Authority and senior police officers. Whilst not wishing to suggest that they subscribe to the view that racial tension within schools or colleges is of a significant degree or increasing, the police are hopeful that headteachers and others feel able to seek their assistance and advice not only if incidents occur but in anticipation of them. Normally, educational establishments should involve local community contact police officers, details of whom are listed below. *In exceptional circumstances*, where speed may be essential, contact with the police should be made by recourse to the '999 system'.

4. A multi-cultural approach to education will bear fruit in the long term, but there is some action which can be taken which may have an immediate effect.

5. Some action which can be taken may have an immediate effect:

   (i) The swift removal of graffiti and in this context, racist graffiti, on and around buildings. The Direct Works Department contains a team of staff known as the 'graffiti squad'. They are usually able to remove graffiti of an obscene or racist nature within twenty-four hours of being told of its presence. This facility is made available either by sending a Repair Note to the Area Maintenance Depot of the Direct Works Department or by telephoning the Works Service Unit 223 7222, extension 158 or 153 and following up with a Repair Note to the depot.

   (ii) The prevention of the distribution of racist literature within or at the gates of schools, colleges, youth clubs and so forth.

6. The action outlined in this letter has previously been fully discussed with the teaching associations and has been circulated to non-teaching staff associations for comment.

7. I am copying this letter to the Chairs of Governors of all establishments and to community groups.

8. Heads and Principals will note that I have enclosed two extra copies of this letter. This is to facilitate wide circulation among the staff of establishments, both teaching and non-teaching.

Yours sincerely

G Hainsworth

By 1983 according to Gordon Hainsworth:

"The community consultation meetings continued and a Racial Tension Working Party had developed within Crown Square. I did not at first attend meetings of the Racial Tension Working Party, but after the Head of Services Branch left the authority I formed a new group to replace it – the Equal Opportunities Group – which I have chaired since then (early 1984). Its bi-monthly meetings have examined reports of incidents with racial aspects and, at the same time, it has sought to co-ordinate work on racial issues within the Department and the service at large. Its main purposes of collecting information on racist incidents and how they have been dealt with remain, but the group also took on the responsibility of co-ordinating the approach towards race throughout the service.

The present political administration took over in May of 1984. At this time, the researcher Barry Troyna produced some work on the development of the Manchester City Council policy on multi-cultural education. In brief, he stated that although the *City Council and Education Committee had policies on multi-cultural education, schools were not really aware of the details and implications thereof.*" (Our emphasis).

Gordon Hainsworth says that in 1984 he initiated moves which led to the establishment of the Education Development Service (EDS), which was to be a force for curriculum change. Various separate groups of detached teachers' support units were merged to become one distinct group for curriculum and institutional development.

In 1984 the City Council approved the following statements within the policy framework for the education service:

"We are committed to the development of a programme of positive action in our education provision to tackle the under-achievement of women and girls, members of ethnic minorities, working class families

302

and disabled people. All our institutions will oppose racism and sexism and should be multi-cultural and non-sexist in their practices."

By 1984, we were told, it became clear that the City Council were committed to an overall policy of equal opportunities. Within this, the emphasis moved from a multi-cultural position to an anti-racist position. The Equal Opportunities (Ethnic Minorities) team was formed within the EDS with a view to co-ordinating work on anti-racism. Statements on anti-racism and proposals for anti-racist training were produced and discussed with employees from ethnic minorities, but we were unable to get agreement to an overall policy on anti-racist training. Over a period of time, work on anti-racist training proceeded in part through the EDS and in part through establishment in-service training (INSET), but in the absence of an overall agreed policy. Meanwhile the Equal Opportunities Group continued to meet and deal with racist incidents as they arose.

Then in 1984, an Anti-Racist policy was developed by Manchester City Council.

"Manchester Education Committee employ over 20,000 people within this city. As an employer committed to confronting racism and its damaging effects on all Mancunians, the Committee expect their employees to uphold this commitment. All employees, both non-teaching and teaching and of every grade are expected to contribute fully to an education service founded on equal rights, equal opportunities and mutual respect.

The Committee expect their employees to behave in a non-racist way towards the public, other employees, and students. More than this, employees are encouraged to be critical and/or to help change institutional practices and procedures that work against equality. Racist abuse, harassment and discrimination is not acceptable. Employees must know that such behaviour will be subject to disciplinary action possibly leading to dismissal."

This punitive rather than informative model of anti-racism, takes little account of the everyday experiences of Asian, Black and White Mancunians, and does not draw on their positive experience, nor was it drawn up in the way in which one Manchester Head had drawn his school's policy by going to students' parents and listening to what they wanted. A school is a community. That community should be listened to.

303

Equal Opportunities Working Party and the issue of class

In March 1985 the Education Department Equal Opportunities Working Party was established, with the following terms of reference, approved by the City Council:

(a) "review the service and departmental employment practices in the light of the council's equal opportunity policy.

(b) develop the detail of policies to combat all direct and indirect discrimination within the service on the grounds of race, sex, disability and sexual orientation

(ⅽ) fully involve representatives and members of the groups covered by the equal opportunities policy in formulating the departmental policy.

(d) to oversee the implementation of the Council's policy on Equal Opportunities in Employment within the department."

The policy draft that was eventually presented to the City Council does not just deal with discrimination on grounds of race, sex, disability and sexual orientation but also with class, and dealt with it as follows:

7   *CLASS*

7.1 This section does not try to define or analyse class. It uses the terms "class", "working class" and "middle class" as they are generally understood. Prior to 1980 the Registrar General's definition of 'social class' meant status within the community. Since 1980 the office of Population Censuses and Surveys has abandoned the notion of status. Subsequently the Registrar General's definitions of social class groups are more closely linked to band together people of broadly similar occupational skills. Occupational skills is a less emotive term than "status in the community" and reflects more the socio-economic circumstances which might have been influenced by educational background, qualifications, training or access to 'education'.

7.2 Class and class perceptions have an important effect upon education. During the 1950's, it became clear that the 1944 Act's theme of 'equality of educational opportunity' was not working Working class children were finding access to equal opportunity in education difficult and the gradual introduction of the comprehensive school was an attempt to correct disadvantage. This still has not worked. Many children in the 1980's still suffer from disadvantage. Practices such as streaming used by school systems further disadvantaged working class children by fixing

304

expectations. Disadvantage can be reduced by avoiding streaming in schools. Teachers need to be aware of their effect on children and parents with working class backgrounds. Teachers are seen to be middle class and although many teachers may themselves have working class origins children will perceive them as from another, different class. Teachers need to be aware of their own inbuilt perceptions based on class attitudes and to be aware of how these are transmitted. Certain actions by those in authority can give the impression that a student or student's background or culture is inferior. Attitudes to work, leisure, religion, food and family can imply that anything other than the "middle class norm" is of less value. There is also the danger of stereotyping groups of children and adults because of perceived similarities when in reality there are considerable variations."

They went on to deal with the issues they felt were raised by class:

7.4 More than one issue is involved:

   (a) introducing students and teachers to the idea of social mobility; making teachers aware that students are not bound by their social class in any deterministic manner;
   (b) countering a traditionally negative perception of the working class contribution to society;
   (c) fostering a pride in membership of the working class;
   (d) providing a positive environment in which to view working class contributions to culture and society's values.

7.5 Mobility might be seen as contradicting a positive image of a working class background. This authority believes there need to be no conflict for a student, provided institutions are sensitive to the issues, and the authority is committed to combatting classism throughout the service.

7.6 Teachers need to ensure that all students regardless of class and cultural backgrounds are given equal consideration not just by their peers but also by other teachers."

The authors of the policy draft felt that the institutional structures should respond to the problems:

"Institutions need to:
(a) avoid the stereotyping of students either from different 'social classes' or genders from the beginnings of Nursery and Infant Education through to the option year of secondary education

305

and post-16 in the variety of courses available for academic and vocational orientated students;

(b) make themselves aware of the possible damage done when the value system presented is one which makes sense only to those that have formulated it;

(c) ensure that teachers present positive images of all people irrespective of class;

(d) ensure that teaching materials and books should present positive images of all cultures;

(e) help students to understand the meaning of social class in its historical content.

Issue of "class" left out

When the working draft was presented it did not find favour with the leadership of the City Council.

The issue of class was dropped. For some councillors it was cleary too controversial and, unlike issues of sexism or racism, it did not easily lend itself to any "all party" consensus. In our view this is a regrettable decision, because class discrimination and the way to overcome it and foster class mobility has been central to all education policies since 1944.

To deal with sex and race, but not class, distorts those issues. Disadvantage can only be dealt with if it slots neatly into a race or sex pigeon hole. All grievances, if they are to be remedied, become issues of racism or sexism, even when their causes are much more complex. This ostrich-like analysis of the complex of social relations leaves white working class males completey in the cold. They fit nowhere. They become all time losers. Their interests as a group are nowhere catered for. That, surely, is a recipe for division and polarisation, particularly in the area of anti-racist policies.

The City Council's decision also creates an interesting situation as far as education initiatives are concerned:

"Manchester's use of Section II funding has increased dramatically in recent years, a fact which the Minister of State for the Home Office drew to the attention of those attending an MCCR meeting when he explained that funds for the City had increased from £118,000 in 1979/80 to £2.2 million in 1982/83" – (D Gibson 1985).

Meanwhile in Poundswick country, a group of Heads of infant, primary and junior schools in Benchill and Woodhouse Park, produced an update of a report compiled in 1984 on "Educational and Social Deprivation in the Benchill/Woodhouse Park area". It stated:

306

PURPOSE OF REPORT

To update a similar report compiled in 1984.

To outline the extent of the problems experienced by the Benchill/Woodhouse Park Schools.

To stress to the Manchester Education Committee the need for special staffing initiatives to counter the problems of educational disadvantage.

EQUAL OPPORTUNITIES IMPLICATIONS

This report has significant equal opportunities implications.

The City Council's policies on equal opportunities in terms of working class children and deprivation are not being implemented in this area.

The deprived working class children of poor familiies in Benchill/Woodhouse Park are not being afforded the same educational opportunities as similar children in the Inner-City areas.

RECOMMENDATIONS

Immediate action to improve the staffing situation in schools in the Benchill/Woodhouse Park area in accordance with the City Council's equal opportunities policy statements (Annex 1).

The report concluded as follows:

"In 1984 the Headteachers concerned in the compilation of the report made the following concluding statement:

"It is the contention of the Headteachers concernd with this report that the present resources and staffing available to the schools in this area is totally inadequate to deal with the large and increasing number of children suffering from social and educational deprivation."

Since that statement was made the situation in terms of resources and staffing is unchanged whilst the situation in terms of social deprivation has continued to deteriorate.

Large numbers of our parents are unable to cope with their problems. Their children are suffering.

They need extra help.

Large numbers of children in the schools are suffering in educational terms because of inadequate resources to deal with their special needs.

They need extra help.

The teachers in the schools are facing increasing numbers of

307

disruptive, emotionally disturbed and educationally deprived children in their classes.

They need extra help.

The Heads of the schools are rapidly becoming the highest paid social workers in the city at the expense of the job they are paid to do and with decreasing amount of support in terms of NTA time, Educational Psychologist time and EWO time.

They need extra help.

Inner-city schools have major problems with social and educational deprivation.

Some extra help is available to them through Section II teachers and home/school liaison teachers.

Inner-city schools deserve the extra help they receive although in many cases the extra staffing is still insufficient.

Schools in the Benchill/Woodhouse Park area have similar and in some cases even worse problems (Annex 4) No extra help is available.

The Headteachers believe that a minimum of a basic PTR of 1:25 together with extra provision for social deprivation and home/school liaison is necessary for schools in this area.

The Headteachers of these schools call on the Education Committee to implement staffing improvements in accordance with the City Council's equal opportunities policy statements."

Here, then, are a group of Headteachers posing a challenge to the Education Committee to address the issue of equal opportunities in relation to class. Those headteachers all have the problem of white working class racism to deal with in that area.

Furthermore, Section II funding, as we have seen, is intended for a very particular purpose as the wording of the section indicates, but is increasingly used for a far wider purpose. Few local authorities, it seems, keep to the letter of the law and a blind eye is turned to the mild abuse of Section II funding that goes on everywhere. In inner city areas, in particular, it becomes one of the antidotes to serious social deprivation. In Burnage it is available because of the large number of black students. In an area like Benchill in Wythenshawe – a largely white working class area – there is serious social and educational deprivation, but no extra help is available through Section II. The contrast between Burnage and Benchill highlights the problem in Manchester, but it is not just a Manchester problem. It is a national problem, and the solution lies, not with Manchester City Council, but with Central Government. Extra funding is needed – not limited like Section II – for black and white working class children alike.

Reporting and monitoring racial incidents

Though the inclusion of class was too controversial for the City councillors, the issue of anti-racism was not. According to the Chief Education Officer, the anti-racism policy is necessary:

"My personal view is that the City Council and the Education Committee should have a policy on racism. It should cover anything to do with employment and curriculum development. It should not just be a question of non-discrimination on employment policy, it should affect where teachers and learners work, it should have an impact on the way in which institutions function and in-service training should be targeted to effect change. There should be a four pronged attack on policy, employment and institutional change related to in-service training."

In accordance with this view an improved system of reporting and monitoring racial incidents was introduced by the Chief Education Officer. He has now issued various letters to schools on the subject of anti-racism, reporting racist incidents, and the use of the disciplinary proceedings if employees are found to be guilty of racism. A series of letters and statements dealing with these matters are to be found in Appendix F. They start in 1982 and end up into the new reporting system of 1987, which has extended from racism to other forms of discrimination. It was to the 7 February 1987 letter that John Tummon reacted on behalf of MCCR with the opinion that those reporting procedures were not working with race.

So how are these Reports monitored, what use are they to the Councillors?

According to one Asian Councillor.

"The feedback which I have certainly received is that the mechanism is not working, because people have said they have reported incidents in the school and nothing has been heard of them. Certainly when in public meetings we have asked the Chief Education Officer how many incidents had he received in the last three or four years, and the answer we have received is perhaps one or two, or maybe none. Whereas we know from the community that many, many complaints have been made."

This Councillor continued by saying that:

"even when towards the end of 1986 we widened the reporting mechanism whereby the communities could report through the community representatives to the City Council, or directly to the Education Offices, or to the local councillors, or whatever means they could find to actually report the incidents to the Education Authority. Even after that, we have not really had many complaints registered."

To another Councillor the real reason that underlies this 'under reporting' is the system itself:

"with any system of this sort . . . there is a reluctance with people in many cases to report a complaint. They are afraid they will be regarded as a nuisance, or otherwise be penalised, and things get lost, I am afraid, sometimes in the system. The teacher may want to make a complaint and the Head may not take it up."

According to Richard Leese, Chair of Education, there has so far as he is aware been no progress report presented to the Equal Opportunities Working Party in the Educaton Department by the Incidents Group which is chaired by John Taylor, the Chief Inspector, and there is no annual analysis of reporting to the Incident Group.

John Taylor of the Inspectorate accepts that it is up to the Schools themselves via the Head Teacher to ensure that staff, students and parents know of the Reporting System and how to use the Reports System.

One view of these reports procedures and the effectiveness is as follows:

"It seems that the response within Manchester to what are essentially political problems, is often a bureaucratic one, e.g. procedure for reporting racist incidents, involves the filling in of complicated forms which are not to my mind geared to parents or students. The way the form is structured and the procedure that goes with it indicates that it has been designed for teachers to fill in about students. The Authority's position is that incidents should be solved inside institutions. This raises questions about the Head teachers willingness and ability to take on the issues and the support Head teachers would or would not receive. Also, it is unlikely that students will feel able to report incidents inside schools. By setting up this bureaucratic procedure and by focussing on institutional solutions, it could be said that the Authority has abdicated it's responsibility."

To one former worker in the policy section of the Town Clerk's Department, who had a particular interest in the work of the Equal

Opportunities Unit and was then involved in setting up the Race Unit, an immediate concern was that of all the group representatives that came to work with the Council during the organisation of the forum only a tiny minority were from the ethnic communities. White males predominated both in the Council and as Principal Officers to the Council. To this worker:

> "Perhaps the most worrying factor about the Council's 'commitment' to racial and sexual equality is the hypocrisy which inevitably takes place. Frightened that they might not be acting in accordance with Council policy many officers will take great care to generate written material (leaflets for publication in particular) which have a careful balance of text and multi-ethnic graphics, whilst having no under-standing of or acting upon the wider issues. Meanwhile committee and working party representation – both Councillors and officers – remains predominantly white and male."

Consultation with Community Groups

The Education Department began consulting with community groups in 1978, at about the same time that their multi-cultural education policy document was being put around. Prior to meeting with 'ethnic minority organisations' in their own right, the Educaton Department was guided and monitored by the Manchester Council for Community Relations (MCCR) which acted as the organisation representing the interests of blacks and ethnic minorities.

Since 1978, a number of organisations have held consultations with the Education Department. The most regular groups are as follows:

The Manchester Muslim Association
The Indian Association
The Sikh Association
The Greater Manchester Bangladeshi Association
The Black Church Leaders
The West Indian Organisations Co-ordinating Committee
The Chinese Centre

David Gibson, Principal of Community Education for the Central Area, conducted a study in 1985 of the Education Department's consultations with ethnic minorities. His study reveals that most of those groups plus some fourteen others who fell by the wayside approached the Education Department seeking an opportunity to share perspectives and air grievances about the state of the schooling their children were receiving. The one exception was the Black Church Leaders whose representatives "remained adamant that the Senior Assistant Education Officer had 'pushed the idea'."

The purpose of the consultation was never clearly defined, and therefore some of the groups on the one hand and the education officers on the other hand had conflicting views of what those consultation meetings were for. The Education Department's understanding was that:

"These consultations are in keeping with the Manchester LEA policy on education for a multi-cultural society and it is considered that the exchange of ideas and information is an important aspect of the development of policy in this area."

(Chief Education Officer's letter, 1984).

The groups felt that they wished to determine what was discussed, and have the Education Department provide answers to some of the questions they had concerning anything from wanting a separate school for Muslim girls to the way a teacher dealt with an incident in a classroom.

David Gibson found that "the most regular complaint from the black representatives interviewed is the failure of the meetings to be productive."

The Chairperson of the West Indian Organisations Co-ordinating Committee (WIOCC) told us in evidence:

"As an organisation our aim is to represent the views of the Afro-Caribbean peoples in Manchester, and to enable them to get the best out of the system, to improve themselves and also to inter-relate with the host community. I think the thing is that consultation with the Education Authority has not been very fruitful as far as we can see it. We have had it now quite a considerable number of years, and it would appear that our concept of consultation is totally different from the concept or idea of consultation from education . . .

"We consult on a number of issues, and we appear to be going round in circles, in so far as the issues that are sometimes brought to us are issues education themselves want to discuss with community groups. There are times when they bring issues to us that they want just a nod on from us . . ."

The WIOCC complain that power remains with the Education Department and consultation is done wholly on their terms. The agenda for the consultation meetings is set by the officer within the

Education Department, the meeting is invariably chaired by the Senior Assistant Education Officer or his representative, except in the case of the WIOCC who have their own staff. The minute-taker is also an officer of the Education Department.

Consultation has therefore been, in the main, a process whereby the Education Department engages community groups in endorsing and rubber-stamping policies and procedures which they have already worked out.

The one area in which those groups are now seeking to exert some influence is in relation to Section II posts. The requirement that the local authority consult with black groups before decisions are made in relation to the recruitment of Section II staff now places those organisations in a position where they can exert some influence over the way decisions are made about those posts.

It could be argued that the LEA is adopting a somewhat patronising attitude towards those community groups by appearing to give them a semblance of power while at the same time making it virtually impossible for them to exert that power.

But, in many respects this is simply a reflection of the patronage which those groups themselves represent. The LEA consults with them and shares information and policy documents as necessary. We are given no reason by the LEA for consulting with certain groups and not with others. The consultation is done on the basis of the representative nature of those groups, but the LEA seems to be unconcerned about the fact that it is seen to be aligning itself with groups who are not themselves answerable to those whom they claim to represent. Tokenistic though the consultation is at the best of times, there are occasions, as we have seen during this Inquiry, when schools and the Education Department target such groups and involve them in managing the affairs of black people within the community, with or without their consent.

What is even more important is the fact the LEA fails to ensure that the groups it incorporates into its structures do not exclude huge sections of the population they claim to be representing, i.e. young people and women. Nor does it concern itself with whether or not those groups demonstrate commitment to the Authority's equal opportunity policies.

What then is the political location of that consultative process?

Apart from the fact that many members of the City's Race Committee are drawn from amongst the membership of those organisations, the process itself bears no relationship to the Committee structures of the City Council. Officers do not put forward reports to Committees based on the results of those consultations, and, effectively therefore the consultations have more to do with the Education Department's formulation and implementation of policy than with either the concerns of politicians or the requirements of so-called ethnic minority groups.

If the purpose of the consultation from the Education Department's point of view is as stated above, and if 'a multi cultural society' consists not only of black people or black ethnic minorities, why, in the interests of a relevant and grounded policy, is the consultation not taking place with various white groups also? Is a multi-cultural education policy and the monitoring of it simply something that blacks and ethnic minorities should be involved in? It is significant in this regard that there is no consultation with the Irish community despite the fact that they are the largest ethnic minority group in Manchester, and their children's experience of the education system is at least comparable to that of Afro-Caribbean students.

Conclusions

We see the Education Department's consultation with ethnic minority groups as a larger scale version of the consultations with EMAG's at Burnage High School. As a structure and as a process we consider both to be flawed for identical reasons. In the case of the Education Department, the consultation exercise is essentially consulting while retaining power. The groups consulted have no power to take the department's policies in directions other than it wishes them to go. The process of empowerment of those groups, therefore, is one that is undermined.

In the case of the Ethnic Minority Advisory Group at Burnage, a similar argument obtains. The agenda is set by the school, the notes are taken and circulated by the school, and the group simply provides a forum for the testing out or the approval of initiatives put forward by the school.

We take the view, therefore, that the Education Department's and the Burnage (EMAG) consultation processes should be phased out, and replaced by school and college based development councils involving students, teachers and parents from across the school community. Through the development councils the schools would then feed into the Town Hall. Should parents or students wish to organise independently within their communities, as parents or as students, they should be encouraged to do so without interference from schools or from the Education Department. We return to the proposed new machinery for consultation in Chapter 32.

Although we are critical of aspects of Manchester City's policies, we consider that their formulation and implementation has been an important and progressive step. As we indicate in a later chapter, there is no set recipe and there must always be an element of trial and error in formulating and carrying out such policies. Our criticisms, our plans and our recommendations involve change, some of it more fundamental than the rest, but always it involves building on and adapting to the achievements so far.

There exists a different kind of criticism. We are mindful that in formulating and implementing anti-racist policies, both the City Council and schools in Manchester have been forced to look over their shoulders at what has been called the "white backlash". This backlash has both its practitioners and its theorists. We turn to these in the next chapter.

CHAPTER 29

Education on the Front Line – Parents' Right to Choose?

A matter of days before Ahmed Ullah's murder, the Manchester Evening News published an article by Ray Honeyford, entitled "The Myths of Race". The article was presented dramatically in bold type and with a long sub-text which stated:

"...In May this year, Mr Honeyford who lives in Prestwich, was courting controversy again in another article in the Salisbury Review in which he warned that schools would face utter chaos if they accepted that all cultures in their classrooms should have equal status. Today, Mr Honeyford is on the attack again. This time his target is Manchester City Council and their race unit. Here, in another forthright article, he claims there is no room in today's society for such a unit."

In that article, Honeyford states that:

"Anti-racism as an ideology is impervious to reason. It is rather a form of demonology claiming to occupy the moral high ground... Manchester City Council's decision to create a racial bureaucracy is unwise. You cannot produce substantive policy out of myths. In seeking to do so, the bureaucrats may well produce anger and resentment in the population at large – feelings which would be displaced on to the ethnic minorities, for whom there is a great deal of goodwill in the City... Race relations generally will suffer – and that would be tragic – the City fathers should think again."

Manchester Evening News
.9.86

No doubt, by setting up this Inquiry, "the City Fathers" – and no doubt the Mothers too – would have earned themselves the further displeasure of Mr Honeyford and "the resentment of the population at large" for wasting valuable public money" "to discover racism". Doubtless, also, the Manchester Evening News and the media generally will be at pains to inform Mr Honeyford and the population at large exactly how much valuable public money was spent on this exercise.

317

We have already dealt with the debate between Manchester City Council and the Evening News in respect of the interpretation of Ahmed's killing in Chapter Seven. Against the background of the Honeyford article, that correspondence was interesting in itself.

During the course of this Inquiry, three Manchester schools became the focus of much uninvited publicity, as a vociferous minority of their parents with the sometimes over-zealous assistance of the press, decided to insist on their rights.

The schools in question were Crowcroft Park Primary School, Wilbraham Infant School and St Mark's C of E Primary School.

What parental rights were these schools infringing?

As far as the parents were concerned, each of the schools was denying them their rights to impose on their children a "good, Christian, English education". In each case, a wide range of questions are thrown up. What do the parents want? And why? How, in their estimation, are the schools failing their children and thwarting their aspirations as parents? What is the effect of their action on the internal life of the schools particularly on the staff, the young students and their parents? What are the policies of the Education Committee which provoke this good Christian response? And what is the relationship between good educational practice in its own right, and the practice that results from having multi-cultural or anti-racist education policies? The one issue that hardly arose, however, was what are the rights of the child.

Another way of posing the question is: do parents have a right to bring their children up as racists and sexists or to insist that the school they choose for their children does so? Have schools got a right to provide children with a racist and sexist education or have children the right to an education that is geared not to the satisfaction of narrow sectional interests of religion, race, class, gender, parochialism, or nationalism, but to enable them to establish an identity and, a sense of responsibility for themselves and others; to develop tools and skills for understanding themselves, their individual and group histories; for understanding issues in their communities, in society, and in the world; for understanding conflict – the conflict which exists all around them; and for learning to make decisions and form judgements? Have children a right to an education that is also geared to encouraging a love of discovery, of ideas, of creativity, and geared to cultivating respect for others, their opinions, their rights and their entitlements?

Those questions are critical to the current debate around Kenneth Baker's Education Reform Act. They also need to be borne in mind in any examination of the political content of multi-cultural/anti-racist/

318

anti-sexist education policies.

Sadly, however, a concern about the rights of the child has been displaced in the attack on anti-racism by an almost obsessive concern with the party political origins of multi-cultural and anti-racist education policies. They are attacked as the produce of demon left-wing councils put forward in order to combat the immorality of racism and racial prejudice. Local education authorities, such as Inner London, London Borough of Brent, Manchester, and Sheffield are, therefore, attacked as engaging their employees, their parents, and their students in what Honeyford calls "a form of demonology claiming to occupy the moral high ground".

But the promotion of anti-racism and the advancement of good educational practice in the terms stated above, and of the rights of children in this respect is no more the exclusive domain of people on the left any more than "the moral high ground" is the exclusive preserve of people on the right.

In the end, contesting space on "the moral high ground" is about answering the questions:

"What vision of a future society do we have?"

"What is our view of the society we are assisting our children in shaping and transforming?"

"What is the function of education in relation to that?"

People in education, either as policy makers or practitioners, who dare to ask those questions and be guided by them, often find themselves labelled and placed in a particular camp. This is best illustrated by an extract from the evidence to us of one witness involved in the training of teachers in Manchester:

"In terms of in-service, there is not a very great deal done. The University is the institution that runs the diploma courses and the M.Ed. in this particular field of multi-cultural education. The Polytechnic has an in-service course. There is an input of multi-cultural education. It used to be taken up under "learning difficulties" and that, I think, is indicative of the thinking three or four years ago. It was the only area we could find for a couple of sessions relating to the needs of a multi-racial society. It is, of course, a classically damaging heading. . ."

319

Q. On the question of initial training of teachers at the Polytechnic, why is the overall emphasis on multi-cultural rather than anti-racist education?

A. I think I might best answer that by referring to a comment from a senior member of staff at the School of Education. When we were talking about work for equal opportunities, the reference was that there should not be "thought police" in education. That seems to me quite important, and there is the feeling that there could be indoctrination, that this is a political issue. . .

Q. Is it a political issue, in your view?

A. With a small "p", yes. It seems to me, thank goodness, that there are people from all areas of the political scene, apart from the extreme Right, I think, who would be in a position to act effectively against inequality, even with the present climate of opinion, the present Government. I think it is quite possible for there to be non-Marxist anti-racists. I do not regard anti-racism as purely a Left-wing concern. I think it is very important that the case is clearly and publicly re-established that there can be a non-Marxist anti-racism. I think what has happened, of course, is that it has been associated with the Left-wing in schools and, therefore, in colleges, it is seen very much as a radical concern, a Left-wing concern. I think it is also true that there are a lot of teachers who would consider that education does have nothing to do with politics, and that their work, particularly in education, is concerned with creating a good learning environment, happy relationships, and that to bring in elements of conflict, discord and bitterness would damage the work.

Q. Would you agree with that?

A. No, I would not. I can sympathise with it. I can understand the thinking. It seems to me, though, that if you take that to its extreme, you have established a little haven of peace and the kids know very well, particularly in the inner cities, what is going on in the world, or they have got some ideas anyway that there are conflicts, there is bitterness, there is anger.

   If you are going to work from where the kids are, then you must bring in their life experiences, and that brings in something which many people would regard as political.

Q. So the comment, "We don't want the thought police", that is coming from which source?

A. High sources in the School of Education, management sources. It is one particular comment at one particular time.

Q. Does it represent a general climate of opinion?
A. I would have thought so. . .it indicates a general anxiety that this is a political issue, as I say, of indoctrination, and that it is something which we should treat with great caution.

Q. So would you agree then that it is that climate of opinion that has held back a desirable move towards a more specifically anti-racist rather than multi-cultural approach?
A. Yes, I think that is fair comment. A lot has been achieved, but there is also quite a bit of complacency about what has been achieved."

In the 1960s, white parents became very vocal about the number of black children who were being allowed into inner city schools. They viewed the changing face of the local school population with alarm, and prevailed upon their Members of Parliament and their local councillors to take action. The Department of Education and Science then issued guidelines that no school could have more than 30% black children. Where the proportion of black children would have exceeded this, buses were laid on to disperse the black children to other schools "in order to maintain the racial balance".

The organised power of ordinary working-class West Indian parents forced the DES to abandon its 30% rule, and effectively put an end to bussing. Some white parents subsequently fled the inner cities, leaving in some cases a majority of Afro-Caribbean and/or Asian students in the schools. Those students and their parents combined in an effective black working class movement in education, and challenged local education authorities to make the nature, curriculum and organisation of schooling more responsive to their needs.

Some twenty years later, Mr Kenneth Baker proposes to extend parental choice, allow for open admissions to schools, and give school governors and parents the right to opt out of their local education authorities.

A national curriculum is proposed which, by all accounts, attempts to ensure that no wayward local authorities nor the devotees of their policies could indulge in "policing" thought.

Some twenty years later, Dewsbury parents are insisting upon their "right to have freedom of choice" in deciding whether or not their children should be educated in a school with a majority of Asian students. This is what one of the Dewsbury parents told us in a statement made to the Inquiry:

"I do not want my child to attend Heathfield School for many reasons. The main thing is the difference in culture and religion. We have been told that Heathfield is a C of E school, but it can't be because 90% of the children are Muslim and so our religion is being killed. Our religion is Christianity and it is not taught at that school. Muslim kids have their religion and we have ours – they can have theirs; but we should be able to preserve ours. On the other hand I am not myself a particularly religious person, it's more the cultural aspect. I want R---- to go to a Christian school; I don't want her to learn about other cultures – why should she in Britain?. . .

"Obviously another reason we don't want our children to go to Heathfield is because the balance is all wrong. The Asians are too much in the majority now; I would accept about 25% Asians in the school. There can't be proper mixing when our children are so outnumbered. . .

"I feel that the allegations of racism are nonsense.People don't know the differences between racism and culture it's a matter of culture. . .how can I be accused of being racist, when I am planning to open an Indian Restaurant in the back of my pub?"

Those views were echoed quite substantially in the evidence given to the Inquiry by the parents in each of the three Manchester schools. We will look in some detail at Crowcroft Primary.

Crowcroft Park Primary School

On Thursday May 7th 1987 "The Sun" ran a front page story with the following banner headline:

THE OUTCAST

– MUM TAKES OUT THE ONLY WHITE BOY IN CLASS OF 30 BECAUSE HE CAN'T DO HIS ABC

Alongside a photo of a forlorn seven year old James Shad, the Sun gave their so-called "Exclusive" account of how hard-done-by little James Shad had been at the hands of a primary school in Bow, East London. On an inside page, under the banner headline "ODD BOY OUT" they listed a set of "deficiencies" in James' education. These included: being at the school for three years and yet not knowing his ABC; not being able to write his own name, going hungry because curry was often the only school lunch offered, learning about Third World countries but

322

not about Britain. One of the many quotes they attributed to James' mother was:

> "Asian children at that school get total priority while white kids are left to their own devices. . .the last straw was when he came home talking Indian. I thought he'd end up more fluent in Asian than English."

On Friday May 8th 1987, "AM Weekend" (now re-named "Metro News"), the free, advertising paper of the Manchester Evening News, published an article by Chris Southern which could well have dropped off the pages of "The Sun" except that this time the school was in Manchester and rather than the ABC, it was counting to 10 that some hapless little fellow could not do in English but was fluent at in Punjabi.

This time the unfortunate student is seven, and he is the offspring of a white mother and a black father. . .well, not full black. Let Mrs Ruscoe speak for herself:

> "These days you daren't give a view or you are labelled racialist," says Mrs Ruscoe. "But that is not our point. I am married to a half-caste and my daughter is quarter-caste. I am not racially prejudiced. . . But when you find that your child is nearly seven years of age, can count to ten in Punjabi but not in English, and has great difficulty in reading in English, it's time to stop and say "This has gone too far".

Apart from dreading to think how Mrs Ruscoe would describe her children's children and their children especially if, somewhere along the way, they too were to marry "half-castes" and mess up the fractions, one is led to wonder how a parent can so boldly disown her own responsibility as a parent, and own up to the fact (if indeed it is a fact) that at age 7 her child canot count from one to ten in English but can do so fluently in Punjabi.

What then, are the facts behind that story, and what is Parents' English Education Rights (PEER)?

This is what Mrs Roscoe told us in evidence:

> "At first I was quite happy with the education that R was receiving at the school and I liked both the Headteacher and the other staff. However I became extremely upset and annoyed one day, around June/July 1986, when my son came out of his classroom with a symbol like a star shaped on his hand. I said to him 'what's this' and he said 'we've had a Pakistani party'. I said 'what do you mean' and

he replied 'I don't know, but I had to have this on my hand'. I went into the classroom and I said to Miss B 'who has put this on his hand' and she replied 'It's just to celebrate Eid'. I said 'I don't want this on his hand or anything like it ever again'. My words were, I think *'don't ever disfigure my son again'*. (Our emphasis) She did not seem to know how to react to my anger. I was however extremely upset and I said 'it is disfiguring because, look, it won't come off'. I then decided to see the Headteacher, and I think I got to see her the same day. I asked her what was going on and I said that I did not want him involved in stuff like that, that I don't know about. I also asked why I wasn't told about it. My feelings were and are if I didn't want him to participate in a religious festival – of whatever kind – I should have the right to say so and I should have been informed about the festival to give me that choice. I am not a religious person myself, but I do believe that if the children are to be taught any religion it should be their own first."

"My worries were aroused again, when one day he came home and said 'listen to me'. He then said some words which I didn't understand. I said 'what's that' and he said 'it's 1 to 10 in Punjabi'. I said 'O.K. let's hear it in English'. He got to 6 alright but after that was obviously in difficulties and had to think about it. Unlike the impression given by the subsequent press coverage, he did eventually get to 10, but it was the fact that he was fluent in his counting in Punjabi, whereas he was struggling in English. I was very angry about this; I thought 'Am I in England?' I'm sending him to an English school to teach him to be able to cope with English life and here is my son fluent in counting in a foreign language and having difficulty with his own. I believe in traditional basic education first."

"But all along, too, I was made to feel that I was an isolated case so because of this I backed off again. Gradually other worries began to emerge too. R is not a very good eater and he would come home hungry. I asked him why and he said 'because the food was too hot'. He didn't like it – it burnt his mouth. I understand, despite what the school has said, that on certain days only curry was available. Also a situation can arise where, if a child is late or a slow eater, all the English food may be gone by the time he gets round to it. As a result of this and the other worries I would express my concern in the playground to other parents sometimes and I began to get a response."

"The next thing to happen was when R was in the next class up. He came home one day – some time around the beginning of this year – and called his sister J a nigger in an agrument (J really is quite dark). I was not in the house at the time; my husband Colin just smacked R and put him straight to bed. When I got home and was told about it I couldn't believe it because although J is very dark, especially considering that she is only a quarter caste, previously R did not appear to notice at all and he doesn't generaly miss a trick. So I went up to speak to him about it. I said it was worse than swearing and he said sorry. I said 'where have you got it from', and he said 'from a friend who called it me at school'. So the next day I went in to see Mrs W and told her and she said she was sorry and that she would see the boy about it. I therefore left it at that, although I was extremely unhappy. Later on though, just after PEER had started up, and as a result of more talks with R about religion etc, I began to feel that his behaviour had been due to the school highlighting differences. I felt this partly due to seeing the contents of the draft anti-racist policy. I felt this enforced focus on multi-culturalism produced and produces prejudices. They are standing 5 year olds up in class pointing out differences for instance where people come from – and I feel this makes differences. Children of that age do not notice differences until they are told about them. I feel this is where the name calling stems from. I know that some racism also comes from families themselves, but I do feel that the multi-cultural approach helps because it makes the parents madder and more racist. For instance if kids go home to racist parents and talk about Pakistan or whatever, they would get a racist response."

Q. You raised what you feel are very genuine concerns as a parent?
A. Yes.

Q. Do you feel that the way that some of the newspapers intervened in this was to try and stir up things in a way different from that?
A. One thing that I did feel very, very strongly about with all the papers, which I told them, was the fact that because I had a coloured child and a coloured husband – out of all the photographs that were taken, and there were many, many of us all together and lots of the children on their own, there was only ever my photograph that was put in, and I felt that this was to cover themselves if anyone accused them of printing anything racist, because they could say, "No, because look at this mother". As I said to them, who are they bringing to prove they are not prejudiced? Are they bringing a coloured neighbour or something? I did object to that fact, and it was stressed all the time –

"Mrs Ruscoe's husband is half-caste". What difference has that got to do with it? I have got those views whether or not, and then on the other hand I have been called colour prejudiced and racialist.

Q. Do I understand you to say that as far as you were concerned the press themselves behaved in a racialist way?
A. I would not say racialist, no.

Q. Prejudiced?
A. I don't know. When I rang up and complained to the Sun and Star I was told that these made headlines – these certain headlines that they had used. My son was subject to ridicule for this for weeks; he was heartbroken. I did write to the Head and explained that I had been – not so much misquoted, but the way they had emphasised certain small examples. That was the main thing.

The CHAIRMAN:
Q. Do you think that the press over-stated your case, or just did not state it well enough, or just completely misrepresented it?
A. At certain times they over-stated it, but then after the meeting I rang up, only because we had been asked to do, to give a statement of what had happened, and we did this, and we were refused. They did not want it because the Chair of Governors had already been on and told them all now everybody was satisfied. It was only a very, very small minority that was dissatisfied, so there did not seem any need for them to take a press statement. The very, very small minority was in fact us, which to me does not matter if it is one person that has a different opinion. . .

Ms BHAVNANI:
Q. You talk quite a lot in your statement about home culture and English culture. What do you mean by that?
A. This has been said to me a few times. You are right – when I said I was taught at school – I went to school with coloured children – my main thing is – it is very hurtful – I have got to say the word, the Muslim religion, because that happens to be the religion that he can talk about, and he can talk about that to me and tell me most things about it; but when I was told that he was taught his own and I asked him the simple question, "Are you Protestant or Catholic, R?", that was his answer – "Is that two countries like Bashir's got". He is bright; he does not miss a trick, and I have never, ever, ever as true as I am sat here known him pass comment that his sister

326

is a different colour. You can see by the photographs that she is very, very dark quarter caste, and then for him to come home and start "Nigger" and "Paki", and she's calling him "Paki", and white children are calling white children, and coloured children – it's just not on. . .

Mrs Ruscoe shared her concerns with some other parents whom she found to have similar anxieties about their children's education in the school, and, together, all four of them formed Parents English Education Rights.

The press continued to take a keen interest in the matter. "The Sun" carried the story on May 9th as did the "Star", each with a picture of mother and son.

One of the PEER group told us in evidence:

"We explained to the Head that we had formed a group called PEER and we promised that we would keep her informed as to its activities. She seemed happy about this. We explained that we did not hold her or the staff responsible, but felt that they were equally victims.

Following this, we continued to meet and we put out independent positions. We placed these at local news stations, post offices, cafes etc; these were directed to all people who might back us – whether they had children at Crowcroft or not. After 4 or 5 days we collected all these petitions and found that we had about 400 signatures. In the meantime Kim Ruscoe had also contacted the AM newspaper to ask if they would print a letter from us. She was apparently told that they would not print the letter, but that they would give us front page coverage if we gave them a story. As a result of this conversation, a woman journalist – Chris Southern – came to Kim's house where we all met her.

As a result the AM published our story in it's 79th issue (8/5/87), entitled "A war of words". Once this was printed other journalists contacted us, both at Kim's house and also outside the school. At the same time, perhaps because of this, I felt that the attitude of the teachers at the school was beginning to change. They became increasingly unfriendly, although nothing was said.

The school and the Education Committee responded both to the press and to the parent community of the school.

A letter was sent to the Editor of Manchester Metro News (formerly AM Weekend), with statements for publication from the Chair and Vice Chair of the Governors and the Chair of the Education Committee. The school held two meetings with parents and provided them with information about the school's policies and practices in relation to all its students.

Regrettably, the rebuttal letter sent to AM Weekend was not published. This led the Chair of Governors, quite understandably, to the view that AM Weekend intended their reporting of the PEER viewpoint to be inflammatory.

We take the view that the appearance of the story in the "Sun" on May 7th about the London primary school, the AM Weekend story on May 8th and the "Sun" and "Star" coverage on May 9th was not a coincidence. Education was clearly a critical issue in the general election, and the main political parties were stating their positions on the issue. The question of the future of education in the hands of left-wing authorities like Manchester had been publicly raised by the Conservative government.

Both the London story and the Manchester Crowcroft story were so fundamentally flawed that one has got to ask whether those two young boys and their alleged literacy and numeracy problems were not just cynically manipulated by the newspapers concerned. Whose interest could it serve, for example, to have the whole nation told that the boys in those photos are failures and dunces, unable to count to ten without difficulty at the age of 7? What does it do to a child to be put in a situation where ammunition is given to all and sundry to ridicule him? Why did the journalists concerned not attempt to verify with the schools the accounts given by parents? Above all, what leads parents, who obviously are concerned about their children's welfare, to fall into the manipulative and irresponsible hands of the tabloid press?

The Chair of Governors at Crowcroft provided us with answers to some, at least, of those questions:

"I would say that not enough care was taken in the way the press reported the situation. In my opinion the incident was sensationalised by the press. It is the views of the minority of parents which have prevailed throughout. Many articles have appeared which have shown only one side of the argument. The worst coverage in my opinion was in AM Weekend. Myself and the Deputy Chair wrote to AM Weekend to correct their last article about the meeting for parents at the school, which was held by the Governing Body. We wrote to the Editor to protest at the inaccurate and unbalanced reporting and to say what things were really like. The letter has not been published. In view of the situation I believe that the reporters should have taken more care to verify facts because it was a

328

potentially explosive issue. It is possible that the "Sun" and "Star" got wind of the story through a local reporter or newspaper.

"At a very early stage one of the parent Governors became involved in PEER and he spoke to the press as a parent Governor. In terms of protocol this was quite incorrect behaviour. He said that he didn't realise, but this gave added ammunition to the press because he was a parent and a Governor.

"As Governors we organised a meeting for the parents. This was an opportunity for the Head to explain what the school was doing in areas which had multi-cultural elements. It was also an opportunity for parents to voice their views about practices in the school and LEA policy. We had representatives of the LEA on the platform as well as two Governors and the Head. Teachers came as observers and the other Governors were also there. Everyone else who attended were parents or grandparents or guardians etc. Approximately 50 parents turned up, mostly white parents, a few Asian parents, one West Indian parent and an interpreter was present.

"After the meeting the teachers and the Governors tried to speak to the parents who hadn't spoken. We got the impression that the majority of the parents were reassured, including many of those who had signed the petition. The Governors met after this meeting and concluded this.

"They also concluded that a small number of parents continued to be dissatisfied with the LEA and national education policies. The parents said they were not against the school or the teachers but that it was the policy and policy maker behind what the school were doing that they were dissatisfied with.

We later sent letters to the parents with a note of what was said at the meeting and a slip for them to return to register their satisfaction or concern. In the letter, there was an invitation to them to talk to the Head or myself. Virtually all the returns said they were satisfied. A few were returned saying they were concerned, but what their concerns are have not yet been clarified – they may be unrelated to this issue.

I would like to describe some of the factors I consider may have contributed to the disquiet of parents at Crowcroft Park:

1. *The economic and social conditions of the community itself.* Factors which together mean the area is deprived have an important bearing – low income, poor housing, scant community facilities and people living in very close proximity together. The culture

329

clashes between the white working class and Asian working class are much more marked in areas such as this (i.e. Longsight/ Levenshulme) compared with middle class areas. The white working class in this area may well feel that they are deprived. I think some parents get the impression that special treatment is meted out to non-white children at school. They possibly have aspirations for their children i.e. for their children to get out of the neighbourhood, and resent practices which they believe will impede their own children's education. They look to the school as a way of their children getting on, and perceive the non-white groups in the community as being given special treatment and of somehow rising above them.

2. Another factor which I believe is relevant to the incident at Crowcroft Park is the *attitude to race and racism by the parents.* I would like to repeat some of the comments/views expressed to me in the parents meeting. Firstly, one view was that racial differences shouldn't be emphasised or even recognised. This came from a couple, the woman being white and the man black. Their worry was that the school's policies and practices with regard to other cultures were generating racism. That is by acknowledging different cultures etc. they were creating racism. They felt that if you ignored racial differences then the children wouldn't develop racial attitudes to each other. The school incorporates different cultures/aspects of different cultures into the daily life of the school in such a way that they are respected, rather than in a devisive way as envisaged by these parents. I think that the concerns of these parents were created because of the activity of PEER and probably didn't exist before that. I think PEER worked up a lot of feeling/worry which was unfounded. Secondly, I have the impression that a number of parents feel that their racial identity is under the threat of being changed not only by the presence of other cultures in the community but also by the role which is being given to cultures in the school. The extreme end of this "cultural identity threat" is epitomised by views such as "if people from other cultures come here they should adjust and become like us", no concessions should be allowed, and any change is seen as regrettable, put in "England for the English". These views have been expressed by white-British parents at Crowcroft Park.

We visited the school and had a very full discussion with all the staff. We were impressed by the support the majority of the parents had demonstrated for the policies and practices of the school. 78% of the parents had formally stated they were satisfied with the education the school was providing. What the staff found even more encouraging was that quite a number of the white parents who had signed the PEER petition had telephoned or gone to the school to dissociate themselves from what PEER stood for as they did not see that to be in the best interests of their children.

The school has been attempting to take all its parents along with it and enlist their support in building a unified school community where no one child or group of children is disadvantaged.

Addressing the panel in her personal capacity, the Chair of the Governors discussed with us what she sees as the issues and difficulties for the future:

Q. Do you think that the situation united the staff or created divisions in the staff at the school?
A. From what I have seen, I would say it united them.

Q. And made the staff feel stronger about the correctness of the way they were running the school?
A. That's possible. It's hard for me to say.

Q. I mean, having gone through this particular thing of being suddenly put under the press gaze, the media gaze, and then having the meeting that you have described in your statement, do you think that the school feels more confident about putting into effect its multi-cultural curriculum?
A. No, I wouldn't think so; I would say that the result of the few parents voicing their concerns so vociferously, had two effects. One, to contrast the unreasonable views that some of the parents were putting forward with what they as staff were doing, which has very good intentions and is seen as being good practice educationally.

But on the other side of it I think they probably feel wary about this policy and wonder whether it is being done in the right way. Again, it is difficult for me to speak for them.

Q. Is that how how you feel? Do you feel wary about this policy, as a result of your experiences?
A. I am wary in the sense that I don't think it is over and done with and I think there are going to be further problems and further come-backs. So that when the school is celebrating a non-white British festival, then there may be protests, or there may be

331

problems because of that. But from what I know about the way Crowcroft is practising its multi-cultural policy, I feel that they are doing the right thing. I mean, I wouldn't want to see a change. I am always willing to think about what changes might be better, but I haven't seen any obvious faults in it, or anything which is detrimental to the children, and I feel the role of the school is to teach the children, not the parents and not just to bend parents' prejudices, or whatever.

Q. Are those parents in any way prepared to enter into a dialogue with people who do not share their views, or are they quite rigid?

A. They have been prepared to talk, but they don't seem to be prepared to listen to the answers, or the logic, or the reasoning behind why the school is doing something that they don't like. It is incredibly frustrating to hear the same monologue again and again and again. The head teacher had the set monologue. I and two of the governors had it during the parents' evening when the parents came to the school to talk to the teachers, and so on. We had the same thing, and the head was there and she also went over the same ground. I didn't appreciate then that she had already been through all those things. Then we had the same thing again at the meeting that we specially held for the parents.

So if by "dialogue" you mean taking on board something that the other party says, I would say, no.

Q. Can I take up another thing that you deal with in your statement? You say "Policy makers cannot expect to implement changes which concern sensitive issues as race in schools unless they secure the understanding and support of the parents. I feel that the onus is on the LEA as instigator to secure this support, not the school, which is the instrument of their policy." As I understand the position, although a local education authority like Manchester may put out a policy, or have a policy itself, whether a particular school in Manchester follows that policy, or departs from it, is a decision for that school acting through its management team and its board of governors. So that the decision to implement policy must be a decision, as I understand it, of your governing body and your senior management.

A. I would say that's correct in one sense. I think the LEA produces policy for schools to follow and, if schools depart a long way from policy, they will bring what pressure to bear that they can to bring schools in line. Yes, this school chose to follow that policy, following the guidance of the LEA.

But I still feel that my comment there is that the LEA's put together the policy that it wants schools to follow; it wants them to be their instrument in implementing their policy, and it should help create the ground for the right environment, or whatever, for that policy to succeed. My feeling is that what has happened is that the schools are flagships and they are out on the front line, and they didn't have the back up.

Q. You go on to say "I think that the equal opportunities policies of the Council, and the way these policies have been given first priority, have caused a considerable amount of disaffection amongst Labour voters and others in Manchester".

A. Yes, I think that's relevant to the context in which parents see multi-cultural elements in the school. Obviously this is just my view. But, in my view, the thing that this term of Manchester City Council will be remembered for is its equal opportunities policy. It will be remembered for policies that were put in to help the gay community, to help the black community, and so on, to help disabled people.

But I think what will stick in people's minds was that minority groups were taken on board in a big way, and people who don't belong to minority groups said "Well, they didn't do anything for us". I am not trying to give an analysis of fact in terms of how much poundage per head of Manchester population went into those policies. I don't think that's the point. I think what is relevant is the perception of people. It is just my view.

Mr JOHN:

There is a problem though, is there not? . . . The City Council gives leadership, in terms of policies, within the broad framework of combatting various forms of oppression. That is, the broad arena of its political activity as elected members. The school operates to provide a service in respect of a community, the school community. I mean, the school has got to create that community and . . . to introduce policies and practices, which it sees as being in the best interests of the students, in a sense regardless of what the local authority does. There are schools in Manchester where people have, for example, been doing quite a lot of work, in terms of multi-cultural education, anti-racist

approaches, etc, long before Manchester City Council pro-
nounced on those matters.

So . . . the point is to what extent can the school itself, by
encouraging certain practices, encouraging certain types of
relationships with its students, with its parents, build that
community. So that when policies of one sort or another have got
to be introduced, there is already the basis there for doing that,
regardless in a sense of what the policies are. That for us is the
question that we need to address as a panel.

A. Well, in the case of Crowcroft, while these things, I don't think,
are being specifically addressed vis-a-vis the parents, the school is
very open. I mean, the parents do come in and they do see what
the school has been doing. It has been carrying out the same
policies really over three years. But when this flares up, you
suddenly find that almost 50 parents are prepared to sign a
petition to say that they want an English education.

The CHAIRMAN:

Given that you are a primary school where, if you like, the door
is always open and parents are free to come in and out, and they
are made welcome; but at the same time, in terms of consultation
with the parents – say you introduce some new method of
teaching maths, or a new method of teaching French, or
whatever it is; an issue which affects every child in the school –
would you normally expect to have a special parents' meeting in
order to discuss it?

A. No, you wouldn't. The other thing is that you make this point
about the new maths teaching scheme, or maybe reading scheme,
or something like this. The school did have a display about
reading on the parents' evening when they came in to see the
teachers. But the sorts of comments we got at the meeting were
really people talking about the education they had. To them that
was what proper education is, and that is really how education
should be, in their view. They wanted to roll back the clock 20
years/30 years. That is what I really mean, I suppose, about this
gulf in understanding between what the school is doing and what
is in the parents' minds, or in some of the parents' minds. You
can't quantify really how many of the parents are thinking in the
mode of 20 years ago. Some of them anyway are thinking in
terms of straight rows of desks, prayers in the morning, doing the

times tables, Janet and John books. That is a general sort of thing. How can you take that on board?

The school has been having a go. It was trying to explain the reading scheme, to explain that children these days are supposed to use the pictures to help them learn the words. One mother was saying "Oh, I always cover the picture up. I say 'no, no, you mustn't look at the picture; you have got to read the words'." That is a fundamental conflict between what the kid does at home with the parent and at school.

Q. But you have to start from the assumption that most people are quite reasonable. If it is explained to someone that it is actually quite important not to cover the picture up, and it is explained why it is, then they will see – I mean, if what you are talking about is sensible.

A. Yes.

Q. They will see that.

A. Yes, but that kind of misunderstanding, or lack of information, if you like, I think it just exists right across the sepctrum. So when you have got the case of a child coming home speaking one to ten, very proud of the fact, I am sure, in Punjabi, because he has picked it up from the bilingual instructor, and you try to explain to the parent that (a) it probably means the kid is bright; (b) learning it has probably been good for his linguistic development; and (c) he has not actually been taught it deliberately as policy, you just can't get through. It's very, very difficult.

Q. Do you think that you would have had that same reaction if the child had gone home counting one to ten in French?

A. No.

Conclusion

It is significant that in the case of Crowcroft as with Wilbraham and St Marks, the major concern expressed by parents is about the "totally alien" culture and religion of Asian people. Deep in the psyche of very many white people is the sub-continent of South Asia as a place where Christianity failed to make any impact upon the "benighted heathens of the deep East". The Islamic faith, the Punjabi, Urdu, Sylhetti, Hindi, Gujerati, Bengali languages, and the customs of the people of the sub-continent in this country conjurs up the strongest emotions of distaste in some of the people who gave evidence to the Inquiry.

A parent governor at Crowcroft to whom the PEER parents took their complaints, and who shared their concerns and assisted them in forming PEER, was quite adamant in his evidence to the Inquiry about what the remedy was for situations such as that at Crowcroft:

". . .The Christmas and Easter celebrations in school are very much watered down. In summary we are experiencing a loss of English heritage and identity. On the other hand these policies do not help Asian people either because they are not promoting peaceful relations between Asian people and white people – on the contrary.

With regard to the avoidance of racial tension by means of being "race blind" and sticking to the fact that ethnic minority children are being educated in English schools, I would like to say the following things. Although I feel that this attitude of "race blindness" would help to reduce racial tension and violence etc, it is not the full answer. I believe that the only remedy for racial violence/hatred and discrimination is a change of people's hearts. I am now speaking as a Christian. Since race hatred is a consequence of man's estrangement and his rebellion from his creator and since it has become a fundamental component of fallen human nature, the only true remedy to racial hatred and violence is for people to become re-united to God through Jesus Christ. I am thus advocating that non-Christian people in this country including white and Asian – become united, as it were, by becoming Christian. I am saying that I would like to see people give their hearts to Jesus Christ rather than just make a mere formal confession of Christianity. I am not racially motivated and as such I say that I recognise the importance of respecting other religious faiths, but I must say that other religious faiths cannot provide the answer to human sin in the way that Jesus has through his blood shed on the cross, and in conclusion race hatred is bound up in human sin and is not treatable by any other method.

People can only stop hating each other on a racial basis or any other basis when they come to know God in Jesus Christ, because he takes that element in us which is against God and against each other and begins to transform it into his own image.

As I see it in the scriptures I believe that there is no other route to salvation other than through Jesus Christ."

This parent is one of two parent governors at a school where 38% of children belong to groups other than white British. To quote the school:

"They are children whose families originated from the Afro-Caribbean, India, Pakistan, Bangladesh, Nepal, the Middle East, Turkey and Columbia in South America. And, of course, many of the white British families will have come from Scotland, Wales and Northern Ireland, as well as those with Irish backgrounds."

The fact that some white English parents insist that that 38% be sujbected to traditional English Christian education while at the same time complaining about their white children singing a nursery rhyme in Urdu is more than just English arrogance. Nor is it enough to fit them up with the racist tag.

Comparatively speaking, white working class parents, like the Mrs Ruscoe's of this world, are deprived. Even in terms of what she has told the world about her interactions with her children, let alone the way she describes them, one gets a sense of someone who has little basis on which to root her own identity as a white working class woman. Therefore, the perception she has of her son's school catering directly for the needs and preferences of Asian students, thus indicating the extent to which they and their culture are valued, is in sharp contrast to her own experiences as a young working class woman in school.

She, PEER, and all the other parents who are disaffected from Crowcroft, Wilbraham, St Marks and Dewsbury are not inclined to challenge the usefulness of their own education or examine how oppressive it was to them. Rather, they devote their energies to seeking to have it (or some nostalgically remembered version of it) imposed upon their children. The right of a child not to be caught up in that, with or without the help of the tabloid press, is one which parents, particularly other white parents, students themselves, teachers and policy makers must surely stand up and defend. . . , even if it means contesting the "moral high ground" with the likes of Ray Honeyford and Kenneth Baker.

As the Chair of Governors at Crowcroft put it to us:

> "The role of the school is to teach the children . . . and not just to bend to parents' prejudices, or whatever."

If indeed, we are entrusted with the care of the present so that our children could inherit and take care of a future, then the example of a Crowcroft or a Dewsbury must surely warrant some checks and balances on parents' rights to choose not to respect their children's rights.

CHAPTER 30

The History of Anti-Racist Education

Throughout the evidence, the words "anti-racism" and "multi-culturalism" occur again and again. What do they mean? Where do they come from, and how do they relate to the experiences of students, teachers and parents both white and black?

"Anti-racism" and "multi-culturalism" are seen by many as something to do with the parents from Crowcroft Primary School in Manchester, who have been agitating for an "English education" or the white parents in Dewsbury, Yorkshire, who have been fighting Kirklees Local Authority so that their children are not educated in the same school as Asian students. This is the sort of popular press publicity anti-racism and multi-culturalism obtains; or else it is Maureen McGoldrick, the former headteacher in Brent, who was alleged to have made remarks about not wanting any more black teachers in her school.

This image of anti-racism and multi-culturalism means that we rarely hear about the feelings and views of black students and parents or about the experiences of working class people, both black and white.

Background

What are the roots of anti-racism? How did ideas of anti-racist education develop in Britain? In Chapter 28 we highlighted the development of Manchester City policies on multi-culturalism and anti-racism and, clearly, this has been part of a national development.

After the Second World War, educational reports stressed the "failure of working class children in the education system. Much of the blame for the failure was placed on families, and it was said, for example, that working class women were not as "interested or involved" in their children's education as middle class women. Similar things were said when black people migrated to Britain from the West Indies and from the Indian Sub-continent. They were channelled into run-down areas of the cities and the jobs no-one else wanted, with low pay and long hours. It is not surprising, then, that black families were also viewed in a similar way to working class families – depriving their children and unable to give them the necesary encouragement. Add to this the prevalent racist notion that black people were "backward" and

339

"inferior" to whites, and it is easy to see how black families were then seen as "worse" than white working class families.

When in Rome . . .

After the Second World War, Britain needed labour for its industries and recruited workers from its old colonies, in particular the West Indies and the Indian Sub-continent. But when these workers came, it was strictly on the understanding, so far as the British authorities were concerned, that they should "adapt to English ways". This was the notion or theory of "assimilation". This theory took root in education, where two main problems were identified: first the need for black people to learn English and secondly the need to understand why numbers of black children in a particular school would make adaptation to English ways difficult. At the time "high" numbers of black students in a school were seen as a threat to good education and in the early 1960's the Government laid down guidelines for 30% as the maximum number of black students in a particular school. As a result, many local authorities began the process of bussing black children out of their neighbourhoods.

It is interesting that the little group of parents in Crowcroft and Dewsbury are using these ideas as the rationale for rejecting multi-cultural education. The arguments they are using are nothing new. The idea that numbers of black people make a difference to "race relations" has been put forward by both Labour and Conservative governments to justify policies in both education and immigration. Indeed, the need to control numbers in order to achieve good race relations has been used by successive governments to justify the imposition of further restrictive immigration controls from 1962 onwards. This is how it was put by Mr Maudling, the Home Secretary, when he introduced the Immigration Act 1971:

"the main purpose of immigration policy . . . is as a contribution to . . . peace and harmony . . . If we are to get progress in community relations, we must give assurance to the people, who were already here before the large wave of immigration, that this will be the end and that there will be no further large scale immigration. Unless we can give that assurance we cannot effectively set about . . . improving community relations." (813 HC Official Report [5th Series] COLS 43–44).

The argument in education has always had its counterpart in immigration.

In all inner city schools in the 1960s, great stress was placed on the teaching of English as a second language. The theory was that once black students learnt English and became adapted to and absorbed into the ways of English working class life in Britain, all "racial" problems would wither away, and a new generation of black children would grow up, totally "assimilated". This was the theory underpinning educational policies, which involved limiting the number of black children in schools, bussing children across cities to ensure the right numbers, and testing of children to classify those who were properly adapted and those were were educationally subnormal.

The black community responded strongly by organising campaigns against bussing and against the tests used to classify black children as educationally subnormal, and both these initiatives died away. In the process, assimilationist ideas began to be questioned in educational circles and were gradually replaced by ideas about "tolerating other people's cultures". However, views about the uniformity of "English" culture (as if this existed), and numbers of black people in Britain, and in particular schools, continued to be bandied about from time to time by politicians and others who trot out the arguments about the swamping of the English way of life. The assumption behind these views is that black women, men and children are the "problem".

Live and Let Live . . .

Reports in the late 1960s and early 1970s continued to show the existence of racial discrimination in all areas of social life, especially housing, employment and education, and "integration", with its offer of equal opportunity and cultural diversity, became the new catch word to replace "assimilation". Roy Jenkins, in a famous speech in 1966, said integration was:

> "Not the flattening process of assimilation, but an equal opportunity accompanied by cultural diversity in an atmosphere of mutual tolerance."

"Integration" was not to apply only in the field of education, but also became part of the justification for immigration control, as Roy Hattersley once pointed out:

> "Without integration, limitation is inexcusable. Without limitation, integration is impossible."

341

At the same time that schools were being asked to value other cultures, a growing number of government and CRE reports talked about the fact that Indian, Pakistani and West Indian culture were somehow inadequate. These reports spoke of "culture shock", "cultural conflict" and "generational conflict". The House of Commons select committee on race and immigration in their report in 1969 referred to the "rigid" discipline in Asian households and pointed to the failure of Asian young people to use youth clubs. Titles of studies, some from the Community Relations Commission, gave the game away; these included "THE HALF WAY GENERATION"; "PUNJABI OR ENGLISH"; "IN SEARCH OF IDENTITY"; "DAUGHTERS OF TRADITION"; and so on. The assumptions were that black men and women were "hindering" integration and inhibiting progress, because their "culture" did not enable their children to take advantage of the equal opportunity on offer under this new policy of "integration". Thus, reports cited young Asian girls running away from home, omitting to mention that pressure to conform is not something peculiar to the Asian community. References were made to the "passive" Indian/Pakistani mother, speaking no English and always at home, and the "dominating" Afro-Caribbean mother, always out of the home and always working. These reports and studies perpetuate images in people's minds that black families "therefore do not help education" to do the job schools have to do with the children.

The period of "valuing other cultures" gave rise to a growth of black studies. However, this was unlikely to be very successful in eliminating racism through education, because black studies and the valuing of other cultures had to compete with a growing number of official reports and studies to the effect that black children have identity problems and an inadequate cultural background. It was said, therefore, that education needs to "compensate" for the inadequacies at home, and was to be regarded as in some way "remedial". The result is the narrow emphasis on steel bands and their lack of status compared to other academic subjects. The new initiative, far from solving the problems of racial conflict, contains within it the seeds of further racism.

Multi-cultural education stems from the tradition of "integration". The "saris, steel bands, and samosas" approach, however, soon came to be seen as a merely tokenistic change to the curriculum in schools. At the same time, it was argued that multi-cultural education should really be for all children, in all schools, and not just for black and a few white children in inner city schools. This argument was put forward throughout the 1970s and into the early 1980s and was expressed in its most developed form in the Swann Report "Education for All" in 1985 (Cmnd 9453, HMSO 1985).

However, the experiences of black children and parents were far removed from "multi-culturalism" and what it seemed to mean to people in power. A growing number of supplementary schools, campaigns to protest against the placing of black children in special units and the pressure to look at multi-lingualism as good educational practice, are all indications that somehow "good practice" in education has been divorced from students' and parents' wishes.

The Rampton Committee, which was asked to investigate "the under achievement" of West Indian children did an interim report in 1981, "West Indian Children in Our Schools" (Cmnd 8273, HMSO 1981), and the work of that committee was continued under the new chairmanship of Lord Swann, who widened the investigation and began looking at all ethnic minority groups and education.

The Swann Report was produced in 1985, as we have seen. Then there is the Scarman Report on the Brixton Disorders (Cmnd 8427, HMSO 1981). All these reports put forward various remedies, but none based themselves centrally upon the lives and experiences of young working class people in inner cities, both black and white.

Rampton and Swann

The Rampton Committee was set up to investigate the under achievement among children of Afro-Caribbean origin. It received a large body of evidence about racism and its influence in schools. Although the report still fell into the trap of talking about "ours" and "theirs" by using the title "West Indian Children in *Our* Schools" (our emphasis), it nevertheless felt there was sufficient evidence to stress that teacher attitudes and racism were important factors contributing to the under achievement of black students. However, they only published an interim report. Almost immediately afterwards, the Government replaced Anthony Rampton as Chairman of the Committee by Lord Swann, and widened the Inquiry's terms of reference to include children of South Asian origin and others from ethnic minority groups. This meant, almost inevitably, that differences in cultures, rather than common experiences of class and race, would be highlighted. We have been shown media cuttings in the year before Swann reported and these indicate conflicts of opinion among members of the Committee and a string of resignations. The Final Report came out in 1985. It placed less emphasis on racism and more on cultures and equal value, and made great distinction between the "success" of Asian children (except the Bangladeshis) and children from Afro-Caribbean families. On December 7th 1984, the Times Educatonal Supplement reported:

"Lord Swann, Chairman of the Committee of Inquiry into the education of ethnic minority children, will face a major revolt next week at the last meeting of the Committee. A substantial number of members, including the four West Indians, are unhappy with Lord Swann's rewriting of the chapter on achievement, which they claim no longer reflects evidence presented to the Committee. Lord Swann placed greater emphasis on West Indian family background and life style as reasons why black children do badly at school. Members felt that this undermined findings of the interim report by the Committee, then under the chairmanship of Anthony Rampton, which stressed teacher attitudes and racism as main factors in under achievement."

The Swann Report gave prominence to the notion of "cultural pluralism", the idea that all cultures should be valued equally in society, and recommended that this should be taught to children in schools.

Multi-Culturalism: What Is Wrong With It?

Since the early 1970s, many reports and studies have emphasised the importance of multi-cultural education and the need to learn about and value other people's culture. But it is clear that learning to "value" other cultures is almost impossible when not all cultures are given the same value or are regarded equally. Black people's cultures, whether Jamaican or Bangladeshi, are seen as "interesting", "exotic" or "strange", especially when studied in isolation from questions of power and the standing of these cultures compared to white middle class culture. In our view, culture is not to be seen as some neatly defined category with specific labels for food, dress, music or language, but includes the work patterns and life styles of people and how they deal with employers, landlords, schools, families and so on, in a society which is divided into hierarchies according to such factors as race, sex, class, age and geography. In other words, understanding a famous Manchester boxing champion like Len Johnson (featured in a later part of this chapter) is only possible if we examine how he grew up. His relationship with Annie Forshaw, an Irish woman, and her struggle will help us understand Irish working class culture in all its fullness and richness.

A central tenet of multi-cultural education, and one of the theories

344

under-pinning it, is that racism and racial conflict in Britain are caused by some sort of cultural misunderstanding. If only people understood each other's cultures, then racial conflict would be unnecessary and would wither away. Thus, in the Swann Report, great emphasis is placed on the need to understand the cultures of Britain's immigrant population and to teach these in schools. In this scheme of things, nothing need be said about such disturbing and controversial things as power relations as they have to do with sex, race or class.

It is also clear that understanding culture does not necessarily involve an examination of "culture" in Britain. It is, rather, assumed that the "culture" to be talked about is that of the white middle class. The very different "culture" of the vast majority of people, who have been brought up in an English working class environment, is ignored. It is clear to us, both from the evidence and from the vast literature and documentation put before us, that most of the time when people discuss multi-cultural education they are referring to the cultures of African, Afro-Caribbean and South Asian people.

In practice, it would appear that schools now give a narrow definition to what is "multi-cultural" and essentially, teachers are required to interpret, dilute and clarify a fairly standard set of ideas about how black people live. As a result, multi-culturalism does not in fact deal with or assist in the understanding of the complexity of people's lives and histories and does not draw upon the lives and experiences of the students who are being taught.

In fact multi-culturalism has been much criticised for not effectively coming to grips with the racism and racial harassment experienced in school and the wider community. In the aftermath of the widespread city rebellions in Bristol, Brixton, Moss Side and Toxteth in 1981, it began to look largely irrelevant. As a result of these disorders and the Scarman Report into the Brixton Disorders in 1981, many local authorities began a move to anti-racism and positive action.

A Moral Individual Issue?

The Scarman Report emphasised the desperation and anger of the inner cities and the racial disadvantages. Lord Scarman concluded:

"The evidence which I have received . . . leaves no doubt in my mind that racial disadvantage is a fact of current British life. It was . . . a significant factor in the causation of the Brixton disorders. Urgent action is needed if it is not to become an endemic, ineradicable disease, threatening the very survival of our society . . . Racial disadvantage and its nasty associated racial discrimination, have not yet been eliminated. They poison minds and attitudes: they are, and so long as they remain, will continue to be, a potent factor of unrest."

The Report refers to "the destructive changes" wrought in West Indian family life and to "family break-down", with a very high proportion of single parent families and young people experiencing a sense of insecurity. The report, however, expressly rejects the notion that there is any "institutional racism" in Britain and puts racial disadvantage and racial discrimination down to the acts of individual prejudice and discrimination. Thus, racism in the police force is confined to the prejudiced acts of individual officers. But, as we have seen, the Report did stress "racial disadvantage" and this was latched onto by most local authorities in the aftermath of the 1981 inner city disturbances. Policies to promote positive action on equal opportunities were developed in consultaton with local community leaders. This was the pattern, as we have seen in Manchester. These initiatives created a space for anti-racism and for anti-racist education to be developed.

Equal Opportunities and Racism Awareness

At the corner stone of local authorities' policies on anti-racism were equal opportunities and the recruitment of black employees. Many institutions also took on the issue of racism awareness. Resources were allocated to racism awareness training (RAT) and the Government gave such initiatives their blessing. Four underlying themes can be detected in the post 1981 anti-racist initiatives. The first is that racism is the manifestation of individual racial prejudice rather than being "institutional". Secondly, it creates racial disadvantage and is a recipe for social disorder and is thus morally wrong and should be condemned. It follows, thirdly, that white people should be condemned. It follows, also, that white people should be trained to detect their own individual prejudices with a view to eliminating them. Thus, RAT. Fourthly, anti-racist policies on jobs, housing and education should only be brought into being in consultation with local "community leaders". In many cases, for example in the ILEA in London, anti-racist policy deals not only with race but also class and gender, but never is there any attempt to relate the issues to one another or, in the education context to discuss the respective and combined role of race, class and gender. Although consultation with community leaders is a feature of nearly all these policies, it is a very institutionalised process, and part of a "top down" approach, which does not involve or take into account the ideas and aspirations of the bulk of students or parents. It is symbolic rather than real.

It has become ever more evident to us that anti-racism in symbolic gestures is meaningless and can clearly reinforce racism. If the school does not involve the total community, teachers, ancillary staff, students and parents, both black and white, in the efforts to tackle racism in school, the whole exericse will end in failure.

There is an assumption, at least by some schools and local education authorities, who have taken on the mantle of anti-racism, that black students are "victims" of nasty, immoral racism from white students and that it is enough to have policies which publicly say they condemn it, have procedures for reporting it, send staff to racism awareness training and institute multi-culturalism to the extent of holding Muslim assemblies and so forth. This whole package is keyed into a process of "consultaton" at school or education authority level with a group of self-appointed leaders, who are often neither democratic nor representative, or with some randomly selected individuals from the local community.

Almost inevitably the policies bear little or no relation to black students' experiences or the strategies which they have evolved for dealing with their experiences, and little or no relation to white students' experiences or in many cases their strong commitment to anti-racism. Neither the policies nor the "consultation" process are capable on a practical or theoretical level of embracing the experience or sub-culture of the student population.

Since the assumption is that black students are the victims of the immoral behaviour of white students, white students almost inevitably become the "baddies". The operation of the anti-racist policies almost inevitably results in white students (and their parents) feeling "attacked" and all being seen as "racist", whether they are ferret-eyed fascists or committed anti-racists or simply children with a great store of human feeling and warmth who are ready to listen and learn and to explore their feelings towards one another. The notion that all white people are "racist" is part of the racism awareness training (RAT) model. It plays upon white guilt and its basic premise is that blacks are morally superior to whites who should therefore listen to everything blacks say. Racism is placed in some kind of moral vacuum and is totally divorced from the more complex reality of human relations in the classroom, playground or community. There is no room in the RAT model for class, sex, age or size differences.

In practice, it has been an unmitigated disaster. It has reinforced the

347

guilt of many well-meaning whites and paralysed them when any issue of race arises. They have become the wimps of race relations. It has taught others to bury their racism without in any way changing their attitude. It has created resentment and anger and topped free discussion. It encourages the aspiring black middle class to play the "skin game" and for a few "liberal anti-racist" whites to collude in it. It has put a few unrepresentative blacks into positions of false power without in any way empowering the rest of the black population. In a time of crisis, as at Burnage, the application of symbolic moral anti-racism is almost like pouring petrol on a fire. In short, it is a disaster and soon has the opposite effect, leading to polarisation between black and white and to a potentially greater racial conflict.

At Burnage, as we have seen, the application of a moral anti-racism effectively placed all white students and parents beyond the pale. As Dr Gough put it, they did not have the "particular experience" of black students or parents and it followed, therefore, that they should not be involved or consulted in questions to do with anti-racism or Section II. In their theoretical model "race" becomes paramount and class and gender positions are seen as irrelevant.

The exclusion of white students and their parents from responsibility for any anti-racist education has other side effects. Almost inevitably the white students will perceive black students as seeking "special treatment". In fact, as we saw only too clearly at Burnage, this so called "special treatment" is far removed from the demands black students are making or have made. They are having "special treatment" thrust on them, which they have never asked for or needed.

The fundamental error of these morally based anti-racist policies is that they assume that a complicated set of human relations, made up of many strands, including class, gender, age, size and race, can be slotted into a simple white versus black pigeon hole. It is the problem of white versus black which has to be addressed and dealt with. The other things are assumed and not dealt with. This simple model assumes that there is uniform access to power by all whites, and a uniform denial of access and power to all blacks. Clearly, this is not the case. We do not believe that an effective anti-racist policy can exist unless the other issues are also addressed and dealt with, in particular class and gender.

CHAPTER 31

Good Practice

Manchester Education Department has prepared model anti-racist policies. Manchester Education Department has a city wide system for reporting racist incidents. But a good document does not necessarily mean a good practice. How do schools respond? How do schools develop a good practice? What is good practice? What is there in Manchester on which to build for the future?

Schools' Responses: tackling Racist Incidents

The Head of one Manchester School, which has 45% white, 5% Asian, 35% Afro-Caribbean and 15% mixed race, says that he deals with an average of two or three racist incidents a term. About two years ago the school decided racist incidents needed to be taken very seriously. This meant almost always sending a student home and asking their parents to come in; probably following that with the suspension of the student involved. One reason was to highlight the importance the school attached to such incidents. Initially, the same procedure would be adopted for relatively minor incidents like name calling.

> "I think, certainly the message in one way or another has got through. One hears in conversation, both in the classroom and overheard in corridors and outside, students talking amongst themselves, and referring to incidents as either racist or sexist. In other words, we have done something to raise their consciousness of certain things being acceptable or unacceptable for those reasons."

According to this Head, these incidents are drawn to the attention of the City Council in one way or another, either using the City Council reporting procedures or by referring to it as a racist incident when reporting a suspension. In addition, examining whether an incident is racist or not is a crucial consideration:

> "If names are called or things are said which are clearly racist, if you break up a fight and one boy says, 'I want to get that Paki and do him in' or whatever, that very clearly is racist. If anything like that is said, or if just names are called which are clearly racist, and if there is a pattern of behaviour whereby particular groups of children tend to get picked on and tend to be the victims of name calling or bullying

349

or being pushed around, if, for example, they are Asian children then there would be a suspicion that it might be a racist incident. In other words, that is something we would look at carefully. For example a couple of weeks ago a first year Asian boy was pushed down a flight of stairs in a way that was pretty severe bullying. It wasn't horseplay and he slipped or whatever. The fact that he was an Asian boy made us ask the question, 'Was this just an incident that might have happened between any two boys or was there some dliberate picking on that child?'

This Head views the punitive approach to racial incidents as sometimes ineffective, especially as far as the person who is dealt with in that way is concerned.

"It may well be effective in terms of raising the conciousness of other people and making other people less likely to say things, but for the persons themselves one doubts whether it achieves very much. It may mean counselling immediately before or when they come back to school. That may be effective or talking it through with their parents, but then that is not part of the actual punishment. It may be we deal with issues in that way, that we are less confident that we can deal with it in any other way, that we are exploiting our outrage but we do not actually feel confident talking it through. The other thing I was going to say was that dealing with incidents in a severe way raises consciousness, or was intended to, partly amongst students but partly amongst staff as well. In other words, I think there were some staff, and still are, but to a lesser extent, who would deal with the incident I mentioned before as a straight forward bullying and pushing on the stairs. I hope that staff are more aware now of the possible potential of racist overtones and undertones behind incidents and, therefore, when they deal with them in a possibly non-punitive way they are also dealing with that aspect of it too. In other words, we don't just deal with it as bullying or name calling or whatever, but we are more on the lookout for potentially racist aspects of incidents. Even if they are not always dealt with in the way we started dealing with them two years ago, they are better than they were previously because certain aspects are not ignored."

Again the introduction of a formal anti racist policy was considered to be important:

"I think it is necessary to have the formal statement for staff, students, and parents, and everybody knows that it is an issue we take seriously, exemplified by having a formal statement on racism or sexism or whatever, but that is certainly not enough . . ."

It is clear that any anti-racist policy, which may well involve the above procedures, will be totally ineffective if carried out in a vacuum, *without the involvement of parents and students.*

Parents and Pupils

One secondary Head emphasises that the *processes* involved in drawing up an anti racist policy are as important as the content of the document itself. The process involves people from the whole school community.

"The school has an institutional policy against racism which was drawn up by a party of approximately twenty, which included students, non-teaching staff, teaching staff, parents and governors. Representatives of each of these groups came together to decide on a sensible and acceptable institutional policy."

The process started in 1983:

"One would automatically have looked at the senior girls on the School Council for their views. The school institutional policy against racism if only I'd written it, would have been brilliant. But by choosing that route and getting representatives of parents, teachers, non-teaching staff, governors and students, I had to accept that the high-flown language that would have got me tremendous applause from anybody who read it was out of the question, and something which read far less high-flown but which perhaps they were prepared to agree to and might be implemented would be what I would get. I don't think, unlike some institutional policies against racism, that this will ever be widely disseminated around England as this is what a school can do. I have written loads of things that will look better than that; I am just very proud of the process we went through to get it."

This particular Head felt quite strongly that the setting up of different parents' groups for Asian, white or Afro-Caribbean parents would be counter productive to what the school was trying to achieve:

"I wouldn't set them up at a school; if I had a request from a group of parents to do any such thing, I would obviously have to consider it. I certainly feel that people from different backgrounds often need different ways of responding to their needs. I have not been happy when we have had almost separate anything. If I can give you an

351

example . . . Many groups wish to encourage Asian girls to continue their education (just as we do), and those sets of people often want to come into school and want to encourage the girls to stay on at school, come to youth clubs, or whatever. The request is always "Can we meet your Asian girls to tell them about this?", and in the first year I was here, I think that happened on two or three occasions, and on each occasion it caused serious resentment from the other girls. Why was there a separate group meeting? What was it about? It's not fair, why are they having a meeting and we're not? Therefore, I would be sorry if the route forward is by separate anything. For example, Direct Works have an excellent policy of wishing to encourage girls – and different ethnic groups – to apply for and join the Manchester Direct Works force. The Councillor and the Head of Direct Works came into school probably May/June, or maybe April – and spoke to the whole of the fifth years about that policy, explaining that it would encourage girls to apply, because girls should now be doing non-usual occupations, and also that the policy was about making sure girls from Asian and West Indian backgrounds had a fair chance as well. That was with the white girls there. If that had been said at a meeting of black and brown girls, or just brown girls, it would have been resented outside."

One Primary Head teacher feels that, although white working class children do not suffer racism, they can nevertheless often feel very excluded, particularly if teachers do not treat the children's or their parents' experiences as valuable. This teacher thinks that if you build up trust with parents it minimises the chances of exacerbating racism.

Another primary Head stresses the parent teacher relationship as having been very important:

"I think some teachers get an attitude of mind where they think everything they say is right and that it isn't a dialogue with the parents. They are not listening, not actually listening, to parents or evaluating what they are saying, or thinking perhaps the parent is right. I think teachers need to think, 'is what I'm saying right?' If parents are coming into school there needs to be an open-mindedness, there needs to be an open door in your mind as well as in the school. Parents are often not treated with respect. I have one teacher who can reduce any parent to tears, or angry frustration. My staff think I am soft with parents, but I think, 'Why should we give them a hard time?' "

At the same time this Head is clear about ideas of the role of education and the school's part in this:

"I am totally honest with the parents about my politics and values. One parent actually took his child away from the school because he didn't want him taught about those 'Paki's and niggers that have come to our country'. But if teachers don't relate to parents on a human level they miss out. They miss out because the parents are not on their side. If a parent comes to see me I always listen to them. Teachers don't see what parents are having to cope with. They can go through an inner city area and not see what is there. The trouble with education is that we are still producing middle class education for working class children, we are not latching on to the way children feel and think about school. We are not taking into account the setting of children's lives."

Continuing with this theme, one secondary Head views student involvement as essential. He discusses it in the context of tackling racism:

"I think it is very important that we are there for the students and to raise their awareness of the issues and to make them more confident in dealing with perhaps racism directed against them, and racism they find in society when they become adults. It is a very important part of the job that schools ought to be doing, to equip young people. We cannot do that by treating young people as passive recipients of education or of learning. They have got to be involved as well. We have school councils which are representatives of each tutor group, lower school, middle school, and upper school."

"Agendas are put together from staff or student concerns, very often about all the minutiae of school life, such as school dinners but it does relate to and address students' experiences."

Starting with parental involvement may not be particularly easy. One secondary Head, dealing mainly with white parents, had virtually given up on trying to get them involved. This Head observed:

"My parents, by and large, don't communicate with school; they don't write, they don't telephone. To all intents and purposes, it's safe at my school to treat all my children as orphans. So if they don't react, it isn't because they are supportive; if they don't react, it isn't because they are opposing; it just doesn't come in their culture to get into a dialogue with school. I have had as many letters complaining

353

about my use of the signs of the zodiac on my note paper as I have had about race."

And, pursuing the question of parental involvement in schools:

"I say to my staff, 'I act as though my children were orphans', and my teachers say to me 'You are wrong. We go to their homes and we sit in their lounges and talk about their kids, and we find out that their parents are very interested in their children and what they are doing at the school'. But what they don't see is that they have a role to play as a member of an audience hearing a speech or joining in a discussion. They feel insecure and uncertain and afraid of what is basically a middle-class insitution with different mores. Two years ago we put on a special evening for the parents of the alternative curriculum. Now, to attract them in, we put on a free bar – and we thought we couldn't get a more powerful inducement than a free bar – but we weren't getting any in. We phoned their homes and said 'Please come', and it was very interesting to see that you would get a mum coming through the door with her next door neighbours as supporters and perhaps as many as 10 children in train, and they needed this protective 'gang' around them to make them feel safe in the school. Now, it struck me what a failure that really was, you know, that parents needed this sort of protection before they felt safe enough to attend what was a social evening with a free bar."

On parental involvement in schools, another secondary Head made the following observation:

"One of the first steps is understanding where different groups of parents come from. I am aware that there is a big problem in terms almost of a misperception, certainly, of the role of the school. Different groups of parents may have quite different perceptions of the role of the school and the role of teachers, and their own role in that process. It has been put to me that many Afro-Caribbean parents for example, especially if they themselves had what is characterised as a much more traditional education in Jamaica or the West Indies – would have a different view of the role of the school and the role of teachers. They would have a different perception of the role of negotiation that we have just talked about. Those differences of perception are the first hurdle that we have got to get over, I think, and you certainly cannot do that without a lot of dialogue and a lot of willingness to open up as far as what we are doing and what we are trying to achieve is concerned.

My aim is to positively seek parents out so that possible misunder-standing between our view and the parents' role and their view could be cleared up. That has been an aspiration and I am trying to do that. It has been very difficult partly because of industrial action again. There have been no parents' evenings in the last two years. The aspiration to involve parents more has been there, but the practice has been very little by comparison. . . We found it relatively difficult to get parental responses. That is definitely a problem to understand the reasons why parents are relatively little involved."

Other Heads have been more successful. One describes the procedure he followed.

"I started the school band and we had regular concerts to break the ice with parents. I invited parents into assemblies. Meetings with parents were held to explain what I was trying to do. Also, attempts were made to involve parents in the school life in the classroom. At that time it was quite successful. There was also a bit of what was probably moral cowardice on my part at that time. Some parents, either in the use of language or in their attitudes, were not setting a good example to the children, yet they were the ones who wanted to get into the school and I also wanted them in."

Indeed, this Head said that staff were at this point resistant to change. They didn't want parents in and their attitude was that:

"What happens on the street is nothing to do with us – we are an all white school, so we don't need to tackle racism."

It was only two years later that staff attitudes started to change, at which point tackling racism became even more important. He says:

"This caused a lot of conflict. (There was an element of hard core racism e.g. swastikas on lighters, tatoos etc. in the community). There were two elements – myself as the Headteacher and two of the staff would challenge racist comments when we were in informal situations outside and refuse a light from swastika lighters etc. That made us unpopular with a lot of people. We were three quite tough and very determined people, however. During that stage, as well as making our own statements it was taking the school line out into the racist environment."

At one stage, resistance from white parents regarding curriculum innovations did come through.

"Kids were saying that their parents were still saying racist things. We would say to students 'either you have got to challenge that, or realise that sometimes parents are wrong.' If a kid goes home and says the school says 'you are wrong' there can be difficulties. A couple of parents came in and one said they didn't want their children to learn about other religions and the other said they wanted an English culture. On both occasions, we showed them the work the children were doing. One parent was happy then. The other one still wasn't happy so we said 'this is the way we are doing it, you've got the right to take your children away'. She didn't. This would be about 1983."

We received information and evidence from a variety of schools in Manchester, but it is clear that there are only a few who are tackling issues which *involve* students and parents in more than a tokenistic way. But how do parents view examples of good practice from their point of view?

Parents' Views

Clearly open access to the Head and staff are priorities. One parent spoke of primary schools as "better" than secondary ones. Partly, it appears, because of the easy access and involvement of parents in the life of the school. One Asian mother said:

"I have a seven year old and a four year old. There is not much fighting. When my daughter arrived at school she was picked on, but it wasn't racial. It was the normal sort of teasing and bullying of a new girl. I saw the teacher, who sorted it out satisfactorily. I go to parents meetings, which I find useful, because we parents get to know each other. The school notices only go out in English, and I think it would be useful if they went out in more languages. There is open access to the Head Teacher; no appointment is necessary and I think this is a good thing".

One other Asian parent spoke of the importance of the PTA not being divided on racial lines.

Individually, parents need to be part of the school community. But what about parental involvement on a wider scale? And how can support be best provided?

One Afro-Caribbean parent who has been involved in a parents group told us the struggle she had in being involved in an independent parents group of a primary school. The group met in a community room in the school and had a Creche Worker.

"A few parents, by word of mouth got together, and we decided we were fed up or sick to death of the way the school was operating on the other side I say the other side, because they are operating under two Heads. We decided that if we had a voice we would be able to do something about this school."

As a result, a few parents held a meeting, asked the Headmaster about setting up a parents' group, and made it clear that they did not want a parent teacher association as such.

"Some parents didn't feel they could speak when teachers were around, so we said we didn't want a PTA, we just wanted a parents group to try and see if we could sort out the curriculum in school – to see if we could help out in any way whatever."

From this mother's account it seems clear that the efficiency of the group, their note-taking, and their getting books together made the Headmaster "panic". They typed a set of minutes and asked the Head to run them off. This was when the trouble started:

"Our minutes somehow disappeared and got into the hands of one of the teachers (or so we were told), and all the teachers objected to what was down on the minutes. We were told that we could not have them back and if we pursued the way we were going on, we would come up against a libel case. This, to some of us, seemed like a nightmare we didn't know what we had opened or what we had done."

It was not just their minute-taking that seemed to worry the Head and staff, but the fact that they wanted to be involved in the day to day running of the school and wished to move beyond safe things like fund raising.

"There were disputes, because one or two of the parents (who we called the 'little elite' in the school) wanted a little 'softly softly' approach – the fund raising – and all that bit – and we were saying, 'not in an area like this. Fund raising cannot be the majority thing, we need to get the curriculum and things like that sorted out.' "

Because these parents were critical of the reading material and wanted to be involved in its selection, to see that it "should reflect the multi-ethnic position of the school", the Headmaster had been horrified and treated their actions as criticisms of his staff. The Education Department also reacted. Bill Gulam, one of the Inspectors from the Education Department who had been helping the parents, "appeared" to have been removed and replaced by John Springthorpe, a Senior Inspector who was seen to be "for the teachers" and not the parents. Another employee from the Education Department, who had been assisting the parents, was told "she was being too political with our group, meaning that we didn't have a voice ourselves and Ms X was speaking for us". The Headmaster then left and the parents group "fell apart", and we "didn't have a fighting voice any more." A parent teacher's association was then suggested, but it was not what the parents wanted.

At this point it was decided that this parent should become a parent governor and be involved in that way. She now tries to maintain two way communication and a feed back to and from parents. She makes it clear that she supports parents and "refuses to take the school's word as final".

Conclusions

It is important in good practice to ensure that support is available for parents who want it, and to encourage and support parents' own attempts to organise themselves, defining or co-opting their organisation.

One person involved in a variety of anti-racist work and who gave evidence to the Inquiry says this:

"We've got an anti-racist policy written down. The question is whether it is serious."

"This means it's not all going to be hunky dory, it means you are going to have to deal with these teachers who don't want to change. It means you're going to have to deal with Heads who don't want to change. It means you are going to have to deal with questions of the core curriculum. It can't be met solely by these symbolic measures. Therefore it means that the Education Authority has got to be responsive to the black community generally, not just self-appointed leaders. It means we have got to address the question of what sort of education we are providing to all the youngsters in the schools, because quite clearly education is appalling, it doesn't provide for most youngsters in the schools. It's got to communicate, it's got to listen, it's got to be accountable, and it's got to do it not merely by dictate from on high. It's got to sit down and work through and

358

communicate with parents and all parents and it's got to address the question of what is education about."

Students' Views

In Nigel de Noronha and Salma Ahmad's work, the boys, and not the girls nearly all agreed that teachers did not understand them and seemed evenly divided about whether this mattered or not.

The interviews showed that name calling is widespread, particularly in the boys' schools and indicated that the most successful way of dealing with this harrassment was direct retaliation. There is also a high level of aggression, particularly towards Asians. Reports of violent incidents confirm that most of the victims and their friends perceive racism as a major factor in the attacks. Very few respondents were satisfied with the effectiveness of reporting procedures or any action taken when they did report incidents.

In discussion with the young people who had been involved with the Memorial Committee, many agreed that they should be allowed to report incidents anonymously and if a number of reports were received about particular "racist" individuals, they should be closely monitored.

Good practice, in terms of support systems, came usually from youth workers as far as the students were concerned. There was little evidence from most schools of any provision within the pastoral care system for the victims of racial harassment or violence. This clearly raises questions about all schools being "community" schools and involving many aspects of the wider community.

The issue of organisation was prominent in the minds of these young people who had been involved with the Memorial Committee. Many clearly saw the need for organisation to combat racism within their schools (such as marching together for support through Longsight).

As Nigel de Noronha and Salma Ahmad point out:

"The question of the school's response to such development raises a number of questions about the power relationships between the school and students. The organisation of students against racism should pose far less threat than the organisation of gangs to terrorise younger and weaker students. This is not the case perhaps because such an organisation is not satisfied with staying within the boundaries of activity described by the school establishment."

"The major motive force for change within the schools is contained within regulations and practices designed to deny them participation within any decision-making process. To give students power over their education is an easy thing to say, but the prospect of developing sufficient responsibility amongst any such groups is a daunting one."

Frontline Theatre Group

One example of how this power and responsibility can be encouraged is through curriculum innovations. We were privileged to see one such innovation by a large mixed group of white and black students from three schools who came together to form the Frontline Theatre Group and perform a play called "Struggle for Freedom – The Life and Work of Len Johnson".

Background

The young people were recruited to take part in a cultural and educational experiment run by Frontline Culture and Education, a shoestring organisation, funded partly by the Local Education Authority and staffed by eight volunteers with experience in drama, music and design. It is co-ordinated by Dan Baron Cohen. Frontline spent five months working with the students, researching, writing and rehearsing the play, sometimes putting in a 12 hour day in rehearsal and on design. The whole story was researched and written by the players themselves. The result was a musical play based on the life of the well known Manchester boxer and political campaigner, Len Johnson, who lived from 1902 to 1974.

Two groups of students, mainly Asian and Afro-Caribbean, came from Burnage High School and Ducie Central, and the rest from a mixed Catholic comprehensive, St. Vincent de Paul, where 80% of the students are of Irish background. About 25 male students took part from Burnage and Ducie and 50–60 male and female students from St. Vincent de Paul.

Story

The story of Len Johnson's life was carefully chosen for its local relevance. The child of an African father and an Irish mother, he spent much of his life in the same part of Manchester, now served by three schools, and married a local Irish woman, Annie Forshaw, against fierce opposition from her father and community. Although a highly successful fighter, Johnson never won a title because of the colour bar of the 1920's and 1930's. With his eyesight damaged, he quit boxing and turned to a political career and campaigned for black rights in Britain and abroad, working with Paul Robeson and others, and helping to organise the first Pan-African Congress, which took place in Manchester.

The story of Len Johnson and Annie Forshaw could be locally and immediately researched. Some of the students met local people, including Spanish Civil War veterans, who had known and worked with Len and Annie, who herself became politically active and organised women threatened with redundancy. The themes of racial discrimination, cultural conflict, and the role and rights of women are as real today in Moss Side and Burnage as in the pre-war days of Annie and Len's lives. It is a story in which sexist and racist culture and class conflict are laid open and bare, and the young people themselves have made the connections with these themes very clearly. The whole five month project was run on democratic lines, with teams of writers, composers and designers elected by the other students.

The intial work on the project was done in two two-hour sessions a week in the three schools. Each school took a different aspect of Johnson's life story – the personal, the legal, and the sporting, and came together outside school to create the whole. This project had an almost 100% attendance compared with high levels of truancy in all three schools.

The play has been performed all over Manchester and also in Sheffield, Rochdale, and Norfolk. Parental support and staff support was almost total until near the end, when staff support declined because of controversy over the final scene.

What impact has this had on the students?

We talked with groups of the students involved in Frontline about their perceptions of the play, their schools, and themselves. Almost all talked about the growth in their self confidence and enthusiasm they found in recording and writing up their conversations into the play.

Many reported a better understanding of Manchester history, and the encouragement their experience in the play had given them to be critical and to ask questions in the classroom, when they returned to the schools. For example, one boy felt confident enough to ask for AIDS to be discussed in his Religious Education class. Another boy told us he had previously been used to accepting quietly what he was told, but, because of the themes of the play and his discussion with the other students, he had started to rethink his ideas of "a woman's place being in the home". They learnt through discussion, debate, and research what imperialism, racism, sexism and Pan-Africanism meant and began to appreciate the complexity of their own feelings about all of these things.

How much self growth and confidence there was, is illustrated by the following evidence:

". . . towards the end of the project one girl reported back to us that when she was walking done one of the corridors one of the teachers was taunting her saying the words "racism", "sexism", "imperialism" to her, and she began an argument with the teacher, and said "do you know what imperialism means?" and she said the teacher couldn't answer her.

Making decisions for yourself was clearly a crucial aspect of the students' experience. They saw clearly the connections between the "struggle for Freedom" of Annie and Len – the title they chose for the play – and their own experiences and struggles in the schools they were attending. They told us that they were now more aware of the racism and sexism in their own lives, and they were deeply suspicious of the police.

The 'controversial' Scene 16 was written by the students after the murder of Ahmed Ullah and was very much a metaphor of their feelings about it, about an anti-racism that is compulsorily imposed on students, and about a trend towards greater police involvement in schools. The scene is set in an inner city school in the not too distant future.

The scene shows a school in open revolt against their teacher. The teacher is depicted as someone who is obviously working under great pressure, and is being asked to do something which is patently absurd: in an authoritarian way impose anti-racist policies. In the scene the class start to question why they are being 'forced' to draw black and white hands in friendship – friendship for them did not happen because of compulsion. Teaching in this particular school is supervised by a patrolling policeman who as a schoolboy sat for years beside and protested with those he now arrests. And the boy who is persuaded to join the force, for the security of a steady job, turns into the authoritarian and racist policeman of tomorrow.

The young people did feel that the scene reflected serious concerns about young people and racism, police behaviour and police in school. It is also topical because of the new legislation which involves police in the development of the curriculum. Students are particularly concerned about police access to school records. They discussed these issues in the project, but were certainly not able to do so in school.

Scene 16 caused great controversy. When it was first performed, four teachers who saw it thought it was "outstanding". Teachers who saw it at other performances were also very positive. These were all lower-scale teachers. None of these had any problem at all in identifying the single teacher on stage in Scene 16 as a teacher under pressure, being asked to carry out the patently absurd task of imposing anti-racist policies in an authoritarian way.

But two other senior teachers had very different ideas. Their misreading of the scene was very significant. They saw the single teacher as representative of all teachers and they saw the police officer as a Headteacher, although he was in police uniform. This clearly set off the alarm bells. They told other senior teachers who, although they had not seen the play, nevertheless condemned the scene as being "provocative". As a result the scene was removed from all future performances during the Summer of 1987. We saw it in a private performance specially put on for us by the cast and afterwards we had lengthy discussions with small groups of students.

Conclusions

The themes of student participation and decision-making were constant in the project. It is clear that the students were learning a history that was their own, such as a history of Africa, West Indies, and Ireland. But it was not necessarily the history which the school would think suitable. It was not Henry VIII or Mary Queen of Scots. That may be, but we were told that why the kids responded to the project so well and so enthusiastically was because it was their own history and it was a history of which they had basically been denied.

What struck us was that the students were using the play and its themes as a metaphor for their own lives and were learning about their own culture, about the significance of their friendships and relationships with each other at school and at home, about their attitudes to women and about race and class. In the course of the play they unpack and lay bare the content of sexist and racist culture.

By using the experience of students to examine history, geography, humanities, drama, art, and contemporary themes in students' lives, we clearly have before us the essential elements of good educational practice. The integration of the issues of race, class and gender with the students' lives, the linking of the different parts of their own experience (e.g. as Irish, as women), and their resulting critical questioning and growing self confidence is a testament to the creativity of the project. We see it very much as an example of good practice and as a model of anti-racist practice for the future.

CHAPTER 32

Education, Schooling and Empowerment

There is a lobby amongst parents which suggests that education is too important a task to be left to teachers. That lobby sees parents as having a crucial role to play in the education of their children, both in relation to what they do at home and at the interface between the home and the school.

The classical view of schooling is of a process involving a partnership between school, home and the interests of the wider community, with the school ultimately preparing young people for a fully active and participative life in society.

Implicit in both these approaches to education and schooling is the notion of parents exercising power, and conceding a certain amount of power to the school. There is no suggestion that students should be able to exercise power similarly in relation to their schooling.

Schools, either independently or in response to pressure from parents, make decisions about what should and should not be taught, and how relationships within the school or between the school and the home community should be handled. The evidence we have presented in this report points to the very many ways in which schools regulate the use of power by staff, by parents and by students.

In our view, tackling racism and racial violence in schools is not a task that can sensibly be undertaken without regard for those power relationships. Time and again, we heard evidence from teachers and students about inconsistency on the part of Burnage and other schools in dealing with racism and acts of violence. Similarly, we have had evidence of students feeling aggrieved because of racist and/or violent treatment by staff, and of staff feeling aggrieved because of the racist and violent conduct of students. In the case of black members of staff, an accompanying cause for grievance was the way the school's treatment of those matters seemed to confirm and uphold the racist and violent conduct of students.

We see it as crucial that schools declare unambiguously and openly what their stance is on racism, racial harrassment and violence, and do so in a manner that staff, students and parents can understand. Equally importantly, schools need to signal how they see that concern about racism, racial violence and harrassment having an impact on the curriculum and on the school's relationship with students and parents.

But, how does the school arrive at its formal position on these matters. The evidence we have presented so far points to a process whereby the Education Committee decides on policies which are then adopted by the school, or forms the framework for the school's own defintion of its policies.

Both the City Council and the school at present engage in a consultation process which involves various groups within the black communities. That "consultation" process does not involve school students or parents. Students, parents, teachers and Education Department officers all point in one way or another to the unsatifactory nature of these processes.

We received evidence from a number of sources with suggestions for alternative approaches to the organisation of schooling in relation to all of the above matters. We intend to deal, principally, with three of these submissions, concentrating in some detail on two of them.

(1) *MCCR on monitoring racist incidents*

The Manchester Council for Community Relations (MCCR) submitted "Recommendations on an improved system of notifying, acting on and monitoring racist incidents". In their submission, MCCR warned against the tendency to respond "as if all undersirable 'isms' could be addressed simultaneously in an identical manner".

They point to the 'strong tendency within Manchester City Council thinking' to view racism, sexism and discrimination against sexual and other minorities as "fundamentally flawed" because it attempts to short circuit real differences in the origin and reproduction of different oppressions. Applied to behaviour in educational institutions, that approach is considered very much a problem.

MCCR's view is that much assistance needs to be given to teachers to help them distinguish racist incidents when they occur, and be sure about the relationship between an inter-racial incident and a racial or racialist incident.

(2) *Burman, Collier and Heffernan – developing a strategy on violence and anti-racism*

The second submission was by Burman, Collier and Heffernan, the three educational psychologists who were closely involved with Burnage in the aftermath of Ahmed's murder. The first part of their

366

submission deals with 'Identifying Violence in Manchester Schools', and the second with 'The Implementation of Anti-Racist Policies'.

(See Appendix G)

They make the point that educational establishments are complex hierarchical organisations within which power is invested and wielded differentially. Within such a system, both individuals and groups of individuals can feel violated in a number of different ways.

"Violence can occur as directed from:

Student to staff	Student to parent
Staff to student	Parent to student
Student to student	Student to staff
Parent to staff	Staff to parent"

The authors' view is that within each of those groupings the variables of race, gender, class, disability, age and sexual orientation must be recognised.

They propose a structure for identifying and dealing with violence which involves the whole school, parents, staff, students, Governing body, Headteacher and community groups. Operating in a non-hierarchical way and in a manner that does not reflect the existing power structures within the school, this umbrella group would set itself the following task:

To identify its establishment's definition of violence (personal, institutional, structural), structures of domination within the school, a system for monitoring violence, strategies for dealing with violence, and devise techniques for teaching non-violent solutions to conflict.

In order to inform that process, this umbrella group might wish to subdivide into groups according to particular characteristics, e.g. girls and women (students, parents, staff), ethnic groups (students, parents, staff). These sub-groups would consider the various aspects of violence in the life of the school by reference to their own experience, and feed back into the main umbrella group. These sub-groups could meet with their equivalents from other education establishments and form support networks throughout the City.

The work of such umbrella groups should assist their respective establishments in determining the nature and range of violence within the institution, its techniques for identifying and monitoring violence, its technique for dealing with violence, and its needs for future development.

The umbrella group and its various sub-groups would:

- raise levels of consciousness with regard to the nature of violence.
- empower victims and low-status groups by providing support.
- develop good practice for reducing aggression and violence, and develop non-violent solutions when it does occur.

The umbrella group would be expected to complete its task within a specified period and be a in a position to report to the whole school community, the Governing body, the Education Authority, the Equal Opportunities Unit and the Race Unit.

We share the view of these authors that "a shift of power within the school system is an inevitable and attainable objective".

Moreover, we believe that policies and strategies for dealing with racism, violence, harrassmant, bullying, and so forth should not be seen as solely the responsibility of the school management or the Education Authority but that of students, parents and community bodies as well. Otherwise their implementation will inevitably be riddled with conflict.

We would also welcome the idea of an umbrella working group to define the school or college's policies and strategies, or to negotiate with the Local Education Authority on matters concerning any section of the student population.

We take the view that were such groups to be formed in every school or college, Manchester Education Department's consultation with them would be a far more meaningful and democratic exercise than the current system of consultation.

The success of a policy depends as much on the process that led to its formulation, and people's perceptions of that process, as it does on the vigour with which the policy is pushed forward within the establishment. A consultation process that is rooted in the school community is more likely to be successful than one based on an "ad hoc" selection of local community organisations, who are not necessarily representative or democratic.

3.   Four Inspectors' recommendations to combat racism

The third submission which we discuss was made by a group of Inspectors from the Education Department in Manchester. The

368

group included the Chief Inspector and Inspectors who had carried out the Burnage inspection in 1985. In their submission, the Inspectors made recommendations concerning further work they felt to be necessary at Burnage High School in the light of the inspection findings, as well as recommendations necessary to combat racism and racial violence in Manchester schools.

(See Appendix H)

We concentrate on three aspects of the submissions, as follows:

a) Anti-racism training in linked primary schools.
b) The need for political education – in particular to influence white youth.
c) Ways in which student power is organised, expressed and incorporated into the school organisation.

(a) *linking with primary schools*

In relation to a), the Inspectors propose that linked primary schools should nominate 'key worker(s)' to focus anti-racist staff development/ training at Burnage High School. This would create "a working ongoing relationship between primary and lower secondary school staff."

The Inspectors suggest that anti-racist training is part of a process that does not have a finite end, but needs to have a determined starting point. "Too often" they suggest "the process starts too late, usually in the secondary school. The model suggested is one which should have a primary-secondary continuum".

The Parr's Wood Project

This is not a proposal that the Inspectors need to be tentative about, as an actual example of this 'primary-secondary continuum' already exists.

For the last three years, Manchester has been operating an experimental project funded under the DES Education Support Grant Scheme. Based at Parrs Wood High School, the project is geared to assisting teachers at Parrs Wood High and two of its link schools in developing anti-racist approaches to the curriculum.

The project has involved teachers and students across the schools, as well as the Governing bodies and parents.

369

The project director, Doug Bloom, gave written evidence to us, and we are convinced that in the Parrs Wood Project Manchester already has a tried and successfully tested model on which the City should seek to build.

The Parrs Wood Project has already gone way beyond what the Inspectors propose. It organises in-service training workshops within and between schools. The Project also acts as a catalyst for change within the link schools and in individual departments in the High School. Doug Bloom acts as a co-ordinator of the wok in the High School and in the link schools.

Teachers and students in the link schools know what Parrs Wood High is doing in the area of combatting racism and ethnocentrism, and of developing positive self-images amongst the constituent groups in the student population.

The Project assists staff and students in each of the schools to explore racism and the various ways in which it is perpetuated and indulged through schooling.

In our view the process which the Project inspired and its products are worthy of dissemination, and deserve a much wider exposure within Manchester Schools.

The Inspectors recommend in their submission that "key trainers should be identified in the LEA to facilitate the process" of focussing anti-racist staff development on the primary-secondary continuum. We find it strange, therefore, that the Parrs Wood project which we were told would wind up at the end of July, is now scheduled to end in March, thus leaving no time for the dissemination of its results.

In the light of Elinor Kelly's survey findings, and the evidence of Nigel De Noronha and Salma Ahmad, concerning the experiences of students in the lower years of the secondary schools, we would urge Manchester Education Committee to find ways of enabling other schools in the City to benefit from the Parrs Wood experiments.

(b) *Influencing White Youth*

In relation to the need for political education – in particular to influence white youth, the Inspectors suggest that a potent way of combatting racism is to get young people to identify what they have in common with each other rather than what is different.

They call for representatives from departments and faculties to get together to develop strategies for introducing political education into the curriculum in a co-ordinated way.

They also propose "a young people's 'grouse' group". The group would be similar to a democratically elected school council and would make representation to management on issues affecting the wellbeing of the school community. It would also monitor racist incidents/aggression. The school management would need to be duty bound to reply to this group's grievances.

We have a number of comments in relation to these matters.

Students of whatever background have common interests as students. Those interests are not necessarily the same as that of the school or of parents. The school exercises power over students but also regulates the exercise of power by one student or group of students over others. It is required at all times to guarantee their safety in so far as that could reasonably be expected. The manner in which the school exerts power and regulates it is in our view something that should involve the student body. The idea of a 'grouse' group making representation to management, with management replying to the group's grievances we see as being too negative.

We propose instead a democratically elected school students' union, to be resourced and provided with accommodation from the school's establishment, and from whatever fund raising they might do themselves.

The union would accept its share of the responsibility for the wellbeing of the school, and would therefore be involved in shaping or reviewing school policy.

It would monitor issues of violence, racism and racial harrassment, and, in accordance with the strategies identified through the 'Umbrella Working Group' (on which it would have been represented), form part of the school's mechanism for dealing with those issues.

Concerning the strategy of getting young people to identify what they have in common, we are conscious of the evidence we received from a number of white students. Their experience of being expected to respect the cultural and religious preferences and beliefs of blacks, without anyone exploring their feelings or racist beliefs with them is something we feel the designers of anti-racist policies must be aware of.

When one sweeps away the power that being white in a racist society confers on white students, a great deal is revealed which those students could explore to their benefit. At the very least, it assists them in placing the oppression of blacks in its proper persepective. That, at least, was one of the discoveries of the Frontline group.

(c) *Organising pupil power*

As regards (c) (ways in which student power, can be organised, expressed and incorporated into the school organisation), the Inspectors put their case as follows:

"Disputes between students and teachers are often unfair. A highly educated, mature, often middle-class adult debates against an immature, often less articulate young-person, in a forum which is seen to be on 'the teacher's side'. Judge and jury is often a member of the school senior management team.

This is not fair for the student.

"A student/parent advocacy should be developed. The mechanism could be a teacher or youth worker appointed in each area of the city. The staff appointed would be independent of any individual institution and could be called upon by any parent or young person to act as their advocate in disputes".

We endorse the premise, but disagree with the recommendation. In our view, the form of advocacy suggested here does not square with the notion of giving students more say. It keeps power in the hands of the professional advocate, who may well identify with the school's senior management.

We are not against student and parent advocates but we believe that an independent body of students and an independent body of parents organised in their respective interests should be the groups from whom such 'advocates' should be chosen. In the absence of such groups, a sub-section of the 'Umbrella Working Group' should constitute a 'tribunal' to safeguard the interests of students. Such a 'tribunal' would consist of students, parents and a teacher governor from the same school to which the incident relates.

All the events at Burnage High School which come within the purview of this Inquiry, and the decisions made by the Senior Management of the school and by the Governing Body have affected each and every one of the students in the school and the great majority of their parents. Time and time again we have seen examples of the school, usually through the Headteacher, seeking to protect or advance its interests, however ill-conceived those might have been.

We believe that the school's handling of the aftermath of Ahmed's murder, of Ahmed's funeral, and of the events of February/March 1987 might have been very different if a disciplined, well organised, democratic and vibrant students' union had been operating in that school. The self-regulation that such a democratic formation implies might well have avoided the great disruption of the March events and their aftermath.

The shift of power we recommend is seen as being in the wider interest of the school and its whole community.

We believe that it is in teachers' interests to encourage and assist such self-organisation amongst students and parents. It may well prove to be the only guarantor of social cohesion in the inner-city schools of tomorrow. But it will mean change.

CHAPTER 33

Conclusions

We have set out at great length our summary of the evidence given to us. We now try to draw together the conclusions we have reached. They fall into three parts:

(1) The murder.
(2) Burnage High School.
(3) Manchester generally.

We have been greatly impressed throughout the Inquiry by the co-operation and great goodwill we have received and the care which witnesses have taken over the preparation and the presentation of their evidence. We are anxious that all this effort should not be in vain and that our report should not have its moment of glory and then be shelved, because of financial stringencies or for any other reason. We have felt it important, therefore, to make certain recommendations about the handling of our report.

The full report will be too much for many people and we, therefore, asked Manchester City Council to assist us in preparing a report summary. This has now been done. The summary should be made available to any parent, student, school staff or governor in Machester on request and without charge.

We are anxious that our report be distributed as widely as possible and given to all relevant people. We recommend that all those who gave evidence or assisted the Inquiry in other ways should receive a copy of the full report and a copy of the summary, without charge.

The Advisory Council for Education (ACE) has a wide and competent distribution network of educational information to schools, governors, parents and other concerned persons. We recommend that Manchester City Council arranges the distribution of the report through that body, on whatever terms they may agree.

Many of our conclusions indicate further action. In our opinion these will need regular monitoring and we, therefore, recommend that Manchester Education Department set up the necessary machinery to carry out this monitoring.

To ensure that effective action is being taken or is planned on the matters we deal with in our report, or that there is a good reason for not acting or following up any of our recommendations, we recommend that the Inquiry be reconvened in June, July or September 1988 to check and report on progress. In the interim period the services of the Clerks to the Inquiry and the Solicitors should be retained.

We recommend that a report on progress to date be prepared by the Manchester Education Department for the Inquiry before we reconvene. This report may be written or given orally. Other interested parties who wish to give us evidence or information about progress should contact the Inquiry through the Solicitors.

Evidence was given to the Inquiry in private and many witnesses expressed a wish that their identity should not be revealed. We propose to place an embargo on statements made to the Inquiry and on the transcripts of evidence given to us until the year 2000. We have asked the Solicitors to the Inquiry to arrange for the safe keeping of the documents.

We now turn to our main conclusions.

Delay in Reaching Hospital

1. Although we heard a certain amount of evidence about the possible effect of delay in taking Ahmed Ullah to hospital, we do not regard this as falling within our terms of reference. It is unconnected with any racial aspect surrounding his death (our first term of reference) or with any aspect of violence and discipline at Burnage High School (our second term of reference). However, we have set out in some detail in Chapter 1 evidence given to us of the period from 8.30 a.m. to 9.15 a.m. on Wednesday September 17th 1986, in order to tell the story properly. But we have reached no conclusion.

Darren Coulburn

2. The way the school dealt with Darren Coulburn is clearly within our terms of reference. We were given an almost complete dossier by the school, the Education Department, the Educational Welfare Officer and Social Worker and would like to record our thanks to all these people for their assistance. We summarised Darren Coulburn's history at Burnage High School in Chapter 2 and set out our conclusions in Chapter 5.

3. Our conclusion is that he ought to have been removed from Burnage High School before the beginning of the September term in 1986, because by then it should have been clear that the school

376

did not have the resources or the capacity to give him the help he was so obviously crying out for, but there was no basis for removing him from the school on the grounds that he had shown a propensity to be violent or had given some indication that he was likely to commit murder or grievous bodily harm.

4. In dealing with Darren Coulburn, we are critical of the way in which the school dealt with a boy who was so obviously in need of help. Part of the difficulty was that the school did not bring together all the facts until after the murder (Chapter 5) but we have also come to the conclusion that the handling of his case was adversely affected by the management style of the senior management team at Burnage.

5. As a result, the governors were not informed of the views of Darren Coulburn's teachers. After the burning of the art block, the teacher governors were given no advance notice that the question of Darren Coulburn's exclusion from the school would be discussed. His year head was rebuked by senior management for informing his form teacher in a memorandum of Darren's conviction for arson. Mr Hewitt, the Deputy Head, was asked to monitor his progress after the governors had decided in December 1985 that he should remain in the school, but other teachers were not informed of this, and as a result Mr Hewitt clearly did not get full or up-to-date information on Darren Coulburn, which would have enabled him to carry out efficient or effective monitoring. In short, communications between teachers and senior management and between the school and social workers was haphazard and uncoordinated.

Was the Murder Racialist or Racist?

6. We make a distinction between the terms "racialist" and "racist". Our working definitions are given in Chapter 5. "Racialism" refers to prejudice, beliefs and behaviour based on race, culture or ethnicity and a murder may be "racialist" if it is done for a racialist motive or out of racial prejudice, for example, because the victim is black. The term "racist" has a wider meaning. The murder could properly be described as "racist" if it has been based on a doctrine of racism or reflects the racist structure of society and need not be conscious behaviour as such.

7. In our view there is no evidence to suggest that the murder of

Ahmed Ullah was racialist or that Darren Coulburn stabbed him because he was Asian or because he was looking for a "Paki" to kill. We emphasise that we are not talking here of some marauding gang of National Fronters, of whom Darren Coulburn was one.

8.   At the same time, there was no evidence that the murder would have happened, if Ahmed Ullah had been white or of some other ethnic origin. In our view, the situation, in which the two boys met in fatal combat, would not have taken place if Ahmed Ullah had been white. In our view racism was one of the vital ingredients that brought the two boys together. It was a factor which led Darren Coulburn to bully the smaller Asian boys in Ladybarn Park. It was behind their appeal to Ahmed for help, and his response. And no doubt racism fuelled Darren Coulburn's bitter response to his own humiliation by Ahmed and added potency to his vow for revenge, since in the fatal moment the victim of his attack lost all individual identity and became the symbol of his race – a "Paki".

9.   Although we are clear that the murder was racist as we have defined it, it was also a much more complex event and raised other equally important issues, for example, that Darren Coulburn was a highly disturbed boy with a long history of difficult, delinquent and anti-social behaviour; that he was a known bully; that the carrying of knives in school was not unknown; and that violence of this kind might in part be due to an all male environment and a power structure based upon it.

10.   We see nothing difficult or contradictory for an institution like a school to accept that for Asian students the murder was first and foremost a racist murder and to white students it was merely the work of a highly disturbed boy with a history of bullying and delinquent behaviour and not racist at all. Unless the school could deal with both points of view it was not in a position to allay the fears of Asian students and their parents, who were afraid of further attacks, or of white students and their parents who were afraid of an Asian backlash.

11.   At the meeting held at Burnage High School on the afternoon of the murder, the school and the Education Authority became committed to the view that the murder was racist and did not at any stage publicly acknowledge the other complexities or issues involved and thus the official view of the killing was partial, incomplete and in our view misleading.

12. The repercussions of this partial and incomplete view of the murder by the school authorities led them to ignore the experience and feelings of the white students, for whom Darren Coulburn was someone quite separate and with whom they could not identify, and was a factor leading to a polarisation of white students lumping them into the same camp as Darren Coulburn. Our conclusion is that ignoring the white reaction is as racist as ignoring the black (Chapter 3).

13. The police took the view that there was no racial aspect to the murder and made this clear in the press on the day of the murder and at a well attended meeting at Bangladeshi House on the following day. By failing to recognise or acknowledge any racism in the crime at all, the police outraged the whole Asian community and denied the reality of racism which the Asian community, and in particular Asian youth, were putting forward.

14. It is clear to us that the murder was used as a metaphor for the feelings and experiences of all sections of the Asian community, particularly of the youth, and enabled people to bring together their experiences and to explain and come to terms with the tragedy of Ahmed's death. By denying the validity of that experience and suggesting it was not a fit subject for discussion, at any rate pending the trial of Darren Coulburn, the police assisted in a polarisation of Asian youth, which was later to surface in the events of March.

15. There is nothing in the evidence to suggest that a murder of this kind could only have taken place at Burnage High School. It could have happened in any number of other schools in Manchester or the United Kingdom. What singled Burnage out is the aftermath of the tragedy. Becase of a failure to understand the racist context in which the murder took place, neither the school nor the police were capable of dealing with the great ripple effects that flowed from it. In our view, the events of March 1987 are peculiarly Burnage events and we have concluded that these events can be traced directly to the mishandling of the aftermath of the tragedy.

Handling the Aftermath of the Murder

16. After the stabbing, Ahmed's family were called to the hospital, where they were met by the police, Mr Moors, Ms Aisthorpe and Mr Choudhury, who had been fetched by Ms Aisthorpe. We have

found the assumptions made about the family to be insensitive. It was assumed that they needed an interpreter without anyone having taken the trouble to find out if this was true. The family might have preferred to have been left to cope on their own but they were never given this choice. We have concluded that no white family, who had just lost a son in similar circumstances, would have been treated in the way the Ullah family were treated and their grief would not have been treated as a community matter (Chapter 3).

17. White students from Burnage were stopped from attending Ahmed Ullah's funeral at the very last minute. This decision was taken either by Dr Gough on his own or in consultation with Mr Moors. It was a decision which caused grief and anger.

18. We did not manage to hear all evidence about the manner in which this decision was reached, but from the evidence we have concluded that it was a panic decision, made without proper consultation. It is matched by a failure to hold staff briefings or discussions about the funeral arrangements themselves.

19. The decision had a damaging effect on race relations at Burnage. Apart from denying white friends of Ahmed the opportunity to say goodbye to and mourn their friend, it helped to reinforce a feeling amongst white students that they were somehow to blame for the death and should be kept away from the funeral. Our conclusion is that it is a further link in a chain which leads to a polarisation of students at Burnage along racial lines, a polarisation which would finally surface in the events of March 1987.

The Events of March 1987

20. The events of March 1987 were almost exclusive to Burnage High School. Apart from the short one day spill over in Levenshulme Girls School, no other school in Manchester experienced similar disorder.

21. During the events of March, the student population in the Upper School at Burnage polarised along racial lines, the two main antagonists being Asian students on the one hand and white students on the other. Afro-Caribbean students were involved in initial attacks on Asian students, but later took a neutral position.

22. During the disorders, members of staff at Burnage were able to circulate quite freely amongst all sections of the student population, even when they gathered in large groups.

23. The March events spread out from Burnage High School into the surrounding streets and neighbourhoods and involved members of the white and Asian community who were not students at the school.

24. The incidents which sparked off the disorders were relatively trivial and unimportant in themselves, but the roots of the polarisation are to be found in the way in which the aftermath of the stabbing was handled by the school authorities, the established community leaders, and the police.

25. White students were effectively labelled by the school authorities as outcasts, racists in the same mould as Darren Coulburn, and had been refused permission to go to the funeral.

26. Asian students, who had reacted to the murder by placing on record their own daily experiences of racism in school and in their neighbourhoods, had been slapped down by the police and had been discouraged at every turn by the established community leaders, when they attempted to organise themselves around those issues, which they felt were exemplified by Ahmed's murder. From the experience of the Ahmed Ullah Memorial Committee they learned the lessons of self reliance and self defence. They organised around those principles in Burnage School during the Spring term of 1987.

27. Before the outbreak of disorder, the Asian students had tried to take their grievances to members of the staff at Burnage but had failed to obtain satisfactory redress. They then took things into their own hands.

The School's Handling of the March Events

28. Order was restored in Burnage High School by the withdrawal from the school of a group of white students, who were supposedly part of an Asian students hit list. These students never returned to the school that term or the following term.

29. Some of the heat was undoubtedly taken out of the situation by the introduction into Burnage High School of Geoff Turner and

381

Mukhtar Khares, two senior and experienced youth workers, who worked closely with the core group of Asian and white students. However, the work which they carried out was never acknowledged or followed up by the school.

30. No member of staff asked for or obtained a report or debriefing from either Geoff Turner or Mukhtar Khares about the situation which they had found. As an institution, the school, therefore, never dealt with the grievances of the Asian students or resolved the position of the white students who had been withdrawn for their own safety.

31. As a result the situation was allowed to fester, with many scores unsettled. We have concluded that the failure to resolve the situation created the possibility of racial disorder taking place on a far greater scale than any of the events of March. These disorders would inevitably have involved other members of the white and Asian community and the school would have had no control over them at all.

32. The failure of senior management at Burnage to foresee or understand the potential for far greater conflict as a result of their inaction is, in our view, one of the most serious indictments of senior management at Burnage. We find it sad to see a man such as Dr Gough, who is so committed to the principles of anti-racism, being responsible for one of the most obvious acts of discrimination we have come across in the course of the Inquiry. His failure to see the link between the way the school treated those white students and the potential for racial conflict in the neighbourhood outside the school is, in our view, unforgiveable.

33. Burnage is an all boys school and there is evidence of greater aggressiveness and a greater propensity to solve problems through force and violence than in a mixed school or an all girls school. It is part of a male culture (Chapter 15).

34. Despite the removal of corporal punishment as a sanction, there is still evidence of teachers imposing their authority from time to time through acts of violence against students and a number of these were documented for us. (Chapter 16).

35. It is not altogether surprising that there is a widespread pattern of violence amongst students towards each other, given that Burnage is an all boys school and that there is an important segment of staff

and students who still think of force as the ultimate sanction for imposing teachers' authority. The evidence to us suggests that violence, aggression and the use of force is very much part of the culture of the school. However, it is very difficult to judge whether Burnage is any different from any other all boys' school in a city area. It is a school which has been very much under the spotlight and to single it out as something special would, in our view, be unfair. (Chapter 16).

36. The evidence does suggest that if there is any return to the saction of corporal punishment, there would be a probable escalation of violence at all levels in a school like Burnage. (Chapter 16). A different strategy for dealing with violence is needed and one model has been suggested to us (Appendix G), which we deal with in a later chapter (Chapter 32).

37. The culture of male violence cannot be separated from the culture of racism. Burnage is not just an all boys school, it is also a school in which a large proportion of the student population is Afro-Caribbean and Asian. Racism and racial violence existing in the local community is bound to be reflected in the school itself, both among students and teachers, and so it was at Burnage (Chapter 17).

Racism and Violence at Burnage

38. We received evidence, entirely anecdotal, of daily acts of racial violence and abuse heaped on the Asian and Afro-Caribbean population in the areas of Burnage and Longsight. It is nothing new. Such evidence repeats itself all over Britain, as indicated by an examination of the growing literature on racial harassment and attacks. (Chapter 17).

39. Inside Burnage itself, we had a sufficient volume of evidence to indicate that there have been teachers at the school who have behaved in a blatantly racist manner towards students and members of staff, and have been guilty of racial bigotry. We document such instances in Chapter 17. There is nothing, however, to indicate that this racism dominates all social relations at the school or is widespread amongst the whole staff or that it is fixed or unchangeable.

40. Among students, the picture is similar. Asian students, in particular, have been subjected to a daily dose of racist name-calling and

there is strong feeling that many are picked on because of race. A strong sense of racial identity among both black and white students emerges from the evidence and at dinner time there has tended to be a separation of Asian from White and Afro-Caribbean students (Chapter 17).

41. The elements for the sort of conflict that led to Ahmed Ullah's murder have been in the school for a very long time. So too have the elements that led to the racial polarisation that took place in March 1987. We were, therefore, interested to see whether the school or the local education authority had learned anything from an earlier incident in 1982 which contained a similar mix of violence and racism.

Learning the Lessons of 1982

42. The incidents of 1986 and 1987 are pre-dated by what happened at Burnage in 1982. In January 1982, the son of the Deputy High Commissioner for Bangladesh, who is based in Manchester, was attacked by five fellow students in the Careers Library in a totally unprovoked incident and received serious facial injuries including a fractured cheekbone. (Chapter 18).

43. The school and local education authority blindly denied the existence of a racial element in the violence, but the incident created fear and insecurity within the Asian community around Burnage and Longsight and remained deep in the memory, to be recalled as soon as that community heard of the death of Ahmed Ullah in September 1986. We recall the details of that incident in Chapter 18.

44. Our finding is that neither the school nor the local education authority learned any lessons from this incident or used the opportunity presented by it to deal specifically with the twin questions of violence and racist violence at Burnage (Chapter 18).

45. We take the view that a more vigorous approach to the issue of violence and racial abuse after the 1982 incident would have made both teachers and students more alert to the situation that Ahmed Ullah found himself confronting in September 1986 and would have created a climate in which Asian students would have felt more secure.

46. The failure to deal with the 1982 incident properly made it more likely that when Ahmed Ullah was stabbed in 1986 the Asian community would react with an even stronger feeling that, as a community, they were under racial attack and their reaction would produce the sort of clumsy responses from the school and Education Authority, which we have already examined. In our view, both the 1982 and the 1986 incidents are examples of how common sense and ordinary judgement which schools such as Burnage might well exercise in relation to other matters get displaced by the confusion and lack of logic which the application of doctrinaire multi-culturalism and anti-racism engenders. (Chapter 18).

Anti-Racism and Multi-Culturalism at Burnage

47. Since Dr Gough's arrival at Burnage High School in 1983, many important and, in our view, progressive changes have been made: for example corporal punishment and didactic methods which go with it have been replaced by child-centred education: more women teachers have been employed; and the school has made a commitment to multi-cultural and anti-racist education and has introduced anti-racist policies into the school (Chapter 19).

48. However, the manner in which these policies have been introduced has created a certain amount of distrust among staff and has led to some hardening of existing staff polarisation. (Chapter 19).

49. Extra staffing for multi-cultural and anti-racist development were introduced into the school, using Section II funding, and all Section II staff were eventually grouped together under a new community education department, whose thrust has almost exclusively been concerned with Afro-Caribbean and Asian issues (Chapter 19).

50. We find this to have been a strange use of a community education department, which we would normally expect to enlist the experience of the whole community, white as well as black. The practice of the community education department at Burnage appears to have ignored the notion of "community" as necessarily embracing the white community and multi-culturalism as including the culture of the whole working class, and this we find regrettable. (Chapter 19).

51.   We also find that using Section II staff to "graft on" anti-racist policies can easily lead to a marginalisation of these issues in a school and can absolve from the responsibility for anti-racist education the non-Section II staff, who then tend to see anti-racism and multi-culturalism as being the exclusive responsibility of the Section II staff (chapter 19).

52.   In Burnage the position, in our view, was made worse by the setting up of separate ethnic minority advisory groups (EMAGs) which consisted of Afro-Caribbean and Asian parents only. This was ostensibly done to satisfy Home Office guidelines requiring consultation, but it was unnecessary to satisfy these and the EMAGs were created in the face of good advice to the contrary – advice which in our view should have been followed at Burnage (Chapter 19).

53.   The creation of EMAGs was divisive of both parents and students and made it appear that white parents have no business in the development of anti-racist education, a notion which we reject totally (Chapter 19).

Management Style

54.   In 1985, two investigations were held into the running of Burnage High School, one by the Governors and one by the school inspectorate of the Manchester City Education Department. Both reports identified a serious crisis in staff relations in more or less clear terms, but on both occasions the opportunity to do something about this was missed (Chapter 20).

55.   During the course of our inquiry, we found an atmosphere of great fear amongst staff, many of whom went to great lengths to avoid it being known that they had spoken to the inquiry. This occurred not just with teachers but with the anciliary staff as well. We were very anxious to find the cause of this fear and therefore examined in some detail the management style of the head and deputy heads of the school (Chapter 21).

56.   The management style at Burnage High School, as exercised by Dr Gough and Mr Moors, would have rendered that school virtually unmanageable but for the professionalism and commitment of a large number of able and dedicated staff. Mr Hewitt's position is different in that there was not the same volume of

complaint. Nevertheless, we take the view that he was part of the senior management team and had taken direct responsibility for the "monitoring" of Darren Coulburn, which other staff had not heard of, and for handling the events of March 1987, in which, as we have seen, a number of white students were permanently excluded from the school. In our view, he and the other two senior managers must stand or fall together (Chapter 21).

.57. We were singularly impressed with the way many of the staff below the top level gave their evidence and with the skill and resoluteness with which they had managed a number of crises, often in the absence of any involvement, lead or support from the most senior managers of the school (Chapter 21).

58. With senior teaching staff who have demonstrated a high degree of competence, professionalism and management skills as well as two deputy heads, an astute manager would, in our view, have little difficulty in utilising his or her staff and building a vibrant school community, nothwithstanding that the staff could be expected to contain some who are racist and bigoted. But this was not done at Burnage (Chapter 21).

59. Our finding is that the management style has created an atmosphere of fear and mistrust and has undermined staff attempts to make the school function cohesively; senior management support on discipline is regarded by many staff as inconsistent and there is a lack of openness and willingness to share information. Dr Gough is described by some of his staff as highly intelligent, incisive and quick but rather aloof and remote and his style of management, as insensitive and divisive. We have documented incidents illustrating the management style in practice. (Chapter 21).

60. At Burnage, there emerged two dominant camps whose members have been placed into categories which have become fixed and static. Instead of breaking them up and reconciling the rigid camps, Dr Gough and Mr Moors in particular have tended to view them as those who are for and those who are against, so that they tend to cultivate and nurture people in the one camp and fail to appreciate sufficiently the skills of those in the other. We have also found instances where senior management ought to have been seen giving active support to members of their staff but in fact that support has been absent. (Chapter 21).

61. At many crucial stages in the events we have been examining the views and advice of senior teachers, heads of year and form teachers have been undervalued or disregarded by senior management but they have still had to deal with the consequences of decisions taken higher up. (Chapter 21).

62. But the story does not end there. It has been suggested to us by a number of witnesses that the shortcomings of the management style can and should be overlooked in view of the clear and strong commitment of Dr Gough and Mr Moors to promoting child-centred, anti-racist and anti-sexist policies in the school. If they had to leave, so the argument goes, the anti-racist teachers remaining in the school will be at the mercy of the hardcore of bigots who will then come out of their closet and destroy the modest progress achieved under Dr Gough. We have considered this argument very carefully but have rejected it because:

(i) it ignores the failure of the "liberal" regime to recognise or deal with the racial polarisation which took place in Burnage following Ahmed Ullah's death;

(ii) It overlooks the treatment of the white students in the aftermath of the March events and the possibility of further serious racial disorder recurring and

(iii) It leaves out of account the perceptions and experiences of the black teachers at Burnage, whose experience we document in Chapter 22.

The Experience of Black Teachers at Burnage

63. Both visiting music staff and the Urdu teacher had experiences which were humiliating and degrading. Music staff did not feel able to look to either Dr Gough or Mr Moors for support and appeared to have received precious little help from the head of community studies. If their experiences are anything to go by, the anti-racist policies do not appear to be in any way effective.

64. Ms X, a black drama teacher, struck us as a teacher of enormous courage, child-centred and concerned about parents and students alike whether they were Afro-Caribbeans, white or Asian, but in our view, her position and authority as a teacher was undermined by senior management at the school.

388

65. She worked with at least one of the white students who was excluded from the school after the events of March, 1987 and visited that student's home. Through her work, she presented the school with an opportunity to deal with the mess that had resulted from the March events, but this opportunity was lost when senior management told the teacher that if the student in question came back to the school, there might be trouble.

66. The views and experiences of the black teacher reinforces our findings with regard to the management style at the school. We have no doubt that Dr Gough inherited a group of racist teachers amongst the staff at Burnage, but that was something that any head, having Dr Gough's analysis of British education and British society, could easily have predicted. Equally, we have no doubt that racism remains a problem to be confronted both among the staff and students at the school (Chapter 22).

Dealing with Burnage

67. We have already dealt with the rigidity of the divisions which have arisen amongst the staff at Burnage. We feel that the management style of Dr Gough and his two deputies makes it unlikely that the various divisions amongst the staff groups, can be reconciled but even if such reconciliation is possible, it will not come about under the leadership of Dr Gough and his two deputies. An entirely new top management team must be brought in. We, therefore, recommend that the talents and undoubted commitment of these three men be used elsewhere, where there is not the same history of division and recrimination. Burnage needs and should have an entirely new top management team. (Chapter 22).

68. We do not assume that those amongst the staff who support Dr Gough and his deputies and those who are at odds with them would automatically decide to work together and go forward in a spirit of unity under a new leadership. We take the view that some of the staff will not work happily in a school like Burnage under any leadership, or certainly not in a manner that is conducive to the effective education of the whole school community.

69. In our view the division and argument over the Gough management approach has undoubtedly deflected attention away from the bigotry and racism of some of the Burnage staff and directed it against Dr Gough and Mr Moors in particular. It is regrettable

that they have been unable to deal effectively with what was actually taking place within the staff group, teaching and ancillary, and have attracted a good deal of unnecessary criticism, ridicule and hostility.

70. We take the view, therefore, that even if the leadership at the school were to change, as we have recommended, one would not easily, if at all, manage to bridge the chasms that exist within some sections of the staff. For the sake of the students, the parents and the many hardworking, self-critical and dedicated teachers already in the school, we feel that there is every reason to reorganise Burnage High School and redeploy some of the longer serving staff who were unaffected by the 1982 reorganisation, to give them an opportunity to exercise their skills elsewhere in a quite different environment.

71. We also take the view that in any event Burnage High School poses difficult problems of management in view of its size and its split site and it would be better if the school were reduced in size and put on one site. However, we also understand that there are difficulties in making either of the existing school sites into a viable single school without embarking on considerable capital expenditure on a new school building. We, therefore, express a view but make no further recommendation.

From Burnage to Manchester

The Community Languages Team

72. The experiences of the Urdu teacher and peripatetic music teacher at Burnage echoed elsewhere in Manchester. Both the community language teachers and ethnic music teachers work in intolerable conditions and have unnecessarily low status. They are badly exploited and the issue of their pay and promotion needs to be dealt with as a matter of priority (Chapter 23).

73. In dealing with community languages, we concentrate on Urdu, because that is probably the most spoken community language in Machester. In our view the modern languages inspectorate should see to it:

   (i)   that Urdu is given the status of a modern language and located as a subject within the modern languages department of secondary schools and sixth form colleges;

(ii) that attention should be given to the possibility of employing full time teachers of Urdu to do bilingual work in primary schools;

(iii) that Urdu teachers, whether Section 11 funded or not, should be integrated as part of the modern languages department in secondary schools; and

(iv) that they should be able to offer students the subject in their first, second and third years, as well as fourth and fifth years (Chapter 23).

Racism in other Manchester Schools

74. Random evidence and interviews with students, teachers and parents connected with other Manchester schools tell a tale of constant and widespread racial name-calling and abuse, racial bullying, racial violence and racism which non-white students and teachers have experienced or have assisted others in resisting. We were told, referring to the stabbing, that what had happened at Burnage could have happened at any other Manchester school (Chapter 24).

75. In interviews conducted by Salma Ahmad with Asian girls who attended schools in central and south Manchester, the tale is told of fights involving white girls and occasionally Afro-Caribbean girls against Asians, of racial bullying, name-calling and teasing about dress. In a racist incident, Afro-Caribbean girls did not know what they were doing and would go on anyone's side. Few of these incidents are reported to teachers, often because of fear of reprisals from the bully and her friends (Chapter 25).

76. The evidence from these interviews suggest that Asian girls, no less than boys, attend school in an atmosphere of constant intimidation and amidst an ever present threat to life and limb, notwithstanding that in each of the schools there are clearly spelt out anti-racist policies and teachers who are committed to anti-racism and multiculturalism (Chapter 25).

Elinor Kelly's Survey and Report

77. In order to get a more accurate picture of the overall situation in Manchester schools, we commissioned a survey from the Extra-Mural Department of Manchester University. The survey was conducted by Dr Elinor Kelly with a team of four researchers.

They administered 902 questionnaires to 439 first year and 463 fourth year students in three Manchester secondary schools, located in the south, central and northern districts which encircle the inner city. According to estimates made by the survey team, across three schools, 21% of the students were of black/Asian descent and 22% were of Celtic and European descent, the remaining 57% being classified as "English". One school was an all boys school (School B) and the other two are mixed schools (Schools A and C).

78. The survey was carried out between July and October 1987. The students' answers have been treated as entirely confidential and no identities are revealed. Throughout, the survey has been handled as an exercise involving the collaboration between the survey team, students and their schools. The findings of the survey team are being presented to the teachers and students as interim findings in an on-going process. Dr Kelly and her team expects to participate in meetings with education officers, governors and parents to discuss the implications of the research for school policies and practices. The first working paper on the survey was sent to our inquiry on 6th November 1987 and a substantially revised version was submitted on 17th December and is contained in full in Chapter 26.

79. In the opening pages of the questionnaire, the students were asked to indicate their home language or languages, religion and community on the list compiled. The purpose was to generate the data by means of which the survey team could identify the racial and ethnic categories which were relevant for their analysis of the students' returns. Six categories were identified – Afro-Caribbean, Asian, Celtic, Chinese, English and European.

80. The answers to the opening pages of the questionnaire made it clear that many of the students, especially those in the "English" category had little or no notion of their own ethnicity and were agitated and made insecure by their confusion or else showed anger and resentment at the "irrelevance" of the questions. On the other hand, there was eager response on the part of many other students – among the five "minority" categories – to the questions about their home languages, religion and community.

81. More Afro-Caribbean, Asian and Chinese students report being called names which make then "angry or miserable" than the

white students, although Celtic students also felt themselves to be particular targets for name-calling. Two-thirds of the Asian students report being called names by students outside their friendship group. The report indicates that racial names, such as "Paki", "Nigger", "Black", "Chink" and "Yid" come up as the third most recurrent in type.

82. As might be expected, less girls had fights picked with them than boys, but a higher proportion of Afro-Caribbean boys (79%) and Asians (70%) had fights picked on them than Celtic, European or English boys (61%–63%). Fights were more serious for Asians, Afro-Caribbean and Celtic students than for English and European students, a greater proportion being started by students outside their friendship group.

83. As with the earlier confusion by some students over their ethnic identity, there were also signs that many first year students were confused about whether name-calling or a fight is "racial", but by the time they are 14, the students recognise the term and apply it more accurately.

84. Students judge whether a fight is "racial" by looking at, or hearing about who is involved and by the names which are called. They are not, it seems, so concerned about the specific issues which might be in dispute.

85. Attitudes to racially discriminatory behaviour are not the monopoly of any one group in these schools and there are differences within each racial group in terms of students' experiences and responses. A number of the black/Asian students revealed that they are not particularly aware of, or concerned about racial issues; a number of the white students wrote and talked quite openly about their opposition to all forms of racial discrimination and racial injustice.

86. The survey also looked at differences between boys and girls. There were no significant differences between girls and boys when it came to having heard racial names in school – 78% for both. But when it came to fights, there were marked differences between the two – 37% of girls recorded seeing fights as compared with 51% of boys. These findings were consistent with the figures recorded for boys and girls in relation to the general question about fights in school.

87. The survey revealed no marked difference between the behaviour of the boys in the mixed schools and the boys in the all boys school until the survey looked at racial issues, when it became apparent that a greater proportion of boys at School B (all boys school) had heard racial names or seen racial fights than boys in Schools A and C (mixed schools), although this could be to do with the local catchment area or to the male culture of School B.

88. Figures collected on inter-racial friendships show that only 1 in 4 students claimed that their friends at school have never included someone from a different racial group and that the majority of students have had such friends either often or sometimes. However, there are two points on which the boys in School B differ. For a start, 10% more of these boys state that they have never had such friends and only 12% have often had such friends. Nonetheless, 62% of the students in School B and 73% – 77% of the students in Schools A and C have had friends in other racial groups.

89. The survey also revealed how difficult it is for students in different racial groups to be individuals in these schools. With some notable exceptions, it seems that encounters between Afro-Caribbean, Asian and white students are viewed as group encounters and that many of the students talk and think in ways which type cast each group in a certain way and which their friendships have not penetrated.

90. Only a very small proportion of incidents of name-calling or fighting are reported to teachers. When name-calling was reported, for the most part teachers told the students to ignore the name-callers and carry on as usual. With fights, as might be expected, the teachers respond more strongly.

91. Teachers do not emerge from the survey exempt from blame. Students accused them in a few instances of general name-calling and in a few cases of calling racial names; a few were accused of starting fights with students and some were thought to be racist. These accusations were made by a cross-section of students from Afro-Caribbean, Asian and white groups in all three schools.

92. Whatever explanation is given for the relatively low level of reporting of incidents to teachers, it points towards a disturbing situation in schools and suggests that communication between students and teachers is not good when it comes to these forms of

behaviour. It also suggests that teachers themselves, as people in authority in the school, are in serious difficulty when it comes to dealing with students in these racial groups that are most subjected to name-calling and fighting. Because students feel that, apart from experience, there is no point in complaining to teachers because nothing gets done or they do not know whether anything is done or not, teachers are being deprived of the information which could help them understand racial tensions and judge the level of racial victimisation in their schools.

Secondly, because a sizeable proportion of students believe the teachers are themselves racist, it does not inspire them with confidence to raise the issues with the teachers and look to them for support. This situation clearly results in students being thrown back onto themselves in dealing with simmering tensions by whatever means they find necessary, until, one day, the school wakes up to a serious situation, as has happened at Burnage.

93.   The survey has shown that different racial groups have different experiences, expectations and responses. For example, a higher proportion of students in the three black/Asian categories reported that they had been mistreated at school, by being called names or having fights picked with them. But there was variation between the three categories both as regards student behaviour and teacher response. For example, more Chinese students recorded name-calling than fighting, but fewer had complained to teachers. Among Afro-Caribbean students, more of the boys than girls recorded mistreatment and they indicated some dissatisfaction with teachers' response. It was the Asian students who stood out most markedly as a racial group. They recorded a combination of more frequent mistreatment by other students, higher rates of complaint to teachers about this mistreatment and lower levels of response by teachers to their complaints.

94.   The three white categories were also differentiated in experience, expectation and response. Students in the Celtic category reported having names called and fights picked at rates equivalent to those of the Afro-Caribbean students. But, unlike students in the black/Asian categories, they reported also that teachers had stuck up for them. The conclusion is that even when considering the situation of the Asian students, it is essential to develop a perspective which incorporates differences among white racial groups.

95. The survey undertaken in these three Manchester schools, should be seen as a "trawl by questionnaire" which has thrown up indicators and clues that need to be followed up if the whole school community is to understand and confront the many ways in which racial attitudes and conflicts are burrowing their way through schools. We agree with the basic starting point of the Elinor Kelly survey that racial issues do not start or end with attitudes and behaviour that openly discriminate, but are meshed in with and form part of the routine of what goes on in schools.

96. The student's report suggests that the three schools need to be vigilant, because there is rumbling discontent and disquiet, not just among Afro-Caribbean/Asian students but also amongst whites, most notably the Celtic group, all of whom have reported in a way which suggests that they see the school as being unjustly discriminatory towards them. White students observe these matters very carefully but have conflicting views about what they have seen. Some are bitter and resent the Afro-Caribbeans/Asians and see teachers as being in collusion with them. Others remark on the unfair treatment of Afro-Caribbean and Asian students by both students and teachers. Both are talking about relations and incidents which can and do lead to the formation of groups which, as at Burnage could flare into inter-racial conflicts.

97. Students in these schools have shown themselves to be alert and perceptive when it comes to racial issues. In thinking about the individuals who may become either "victims" or "aggressors" we are, it seems, talking about a small minority. But in terms of the conditions which allow racial victimisation to develop or persist, we are talking about what we can learn from the majority of school students. No racial group has a total monopoly on attitudes or experience; social class and other factors do not stop functioning simply because a school contains different racial groups.

98. In our view the survey has been most helpful, not only in placing events in Burnage in some perspective, but also in indicating one way towards developing effective anti-racist policies by a process of collaboration which involves all students of all ethnic categories. We trust that the three schools and the survey team will be able to negotiate further co-operation between them and that it will be possible to extend the work of the survey team to carrying out fieldwork with teachers and in the localities of the schools.

99. The inspectorate of the Manchester Education Department have been involved with the work of the survey team from the start and will no doubt be concerned to learn the lessons of the survey and to work on how these may be made of more general application in Manchester schools. We would recommend that both they and Dr Kelly produce, separately or together, a progress report to be placed before our enquiry when it reconvenes later this year (see Recommendation 5).

Plant Hill 1984

100. On Tuesday, 13th March 1984, about 20 black youths aged 15–17 arrived at Plant Hill High School, a largely white school, in North Manchester, carrying baseball bats and sticks, broke into three classrooms causing damage, and attacked two teachers who sought to intervene. As a result some 18 youths were arrested and charged with affray, but the charge was dropped against the only white youth arrested.

101. In his report on the incident to the Chief Education Officer, the headmaster of Plant Hill stated his concern about the racial overtones of the incident, but added that "in dealing with this matter with our own students we have been at great pains to ensure it should be seen as a criminal act not as a racial act". (Chapter 27).

102. The incident followed a series of attacks on David McCorkle, a black student at Our Lady's R.C. High School, including an attack on Friday, 9th March 1984 by a group of white youths aged 15–19 from the YTS scheme at Higher Brackley Youth Centre and from Plant Hill School, many of whom were thought to have National Front connections. At the centre of these attacks was a white boy, W.W., a student at Plant Hill, who had previously gone out with a girl whom David McCorkle described as his "friend". On the following Monday (12 March) a further incident occurred between David McCorkle and two of W.W.'s friends (Chapter 27).

103. When David McCorkle went to the Abraham Moss Youth Club on Tuesday, 13th March, it was decided that all would go and see the YTS youth. At Higher Brackley Youth Centre the group of black youths were met by a hail of snooker balls; W.W. did not appear to be there; and so they set off for Plant Hill (Chapter 27).

104. We set out the details of the Plant Hill incident and the particular responses of teachers, governors and the Education Department at some length in Chapter 27. In examining all the documents and reports on the incident and having heard some oral evidence, we were disturbed at the speed with which the authorities appeared to have satisfied themselves that there was no racial aspect to the attacks on David McCorkle, attacks in which he was clearly outnumbered.

105. In our view the gulf between the lived experience of racism of the young black people involved and those in authority, whose overriding concern seems to have been to outlaw that experience is one which breeds a violent response to racial violence. Young black students experience not only the violence of the racist attack, but also the violence of the might and power of the system, which highlights the criminal nature of the black students response but does nothing about the racism and violence which has provoked it and it thus effectively condones the earlier racist attacks.

106. The failure of those in authority to heed the very clear messages coming through from the evidence regarind the Plant Hill incident must inevitably lead to groups of black or Asian youths organising themselves for self-defence and getting themselves involved in the sort of confrontation that characterised both the Plant Hill affair in 1984 and the Burnage affair three years later (Chapter 27).

107. In Chapter 28 we trace the genesis of Manchester City Council's multi-cultural and anti-racist policies for education from 1978 to the present time, including the system for reporting and monitoring racist incidents occurring in educational establishments, the main feature of which has so far been an evident reluctance of people to report racist incidents.

108. The Council's anti-racist policies do not just deal with discrimination on grounds of race but also sex, disability and sexual preference, but the Council has rejected the suggestion of the Education Department's equal opportunities working party, made in 1985, to include "class", since it was felt that this issue was too controversial and did not easily lend itself to an all-party consensus.

109. We find this decision regrettable. Discrimination and disadvantage on the basis of class has been central to all educational policies

since 1945 and to omit it means that there will be a tendency to attribute discrimination and disadvantage to racism and sexism, even where class is the central issue, and to ignore the class element involved.

110. The omission of class also means that the Council's policies will not be addressing the grievances of the white working class majority, meaning that their interests as a group are nowhere catered for. This is vividly illustrated in the case of Manchester by the plight of schools in the Benchill and Woodhouse Park area, which caters for the education needs of deprived working class children of poor families. Since these are almost entirely white, they do not qualify for Section 11 funding and their needs go unmet. In our view, unless the needs arising from the working class location of such schools is recognised, the rest of the City's equal opportunities policies will be of no consequence whatsoever in those areas.

111. The contast between Burnage and Benchill highlights the problem in Manchester between areas which qualify for Section 11 funding and those which do not, but it is not just a Manchester problem. It is a national problem and the solution lies, not so much with Machester City Council, but with central government. Extra funding, not limited like Section 11, is needed for black and white children alike living in deprived working class areas.

112. In formulating its anti-racist and equal opportunities policies, Manchester "consults" with a number of organizations "representing" the interests of black and ethnic minorities. We document the history of this process in Chapter 28.

113. We see the Education Department's consultation with ethnic minority groups as a larger scale version of the consultation with the ethnic minorities advisory groups (EMAG's) at Burnage High School. As a structure and as a process we consider both to be flawed for identical reasons. In the case of the Education Department, the essence of the consultation process is to consult while retaining power and the groups consulted have no power to take the department's policies in directions other than those chosen by the departments. The process of empowerment of those groups, therefore, is one that is undermined.

114. In the case of the EMAG's, which we have already referred to in

conclusion 52 and 53, a similar argument obtains. There the agenda is set by the school, minutes are taken and circulated by the school and the group simply provides a forum for the testing out or the approval of initiatives put forward by the school.

115. We have therefore taken the view that the Education Department and Burnage School (EMAG) consultation processes should be phased out and replaced by school and college based development councils involving students, teachers and parents from across the school community. Through the development councils the schools would then feed into the Town Hall. Should parents or students wish to organise independently within their communities as students or as parents, they should be encouraged to do so without interference from schools or from the Education Department.

The White Backlash

116. In formulating and implementing anti-racist policies, Manchester Education Department and schools in Manchester had to deal with what has been referred to as the "white backlash". The "white backlash" has both its practitioners and its theoreticians and we look at both in Chapter 29.

117. In three primary schools in Manchester – Crowcroft, Wilbraham Infants and St. Mark's C of E, a vociferous minority of parents with the sometimes over zealous assistance of the press, accused each of these schools of denying the parents the right to impose on their children a "good christian English education".

118. In our view, the issues raised are quite fundamental and pose the question whether the child's right to an education which is not geared to the satisfaction of narrow sectional interests of religion, race, class, gender, parochialism, or nationalism, can be overriden by a parental choice to impose such an education on children and to insist that their schools do as the parents have chosen.

119. We reject the formulation of the question as being one of parental choice (implying that this is always a good thing) against a devilish left-wing plot to seize "the higher moral ground" (implying that this is a bad thing), since this formulation leaves out of account the rights of children as against their parents and of our vision of the future society and the role of education in it. In our view, the commitment to anti-racist policies and the advancement of good

educational practice which is not geared to the satisfaction of narrow sectional interests are no more the exclusive domain of people on the left than "the moral high ground" is the exclusive preserve of people on the right.

120. After hearing the evidence of the PEER group of parents in Manchester, one gets the sense of white working class parents who have little basis on which to root their own identity and whose education has given them little or no conception of the value of their own experience as English working class and who, therefore, react angrily and resentfully to a school which, in sharp contrast to their experience, caters directly for the needs and preferences of Asian students, thus indicating the extent to which they and their culture are valued.

121. Instead of challenging the usefulness of their own education or examining how oppressive it was to them, they devote their energies to seeking to have it or some nostalgically remembered version of it imposed on their children. The right of a child not to be caught up in that, with or without the help of the tabloid press, is one which parents, students, teachers and policy makers, white as well as black, must surely stand up and defend, even if it means contesting the "moral high ground". The role of the school is, in our view, to teach the children and not just to bend to parents' prejudices, even if these are elevated into the lofty theory of parental choice.

The History of Anti-racist Education

122. Burnage High School presents a paradox. Its governors and senior management are committed to anti-racist policies in perhaps a more wholehearted way than any other Manchester school. Yet at the same time the school has been the scene of greater racial conflict and polarisation of its students along racial lines than any other school we have heard of. We were therefore concerned to see if an examination of the history of anti-racist policies could shed light on this paradox, and whether there are flaws in the theoretical model so faithfully applied by Dr Gough and his senior management team at Burnage High School. We look at this history in Chapter 30.

123. We found that four underlying themes could be detected in the post-1981 anti-racist initiatives:

(i) that racism is the manifestation of individual racial prejudice rather than the "institutional";

(ii) that it creates racial disadvantage and is a recipe for social disorder and is thus morally wrong and should be condemned;

(iii) racism and racial disadvantage is the result of white people's individual prejudices and white people should therefore be trained under racism awareness training (RAT) to detect their own individual prejudices with a view to eliminating them;

(iv) anti-racist policies on jobs, housing and education should only be brought into being in consultation with local "community leaders".

124. In the field of education, the basic assumption behind many current anti-racist policies is that since black students are the victims of the immoral and prejudiced behaviour of white students, white students are all to be seen as "racist", whether they are ferret-eyed fascists or committed anti-racists. Racism is thus placed in some kind of moral vacuum and is totally divorced from the more complex reality of human relations in the classroom, playground or community. In this model of anti-racism there is no room for issues of class, sex, age or size. We have called it "symbolic" or "moral" anti-racism.

125. In practice, moral anti-racism has been an unmitigated disaster. It has reinforced the guilt of many well-meaning whites and paralysed them when any issue of race arises or has taught others to bury their racism without in any way changing their attitude and has created resentment and anger and stopped free discussion. It encourages the aspiring black middle class to play the "skin game" and for a few "liberal anti-racist" whites to collude in it. It has put a few unrepresentative blacks into positions of false power without in any way empowering the rest of the black population. In a time of crisis, as at Burnage, the application of symbolic moral anti-racism has added fuel to the fire of racism and has quickly turned into its opposite, leading to a polarisation between black and white students and to a potential escalation of racial conflict.

126. At Burnage High School, as we have seen, the application of moral anti-racism effectively excludes white students and parents from the process of anti-racism and absolves them from responsibility for any anti-racist education, but encourages them to perceive of

black students as seeking and being given "special treatment", when such treatment is neither needed nor demanded by black students.

127. We have dealt at some length with the theoretical underpinning of anti-racist policies, as they are currently conceived in many places, because we feel that Burnage High School is perhaps the most vivid example of a school which is attempting to put into practice the theoretical model of anti-racism we have called "symbolic" or "moral" anti-racism. Dr Gough's adherence to this particular theoretical construction is almost perfect and he has pursued it single-mindedly and wholeheartedly but with disastrous results as we have seen (Chapter 30).

Good Practice

128. Not all schools or all heads have been committed to a particular theory and practice of anti-racism, as Burnage, and we have been impressed by the serious genuine and positive approach taken by many schools in Manchester and by the way in which many heads, teachers, governors and parents have shared with us their experiences and have told us of the difficulties, the successes, the failures, the hopes and the aspirations. We have found that their commitment and dedication to the work they are doing gives hope and optimism.

129. Manchester has moved further, we suspect, than many other places in the U.K. in dealing with racism in the schools and the experience already gained has to be kept hold of and built on, not from the top down, but from the involvement of the whole school community. Unfortunately, we have been unable to find any theoretical ready-made model for success. Schools and local authorities need to proceed by an element of trial and error and by listening and talking as some of them have already been doing. To help this process, we have set out in Chapter 31 a selection of the experiences of different schools in dealing with racism and racist incidents as they arise.

We were particularly impressed by the experience arising from the innovation by a large mixed group of white and black students from three different schools who came together to form the Frontline Theatre Group and perform a play called "Struggle for Freedom – The Life and Work of Len Johnson". The themes of student participation and decision making were constant in the project and it is clear from the evidence given to us that the students were learning a history relating to their own experience, which they responded to with great enthusiasm. What struck us was that the students were using the play and its themes as a metaphor for their own lives and were learning about their own culture and the significance of friendships and relationships with each other at school and at home, and in particular about attitudes to women, race and class. In the course of the play they unpack and lay bare the content of a sexist and racist culture.

130. By using the experience of students to examine the history, geography, humanities, drama, art and contemporary themes in students' lives, we consider that we have before us the essential elements of good educational practice, in which the issues of race, class and gender are integrated with the students' lives and the different parts of their own experience, for example as Irish or as women, are linked together and result in a critical questioning and growing self-confidence. For these reasons, we see the Frontline project very much as an example of good educational practice and as a model of anti-racist practice for the future.

131. The murder of Ahmed Ullah, the earlier incident at Burnage in 1982, the Plant Hill affair in 1984 and many other incidents we have referred to in this report throw into focus the twin questions of violence and racism in schools. Neither issue can be shirked. Both affect the quality of education and both need to be dealt with. We see it as crucial that schools declare unambiguously and openly what their stance is on racism, racial harrassment and violence, and do so in a manner that staff, students and parents can understand. Equally importantly, schools need to signal how they see that concern about racism, racial violence and harrassment having an impact on the curriculum and on the schools' relationship with students and parents.

132. But how does the school arrive at its formal position on these matters. The evidence we have presented so far points to a process whereby the education committee decides on policies which are then adopted by the school, or form the framework for the schools' own definition of its policies. In arriving at these policies both Council and school might engage in a consultation process, which no-one giving evidence to us has found particularly

404

satisfactory. We have already looked at the experience of the Frontline Theatre Group and the collaborationist and developmental methods used in Elinor Kelly's survey in three Manchester schools. These are all pointers to the future and indicators of processes which enable greater involvement of school students in the formulation of these policies. We also received evidence from a number of other sources with suggestions as to alternative approaches to the organization of schooling in relation to all the above matters. We set out some of these suggestions in greater detail in Chapter 32.

133. Three educational psychologists made a submission in two parts. The first dealt with "identifying violence in Manchester schools" and the second with "the implementation of anti-racist policies". We have included their submissions in full in Appendix G. They propose a structure for identifying and dealing with violence by setting up an umbrella group of parents, staff, students, governors, head teacher and community groups.

134. This umbrella group would operate in a non-hierarchical way and in a manner which does not reflect the existing power structures within the school. Its function would be to identify what each school means by violence (personal, institutional and structural), and what are the structures of domination within the school, and it would create a system for monitoring violence and strategies for dealing with it and would devise techniques for teaching non-violent solutions to conflict.

135. (i)   raise levels of consciousness with regard to the nature of violence;
(ii) empower victims and low status groups in schools by providing support;
(iii) develop good practice for reducing aggression and violence and develop non-violent solutions to conflict when it does occur.

136. We would welcome the idea of an umbrella working group or development Council to define the schools' or colleges' policies and strategies and to negotiate with the local education authority on matters concerning any section of the student population. We consider that if such groups were formed in every school or college, Manchester Education Department's consultation with them would be far more meaningful and democratic than the current system.

137. We also received submissions prepared by a group of inspectors from the Education Department in Manchester including the Chief Inspector and inspectors who carried out the Burnage Inspection in 1985. We reproduce their recommendations in full in Appendix H.

(a) *Links with Primary Schools*

138. They propose that links be forged between primary and secondary schools by the nomination of a key worker or workers to link primary schools with secondary schools in the area of anti-racist training. This is in line with evidence we received from the Project Director of an experimental project already under way under the DES Education Support Grant Scheme at Parr's Wood High School and two linked primary schools in south Manchester.

139. We have been impressed by the Parr's Wood scheme and would suggest that Manchester already has a tried and successfully tested model on which the city should seek to build. In our view, the process which the project has inspired ought to be given greater publicity within other Manchester schools and ways should be found through the Education Department to enable them to benefit from the Parr's Wood project (Chapter 32).

(b) *Dealing with White Youth*

140. The inspectors suggest that a potent way to combat racism is to get young people, especially young white people, to identify what they have in common rather than their differences. This is fine, but we believe that the designers of anti-racist policies must be aware of the experiences of a number of white students who gave evidence to us of being expected to respect the cultural and religious preferences and beliefs of black and Asian students without anyone exploring their feelings or racist beliefs with them.

141. The inspectors also propose a "grouse group" similar to a democratically elected council which would be confined to making representation to management about grievances and monitoring racist incidents.

142. In our view a "grouse group" making representations to management with management replying to the group's grievances is too negative and instead we propose a democratically elected school

students union, to be resourced and provided with accommodation from the school's establishment, and from whatever fund raising they might do themselves.

143. The students union would be part of the "umbrella working group" or "school development council" and would have a share in the responsibility for the well-being of the school and would be involved in shaping and reviewing school policy on such issues as violence and racism (Chapter 33).

144. If a disciplined, well organised, democratic and vibrant student union had been operating at Burnage High School, the school might have been able to avoid the great disruption of the events of March 1987. We believe that the rather belated attempt by that school to set up fifth form student councils was a limited recognition of this need.

(c)   *Giving Pupils and Parents More Say*

145. The inspectors propose that a teacher or youth worker should be appointed in each area of the city to act as an independent advocate for students and parents in any dispute with the school or education authority.

146. We agree with the proposition to have student or parent advocates, but we believe that they should be chosen by independent students' or parents' organisations and that there is a strong case for the umbrella working group or development council to be empowered to constitute a dispute tribunal in suitable cases. The tribunal would consist of students, parents and a teacher governor, as well as a representative of the school management (Chapter 33).

APPENDIX A

A PRIVATE AND CONFIDENTIAL REPORT
OF THE SUB-COMMITTEE TO THE
BOARD OF GOVERNORS
OF
BURNAGE HIGH SCHOOL

CONTENTS

410

1. THE SUB-COMMITTEE

The following report has been agreed by the five Governors who participated in the consultation process.

1.1 A Sub-Committee of the Board of Governors of Burnage High School for Boys was formed at the Board's special meeting on Monday 8 July, 1985.

1.2 Its terms of reference were: that it should undertake a process of consultation, especially with the Staff of the School, following a report to Governors of discontent of a serious nature among them.

1.3 The following Governors were appointed to the Sub-Committee: B Glaizner, Z Jamal, A R Johnson, A Jones, D Kealey, K McWilliam and J Marshall. Messrs Jamal and McWilliam were unable to participate for reasons of time.

1.4 The first meeting of the Sub-Committee took place immediately after the special meeting noted above.

    1.4.1 B Glaizner was appointed as Co-ordinator for the Sub-Committee.

    1.4.2 A protocol and a general time-table for consultation was agreed. The time-table forms Appendix 1 of this report.

    1.4.3 The Co-ordinator was asked to prepare and send a letter to all members of Staff of the School, in accordance with agreed terms. (Appendix 2)

    1.4.4 The Co-ordinator asked the Registrar of the School to send out the letter to all Staff and to prepare a detailed time-table for each of the three days when personal consultations were to take place, in accordance with the protocol set out in the letter. These time-tables were made available at both Upper and Lower School Offices.

    1.4.5 Due to the exigencies of the consultative process it was decided to alter the initial arrangements. Members of Staff were duly notified. The time-table for the whole process forms Appendix 3.

2. SUMMARY

2.1 There are, and have been for some time, serious problems within the School which have resulted in an ever-widening breach between the teaching staff and the Senior Mangement.

2.2 The non-teaching Staff are affected to a lesser degree by the problems but have expressed their concern.

2.3 The consequences of the problems are:-

2.3.1 Very low morale among the majority of the Staff.

2.3.2 A significant lack of confidence of the majority of the Staff in Senior Management.

2.3.3 A factionalisation of the Staff.

2.3.4 An atmosphere of mistrust, allegation and innuendo.

2.3.5 A significant number of teachers actively seeking new positions elsewhere.

2.3.6 An alleged deterioration in the behaviour of the boys.

2.4 The problems are exacerbated by the industrial disputes.

2.5 The problems are worse in Lower School.

2.6 Criticism of the Senior Management Team by the Staff is directed almost entirely to the Headmaster (Dr Gough) and the Deputy Headmaster (Mr Moors). Some other members of the Team are in fact praised.

2.7 There are members of the staff who are content but they are greatly outnumbered by the discontented.

2.8 The problems stem from the transition over the past eight years from a rather autocratic, traditional and stable regime to one encompassing the more progressive requirements of central and local government and of educationalislts. The requirements of authority were urgent and the time, resources and money available were inadequate. The changes were therefore too rapid and too intense for some members of the Staff, particularly those who were bacially unreceptive to change, and the seeds of a division between traditional and progressive methods were sewn.

2.9 Imposed on that situation was a period of changes in the Management Team. Mr Marshall introduced the first of the changes but only remained in office for four years. Mr Walmsley, acting as caretaker Head accepted that status quo for one year. The main changes of the re-organisation of 1982, the abolition of corporal punishment and the directives toward anti-racism, multicultural education, Section 11, etc, fell to Dr Gough for implementation.

2.10 The Staff had therefore experienced a period of some years of basic changes, changes in the direction and management of those basic changes, and changes in philosophy. They required leadership, guidance and an agreed policy. They required to be consulted in the formulation of that policy, to have their opinion sought and respected, and to be supported in their endeavours by the Senior Management.

2.11 Dr Gough introduced measures to implement the mandatory requirements placed upon him, together with measures which he himself wished to incorporate, and these were accepted by members of the Staff with enthusiasm. To the majority they were not acceptable in the manner in which they were presented. The pace of the changes aggravated matters.

2.12 Some members of the Staff are fulsome in their praise of Senior Management and examples are quoted of their sympathetic and caring attitude in private and personal matters.

3. CONCLUSIONS

3.1 There is no doubt that serious problems exist in the School and that urgent action is required to resolve them.

3.2 Senior Management has been the focus of many criticisms, some serious, some trivial, and whilst it is recognised that much progress and good work has been achieved in recent years, they must carry a large share of responsibility for the present situation.

There must be a fundamental change in the attitude of Senior Management to the processes of management, communications and staff relationships at all levels and that change in attitude must be clearly visible.

Such a change on the part of Dr Gough and Mr Moors may be traumatic and they will require much support from the rest of the Management Team and from their senior Staff; whether senior in age, experience or position.

3.3 Responsibility for the present situation does not lie entirely with the Senior Management. It is obvious that, over the years in question, some members of the staff have been opposed to

413

some or all changes and have adopted positions of intransigence. It is doubtful whether these people would have allowed themselves to be persuaded by any approach and they have constituted an obstructive and disruptive element.

3.4 There has been over-reaction, over-sensitivity and pettiness to some degree in the attitude of some members of the staff toward the Senior Management.

3.5 No solution is possible unless the Staff react positively to changes in attitude by Senior Management. Entrenched positions must be abandoned and new approaches to many facets of the School operations must evolve by consultation, discussion and reason. If management is to be democratised, staff must recognise their own responsibilities in that process. Those responsibilities must be clearly communicated.

The changes in attitude asked of some members of Staff will be minimal and these individuals can play a vital role in what will be for others a much more difficult process.

Those members of Staff of whom significant changes in attitude and philosophy are asked will require a significant degree of application. It is considered that, given the changes in management policy and the support of their colleagues, they will provide that application in the interests of themselves, the School and their pupils.

3.6 It is considered that a large proportion of the Staff who are at present discontented, would embrace more readily the processes of change if they are presented by Senior Management in a manner which shows due consideration of their opinions, endeavours and achievements.

3.7 Time should be made available (say one week) at the earliest possible date(s) in order that the entire Staff, including Senior Management, may spend it in School in consultation, discussion and debate, to formulate agreed policies, including, but not limited to:-

> Communication;
>
> Discipline and codes of conduct;
>
> Philosophies and policies.

3.8 An extended period of stability in policies and management personnel is essential to the resolution of the problems.

3.9 Both Upper and Lower Schools are physically run down, decrepit and depressing. The equipment is numerically and technically inadequate and books and other material are grossly under supplied.

The physical environment is conducive to discontent and unhappiness.

A major refurbishment is urgently required.

3.10 Some increase in staffing for special purposes is called for, specifically, a person with seniority to support the Section 11 staff; a person, professionally qualified, and with due seniority, to take charge of the proposed Withdrawal Unit. There should be a review of the establishment for the Senior Management Team to ensure that all management responsibilities are adequately covered.

3.11 Members of the Sub-Committee gained an appreciably increased understanding of the School, from many aspects, as a result of the consultation process.

New Governors should be provided with some kind of an induction course so that they can quickly become familiar with details of the School.

They should be provided with the correct documentation that would enable them to acquire a knowledge of the School's history.

3.12 Governors should be provided with information about the current state of the School, such that this information would enable them more readily to enquire or to intervene, as the case may be.

3.13 There is a need for a review at the end of the school year 1986, but the "healing" process and process of adaptation to change must be seen in the much longer term. Annual reviews will need to continue over a period of time.

3.14 The Sub-Committee is impressed by the overall level of dedication and professionalism which exists in the School. It is the Sub-Committee's conclusion that the Senior Management and Staff have the ability to make the healing process a success.

4. HISTORICAL PERSPECTIVES

4.1 It became clear early on that the Sub-Committee's capacity to understand matters depended to some extent on a knowledge of certain events which had taken place over a period of about two decades, ie since the change from a Grammar School.

4.2 A number of significant changes took place from 1967 onwards.

4.2.1 The School ceased to be a Grammar School and it amalgamated with the Ladybarn Secondary Modern School. The Grammar School site became the Upper School and the Secondary Modern site became the Lower School. Thus Burnage became a High School for Boys on split site, with several attendant problems.

4.2.2 Upper School was better equipped and in a better condition than Lower School. Improvements that might have been made were not made, either they were not sought or they were not allowed; it must be noted that educational funding at this time was more generous than is at present possible.

4.2.3 The Staffs of the previous two schools were amalgamated. Because of the requirements at the time, Staff at Upper School were more qualified, in a formal sense. As a result most managerial appointments went to Staff at Upper School. A special designation, Head of Lower School Department, was conceived to give due status to those at Lower School who had the requisite experience but not the formal qualification to become Scale 4 Heads of Department. Furthermore, these appointments were not career appointments.

4.3.1 Over a period of time the conclusion of the School's pupil population changed. Thus there were created further demands for change in teaching.

4.3.2 More latterly, at the instigation of the LEA, the Board of Governors and the Headmasters, curriculum changes have occurred along with pressure to change teaching styles. Fundamental changes in the philosophies of education, such as multicultural education, SENIOS, anti-racism and anti-sexism initiatives and "365" have marked the departure from traditional education. In addition, and consistent with nationally recognised practice, a reformation of teaching style has been demanded such that each child's personal and social needs are recognised and catered for in the teaching process.

4.3.3　　Nationally it has been recognised that pupils whose immigrant parents might be unfamiliar with the English language and/or culture, present special difficulties for teachers, who have to cope with large classes. The School has been able to employ three Section 11 teachers to assist all staff with these problems. Their duties are strictly defined by Central Government.

5.　DETAILED REPORTS

5.1　COMMUNICATION

Elsewhere in this document details of the very significant changes which have taken place in recent years in all aspects of Burnage High School life are noted. The failure of communication pertaining to those changes, between Senior Management and Staff, constitutes a major cause of the present discontent. Consultation, discussion and reason appear not to have been sufficiently applied at the inception of the changes and are not sufficiently applied now.

The major share of responsibility for the failure of communication would appear to lie with the Senior Management Team, and with the two most senior members of that team in particular. Nevertheless, if management is by a team, the whole must face the criticism and bear the responsibility.

However, the responsibility does not lie entirely with the Senior Management. It appears that over the years in question, some teachers have been opposed to some or all of the changes and have adopted positions of intransigence. Thereby they have constituted an obstruction and disruptive element with which communication would always have been difficult.

It is convenient to examine communication within the School from three view points:-

5.1.1　　A Split Site School

The School is on a split site and this presents a

417

fundamental difficulty in communication. Nevertheless, the School had been operating for a considerable number of years on such a basis and during most of that time communication within the Staff and with the Senior Management apparently was adequate. It is not adequate at present. It is a problem which can be handled by good management and goodwill, qualities which in the last few years have not been forthcoming in sufficient degree.

5.1.2   Vertical Communication within the Staff

This has been acceptable to a minority of the Staff but completely inadequate where the large majority is concerned. The lines of communication are held down fundamentally by statute, but local conditions and requirements in a particular school are the responsibility of the management of that school and should overlie the fundamentals. The Burnage Management has not been able to fulfil that responsibility and these lines of communication are unclear and frequently unused.

Exacerbating the communication problem again is the intransigence of those members of staff who lock themselves into specific ideologies of teaching. If the individuals in a vertical line of communication are all of the same persuasion, communication is relatively easy. Unbending dissidents immediately cause a blockage and the line of communication becomes inoperative.

It is considered that in some instances vertical communication of a sort is maintained by the bypassing of certain steps in the line, with and without the knowledge of Management. Such practices lend themselves to the communication of biased ideas, incorrect information and rumours, and are a further source of discontent.

5.1.3   Horizontal Communication within the Staff.

This would normally be along both professional and personal lines, and the two should be interactive. In the present atmosphere of mistrust and discontent factions have been allowed to form within the Staff and suspicions of tale-carrying and "informing" abound. The result is to inhibit both lines and at the same time generate new problems.

5.1.4   Information relating to communication was prominent and repetitive during the consultative process and we consider it relevant to list here the "negative" and "positive" aspects that were given to us.

Negative

5.1.4.1   It is not necessarily the policies of Senior Management with which the Staff disagree, but the poor manner by which they have been communicated to them.

5.1.4.2   Many Staff stated that the Headmaster tends to consult only with those who share his views.

5.1.4.3   Some Staff stated that the Headmaster gives different information on the same subject to different people. They stated that he is selective in the information he communicates and to whom, to the exclusion of Staff with the right and need to know.

5.1.4.4   There appears to be a small hard core of Staff who will not listen or respond regardless of the initiatives taken.

5.1.4.5   Staff would appreciate more personal and informal communications with the Headmaster and Deputy Headmaster. This need constitute merely a greeting, use of a first name, an inquiry after health or family, etc. For such communication to be possible the Headmaster and Deputy Headmaster would need to be seen about the School on a more regular basis.

5.1.4.6   Some Staff see the Headmaster as an "ivory tower theorist", must prone to issuing written directives and consultative documents, who cuts himself off from direct communication with the majority of his Staff. They are critical of the sheer volume of paper.

5.1.4.7   Some newer Staff say that they were not invited to a personal meeting with the Headmaster on taking up their posts and that it was as long as eighteen months in one case before a greeting was exchanged. These factors tend to direct the young teacher to identification with their Departments rather than with the School as a whole and to an adherence to policies of the Head of their Department without the benefit of exposure to other senior viewpoints.

5.1.4.8 Visits to the School over the past year by members of the Inspectorate did not yield any discussion of their reports with the teachers concerned. The reports were only discussed between Inspectors and the Headmaster. The Staff feel that if they are to benefit by change or improvement they should receive feed-back from the Inspectorate.

5.1.2.9 Some Staff in Lower School believe that the Deputy Headmaster is far better able to communicate with the boys than with the Staff. They feel that Senior Management should be able to communicate well with both groups.

5.1.4.10 Staff have indicated that they consider Departmental Reports to have been altered before submission, via the Headmaster's Report, to the Governors.

5.1.4.11 Staff state that they are often not consulted, nor even informed, beforehand of occurrences bound to disrupt classes. Such occurrences could be room changes, decorating, building or other work. They obtain the relevant information by fait accompli, by rumour or from the individual carrying out the work.

5.1.4.12 Staff stated that the introduction of something as important as Section II staff and any explanation of their function were not communicated to them. Even now most Teachers in Lower School seem unaware of the brief given to the Section 11 Unit and of the roles which they are expected to play by assisting with teaching resources and accepting reduced timetables.

5.1.4.13 Some Staff say that on occasions they have been treated in an unprofessional manner by Senior Management. They say that the Headmaster has communicated his displeasure to them by haranguing and shouting.

5.1.4.14 Staff say that details of internal promotions and

recruitment have not been communicated to them either before or after decisions have been taken.

5.1.4.15 It is considered by some Staff that the content of conversations between members of Staff in the Staffroom is reported to the Headmaster. It is further thought that such procedure is not discouraged.

Positive

5.1.4.16 The School Diary system introduced by the Headmaster is seen by some Staff as a very useful addition to the School communications system, if operated properly.

5.1.4.17 In Lower School the Deputy Headmaster (Mr Moors) has excellent communication with the pupils and knows the names of many of them.

5.1.4.18 The Deputy Headmaster is regularly available to Section 11 Staff for consultation and advice. His responses and views are quickly forthcoming in a helpful and direct manner.

5.1.4.19 The Headmaster has dealt with the personal and private problems of individual members of Staff in a sympathetic and caring way.

5.1.4.20 A number of Staff state that the Headmaster is readily available for discussion and advice and that he consults them on a regular basis. Some newer members of Staff stated that the Headmaster and other members of the Senior Management Team, have observed their lessons and have engaged in helpful discussions afterwards.

5.1.4.21 Some Staff, mainly in Upper School, maintain that Senior Management does have plans to approach areas of concern in the School and that these plans have been developed by consultation with members of Staff. They also stated that these plans are being communicated effectively.

5.1.4.22 Many members of Staff have responded positively to the present consultative process involving the Governors.

5.1.5   Objectives

5.1.5.1   Short Term

5.1.5.1.1 To establish by consultation and discussion a system of lines of communication which can be agreed by the majority and accepted by the minority, can be written and distributed, and to which reference can be readily made by Staff and Management.

5.1.5.1.2 To ensure that, even though the system may not initially be perfect, it is followed and is seen to be followed, and that its imperfections are discussed and resolved by both Management and Staff.

5.1.5.1.3 For the Headmaster and Deputy Headmaster to accept and be seen to accept that greater contact by them with the Staff, at all levels and across all departments, formally and informally, is a fundamental requirement.

5.1.5.1.4 For the Senior Management and Staff to accept that covert communication of any sort is anathema to good working relationships and for all to ensure that it does not occur.

5.1.5.2   Long Term

5.1.5.2.1 On the basis of the short term objectives, to develop an atmosphere where all are seen to be striving for the same ends, albeit sometimes by slightly different routes, and where there is continuing communication vertically and horizontally, and frank interchange of ideas and criticisms.

5.1.5.2.2 To arrive at a formal communication system involving the written and spoken word which is designed for Burnage, its pupils, its Staff and its Senior Management.

5.1.5.2.3 In parallel to the formal communication system, to develop an informal atmosphere in which professional and personal communication can take place without inhibition.

5.1.5.2.4 Constantly to monitor the state of communication of all types within the School, and to take early action to deal with problems, anomalies and new ideas.

5.1.6   Recommendations

5.1.6.1   Short Term

5.1.6.1.1 Time should be made available (say one week) at the earliest possible date(s) in order that the entire staff, including Senior Management, in School, in consultation, discussion and debate, to formulate an agreed policy on communication and other matters.

5.1.6.1.2 A system of Assemblies should be adopted and should be as extensive as time and space permit. The Headmaster and Deputy Headmaster should be actively involved.

5.1.6.1.3 The Staff Room Calendar concept should be developed.

5.1.6.1.4 The Newsheet concept should be developed and could prove invaluable provided that it does not become an administrative burden and provided that it can be produced with enthusiasm.

5.1.6.1.5 As part of a wider inspection exercise, the Inspectorate should be requested to address themselves to communication in practice in the School.

5.1.6.1.6 The Governors should take steps to ensure that their lines of communication are clear in order that they may be better and more quickly informed.

5.1.6.1.7 Teacher and non-Teacher Governors should be encouraged to communicate more freely at Governors' meetings.

5.1.6.1.8 A representative of the Manchester Education Committee should be asked to communicate the policies of the LEA to the teaching and non-teaching staff at Burnage. Time for questions and discussions should be available.

5.1.6.2   Long Term

5.1.6.2.1 If the short term recommendations are implemented, it is further recommended that the results must be constantly monitored over the long term by a review body set up for that purpose.

5.2 DISCIPLINE

5.2.1 Background

In 1981 the then Headmaster, Mr John Marshall, and his Senior Management, decided to reduce the level of corporal punishment in the School. At this time a petition was circulated amonst the Staff to protest at the decision. Present unrest over discipline seems to have started here: many Staff were unsure as to how they could teach their classes, in a controlled atmosphere, without the sanction of corporal punishment and using instead the new educational philosophies. In 1982, corporal punishment was prohibited by the LEA in all Manchester schools.

In July 1984, concern over a decline in standards of behaviour, identified by a majority of Staff based at Lower School, and some based at Upper School, led to a joint three-unions meeting. As a result of this meeting an agreed statement was sent to the Headmaster, outlining the concerns which had been expressed. In June 1985, representatives of the NAS/UWT met with Dr Gough to express their continuing concern about various matters relating to discipline. In July 1985, the NAS/UWT welcomed the Headmaster's document on "Standards of Behaviour in School". This document appears generally to have been well received by most Staff as the basis for future discussions regarding some serious practical difficulties. It is possible that over the past two years disciplinary problems have been aggravated in the school because it has been difficult for Staff to meet on a sufficiently regular basis in order to formulate an agreed approach to diciplinary procedures.

5.2.2 Introduction

A majority of the Staff in Lower School, and some Staff in Upper School, feel there has been a fall in the standards of discipline in the last two years. These Staff have identified the following: an increase in swearing; violent behaviour shown to younger boys by older boys; aggressive behaviour on the corridors; a refusal by some boys to adhere to recognised rules governing smoking and school uniform; a small, but powerful, disruptive element in individual classes; slowness in production of detention work or no work produced at all. There are some Staff, however, mainly at Upper School, who have noted a decrease in disciplinary problems and who also point out that Burnage has better standards of discipline than many other schools.

Finally, there are Staff who fall between these two viewpoints in their assessment of the disciplinary situation which exists at Burnage.

Thus, there are a multiplicity of opinions in the School on the subject of standards of behaviour. The Sub-Committee believe that nearly all opinions expressed are genuine sentiments, not maliciously offered, but indicative of individual experiences and collective opinions, possibly measured against criteria of assessment.

This variation in perception and lack of a firmly based and cohesive policy on discipline – understood and supported by all – makes the overwhelming plea for consistency of approach and understandably difficult goal and, acceptalble by all those involved with the School. In order to arrive at this situation the differing viewpoints and concerns of all members of staff need to be recognised, and given equal right, in order to clear the ground for a way forward to be found.

5.2.3   The following points raised by Staff who believe there has been a fall in the standard of discipline in the School:-

5.2.3.1   Staff do not see any improvement in the standards of behaviour since July 1984, when the first concerted effort was made by them – and their union repre-sentatives – to elicit a response and action from Senior Management. It has been stated that there has been an increase in incidents in this past year when Staff have been verbally abused by pupils, and physically assaulted by pupils.

5.2.3.2 Staff feel that Senior Management have placed most of the responsibility for maintaining discipline on Teachers. In this context, for example, Staff feel that they should not have to specify the punishment, once an incident has moved outside the classroom, in the same way they would if it was contained within the classroom.

5.2.3.3 There is a lack of consistency in the application of discipline. Thus Teachers are seen to be acting independently, rather than as part of a corporate body, when they insist on adherence to certain standards. Inconsistency of treatment has aggravated the discipline problem, leading to some boys believing they can challenge the staff and get away with it.

5.2.3.4 It is maintained that many incidents of indiscipline go unreported to the Management because Staff believe the incident might reflect adversely on themselves. Teachers fear the charge of "incompetence" or "inexperience" in situations where they do not believe such criticism is justified.

5.2.3.5 Staff feel that when they do try to implement disciplinary measures they are not sufficiently supported by Senior Management. They believe that in such cases the version given by the boy(s) of a particular event is more readily believed than is the decision given by the Teacher(s) concerned ie, a sense exists that Management favours the boy in most disciplinary matters. The Staff feel that this approach undermines discipline and Staff morale, particularly in Lower School.

5.2.3.6 Staff have indicated that they believe there is a double standard in Lower School for the treatment of individual boys. (Sometimes, but not always, there is a racial distinction in favour of ethnic minority boys).

5.2.3.7 Because of the lax attitude towards discipline, identified by Staff as coming from the top, they feel that too much time is spent on the minority of disruptive pupils to the detriment of the rest. This minority of disruptive pupils are thus able to wield an influence out of all proportion to their numbers. They are seen as "winners" by their peers. Their actions have actually led to truancy by some boys who are well-behaved, thus creating a "loser" syndrome.

5.2.3.8 Staff said that they would not risk separating boys who are fighting because they do not believe they will get support from Senior Management if an accusation is made against them by the boys concerned.

5.2.3.9 Criticisms have been made of the present detention system which is not seen to be working effectively.

5.2.4 The following are points raised by Staff who believe there has been a decrease in disciplinary problems in the School.

5.2.4.1 Staff believe that Burnage has been able to avoid ugly scenes of pupil disorder. The problems of discipline at the School are seen as neither unique nor worthy of special concern.

5.2.4.2 Staff stated that statistics for the School show that corporal punishment was an ineffective method of enforcing discipline.

5.5.4.3 Staff maintain that constructive efforts have been made toward minimising truancy by establishing a special programme with the help of outside agencies within the Authority. Unfortunately, these efforts have been frustrated by some Staff, even though they were involved from the start.

5.5.4.4 Assistant Year Heads have been introduced to involve more Staff in active pastoral work. They have worked hard, as have the Year Heads, but the role of HOY is still viewed by the majority of Staff in Lower School as a policing role. Problems which should be solved inside the classroom are sent, instead, to Head of Year or even to the Head of the School.

427

5.2.4.5   A successful Unit in Upper School has been established, staffed on a voluntary basis, and moving away from punitive techniques toward counselling and remedial techniques.

5.2.4.6   The School detention system has been improved by involving the Headmaster and Heads of School. Better communication has been achieved with parents concerning detention.

5.2.4.7   Boys are still excluded and suspended from School, but only after every effort is made to help the pupils concerned. It is now recognised that the child must appreciate the reasonableness of any action.

5.2.4.8   It is maintained that since 1982 there is concrete evidence of the success in changing attitudes to discipline, and the instituting of new procedures, in Upper School. A member of the Senior Management Team offered the following statistics on really serious problems in Upper School: 1982/83: 22 pupils; 1983/84: 19 pupils; 1984/85: 12 pupils to date.

5.2.4.9   It is believed by some that the child-centred approach, adopted by the present Senior Management is the one which in the long run will achieve positive results. However, there is concern about the way that every innovation of a child-centred nature over the last five years has been greeted with derision and hostility by the disaffected members of Staff. These Teachers are said to have blocked innovations such as the idea of form tutors as counsellors. They have refused to use materials provided by senior management on counselling techniques and refused to use the time for counselling allowed within the form period.

5.2.5   Objectives

5.2.5.1   Short Term

5.2.5.1.1   Recognition that the discipline problem is worse in Lower School than in Upper School.

5.2.5.1.2   Recognition that the majority of Teachers, regardless of their educational preferences, see themselves as child-centred.

428

5.2.5.1.3 An agreed policy must be formulated with regard to standards of behaviour in the School and the methods used to deal with these. The majority of Staff are competent, dedicated, and keen to arrive at such a policy; they believe the majority of pupils are not beyond control, and that all but a few are well behaved. Staff must begin immediately to work together in a constructive atmosphere in order to achieve good professional practices with regard to discipline.

5.2.5.1.4 The Headmaster's recent document, "Standards of Behaviour in School" is accepted as a useful starting-point for discussion by most Staff, regardless of their educational preferences. Even so, reservations have been expressed by people on both sides of the disciplinary debate. The Sub-Committee believe that all Staff must make an attempt to put aside these reservations and start working together, in an atmosphere of trust, to find some acceptable meeting-points between the punitive approach to discipline and the remedial approach.

5.2.5.1.5 It is important that all Staff demonstrates their willingness to discuss their strengths and weaknesses in order to identify particular problems.

5.2.5.1.6 Staff should re-emphasise their recognition that no form of physical punishment should occur in the correction of pupils.

5.2.5.2 Long Term

5.2.5.2.1 Pupils should achieve a sense of community responsibility and self-discipline because the School guidelines on this are seen to be agreed and adhered to by all Staff. Pupils will receive consistency of treatment and, as a result, both they and their parents should prove more supportive of the School generally.

5.2.5.2.2 Because of an effective policy on discipline most disciplinary problems of a minor nature will be solved within the classroom.

5.2.5.2.3 Staff will gain confidence about their ability to maintain discipline because they are supported by

Senior Management, in a consistent way, over a period of time. Support for Staff will also come from their peers, and Middle Management.

5.2.5.2.4 Those disciplinary matters which cannot be solved in the classroom must be processed up an agreed line. The steps for doing this should reach, if necessary, to the Headmaster. All Staff who are involved should be kept informed of the actions taken.

5.2.5.2.6 Staff will operate a reward system, as well as a sanction system.

5.2.5.2.7 Staff will be encouraged to become more involved in, and trained in, pastoral work and counselling.

5.2.6   RECOMMENDATION

5.2.6.1   Short Term

5.2.6.1.1 Senior Management should fully endorse the Government's statement that: "Teachers have a difficult job to do. They must be supported and they must know they are supported".

5.2.6.1.2 Full, frank and constructive discussion must begin in September with the aim of achieving agreed procedures on discipline which can be implemented from January, 1986, onwards. All Staff must take part in this process. Discussions will use the Headmaster's document, "Standards of Behaviour in School." as a starting-point.

5.2.6.1.3 Assemblies should be used as a means of presenting the boys with the standards of behaviour that are expected by the School and the community.

5.2.6.1.4 Senior Management should ascertain the financial and staff resources available for the proposed Special Support Group and Withdrawal Unit.

5.2.6.1.5 Priority must be given to setting-up a Withdrawal Unit (or Units) staffed by professional staff, who are new appointments. There is a need to gain a consensus of opinion about the function of the Withdrawal Unit.

5.2.6.1.6   Guidelines must be produced which are agreed as a procedure for dealing with fighting among boys outside the classroom, or aggressive behaviour by older to younger boys. For example, should Teachers intervene independently in a fight amongst boys, or should they seek the help of a colleague or Senior Staff before taking action?

5.2.6.1.7   Consistency of approach to discipline must be aimed for. This can only be in the best interests of Staff, Senior Staff, Senior Management, Boys and Parents.

5.2.6.1.8   The sanction of suspension and exclusion should be maintained.

5.2.6.1.9   The Sub-Committee believe that the following points merit consideration during the discussions which will take place from September onwards.

5.2.6.1.10 Are there sufficient Staff across the whole range of year and subject requirements who are willing to accept referrals from the proposed Special Support Group into their class groups?

5.2.6.1.11 Is there a need to set a maximum time limit for a pupil to be with the Special Support Group?

5.2.6.1.12 Is it practicable or desirable to have a third-year prefect assigned to each Staff member of the Special Support Group?

5.2.6.1.13 If no new Staff are available to run the proposed Withdrawal Unit, can the School manage to establish such a Unit with its present staffing resources? Would such a decision be a sensible one? If not, can the School manage with only the Special Support Group and other procedures outlined in the Headmaster's document?

5.2.6.1.14 Is the proposed system of discipline panels practical?

5.2.6.1.15 Should some disciplinary offences be regarded as more serious than others? For example, swearing at, and in front of, Staff. This problem is certainly one which many Staff are particularly concerned about.

5.2.6.1.16 Does the proposed new system take into account the generally acceptable opinion that behavioural problems in Lower School are different, and worse, than those in Upper School?

5.2.6.2   Long Term

5.2.6.2.1 Ultimately it is possible that a gradual reduction of punitive methods can lead to a gradual increase in remedial and counselling methods.

5.2.6.2.2 Final sanctions to deal with extreme disciplinary offences must be maintained.

5.2.6.2.3 Staff, on a volunteer basis, should be officially appointed as home liaison officers. These Staff should be given in-service training.

5.2.6.2.4 The Withdrawal Unit (if instituted) should be maintained on a long term trial basis, eg, for up to five years. Careful monitoring should take place, including end of term and end of year reviews. These should include a wide spectrum of opinion from inside and outside the School. For example, Governors should be involved in the monitoring process and the Inspectorate.

5.2.6.2.5 A general assessment of the disciplinary patterns of the School should be presented to the Governing Body at the end of each year. Governors should, in any case, make efforts to keep themselves fully informed of any problems which arise during the year in connection with standards of behaviour in the School.

5.3   STAFF RELATIONSHIPS

5.3.1   Introduction

With few exceptions there appears to be a deep sadness at the apparently widening divisions between working colleagues. Normal professional interactions which should be taking place on a day to day basis are being stifled by fear and mistrust. Healthy discussion and constructive disagreement is not occurring in a free and open manner. Whilst a small minority of Staff, including Middle and Senior Management, appear to have irreconcilable doctrinal/ideological differences, the overwhelming opinions

432

appear to be that these differences are not the cause of the deteriorating staff relationships. Most might be willing to accept and respect differing viewpoints to their own. Most (albeit some with reluctance) might be willing to move with the times and to embrace modern philosophies, particularly the child-centred approach to education.

The belief by some Staff that serious breaches of professional confidence have been perpetratcd by Senior Management has helped to create the atmosphere of mistrust. The potentially reasonable attitudes to change of the majority have been tarnished by the suspicion that a questioning approach to Management initiatives will be treated with hostility and alienation. This has led to grouping of "sympathisers" and discussion falling only on "friendly ear". Poor communications exacerbate the problems and further mistrust appears to have been created as information is distorted by rumour.

Senior Management has expressed the view that there has been, and still is, a resistance to change by a number of Staff, some in senior positions, which has in the past made progress difficult and at times impossible. The Headteacher has explained how he has felt the need to adopt a more positive approach to instigating initiatives which, due at times to severe external pressures, have demanded a rapid response.

Certain incidents have occurred, which have generated an intensity of antagonism between some members of Staff and Senior Management and between members of Staff themselves, which may present major difficulties in the search for reconciliation. There may always remain a residue of intractable grievances which only mature reasoning will give historical perspective. They must not be allowed to fester to the detriment of all that is good.

The so-called stereotyping and polarisation along ideological lines is less significant and straightforward than appears at first sight. This is evidenced in consultations where many individuals have particular viewpoints contrary to the apparently obvious divisional categorisation and yet are willing to align themselves with an overall group presentation.

Indicative Comments

Some indicative comments are given below as an indication of the generally depressing and confused state of Staff relationships:-

"I have never faced this sort of thing before – the attitude of them and us. I tend never to go into the Staff Room as a result".

"Staff aren't given credit for the fact that most of them are actually very caring people".

"Individually people are kind and caring".

"I've never come across such personal bitterness and animosity as exists here".

"There is such a lot I could learn from other Staff members, but I am fearful. It is easier to do nothing".

"There is a need for recognition of people's different qualities; people need to feel they have status. There must be growth of understanding and affection".

5.3.3   Points raised during the Consultation Process.

5.3.3.1   Taking a more detailed look at the results of the consultations, the Sub-committee has been made aware of the differences that exist between Upper School and Lower School attitudes. At Upper School there appears to be more cohesion in Staff relationships, coupled with a more unified viewpoint toward current educational policies. This should not be overstated as there still appearently exists an underlying sense of divisiveness in Staff relationships. Even so, groupings are less easy to discern.

Lower School divisions and groupings are, however, more overt and the feelings appear to be that everyone knows who is in which group.

5.3.3.1.1   One such group, having good relationships with each other and supportive of each other's views, are very discontented with a variety of things, including discipline, communication, management, but in

434

particular who feel strongly on a personal level, antagonistic toward Dr Gough and Mr Moors. They appear to assume that those who do not voice opposition to their views are in agreement with them.

5.3.3.1.2 Virtually all others external to this group do not see themselves as a group in the context of problems in Lower School. They appear keen to make an effort to change the present stalemate situation but they believe that "traditional" members of Staff are not given enough support by Senior Management. This "group", diverse in its make-up, are very unhappy with the atmosphere of Dr Gough and Mr Moors, although they appear somewhat offended by the personal nature of criticism suggested by others. Their own criticism is on a much more low key basis, but nevertheless they appear to be unhappy with various aspects of management style.

5.3.3.1.3 A small third group exists in Lower School who are not critical of Senior Management or particular members of Senior Management. They appear to have excellent relationships with Senior Management and report plenty of advice and support from the Headmaster and Deputy Headmaster (Mr Moors). This group finds it difficult to deal on any level with the intensely critical and disaffected group. They appear to have been worried by the racist and sexist attitude of some of the Staff and with the cartoons and offensive notices which have been displayed on the so-called Censor Free Notice-Board in the Staff Room. They recognise, however, that an overly adamant condemnation of anyone who does not see anti-racism intitiatives and multi-cultural education as the most important aspects of school life, is not desirable. They see that the very difficult situation of staff relationships is not helped by the extremely critical treatment of even a trivial remark and a lack of sense of humour and unwillingness to make allowances will only add to the difficulties.

5.3.3.2 In addition to the above, a view is expressed that

stereotyping of individuals is encouraged by (a) the group supporting the new policies; (b) the group opposed to the new policies; (c) Senior Management, particularly Dr Gough and Mr Moors.

5.3.3.3   There is a belief that Staff relationships are further undermined by a "divide and rule" policy adopted by management which appears to encourage a minority group who are ready to embrace new educational philosophies whilst appearing to deal unfairly and to react with hostility to any dissenting voices.

5.3.3.4   One of the most common complaints and one which, if substantiated is quite unacceptable and inexcusable is that personal and professional confidences are breached on a fairly regular basis. Staff gave examples which they felt demonstrated the Senior Management and, in particular, the Headmaster, had not respected the context of what they themselves regarded as confidential information. It is clear that credibility in this area must be restored and this is a crucial factor in improving Staff relationships.

5.3.3.5   A very significant number of consultations revealed the feeling that the Headmaster has become remote. There was some suggestion that the Headmaster should take on some teaching duties as this would enable him to keep in touch with the day to day problems experienced at classroom level. This would assist him more fully to understand the Teacher's difficulties. However, many expressed the view that probably it was impracticable for the Headmaster to teach in today's climate but felt it absolutely essential for him to become more actively involved in school life generaly. The Headmaster's remoteness, albeit through "open door" policy is more noticeable in its effect at Lower School.

5.3.3.6   Several members of Staff expressed disappointment at the lack of gratitude and recognition for their input to the School, particularly for extra curricula efforts and it is noticeable that fewer Staff are now prepared to give of their time due to what they appear to feel is disinterest by some of the Senior Management.

5.3.4   Comments

The teaching profession consists of caring people and the vast majority of these people are professionals dedicated toward the paramount interest of their pupils.

It has been suggested that Child-Centred may be helpfully termed Person-Centred. This is an agreeable notion and may offer a direction of hope; after all, a Teacher is a person.

Greater effort will be required in future to help pupils with problems, by trying to understand them and their backgrounds. Some Teachers will need to begin analysis of pupil/teachers confrontational situations, to question their own contribution and critically to assess how best they should conduct themselves. They will need to improve their relationships with pupils to prevent recurrence of escalation of problems.

All concerned should ponder on the present depressing state of affairs and the effect it is having on their children. They should use the same criteria towards their colleagues as is intended will be used toward the pupils and gradually, painfully perhaps, Staff relationships will improve.

5.3.5   Objectives

5.3.5.1   To halt the decline in Staff relationships.

5.3.5.2   To desist from encouraging polarisation on views or stereotyping of individuals.

5.3.5.3   To adopt less aggressive attitudes toward differing points of view.

5.3.5.4   To explore ways of dissipating polarisation into professionally acceptable differences of opinion.

5.3.5.5   To be more tolerant of each other's opinion and difficulties and to show due respect to one another.

5.3.5.6   To concentrate immediately energies towards the educational needs of the pupils now in school.

437

5.3.5.7   To produce an unequivocal statement on school direction, policies and curriculum.

5.3.5.8   To determine, as a prime objective, that pupils now in the schools do not suffer any further harm as a result of the poor staff relationships which currently exist.

5.3.5.9   To begin the process of re-building a trusting, working relationship by all.

5.3.5.2   Long Term

5.3.5.2.1 To restore trust between Senior Management, Middle Management and other Staff.

5.3.5.2.2 To develop an atmosphere in which people will thrive rather than flounder, on the basis of mutual respect for each other's opinions.

5.3.5.2.3 To develop a school to which all would be proud to send their child.

5.3.6   Recommendations

5.3.6.1   Short Term

5.3.6.1.1 Communications system must be improved.

5.3.6.1.2 Discussions to be set up with representatives of Senior Management, Unions, and possibly Governors, to formulate a common approach which will help to reverse the declining trend in Staff relationships.

5.3.6.1.3 The Headmaster must immediately be seen to take a more active interest in day to day activities of school life.

5.3.6.1.4 September, 1985, to January, 1986, would be seen as a period for laying foundations for the future of the School, for openly and frankly identifying problems of staff relationships and for making a determined effort to improve the situation.

5.3.6.1.5 Certain particular incidents on which reconciliation appears difficult may need to be readdressed, possibly with Governor's mediation.

5.3.6.1.6 Restoration of trust is a short and long term objective. An assurance from Senior Management regarding confidentiality may at least offer a starting

438

point in developing better relationships.

5.3.6.1.7 Section 11 Staff should be given additional support from their colleagues.

5.3.6.2 Long Term

5.3.6.2.1 The development of proper and mutually supportive professional relationships should be a permanent aim.

5.3.6.2.2 The Headmaster should extend his personal contact with staff adjustment difficulties with more sympathy and understanding.

5.3.6.2.3 The Senior Management must approach staff adjustment difficulties with more sympathy and understanding.

5.3.6.2.4 The formation of a Staff Relationship Committee, using particular members of Staff, and Management, who have been identified as commanding the utmost all round respect and trust. The specific brief would be to encourage better staff relationships. Constant monitoring of opinion and feedback to all interested parties will be essential. The Newsletter is seen as a very useful medium through which opinion could be channelled and it should contain a wide variety of views. This Committee's activities could embrace pastoral and remedial services to all Staff, transcending the traditional and hardening divisions. Care, patience and tact will be vital – good relationships cannot be forced, but may flourish if carefully nurtured over a long period.

5.4 EDUCATIONAL PHILOSOPHIES

5.4.1 A significant degree of divergence of opinion among Staff is apparent in respect of the relative merits of various philosophies practised in the School. At the extremes are the "traditional" high academic, disciplinarian approach on the one hand, and the progressive, child-centred, multi-cultural, anti-racist approach on the other. There are many gradations between these two extremes evident within the Staff.

439

5.4.2　　　The policy of the LEA is to implement in Burnage the latter approach and Dr Gough and his Senior Management Team were charged with introducing the policies thereby invoked. This they have endeavoured to do with enthusiasm. Throughout they have encountered significant opposition from some members of Staff and have been unable to overcome that opposition. This inability may have led to managerial practices about which many Staff complain and these in turn may have led to greater intransigence on the part of some members of Staff opposed to the basic policies.

5.4.3　　　Differences of opinion on the details of educational philosophies occur in most schools and handled sensibly can constitute a healthy debating situation. In Burnage the differences of opinion regarding the philosophies do not appear to be a root cause of the present problems and given goodwill and more suitable management they could well be resolved. These qualities have been found wanting and the differences allowed to escalate.

5.4.4　　　It appears that the educational policies of the Senior Management are accepted by some members of Staff with enthusiasm. To many, however, they are not acceptable in the manner in which they are presented.

5.4.5　　　Many Staff feel that their viewpoints were not taken into account by the Senior Management when planning the policy initiatives and they therefore perceived that they were disregarded in the context of the changes taking place. Some members of Staff consider that a balance of philosophies could have been achieved given the right atmosphere.

5.4.6　　　In turn Senior Management has reported that it has encountered an unwillingness to try the new ideas among some members of Staff.

5.4.7　　　Some Staff have locked themselves into positions of intransigence and it is doubtful whether these people will allow themselves to be persuaded by any approach and they have constituted an obstructive and disruptive element.

5.4.8   Some Staff state that the didactic "traditional" method yielded good academic results which can be tangibly demonstrated by examination success. Others maintain that the child-centred approach is a preferable replacement for that method since it has the capability of bringing out the best in all children.

5.4.9   What has alarmed the Sub-Committee is the serious lack of in-service training which, given the difficulties involved, should have been foreseen as a need by both Central and Local Governments. Even among willing Staff we obtained diverse definitions of the term "child-centred approach". Among those who appeared to be "traditional" many were convinced that being "child-centred" was a natural part of any teaching method.

5.4.10   Objectives

5.4.10.1   Short Term

5.4.10.1.1 Teachers should examine their own attitudes in relation to the educational policies and philosophies promulgated by the LEA and by the School.

5.4.10.1.2 There must be a readiness to come to terms with concepts underlying these policies at a professional level.

5.4.10.1.3 It must be understood by all that genuine difficulties of various kinds will continue to exist and there must be a willingness to allow debate and for apprehensions and doubts to be freely expressed. All this can take place for mutual benefit only in an atmosphere of the betterment of their pupils.

5.4.10.1.4 Therefore the present divisions within the School must be recognised for what they are: counter productive and inimical to the aims of all teachers who wish to work in a congenial atmosphere for the betterment of their pupils.

5.4.10.1.5 There exists a need for clear definitions and statements to be given about the objectives for each of the educational philosophies. Each of the following should be so treated: The child-centred approach; the multi-cultural education; the anti-racist initiative;

the Anti-Sexist Initiative; PSE; Section 11 teaching: SENIOS: "365" vocational training. The statements should be prepared by the Senior Management Team and promulgated to each Teacher, as soon as possible.

5.4.10.1.6 The Sub-Committee believes that the preparation and dissemination of this information in written form will assist Teachers to come to terms with the professional demands made upon them. It would also act as a force for the on-going discussions and consultation process directed towards the formulation of a school document (ie, Staff Handbook).

5.4.10.2 Long Term

To ensure the willing acceptance and the preparation by the staff of the educational policies recommended by the LEA and formally adopted by the Governors and Management of the School.

5.4.11 Recommendations

5.4.11.1 Senior Management to devise and promulgate statements about definitions and objectives of each policy, as indicated in point 5.4.10.1.5 above. A high priority should be given to this task.

5.4.11.2 Upon receipt of these statements, Teachers should seek to reconcile their differences with the stated objectives, at a professional level, so that they may carry out their teaching duties and assignments more effectively in the best interests of their pupils.

5.4.11.3 Further support should be given to Section 11 Staff by the appointment of a Teacher experienced in this field who should be given a measure of seniority.

5.4.11.4 In-service training should be provided so that Teachers acquire a clearer understanding of what is expected of them and the skills necessary to meet those requirements.

5.4.11.5 The Inspectors should continue their process of observation, assessment and advice. Their findings and recommendations should be made available to the School, and the Board of Governors, as soon as possible.

5.4.11.6   It is essential that the Inspectors inform individual members of Staff about any matter affecting them personally, as soon as possible.

5.5 MANAGEMENT

5.5.1   Senior Management

5.5.1.1   It is in the functioning and methods of Senior Mangement that a major cause of the current problem arises. The criticism is directed almost entirely to the two senior members of the Management Team. However, as stated elsewhere in this Report, if management is by a team, the whole must accept responsibility to some extent.

5.5.1.2   Examination of the recent history of the School shows that several fundamental changes have taken place very rapidly in difficult conditions, and against some opposition from a section of the Staff. It is evident that, to bring these changes into effect with minimal disruption, staff management of a high order is required.

5.5.1.3   There should be consultation and discussion at all levels and transcending levels. Any suggestion of coercion and manipulation should be avoided and the beliefs and opinions of all the Staff must be seen to be registered and considered.

5.5.1.4   In an environment of highly intelligent people, holding a variety of views, some very strongly, a very open, frank and receptive approach by Senior Management to Staff is required. There is an overriding need for honesty and polite straight talking. Such an approach does not appear to have been forthcoming.

5.5.1.5   It may well be that at the initiation of its innovatory processess, Senior Management attempted to adopt such an approach but found itself confronted by entrenched positions on the part of some members of Staff. They may have decided that to bring about the changes which they, and the authority required, they would have to adopt more covert policies. If so, they appear to have been wrong, and the present situation emphasized this.

5.5.1.6   The gathering of information by any management is of prime importance, but it is best obtained by direct approach to staff members or direct contact with them, individually or collectively, on a personal or a professional basis. If Staff perceive that information is reaching Management by diverse means, and particularly if Management is believed to be accepting such information, using it, and encouraging more information to arrive by the same or similar routes, then dissent and confrontation are inevitable. The use of information, however gained, should not be directed to undermining the confidence or stature of individuals. It should be used with considerable circumspection.

5.5.2   Middle Management

5.5.2.1   Middle Management has some criticism of the actions and policies of Senior Management, but there is also approbation.

5.5.2.2   The lines of responsibility are sometimes not clear and their usage uncertain. There is a need for clarification and enforcement of the processes and responsibilities in some areas of Middle Management.

5.5.2.3   It is extremely important to ensure that Middle Management functions in accordance with the policies laid down. Failure to do so can create problems of management above and below. An onus of responsibility therefore exists for Middle Management to be sure that policy statements are accurately transmitted to the Staff who operate within the purview of their responsibility.

5.5.3   Staff

An attitude of intransigence by some Staff in respect of philosophies and methods which required to be introduced appears to have been a significant obstacle to good management and some pettiness has been observed. There are some management decisions which are the perogative of management and should be recognised as such by the Staff.

5.5.4   Information relating to management matters formed

a large part of that imparted to us during the consultative process. We consider it useful to list here the "positive" and "negative" aspects which were presented to us.

Positive

5.5.4.1 Among the Senior Management Team are individuals who command the utmost respect and trust by the staff in general. These people could well have an important role to play in the solution of the problems.

5.5.4.2 Section 11 and 365 Staff received support, guidance and encouragement from the Senior Management Team and in particular from the Headmaster and Deputy Headmaster.

5.5.4.3 Mr Moors is considered by the Staff as having as his first concern the welfare and education of the pupils by whom he is highly regarded.

5.5.4.4 The Headmaster has shown much sympathy, under-standing and support to members of Staff experiencing personal and private problems.

5.5.4.5 It is apparent that there are members of the Middle Management structure who also command a great deal of respect and trust.

Negative

5.5.4.6 Many of the Staff stated that they had no confidence in the judgement and leadership of the Headmaster. These Staff feel that their own contribution to the School is not valued, recognised or appreciated.

5.5.4.7 Some Staff stated that the Headmaster and Deputy Headmaster have adopted a strategy of supporting and encouraging only those members of Staff whose views they regard as ideologically correct.

5.5.4.8 Many members of the Staff who complain that they are lacking in support and leadership from the headmaster say that they are sympathetic to the changes which are required but antagonised by the methods of management.

445

5.5.4.9 Some Staff complain that individual members of Staff are taken to task by the Headmaster for remarks made in the Staffroom and reported to him.

5.5.4.10 Other Staff complain that the Headmaster appears to adopt a policy of "divide and rule" and that Staff are manipulated toward that end. Information gleaned by the Headmaster by diverse means is said to be used to disparage and divide and has contributed significantly to a polarization of Staff attitudes.

5.5.4.11 Some Staff say that they avoid confrontation with misbehaving pupils because they cannot be sure of management support.

5.5.4.12 A meeting between Senior Management and the Staff in December, 1983, addressed the question, "Would you have your child come to Burnage High School and if not, why not?" The consensus of opinion among Staff was that they would not although the reasons for this consensus were never stated.

5.5.4.13 A joint meeting with the unions in July, 1984, addressed standards of behaviour and disciplinary procedures in the School. A working party was set up subsequently, but the NUT decided to withdraw because it disagreed with the objectives. The working party was later abandoned.

Some Staff consider that the Headmaster was not committed to the objectives and undermined the confidence of some members of the working party by obtaining information about their proceedings which they regarded as confidential at that stage.

It is considered that union action during this period also contributed to the demise of this initiative.

5.5.5 Objectives

5.5.5.1 Short Term

5.5.5.1.1 To begin the process of building up Staff confidence in Senior Management and Senior Management confidence in the support they can expect from Staff.

5.5.5.2 Long Term

446

5.5.5.2.1　To establish a continuing atmosphere where Senior Management and Staff can work together harmoniously in the interests of the whole School.

5.5.5.2.2　To achieve an acceptable management structure which receives the respect and co-operation of all.

5.5.6　Recommendations

5.5.6.1　Short Term

5.5.6.1.1　From the outset, the Senior Management Team should reassess their management style and its effects.

5.5.6.1.2　The Sub-Committee recommends that the Headmaster and Senior Management Team give the highest priority to completing their policy document (intended to be the Staff Handbook). This document should form the basis of discussion and consultation by all concerned, including the Board of Governors. The objectives would be for the document to be ready for ratification by the Board of Governors by January, 1986.

5.5.6.1.3　Management must recognise its responsibility to explain to all Staff their role in the management task.

5.5.6.1.4　Equally, Staff must recognise that they have a role in the task of management of the School and must therefore be prepared to take on the appropriate responsibility.

5.5.6.1.5　Management should ensure that "in-service training" must be relevant to the School's need, and to each individual teacher's needs. In this context a definition of the child-centred apprach can usefully be applied in a different form, ie there is a need to "start where the teacher is at, rather than where the management would like the teacher to be."

5.5.6.1.6　Members of Staff with senior responsibilities should be allowed to send out letters over their own signature.

5.5.6.1.7　All Staff should try to understand that managing a School of the size of Burnage, with its split site, is a complex and difficult task.

447

5.5.6.2 Long Term

Senior Management should seek professional advice regarding the availability and desirability of in-service management training.

5.6 PROMOTIONS AND APPOINTMENTS

Most staff in state schools have experienced a lowering of morale as internal promotions have been restricted by lack of money over the past few years. The present situation, where most teaching unions are taking industrial action over low rates of pay (amongst other factors), is indicative of why the promotion policy in schools must be seen to be fair to all Staff. Scale rates are unlikely to be increased by any substantial amount in the near/middle future and thus teachers look to promotions as a way of improving their financial as well as career prospects. The situation at Burnage seems, however, to be additionally aggravated by certain factors. Unhappiness with the School, and the promotions policy, have apparently led to almost half the Staff attempting to leave the School during the last year; often they have applied for posts which will not involve promotion.

At the end of this term a number of Staff are leaving: numbers quoted vary from 7/12/19. Whilst all schools expect some turnover of Staff at the end of the year, these numbers appear to be sufficiently high as to introduce an element of instability in staffing resources at Burnage. Staff seem to be leaving on a basis which tends to reinforce the claim that there is a strong element of dissatisfaction with conditions at Burnage, eg transferring to another school, on the same scale; leaving the teaching profession altogether; leaving without another job to go to.

Many Staff have expressed the view that if they believe they are doing a good job they should not feel inhibited from saying so, and from putting themselves forward for promotion. They point out, however, that there is now a high degree of apathy over promotions because people feel it is pointless to apply. Some Teachers say they feel trapped at Burnage. If Staff do feel alienated, it is clearly difficult for them to contribute to the school in a positive way. Essentially, many Staff at Burnage see the promotion and recruitment policy of the Senior

448

Management as operating unfairly. It is thus vital that this perspective is clarified.

5.6.1   The major points raised in the consultative process which dealt with promotion and recruitment policy are indicated below, listed under negative and positive headings:-

5.6.1.1   Negative

Promotions are not published on a regular basis. It is claimed by Staff that at one time all promotions were published at the end of each term/end of each year.

5.6.1.2   Some Staff expressed concern about the apparent lack of openness on promotions. As a result rumours circulate, creating an unhealthy atmosphere. Instances have been identified where staff were asked not to tell people when they received an additional scale point.

5.6.1.3   Many Staff believe that there is an active policy of promoting internally, and recruiting externally, Staff who will be supportive of Dr Gough's views. Questions are asked at interviews which indicate clearly the type of person the interviewing panel are looking for. This is not, of course, unusual in an interviewing situation, but some people have indicated that the questions are too leading, and too indicative of how a person is expected to respond to specific issues. This does not help people to answer honestly because they feel inhibited by the way in which the interview is being directed.

5.6.1.4   Staff believe that internal promotions are made on the basis of ideological preferences rather than on the basis of individual merit. It has been stated that the School is harmed, in the context of promotions, by a small minority of Staff who have "sought to gain preferment by unprofessional practice, or by taking advantage of Dr Gough's style of management."

5.6.1.5   As an example of lack of information, people have quoted the appointment of a new Head of Lower School as from April this year. Everyone interviewed who mentioned this situation, emphasized that they are not opposed to a personal basis to the particular member of Staff. They have expressed concern, however, that this appointment was not explained to Staff and many people were dismayed to see valuable promotion points allocated for another addition to the Senior Management Team.

5.6.1.6   It is possible that some male Staff feel antagonised by the introduction in the past three years, of more women teachers into the School. They appear to think a deliberate policy of positive discrimination, in favour of women, has taken place.

5.6.1.7   New women members of Staff are usually young and are appointed at Scale 1, whereas the senior Staff are mainly men. Some of these younger women teachers have stated that they have experienced sexist antagonism from certain male members of Staff.

Positive

5.6.1.8   Senior Management maintain that Staff have been, and will continue to be, encouraged to apply for promotion.

5.6.1.9   The rapid increase in women members of Staff, appointed solely on merit, has corrected a sexual imbalance amongst the teaching Staff. Women Staff have increased by approximately 200% since 1982, ie they now number about 30.

5.6.1.10   Senior Management maintain that Staff have been promoted and/or recruited on the basis of qualifications and suitability for the post; also on their performance at interview.

5.6.1.11   Some Staff maintain that they view the promotion and recruitment policy at Burnage as operating in a fair and open way.

5.6.1.12   Specialized Staff have been recruited who have added considerably to the quality of education at Burnage, eg Section 11 Staff; Hearing Impaired Staff.

5.6.1.13   It is maintained that Staff have been given additional promotional points in recognition of valuable pastoral, administrative and teaching contributions on the School.

5.6.2   Objectives

5.6.2.1 Short Term

5.6.2.1.1 Staff must be made absolutely confident that promotion and recruitment policy is on the basis of merit and suitability for the job.

5.6.2.1.2 Staff should also be made aware of the promotion and recruitment aims of Senior Management.

5.6.2.2.1 Promotion and recruitment policy must be seen to be operating on a fair and open basis over a period of time. As a result of this, confidence in members of Staff who are promoted, and new members who are recruited, will be considerably enhanced and add to the overall atmosphere of trust and co-operation within the School.

5.6.2.2.2 Monitoring of promotion and recruitment policy should continue as a normal part of the procedures of the School.

5.6.3   Recommendations

5.6.3.1 Short Term

5.6.3.1.1 Staff must be reassured, by a categorical statement, that promotion and recruitment policy at Burnage is on the basis of merit and suitability for the job.

5.6.3.1.2 Promotions and new appointments should be published, on a regular basis, from September, 1985, onwards.

5.6.3.1.3 Staff must be made aware that the appointment of women Staff over the past years has been solely on the merit of their applications and performance at interview.

5.6.3.1.4 A clear policy on promotion and recruitment should be communicated to all Staff. Job descriptions should be made readily available.

5.6.3.1.5 Staff should be aware that it is inevitable that, once the School's curriculum and direction have been determined, recruitment/promotions must be compatible with them. Providing this is an overtly understood position it is up to all to equip themselves accordingly. In this context, where practicable, Teachers should be encouraged to apply for secondment and in-service training.

5.6.3.2   Long Term

5.6.3.2.1   The Governors should continue to be kept informed, on a regular basis, of action on promotion and recruitment.

5.6.3.2.2   Appointment panels should always include a representative from the Governing Body, by arrangement with the Chair of Governors.

5.6.3.2.3   Membership of the appointing panels should be published.

5.6.3.2.4   Staff should continue to be encouraged to apply for promotion if they are possible contenders. Staff should also be encouraged to discuss their promotion prospect with their Heads of Department who should, if appropriate, consult with the Headmaster.

5.7   ENVIRONMENTAL MATTERS

5.7.1   Introduction

There is absolutely no doubt that the depressingly poor environmental conditions and resources have played a major role in producing the frustrations and low morale that exists within the School today.

It appears that the decline in resources and deterioration of the School environment can be traced back to the reorganisation of the secondary school system in 1967. As Burnage was not reorganised not only did old-established traditions persist but so also did the furniture, resources and general fabric of the buildings. There was no major injection of capital at that time as with other schools which had been forced into reorganisation. The situation is more serious in Lower School where, as Ladybarn Secondary Modern School, prior to reorganisation, furniture and equipment were already inferior to those at Upper School.

It is no credit to the LEA that the School has been

452

allowed to deteriorate into the abysmal place it now is.

Of all the diversity of opinion with which we were presented, the most unified area of agreement is that directed toward the extremely poor environment which exists in both schools.

The views expressed in consultations have been echoed by the local Inspectorate and Governors alike.

The LEA are providing limited funds in order to improve the physical resources of the Lower School in particular and the Upper School Science Laboratories if possible. In the LEA's own words "the money is not available to do all that is necessary." This is not an acceptable starting point for recovery. Education is the nation's prime resource and yet pupils and staff at Burnage High School are being treated like second class citizens.

The split site school, created in the interests of economic expendiency in support of a particular educational philosophy, has always been, and will always remain, very unsatisfactory. Many of the difficulties which exist today at Burnage are exacerbated by the managerial complexities, communication difficulties and commuting problems inherent in a split site arrangement. There is no doubt that Burnage needs a complete overhaul as soon as possible.

5.7.2   Specific Points

Some particular areas concerning the general fabric and facilities include:-

5.7.2.1   Decorative condition of the Lower School is appalling.

5.7.2.2   Furniture is very old and hence lacks the flexibility of use needed for modern methods of teaching.

5.7.2.3   Both schools are overcrowded for the activities expected to take place.

5.7.2.4   Lower School and Upper School toilets are extremely unpleasant and a possible health hazard.

5.7.2.5   The Halls are too small for many activities.

5.7.2.6   Music teaching facilities in Lower School are so unsatisfactory as to be virtually non-existent.

5.7.2.7   Showering facilities in both schools are totally inadequate.

5.7.2.8   Sports facilities are insufficient.

5.7.2.9   It was reported by one member of Staff that the whole of the fourth year are taught English from only one set of books.

5.7.2.10   It is relevant to note that the Inspectors pointed out to the Sub-Committee that they consider there is an insufficient range of materials available to cover the spectrum of abilities being taught at Burnage. They noted, in addition, a total lack of certain essential demonstration equipment, particularly for Mathematics and French.

5.7.2.11   The Inspectors also say teaching is constrained at Burnage by very poor resources, lack of space and poor furniture.

        The Sub-Committee wish to state that it is to the great credit of certain staff members that the School quadrangles, planted with flowers and shrubs are preventing the School presenting an even bleaker image than it does.

5.7.3   Objectives

5.7.3.1   Short Term

5.7.3.1.1   To ensure decorative conditions are improved as soon as possible.

5.7.3.2   Long Term

5.7.3.2.1   To improve the fabric of the School to acceptable present-day standards.

5.7.3.2.2   To resource the School fully in all areas commensurate with the needs of some 1,600 pupils.

5.7.4   Recommendations

5.7.4.1   Short Term

5.7.4.1.1   The Inspectorate should be urged by the Governors to press for the commencement of improvement work immediately. It is noted that refurbishment works are not due until the 1986/87 programme. In view of what is being asked of staff elsewhere in this Report, the Sub-Committee regards this as totally unacceptable. The Governors should communicate this view urgently to the MEC.

5.7.4.1.2 A full and detailed inspection of both Lower and Upper School fabric and resources should be initiated as soon as possible. This inspection should be the responsibility of the LEA who should be asked to report back their findings to the Governors. The report should take account of all statutory obligations and Health and Safety Regulations.

5.7.4.2 Long Term

5.7.4.2.1 Governors, Senior Management and Staff should agree on an order of priority for corrective actions.

5.7.4.2.2 Governors should make themselves aware of conditions in both schools. It is imperative that all Governors make time to inspect conditions at first hand.

APPENDIX 1

Dr B Glaizner
24 Park Range
Rusholme
Manchester
M14 5HQ

July 1985

PRIVATE AND CONFIDENTIAL

Dear Colleague

I am writing on behalf of the Board of Governors of Burnage High School for Boys, and a special Sub-Committee of the Board.

At their meeting on 2 July 1985, the Governors decided to undertake a process of consultation with the School. They subsequently appointed a Sub-Committee of Governors for this purpose. None of its members are members of the Staff at the School.

The Governors have resolved that this matter is to be treated as *confidential*. All concerned, whether members of the School Staff or not, are asked to respect this wish for confidentiality, until the Governors decide to raise this embargo.

The consultation process will concern all members of Staff at the School; those members of the Manchester Education Committee and its staff who are involved with the School. and those Union Officers who need to be consulted by their members. No others are to be party to knowledge of these proceedings.

Concern has been expressed to Governors by some Union representatives about the need for privacy and confidentiality for individuals who choose to consult us. The Governors wish it to be understood by everyone that our proceedings will be strictly confidential. When the Sub-Committee reports to the full Governing Board every effort will be made to avoid identifying individual members of Staff. We will use general terms such as: "the teachers;" "some teachers;" "the inspectors," etc.

The Sub-Committee is prepared to receive either oral or written (hand or typewritten) submissions, or both. Meetings have been arranged, or will be arranged with (a) the Senior Management Team,

456

(b) the separate Staff Unions on separate occasions, where their members can present and discuss their corporate views, (c) individual members of Staff or small groups of them, (d) the members of the Inspectorate involved with the School.

Written evidence may be presented in addition to an oral submission or instead of one. If a paper is handed to a Governor, by its author, during a consultation then it can be unsigned. Written evidence can be sent through the post to the Sub-Committee's Co-ordinator, whose name and address are at the head of this letter. Such submissions must be signed. Anonymous letters received, except as already indicated, will be destroyed unread.

The Board of Governors see these consultations as being part of a constructive process. It will therefore be of great value if the evidence given to us consists of opinions supported by facts. While opinions alone may have a use as indicators of morale, it will be a knowledge of the facts and people's perceptions of them that will help Governors to fulfil their responsibility: to bring about a successful conclusion to the whole process.

Written submissions will be seen by members of the Sub-Committee only. When we have decided that our deliberations are at an end, then one of our members will undertake to destroy the papers.

We wish to emphasise that participation in this process is entirely voluntary. We would like to hear the views of all staff, however, it will be assumed by us that people not taking part are, in general at least, satisfied with things as they are.

Appended herewith is a list of the names of the Governors who are members of the Sub-Committee. We also provide an overall timetable for the consultative procedure. It will be seen from this that time has been set aside for personal consultations. It would help us to know if someone wishes to see us at a particular time. We do not wish to know who it is, only if someone wants to meet us. The School's Registrar has three separate timetables, one for each of the three days set aside, mainly for personal consultation. You will see that these timetables have been divided into ten-minute periods. If you wish to meet us then please indicate (as detailed below) your preference for time. You may agree that twenty minutes is sufficient. Please allow a ten minute interval between the end of someone else's time and the beginning of your own time. (We need our "free periods" too!).

It is proposed that Governors will normally act in pairs, but if you wish to see one Governor alone then please write the letter "S" against the first ten-minute period. The Governors will be present in both

457

Upper and Lower Schools. Please use a letter "U" or "L" to indicate where you wish to meet us. The timetable has three columns, since we hope to be able to operate three consultations simultaneously for much of the time.

The Governors believe that Burnage, justifiably, has a good reputation as a school. Generally, it may be said that it has acquired this reputation because of the dedication of the Staff, who work for the betterment of its pupils. The Governors earnestly wish to assist those concerned with the School to improve upon its present position, because we share a common purpose.

The present consultative process is directed towards this end.

Yours sincerely,

Ben Glaizner
Co-ordinator
Sub-Committee of the Board of Governors
Burnage High School for Boys

Copies to: The Chair of the Board of Governors
All other Governors
The Clerk of the Board
All members of Staff
The Senior Inspector for Secondary Education

There will be two sets of timetables, one in Lower School Office with Mrs Jean Ashton and another in the Upper School Office with Mrs Wallace.

APPENDIX 2

PLANNED GENERAL TIMETABLE FOR THE SUB-COMMITTEE

Tuesday	16 July	17.30	Senior Management Team
Wednesday	17 July	09.30–17.30	Meeting Staff
Thursday	18 July	16.00	Meeting a Union
Friday	19 July	09.30–16.00	Meeting Staff
Friday	19 July	16.30–17.30	Inspectors
Monday	22 July	19.00	Meeting a Union
Tuesday	23 July	09.30–17.30	Meeting Staff
Tuesday	23 July	19.00	Meeting a Union
Thursday	25 July	16.30	Senior Management Team
Saturday	27 July	10.00–14.00	Preparation of Report

APPENDIX 3

ACTUAL TIMETABLE OF THE CONSULTATIVE PROCESS:
July/August 1985

Tuesday	16 July	09.30 – 17.30	The Senior Management Meeting
Wednesday	17 July	09.30 – 17.30	Individual Consultations
Thursday	18 July	16.00	NUT Meeting
Friday	19 July	09.30 – 16.00	Individual Consultations
Friday	19 July	16.30	The Inspectors' Meeting
Tuesday	23 July		
Upper School		09.30 – 15.40	Individual Consultations
Lower School		09.30 – 13.00	Individual Consultations
Upper School		16.00	NAS/UWT Meeting
Wednesday	24 July		
Lower School		13.30 – 16.30	Individual Consultations
Thursday	25 July	16.30	Sub-Committee Meeting
Friday	26 July	16.30	Meeting with Dr Gough and Mr Moors
Saturday	27 July	10.00 – 15.00	Sub-Committee Meeting
Monday	29 July	16.30	Sub Committee Meeting
Thursday	1 August	14.00	Sub-Committee Meeting
Monday	5 August	16.30	Sub-Committee Meeting
Tuesday	6 August	16.30	Sub-Committee Meeting
Thursday	8 August	17.30	Sub-Committee Meeting
Friday	9 August	17.30	Sub-Committee Meeting

APPENDIX 4

Some Quotations from Teachers and Management:-

"In achieving so much in such a short period of time we have also made mistakes – perhaps avoidable mistakes when looked at with hindsight."

"Change has to be workd for, worked for hard, and its effects constantly monitored."

"If people trust you, believe in you, then you can bring them round."

"There is mistrust: upwards; sideways; and down."

"It has been a very tense school for a long time. What would have been contained within the classroom in a better atmosphere, just is not contained at Burnage. No allowances are made on either side."

"There's an awful lot of shouting going on at this school.'

"There is just too much cynicism."

"For the first time I, as a teacher, feel very very vulnerable. I feel if I have a confrontation with a child I will be seen as the instigator of the trouble."

"I've taught in tough schools but this lot knocked me for six. It is a confrontation situation. I ask myself, will I snap? If I do, my career could be at an end."

"I've had enough. I don't want butterflies in my stomach as I drive to school in the morning; not knowing what I am going to meet."

"I was impressed when I came here by the Burnage children. They are polite and orderly. It's been a delight to be here. I've experienced no violence at all."

"The majority of pupils at Burnage are smashing."

"Something radical is needed. Staff see themselves in one camp or the other. They feel trapped and frustrated."

"I often feel as if I'm trying to run in water knee deep. There is a genuine sense of weariness here."

"Is there really a need for this consultation? After all the situation at Burnage is no worse than in other schools."

"Management gave me consistent support throughout my first year here."

"Lip service is paid to pastoral care in the school, but in practice we lurch from one crisis to another."

"The Year Heads very successful at man-management. They are first rate at mobilising people."

"I've seen an accelerating cycle of decline in this School. Various parts are getting out ot harmony, one with the other. We're in the wrong gear much of the time."

"This place needs to become teacher-centred for a time."

"There is a need for recognition of people's different qualities; people need to feel they have status; there must be a growth of understanding and affection."

APPENDIX B

**A PRIVATE AND CONFIDENTIAL REPORT
OF THE
BOARD OF GOVERNORS OF
BURNAGE HIGH SCHOOL**

CONTENTS

464

Preamble

The Governors have carried out their brief to the best of their ability and in doing so have received information on all aspects of the School and its operations. Some information was verbal, some written; some was provided by individuals, some by small groups; some was provided by larger groups. Wherever possible we have used information which has been corroborated from other sources, but we have not sought to prove or disprove in any legal sense.

Confidentiality was a prime factor in their brief and they have made great efforts to preserve it. Time will show, we trust, that as far as it lay in their power they succeeded.

We are conscious, however, that the consultation process itself may have further crystallised opinion.

We wish to express our appreciation of the support and confidence given to us throughout our consultative process by the many people who have made their views known to us.

1. CONCLUSIONS

1.1 There are, and have been for some time, serious problems within the School which have resulted in breaches between some of the teaching staff and the Senior Management and between some of the teaching staff themselves. The non-teaching staff are affected to a lesser degree by the problems but have expressed their concern. The problems are exacerbated by the industrial disputes. The problems appear to be worse at Lower School.

1.1.0	The problems as stated during the consultation were:
1.1.1	Very low morale among the majority of the Staff.
1.1.2	A lack of confidence of many of the Staff in Senior Management.
1.1.3	A fractionalisation of the Staff.
1.1.4	An atmosphere of mistrust, allegation and innuendo.
1.1.5	An alleged deterioration in the behaviour of the boys.
1.1.6	There are members of Staff who are content but they appear to be greatly outnumbered by the discontented.
1.1.7	The problems stem from the transition over the past eight years from a rather autocratic, traditional and stable regime to one encompassing the more progressive requirements of central and local government and of educationalists. The requirements of authority were urgent and the time, resources and money available were inadequate.
1.1.8	Imposed on that situation was a period of changes in the Management Team, Mr Marshall introduced the first of the changes but only remained in office for four years. Mr Walmsley, acting as caretaker Head accepted the status quo for one year. The main changes of the reorganisation of 1982, the abolition of corporal punishment and the directives toward anti-racism, multicultural education. Section II, etc. fell to Dr Gough for implementation.
1.1.9	The Staff had therefore experienced a period of some years of basic changes, changes in the direction and management of those basic changes, and changes in philosophy.

1.1.10   Dr Gough introduced measures to implement the mandatory requirements placed upon him, together with measures which he himself wished to incorporate, and these were accepted by some members of staff with enthusiasm. To the majority they were not acceptable. The pace of the changes may have aggravated matters.

1.2.1   Senior Management has been the focus of many criticisms, some serious, some trivial, and whilst it is recognised that much progress and good work has been achieved in recent years, they must carry a share of responsibility for the present situation.

Senior Management should examine its style and methods to see what changes are necessary.

1.2.2   There has been over-reaction, over-sensitivity and pettiness to some degree in the attitudes of some members of the staff toward the Senior Management.

1.2.3   Entrenched positions must be abandoned and new approaches to many facets of the School operations must evolve by consultation, discussion and reason. If management is to be democratised, staff must recognise their own responsibilities in that process. Those responsibilities must be clearly communicated.

The changes in attitude asked of some members of staff will be minimal and these individuals can play a vital role in what will be for others a much more difficult process.

Those members of staff for whom significant changes in attitude and philosophy are asked, will require a significant degree of application. It is considered that with changes in management approach and the support of their colleagues, they will provide that application in the interests of themselves, the School and their pupils.

1.2.4   There must be a halt to the decline in staff relationships.

1.2.5   It is considered that a large proportion of the staff who are at present discontented, would embrace more readily the processes of change if they are presented in a manner which shows due consideration of their opinions, endeavours and achievements.

1.2.6   Time should be made available at the earliest possible date(s) in order that the entire staff, including Senior Management, may spend it in School in consultation, discussion and debate, to formulate agreed policies, including, but not limited to:

Communication

Discipline and policies

1.2.7   An extended period of stability in policies and management personnel is essential to the resolution of the problems.

1.2.8   Both Upper and Lower Schools are physically run down, decrepit and depressing. The equipment is numerically and technically inadequate and books and other material are grossly under supplied.

The physical environment is conducive to discontent and unhappiness.

A major refurbishment is urgently required.

1.2.9   Some increase in staffing for special purposes is called for, specifically, a person, professionally qualified, and with due seniority, to take charge of the proposed Withdrawal Unit. There should be a review of the establishment for the Senior Management Team to ensure that all management responsibilities are adequately covered.

1.2.10   There is a need for a review at the end of the school year 1986, but the "healing" process and process of adaptation to change must be seen in the much longer term. Annual reviews will need to continue over a period of time.

1.2.11   The Governors are impressed by the overall level of dedication and professionalism which exists in the School. It is the Governors' conclusion that the Senior Management and staff have the ability to make the healing process a success.

2. HISTORICAL PERSPECTIVES

2.1 It became clear early on that the Sub-Committee's (which carried out the consultation process) capacity to understand matters depended to some extent on a knowledge of certain events which had taken place over a period of about two decades, i.e. since the change from a Grammar School.

2.2 A number of significant changes took place from 1967 onwards.

2.2.1 The School ceased to be a Grammar School and it amalgamated with the Ladybarn Secondary Modern School. The Grammar School site became the Upper School and the Secondary Modern site became the Lower School. Thus Burnage became a High School for Boys on a split site, with several attendant problems.

2.2.2 Upper School was better equipped and in a better condition than Lower School. Improvements that might have been made were not made, either they were not sought or they were not allowed; it must be noted that educational funding at this time was more generous than is at present possible.

2.2.3 The Staffs of the previous two schools were amalgamated. Because of the requirements at the time, Staff at Upper School were more qualified, in a formal sense. As a result most managerial appointments went to the Staff at Upper School. A special designation, Head of Lower School Department, was conceived to give due status to those at Lower School who had the requisite experience but not the formal qualification to became Scale 4 Heads of Department.

2.2.4 The Senior Management Team has been understaffed for a significant part of the time under consideration. On Dr Gough's appointment there were only two Deputy Headteachers and one Senior Teacher. This state of affairs compares unfavourably with other schools of a similar or lesser size where there would be three Deputy Headteachers and up to four Senior Teachers.

2.3

2.3.1 Over a period of time the composition of the School's pupil population changed. Thus there were created further demands for change in teaching.

469

2.3.2　　More latterly, at the instigation of the LEA, the Board of Governors and the Headmasters, curriculum changes have occurred along with pressure to change teaching styles. Fundamental changes in the philosophies of education, such as multicultural education, SENIOS, anti-racism and anti-sexism initiatives and "365" have marked the departure from traditional education. In addition, and consistent with nationally recognised practice, a reformation of teaching style has been demanded such that each child's personal and social needs are recognised and catered for in the teaching process.

2.3.3　　Nationally it has been recognised that pupils whose immigrant parents might be unfamiliar with the English language and/or culture, present special difficulties for teachers, who have to cope with large classes. The School has been able to employ three Section II teachers to assist all staff with these problems. Their duties are strictly defined by Central Government.

3. RECOMMENDATIONS
3.1 Communication

3.1.0　　*Introduction*
Elsewhere in this document details of the very significant changes which have taken place in recent years in all aspects of Burnage High School life are noted. The failure of communication pertaining to those changes, between Senior Management and Staff, constitutes a major cause of the present discontent. It is therefore important to establish by consultation and discussion a system of lines of communication which can be agreed by the majority and accepted by the minority. This will ensure that, even though the system may not initially be perfect, it is followed and is seen to be followed, and that its imperfections are discussed and resolved by both Management and Staff. However it is essential that in parallel to the formal communication system, there develops an informal atmosphere in which professional and personal communication can take place without inhibition.

3.1.1 *Recommendations*

3.1.1.1 Time should be made available at the earliest possible date(s) in order that the entire staff, including Senior Management, in School, in consultation, discussion and debate may formulate an agreed policy on communication and other matters.

3.1.1.2 The system of Assemblies should be further developed and should be as extensive as time and space permit.

3.1.1.3 The staff room calendar concept should be developed.

3.1.1.4 The Newsheet concept should be developed and could prove invaluable provided that it does not become an administrative burden and provided that it can be produced with enthusiasm.

3.1.1.5 As part of a wider inspection exercise, the Inspectorate should be requested to address themselves to communication in practice in the School.

3.1.1.6 Teacher and Non-teaching staff Governors should be encouraged to communicate more freely at Governors' meetings.

3.1.1.7 A representative of the Manchester Education Committee should be asked to communicate the policies of the LEA to the Teaching and Non-teaching Staff at Burnage. Time for questions and discussions should be available.

3.1.1.8 Governors should be encouraged to involve themselves in School, eg adopt a Department.

3.2 Discipline

   3.2.0 *Introduction*

   3.2.1 In 1981 the then Headmaster, Mr John Marshall, and his Senior Management, decided to reduce the level of corporal punishment in the School. At this time some staff petitioned against the decision. Present unrest over discipline seems to have started here: many Staff were unsure as to how they could teach their classes, in a controlled atmosphere, without the sanction of corporal punishment and using instead the new educational philosophies.

3.2.2   There is a multiplicity of opinion in the School on the subject of standards of behaviour.

3.2.3   Nearly all opinions expressed are genuine sentiments, not maliciously offered, but indicative of individual experiences and collective opinions, possibly measured against differing criteria of assessment.

3.2.4   This variation in perception which suggests a lack of a firmly based and cohesive policy on discipline – understood and supported by all – makes the overwhelming pleas for consistency of approach an understandably difficult goal to achieve.

3.2.5   In order to arrive at this situation the differing viewpoints and concerns of all members of Staff need to be recognised, and given due weight, in order to clear the ground for a way forward to be found.

3.2.6   *Recommendations*

3.2.6.1.1   Senior management should fully endorse the Governors' statement that, "Teachers have a difficult job to do. They must be supported and they must know they are supported".

3.2.6.1.2   Full, frank and constructive discussions must begin in September with the aim of achieving agreed procedures on discipline which can be implemented from January, 1986, onwards. All Staff must take part in this process. Discussions should use the Headmaster's document "Standards of Behaviour in School" as a starting-point.

3.2.6.1.3   Assemblies should be used as a means of presenting the boys with the standards of behaviour that are expected by the School and the Community.

3.2.6.1.4   Those disciplinary matters which cannot be solved in the classroom should continue to be processed up an agreed line. The steps for doing this should reach, if necessary, to the Headmaster. All Staff who are involved should be kept informed of the actions taken.

3.2.6.1.5   Staff should be encouraged to become more involved in, and trained in, pastoral work and counselling.

472

3.2.6.1.6 Senior Management should ascertain the financial and staff resources available for the proposed Special Support Group and Withdrawal Unit.

3.2.6.1.7 Priority must be given to set-up a Withdrawal Unit (or Units), staffed by professional staff, who are new appointments. There appears to be a need to gain a consensus of opinion about the function of the Withdrawal Unit.

3.2.6.1.8 Guidelines should be produced which are agreed as a procedure for dealing with fighting amongst boys outside the classroom, or aggressive behaviour by older to younger boys. For example, should Teachers intervene independently in a fight amongst boys, or should they always seek the help of a colleague or senior Staff before taking action?

3.2.6.1.9 Consistency of approach to classroom management and discipline must be aimed for. This can only be in the best interests of Staff, Senior Staff, Senior Management, Boys and Parents.

3.2.6.1.10 The sanction of suspension and exclusion should be maintained for serious offences.

3.2.6.1.11 The Governors believe that the following points merit consideration during the discussions which will take place from September onwards:

3.2.6.1.12 Are there sufficient Staff across the whole range of year and subject requirements who are willing to accept referrals from the proposed Special Support Group into their class groups?

3.2.6.1.13 Is there a need to set a maximum time limit for a pupil to be with the Special Support Group?

3.2.6.1.14 Is it practicable or desirable to have a third-year prefect assigned to each Staff member of the Special Support Group?

3.2.6.1.15 If no new Staff are available to run the proposed Withdrawal Unit, can the School manage to establish such a Unit with its present staffing resources? Would such a decision be a sensible one? If not, can the School manage with only the Special Support Group and other procedures outlined in the Headmaster's document?

3.2.6.1.16 Is the proposed system of discipline panels practicable?

3.2.6.1.17 Should some disciplinary offences be regarded as more serious than others? For example, swearing at, and in front of, Staff.

3.2.6.1.18 Does the proposed new system take account of the generally accepted opinion that behavioural problems in Lower School are different, and more difficult than those in Upper School?

3.2.6.1.19 Ultimately it must be possible that an increase in punitive methods, can lead to a increase in remedial and counselling methods.

3.2.6.1.20 Final sanctions to deal with extreme disciplinary offences must be maintained.

3.2.6.1.21 The Withdrawal Unit (if installed) should be maintained on a long term trial basis, eg for up to five years. Careful monitoring should take place, including end of term and end of year reviews. These should include a wide spectrum of opinion from inside and outside the School. For example, Governors should be involved in the monitoring process as should the Inspectorate.

3.2.6.1.22 A general assessment of the disciplinary patterns of the School should be presented to the Governing Board at the end of each year. Governors should, in any case, make efforts to keep themselves fully informed of any problems which arise during the year in connection with standards of behaviour in the School.

3.3 Staff Relationships

3.3.0 *Introduction*

3.3.1 With few exceptions there appears to be a deep sadness at the ever widening divisions between working colleagues. Normal professional interactions which should be taking place on a day to day basis are being stifled by fear and mistrust. Healthy discussion and constructive disagreement is not occurring in a free and open manner.

3.3.2   The belief by some Staff that confidence have been breached by Senior Management has helped to create the atmosphere of mistrust. Poor communications exacerbate the problems and further mistrust appears to have been created as information is distorted by rumour.

3.3.3   Senior Management has expressed the view that there has been, and still is, a resistance to change by a number of Staff, some in senior positions, which has in the past made progress difficult and at times impossible. The Headmaster has explained how he has felt the need to adopt a more positive approach to instigating initiatives which due at times to severe external pressures, have demanded a rapid response.

3.3.4   Certain incidents have occurred, which have generated an intensity of antagonism between some members of the Staff and the Senior Management and between members of Staff themselves, which may present major difficulties in the search for reconciliation. There may always remain a residue of intractable grievances to which only mature reasoning will give historical perspective. They must not be allowed to fester to the detriment of all that is good.

3.3.5   *Recommendations*

3.3.5.1 Communications systems must be improved

3.3.5.2 Discussions to be set up with representatives of Senior Management, Unions, and possibly Governors, to formulate a common approach which will help to reverse the declining trend in staff relationships.

3.3.5.3 September 1985, to January 1986, would be seen as a period for laying foundations for the future of the school, for openly and frankly identifying problems of staff relationships and for making a determined effort to improve this situation.

3.3.5.4 Restoration of trust is an objective. An explanation of the process from Senior Management regarding confidentiality may at least offer a starting point in developing better relationships.

3.3.5.5.   Section II Staff should be given additional support from all their colleagues.

3.3.5.6   The development of proper and mutually supportive professional relationships should be a paramount aim.

3.3.5.7   The Headmaster should extend his personal contact with Staff as far as possible.

3.3.5.8   The Senior Management and staff should approach the adjustment difficulties that may be experienced by some Staff with more sympathy and understanding.

3.3.5.9   The use of a Staff Relationships Committee, using particular members of Staff, and management, who have been identified as commanding the utmost all round respect and trust. Their specific brief would be to encourage better staff relationships. Constant monitoring of opinion and feedback to all interested parties will be essential. The Newsletter is seen as a very useful medium through which opinion could be channelled and it should contain a wide variety of views. This Committee's activities could embrace pastoral and remedial services to all Staff, transcending the traditional and hardening divisions. Care, patience and tact will be vital – good relationships cannot be forced, but may flourish if carefully nurtured over a long period.

3.4 Educational Philosophies

3.4.0   *Introduction*

3.4.1.   Teachers should examine or re-examine their own attitudes in relation to the educational policies and philosophies of the LEA and of the School.

3.4.2   There should be a readiness to come to terms with concepts underlying these policies, at a professional level.

3.4.3   It should be understood by all that genuine difficulties of various kinds will continue to exist and there must be a willingness to allow debate and for apprehensions and doubts to be freely expressed. All this can take place for mutual benefit only in an atmosphere of good will and respect for colleagues who have different opinions.

3.4.4 Therefore the present divisions within the School should be recognised for what they are: counter-productive and inimical to the aims of all teachers who wish to work in a congenial atmosphere for the betterment of their students.

3.4.5 *Recommendations*

3.4.5.1 There exists a need for a re-iteration of clear definitions and statements to be given about the objectives for each of the educational philosophies. Each of the following should be so treated: The "child-centred approach"; multicultural education; the anti-racist initiative; the anti-sexist initiative; PSE; Section II teaching; SENIOS; "365" vocational training. The statements should be prepared by the Senior Management Team in consultation with the staff involved.

3.4.5.2 Upon receipt of these statements, Teachers should seek to reconcile their differences with the stated objectives, at a professional level, so that they may carry out their teaching duties and assignments more effectively in the best interestsof their students.

3.4.5.3 In-service training should be provided so that Teachers acquire a clearer understanding of what is expected of them and the skills necessary to meet those requirements.

3.4.5.4 Time should be made available for small group seminars to take place when aspects of modern educational philosophies can be discussed, and the experience of individuals can be shared.

3.4.5.5 The Inspectorate should continue their process of observation, assessment and advice. Their findings and recommendations should be made available to the School, and the Board of Governors, as soon as possible.

3.4.5.6 It is essential that the Inspectors should continue to inform individual members of Staff about any matter affecting them personally, as soon as possible.

3.5 Management
  3.5.0   *Introduction*
  3.5.1   In an environment of highly intelligent people, holding a variety of views, some very strongly, a very open, frank and receptive approach by Senior Management and Staff is required. There is an overriding need for polite straight talking.

  3.5.2   This should begin the process of building up Staff confidence in senior Management and Senior Management confidence in the support they can expect from Staff.

  3.5.3   *Recommendations*

  3.5.3.1 The Goverors recommend that the Headmaster and Senior Management Team give the highest priority to completing the policy document (intended to be the Staff Handbook).
           This document should form the basis of discussion and consultation by all concerned, including the Board of Governors. The objective would be for the document to be ready for ratification by the Board of Governors by January 1986.

  3.5.3.2 Management should explain to all Staff their role in the management task.

  3.5.3.3 Equally, Staff should recognise that they have a role in the task of management of the School and must therefore be prepared to take on the appropriate responsibility.

  3.5.3.4 Teachers should be encouraged to apply for secondment and in-service training which will benefit both the School and their own careers.

  3.5.3.5 All Staff should try to understand that managing a School of the size of Burnage, with its split site, is a complex and difficult task.

3.6 Promotions and Appointments
  3.6.0   *Introduction*
  3.6.1   It is felt by some members of staff that the promotion and recruitment policies of the School have not been perceived to be operating on a fair and open basis.

The evidence shows that the contrary is true.

3.6.1.1 Governors to be satisfied that promotion and recruitment policy at Burnage is on the basis of merit.

3.6.2 *Recommendations*

3.6.2.1 Information about promotions and new appointments should continue to be published, on a regular basis.

3.6.2.2 A clear statement of existing policy on promotion and recruitment should be communicated to all Staff. Job descriptions should continue to be made readily available.

3.6.2.3 Appointment panels must include a representative from the Governing Body except in exceptional circumstances by arrangement with the Chair of Governors.

3.6.2.4 Membership of the appointing panels should be published, once the interviews have taken place.

3.6.2.5 Staff should continue to be encouraged to apply for promotion if they are possible contenders. Staff should also be encouraged to discuss their promotion prospects with their Heads of Department who should, if appropriate consult with the Headmaster.

3.7 Environmental Matters

3.7.0 *Introduction*

3.7.1 There is absolutely no doubt that the depressingly poor environmental conditions and resources have played a major role in producing the frustrations and low morale that exists within the School today.

3.7.2 It appears that the decline in resources and deterioration of the School environment can be traced back to the reorganisation of the secondary school system in 1967. At Burnage not only did old-established traditions persist but also did the furniture, resources and general fabric of the buildings. There was no major injection of capital at that time as with some other schools. The situation is more serious in Lower School where, as Ladybarn Secondary Modern School, furniture and equipment were already inferior to those at Upper School.

479

3.7.3   It is no credit to the LEA that the School has been allowed to deteriorate into the abysmal place it now is.

3.7.4   Of all the deiversity of opinion with which we were presented, the most unified area of agreement is that directed toward the extremely poor environment which exists in both schools.

The views expressed during the consultations have been echoed by the local Inspectorate and Governors alike.

The split site school, created in the interests of economic expediency in support of a particular educational philosophy, has always been, and will always remain, very unsatisfactory. Many of the difficulties which exist today at Burnage are exacerbated by the managerial complexities, communication difficulties and commuting problems inherent in a split site arrangement. There is no doubt that Burnage needs a complete overhaul as soon as possible.

3.7.5   *Recommendations*

3.7.5.1   The Inspectorate is urged to press for the commencement of improvement work immediately. It is noted that refurbishment works are not due until the 1986/87 programme. In view of what is being asked of Staff elsewhere in this Report, the Governors regard this as totally unacceptable.

3.7.5.2   A full and detailed inspection of both Lower and Upper School fabric and resources should be initiated as soon as possible. This inspection should be the responsibility of the LEA who should be asked to report back their findings to the Governors. The report should take account of all statutory obligations and Health and Safety Regulations.

3.7.5.3   Governors, Senior Management and Staff should agree on an order of priority for corrective actions.

3.7.5.4   Governors should make themselves aware of conditions in both schools. It is imperative that all Governors make time to inspect conditions at first hand.

APPENDIX C

David McCorkle –
Manchester 8

Our Lady's RC School *Blackley*
ex St Chad's
At Our Lady's since the age of 11

On the way home on Friday, 9.3.84 I was walking through the park with my friends, three white youths, aged 14/15 also pupils at the school, Mike Fitzpatrick, Paul Harrigan and Michael Cassidy.

A load of guys aged between 15 and 19 started coming at me from all directions. There were about thirty to forty of them. They were YTS Youths from Higher Blackley Youth Centre and from Plant Hill School.

One guy called Wayne Ward came up to me and threw some gravel in my face and started fighting me.

The day before I heard from one of my friends that Wayne Ward had been calling me names, coon, nigger, etc. So I told him to come up and we'd sort it out. He came up to our Lady's with two of his friends and we sorted everything out. We sorted it out verbally, and then we each went our own way.

The girl Wayne Ward used to go out with told me that he'd been calling me names. She is the friend I referred to earlier.

At first it was he and I alone fighting. Then some of the other white guys started fighting me, kicking me, punching me, and chucking stones at my head.

Wayne Ward kicked me while I was on the ground. Michael Fitzpatrick kicked him back and he started fighting Michael. Loads of Wayne Ward's friends started fighting Michael and the others were on top of me.

Some kids must have alerted the teachers, or they may have been driving past, and my ex PE Teacher came, Mr Rearden and the metalwork teacher, Mr Alson. They tried to drag me and Michael Fitzpatrick out of the fight, but the other guys started fighting the teachers as well, punching and kicking them. They finally dragged us out, and the other youths started to run off.

We got taken back to school and I wanted to phone the police but the headmaster wouldn't let me. I started arguing with him but he still wouldn't let me. The two teachers told the Head that they'd got beaten up as well.

I told the Head I wanted to phone my brother and he wouldn't let me do that either. The Head didn't get in touch with my mum but the Art teacher, Mr Moran did. He gave me and Michael a lift home. When we got there, my brother who is 19 was at home, my mum was not. She was at work. The teacher told him what had happened. He didn't tell him what the school intended to do about it.

When the Head wouldn't let me ring the police I started going mad. I even swore at him, he told me he wouldn't have that sort of conduct and

I should go home and cool down. I was never told to go home and think over the matter of involving the police.

On Monday 12.3.84 I went to school late to avoid the rush and avoid the guys I would normally meet in the morning. I was walking up this particular road, on my own, and I saw these two guys. I recognised them as friends of Wayne Ward who had been fighting me the Friday before.

One of them came up to me and was about to attack me so I punched him in the jaw. The other one went for me but I ran away, and one of them threw a heavy object at my head. It caught me on the back of my head. The bump is still there. My head was badly bruised. I kept on running, and went straight to Victoria Avenue, and caught a bus on Middleton Road to Cheetham Hill. I didn't go to school. I went home.

On Tuesday I came down to the Abe Moss Youth Club, and by the time I got down there everybody knew that I had got beat up.

They were asking me if I was going up to Higher Blackley and Plant Hill to sort the matter out.

We all decided to go and see the youths at YTS, because we didn't think it was on that they should attack me every time they saw me.

We went to the YTS place, at Higher Blackley Youth Centre, about 22 of us, and we were met by a hail of snooker balls, which kept on coming through the windows of the Higher Blackley Youth Centre. One of our lot got hit on the head and was injured. We got through one double door and could get no further because of the missiles coming at us. We didn't see Wayne Ward, so we went off the Plant Hill School.

Some of us entered the school premises and were checking through the classrooms looking for Wayne Ward. We didn't know where the 4th and 5th years were so we were just looking through all the classrooms.

Two teachers stood in our way and asked us what we thought we were doing, so we just went past them and continued going through the School.

We broke one window only, and that was to get out of the school. We all left the school after about ten minutes and ran off.

The police came at us over a piece of waste ground about five minutes from the school. I wasn't caught, nor was my friend Richard. The police have not talked to me about the incident.

Since then, I've been back to the school only for about one month to six weeks, because Wayne Ward and the rest kept on coming back to the school.

An EWO organised for me to attend at a Gym in town where you do sports, etc., all day. I stayed there only about one week because I didn't like it. Since then I've been doing maths and English at Abraham Moss College. Sheila Farrell, the Youth Worker at Abraham Moss arranged it and told the EWO.

I understand that in the last two weeks, Wayne Ward and a couple of his other friends have been back to Our Lady's in one of the pre-fab buildings. They punched the teacher, Miss Goughlin, in the face, and beat up Andrew Scottie, a white guy; and also beat up a half-caste guy at the school, just outside the gates, in the last month.

I don't know what action the school has taken about all this.

About two weeks after I'd been beaten up going through the park, I asked the police to come to the school to take some action about my being beaten up, and sort out Wayne Ward. Two policemen interviewed me in the presence of Mr Godlington, and said that they knew Wayne Ward, he was a bit of a troublemaker, and they'd had him already for a couple of things. But it was too late for them to do anything about his assault on me because I did not report it at the same time.

I told the police that two teachers had also been beaten up by Ward and his gang. They didn't seem bothered, and Godlington said nothing.

I asked Mr Rearden if he would come to Court on behalf of the guys charged with affray, and say that he had got beaten up at the same time as me. He said he would but that I should ask the Head first because after all it was his job to sort those things out.

I haven't raised it with Godlington.

Statement given to Gus John, on behalf of the Chief Education Officer on November 29th, 1984.

Signed: D McCorkle

CC: DC Davies, John Taylor, Adge Warm, BB Waldon, Betty Luckham, Bill Gulam and Gus John.

APPENDIX D

REPORT TO THE CHIEF EDUCATION OFFICER Problems Experienced at PLANT HILL HIGH SCHOOL on Tuesday 13th March 1984

On the above date the School experienced considerable problems with intruders which led to injuries to staff and police involvement. During the afternoon of Tuesday, 13th March 1984 a group of about thirty youths were seen approaching the School from the playing fields. We later discovered that they had come from the direction of Higher Blackley Youth Club to which they had caused serious damage. The youths entered the School building in two groups.

One group entered Practical Block 2, the other group entered the Classroom Block. The members of staff on the first floor of Practical Block 2 locked their classroom doors while informing the general officer. Two members of staff, Mr F G Wilkinson and Mr P R Wood, immediately went to the main corridor and met the other group of youths entering the Classroom Block. Mr Wood, realising the situation could not be controlled by staff, immediately went to telephone the Police while Mr E Wilkinson endeavoured to persuade the youths who were carrying offensive weapons to leave the premises. The youths acted violently towards Mr Wilkinson and met up with the group entering the building from Practical Block 2. They then went into Mr Wilkinson's room in which there were half a dozen 4th Year students and caused considerable damage. One large window was smashed, tables were turned and damaged and one of the television links to the computer was knocked over. Two of the 4th Year students who tried to stop the youths were attacked and received minor injuries. One of them had his coat stolen. The two students concerned were Robert Cadwell and Wayne Skelton. Mrs V Goldberg who was in the room and beneath Mr Wilkinson's room heard the noise and assumed some students of ours were having a fight. She told her class, a 2nd Year group, to sit quietly while she went to see what the disturbance was. As she went up the stairs she was met by the gang of youths. They charged towards her and pushed her against the wall threatening to smash her face. One of them tore off her glasses and broke them. As they could not get out of the door by the bottom of the staircase because it was closed they charged into Mrs Goldberg's room, overturned desks, knocked aside students including slamming the fingers of one of them in the desk, threw chairs through the windows and then left. The class were terrified and ran out of the room.

The Police were already aware of the youths being in the area when they were contacted by the School and were on their way to the School within minutes. When I was notified of the incident I was at the other end of the building and by the time I arrived on the scene it was all over. It all occurred between approximately 2.05 and 2.10 pm. The youths ran off towards Pike Fold Junior School and eighteen of them were rounded up by the Police, taken to Collyhurst police station and charged with causing an affray.

Mrs Goldberg was taken to the staffroom immediatey as she was in a stressful state and dealt with by other colleagues. A Police Officer later arrived to interview Mr Wood, Mr Wilkinson and Mrs Goldberg and all the class who were present in Mrs Goldberg's room. The Officer also interviewed Skelton and Cadwell. All these interviews took place in the presence of senior members of staff. Later that afternoon Mrs Goldberg and Mr Wood went to Collyhurst Police Station to make a further statement.

My concern for the rest of the week was to maintain calm. Obviously parents of students at this School were very concerned and I therefore sent a letter to all parents, a copy of which is enclosed. I spoke to all years in the School advising them not to react to rumours and to ensure that their behaviour remained impeccable. I also contact other local schools to warn them of the problems we had had. Staff agreed to patrol the building, grounds and the immediate surroundings of the School during lunch time and after School. I also asked Police to keep the School under surveillance on both Wednesday and Thursday 14th and 15th March. There was a heavy Police presence in the area.

On Thursday 15th March, the School received information that a group of youths from North Manchester Boys, Our Lady's, Abraham Moss and Moston Brook were to attempt to come into School that afternoon. All staff were alerted but nothing happened.

The exact causes of the attack by intruders are not known but it does appear that they could result from a fight between a student at the School and a black youth from Our Lady's High School on Friday, 9th March.

One of my concerns has been the racial overtones of the incident as all the intruders were of West Indian or Pakistani origin but in dealing with this matter with our own students we have been at great pains to ensure that is should be seen as a criminal act not as a racial act.

Unfortunately the incident has attracted some undesirable publicity as far as the School is concerned as rumours have been rife in the district and many people have assumed that it was our students who were guilty of the affray. However, I have tried to maintan a low key aproach to publicity. I believe we have learnt a number of lessons from this incident and as a result we have introduced certain precautionary measures in case of future incidents. However, one of the great problems is that the School is very open and exposed. Another problem is that during last week when staff were stationed in various parts of the School grounds or on the streets it would have been impossible to communicate back to School if there had been any problem. This would particularly have been the case with myself as I stationed myself in the area where intruders were likely to come. Dramatic as it may seem I believe there would be some advantage on our campus if a "walkie talkie" device could be used.

I am sending copies of this document to all members of the Governing Body, to the Heads of the feeder primary schools and the Secretaries of the professional associations who have asked for it.

Finally, I think it only right that I should commend the high professional standards and support my staff have shown during this most difficult time especially as it coincided with a high rate of staff absence.

R E Speller
Headmaster

APPENDIX E

To Clerks School Governing Bodies –
  Our Lady's RC High School
  Plant Hill High School
  Abraham Moss High School

Dear

Arrest of 17 black youths on charge of affray following incident at Plant Hill High School – 13 March 1984

1. Following the incident at Plant Hill High School on the afternoon of Tuesday 13 March 1984, eighteen youths were arrested and charged. Charges were dropped against the one white youth involved and seventeen black youths are due to come before the Crown courts on a charge of affray. I write to inform your governing bodies that solicitors for the defence intend to raise the issue of mitigating circumstances and with information now at my disposal, it is the Committee's wish and my intention to assist defence counsel in their efforts to establish support for such a plea.

2. Concern in these offices over incidents of a racial character was reflected in the letter sent to Heads of Schools and Colleges on 14 May 1982. A list of 16 reported incidents involving schools and/or young people in the North of the City has been compiled and a copy is enclosed. A separate report of like incidents recorded by the Housing Department is also attached. Counsel for the defence will therefore now be seeking to set the events of 13 March 1984 in the overall context of racist activity in the north of the City.

3. More particularly, the events of 13 March 1984 will be set in the perspective of the sequence of events reported by witnesses directly involved. Evidence, for example, already submitted by X, a pupil of Our Lady's constitutes a summary version of events culminating in the Plant Hill incident.

    8.3.84 X said that WW had been calling him names – "coon", "nigger" – so X told him to come and sort it out: this was done verbally at Our Lady's when WW turned up with two of his friends, then each went his way.

    9.3.84 X, the black youth involved, was walking through a park with three white friends and saw a number of youths about 15 to 19 from the YTS scheme at Higher Blackley Youth Centre and from Plant Hill School approaching. One of them WW, on getting close to X threw gravel in his face and started attacking him; afterwards the other YTS youths joined in the attack. WW kicked him while on the ground. The fight continued and only stopped when two teachers from Our Lady's High who were passing intervened. The teachers took X back to school; X and his friend were subsequently given a lift home by a member of staff.

12.3.84 X on his way to school, late, in order to avoid meeting with his earlier assailants, saw two lads, friends of WW approaching him. One of them got near and was about to attack, so X punched him and ran away; a heavy object was thrown and hit him on his head which was badly bruised. X continued running, caught a bus and returned home.

13.3.84 X went to Abraham Moss Youth Club: by the time he arrived everyone knew that he had been beaten up. Those present asked if he was going to Higher Blackley and Plant Hill to sort the matter out. It was decided that all would go to see the YTS youths because they thought that X had been wronged.

About 22 Black Youths from AMC went to Higher Blackley Youth Centre. The YTS youths there seemed to have been expecting some response from the black youths and appeared to recognise them as they approached the building. A hail of snooker balls were showered on the approaching group by those inside the building: a number of windows were broken in the process. One of the black youths was hit on the head and injured. The group entered through a double door but could get no further because of the missiles. There was no sight of WW so the group set off for Plant Hill School where other youths involved in the attack of 9.3.84 were based. The group entered the school, checking through the classrooms looking for WW. Two teachers stood in the way and questioned them, but that did not deter them. One window was broken in order to get out of the school. The group left the school after about ten minutes and ran off. The police came at the group over a piece of waste ground. X was not caught nor was his friend R. He has not been questioned by the police about the incident of 3.3.84. X has not attended school for 4 to 6 weeks because WW and his friends kept coming back to his school. X is studying Maths and English at AMC.

4. Discussions with youth workers, the group of young people themselves and their parents have revealed that apart from incidents of a racial nature in and around schools, some of these young people and their parents have been subjected to physical and verbal abuse by white young people and adults, many of whom are thought ot have connections with the National Front. Apart from feeling that X had been wronged, many of those involved in the incidents at

Higher Blackley and Plant Hill agree that because of the attack experienced by X was to leave the way open for further attacks, to which any members of the group may have been subject.

5. My purpose in writing to you is not to comment on matters which may shortly be sub-judice but to advise Governors and Schools of the Committee's intention to afford the department's resources to assist Counsel for the defence of the youths in establishing the context of racial harassment and provocation in which the incident at Plant Hill High School arose.

Yours sincerely

G Hainsworth

APPENDIX F

LETTERS FROM CHIEF EDUCATION OFFICER
RE: RACIST INCIDENTS 1982–1987

S/C/14001/EB/YB   Mr Cant
February 1987   DIRECT LINE:
                        061-234 7155

To: Heads of Establishments/Centres/Branches
    within the Education Department
    Chairs, Schools/College Governing Bodies

For the Personal Attention of the Head/Principal

Dear Colleague,

EQUAL OPPORTUNITIES : REPORTING OF INCIDENTS

1. I have written to you on several occasions, most recently on 7 April 1986 asking for all racist incidents to be reported to me. This has proved valuable in monitoring progress in combatting racism and disseminating good practice throughout the service. These are the prime purposes of the reporting process.

2. The action taken by establishments, centres and branches on racist incidents is reported to an Incidents Group chaired by the Chief Inspector, and in turn to the Education Department's Equal Opportunities Group which I chair.

3. The present Racial Incidents Group is now extending its role to receive reports of incidents relating to other aspects of equal opportunities. It will continue to deal with reports of action taken on incidents relating to race, but will also encompass reports of incidents relating to sexism, and disability. The group will be known as the Incidents Group and will continue to be chaired by the Chief Inspector.

4. The issues in dealing with discrimination against lesbians and gay people are complex and very sensitive. They are currently under discussion and an agreed procedure will follow in due course. Lesbians in Education and Gay Men in Education now meet regularly and information will be notified in the Bulletin or can be directly obtained from Paul Fairweather (telephone 234 3256) and Chris Root (telephone 234 3251) who are Equal Opportunities Officers for Gay Men and Lesbians.

5. As I have emphasised in previous letters it is important that appropriate action should be taken as soon as an incident arises: the

head of an establishment should not wait until it has been reported to the Incidents Group. The most effective reports are those which describe the action taken by the establishment and can provide a model of good practice for those tackling similar incidents elsewhere. The onus to investigate, take action and report on incidents is on the head of the establishment – it is fundamentally a management task. Where, on consideration of a report of an investigation by an establishment, I believe further enquiries and/or action is required those enquiries will be conducted by the Inspectorate working with management at the establishment. The end product of such a joint investigaton remains a matter on which the latter (including governors where appropriate) will need to take action.

6. The purpose of having a system of reporting on incidents is to enable the education service generally and institutions and their staff in particular, to promote equal opportunities more effectively. To help you do this I enclose a supply of forms on which incidents should be reported. From past experience I must emphasise that in reporting incidents, time is of the essence. The report should be made, and the form completed by people actually involved immediately while everything is fresh in their minds. The Incidents Group will be pleased to receive any suggestions for improving the form as experience in operating the reporting process is gained.

7. It is essential that everyone involved with your institution/department (that is, teaching, clerical/administrative, technical, catering, lunchtime organisation, caretaking and cleaning, gardening and grounds staff, pupils/students, governors and parents) know and are confident that the institution is actively seeking to combat discrimination of all kinds. To this end you will need to make the reporting process known to all these groups, and to display the notice attached wherever appropriate so that all staff, pupils/students, governors and parents can see it. You will see that the notice provides, as the previous version did, for people to refer directly to me if action is not taken in their establishment/centre/branch. Forms for reporting an incident should be made available from your school/college/centre office.

8. Please nominate a senior member of staff to take responsibility for equal opportunities issues and policy development within your organisation, including the co-ordination or reporting of incidents, and let me know who has been nominated on the attached slip. It

may also be appropriate for that named person to have other colleagues to assist and support in responding to equal opportunities issues.

9. Some institutions and departments have been uncertain as to what constitutes an incident or when it is appropriate for an incident, and the action taken on an incident/issue, to be reported to me. I hope the following examples will illustrate the kinds of incidents which have arisen and been reported in the past:

— name-calling between students/students and staff (or vice versa);
— physical attacks or intimidation along race or sex lines;
— complaints by parents and/or students about the establishment promoting 'equal opportunities' eg the introduction of 'Multi-faith Manchester';
— allegations that a school's 'option' arrangements are unfair to girls;
— restrictions on school visits for disabled students;
— display of 'page 3' pin-ups or 'girlie' magazines;
— complaints that a colleague has been speaking offensively about, eg a group of black youngsters at a youth centre;
— defaced notices for meetings concerned with Equal Opportunities.

This list is not intended to be exhaustive. The important point is that such, or similar matters need to be investigated so that the underlying substance of an incident can be explored and the establishment be seen to be taking action against discriminatory practice in whatever form.

10. If you have any queries please write to me. The Incidents Group is anxious to help institutions deal with incidents effectively and an important part of this is an efficient recording/reporting process. I am copying this letter to community groups, union secretaries, and the Diocesan Authorities.

11. Please share the contents of this letter with all staff and retain it for future reference.

Yours sincerely,

MANCHESTER CITY COUNCIL EDUCATION COMMITTEE
EQUAL OPPORTUNITIES
REPORT OF AN INCIDENT

This form should be completed as soon after the incident as possible while events are still fresh in the reporter(s)/witnesses mind.

The following incident is believed to have equal opportunities implications in the following Policy Area(s) (please indicate).

RACE   GENDER   DISABILITY

Name of establishments: _____

Name of reporter: _____

Position of reporter (employment): _____

Date of incidents: _____ Time: _____

Location of incident: _____

Name of those principally involved, and their position:

_____

_____

_____

Description of incident:

_____

_____

_____

_____

(Please attach extra sheets of lined paper if needed)

Any witnesses (staff, students or members of puplic):

Name: _____ Contact At: _____

_____

_____

_____

_____

497

Name and position of senior member of staff to whom incident first reported:

_____

Signature of reporter: _____

Signature of Head of Establishment: _____

Date of this report: _____ Date sent to CEO: _____

_____

Please indicate below any action taken following the incident:

_____

Action taken

_____

_____

Name   Date   Signature

_____

Action taken

_____

_____

Name   Date   Signature

_____

Action taken

_____

_____

Name   Date   Signature

_____

PLEASE RETURN THIS FORM MARKED FOR THE ATTENTION OF THE CHIEF EDUCATON OFFICER

To: Headteachers and Principals of all Education Establishments

Dear Headteacher/Principal,

RACIAL TENSION

1. The specific knowledge which we have in the Education Department about the extent of racial tension within, and impacting on, educational establishments is limited. I intend to monitor its occurrence.

2. Any serious instances indicative of racial tension should now be reported to me; please address any letters to the Chief Education Officer, marked for the attention of Mrs B Luckham, Services Branch. We should like to know about instances such as the scrawling of graffiti, the distribution of racist literature, threats to or actual disruption of social events, physical attacks upon individual pupils or staff (teaching and non-teaching) or groups where an explanatory factor may be the ethnic origins of the parties involved, and racial abuse directed by pupils or students towards staff or vice versa. I appreciate that some people may feel that the monitoring of such events may contribute to their happening; I do not share that view and anticipate that headteachers, principals, and others will ensure that it is not the case.

3. In some instances you will obviously decide in addition to letting me know about them, to involve the police or other agencies or individuals as appropriate. There have been discussions between officers of the Authority and senior police officers. Whilst not wishing to suggest that they subscribe to the view that racial tension within schools or colleges is of a significant degree or increasing, the police are hopeful that headteachers and others feel able to seek their assistance and advice not only if incidents occur but in anticipation of them. Normally, educational establishments should involve local community contact police officers, details of whom are listed below. In exceptional circumstances, where speed may be essential, contact with the police should be made by recourse to the '999 system'.

4. A multicultural approach to education will bear fruit in the long term, but there is some action which can be taken which may have an immediate effect.

COMBATTING DISCRIMINATION

The Education Committee and City Council are working to combat discrimination.

If you work or study in an educational establishment/centre and see a situation involving possible discrimination – on whatever grounds – you should report this to the head of the establishment/centre. The head should take appropriate action and report both the original incident and the action taken to the Chair of Governors and the Chief Education Officer.

You can get a form on which to report the incident from the school/college/centre office.

If you report an incident, and no action has been taken within 10 working days, you should write directly to the Chair of Governors (you can get the address from the school/college/centre office) and the Chief Education Officer, Education Department, Crown Square, Manchester M60 3BB.

'Incidents' may involve you, or other people, adults or children.

Please help us to fight against discrimination.

Gordon Hainsworth
Chief Education Officer
1987

Dear Colleague,

RACIAL INCIDENTS

1. I wrote to you in April 1985 setting out procedures for reporting racist incidents occurring within or affecting education estalishments. Although some colleagues have submitted regular reports of incidents in or around their establishment – and these have been valuable, particularly where follow-up action taken has provided an example for others to consider when faced with similar issues – I am concerned that reporting procedures are not being followed consistently, in part because staff may be unfamiliar with, or unaware of, such procedures. I am writing to re-emphasise the value of making a report on incidents of racism, whether individual or institutional, and ask that all members of staff (teaching and non-

500

teaching) are advised of reporting procedures by posting the attached notice prominently within your establishment. I do not believe that the recent fall-off in reporting by institutions can necessarily be taken as an indication that racist incidents are no longer occurring.

2. Whenever a situation with possible racist overtones is recognised the member of staff involved should report this to the Head of the Establishment who should then submit a report in writing to the Chief Education Officer and Chair of the Governing Body. Any action which follows should be reported by the Head of the establishment to the member of staff who raised the issue. If no action has been taken within one month of an incident being reported, the member of staff involved may report in writing directly to the Chief Education Officer and the Chair of the Governing Body and ask for action to be taken. Initial and follow-up reports should be marked for the attention of Mr Jobson (SAEO – Schools) in the case of the Schools sector, or Dr Jones (SAEO – Continuing) in the case of continuing/community education establishments.

3. I also should like to remind colleagues of advice previously given. It is important to stress that appropriate action should be taken as soon as an instance of racism is recognised: the head of an establishment should not wait until it has been reported to me. In fact, as mentioned above, the most helpful reports are those which describe the action taken subsequently. It will often be appropriate to involve other agencies or individuals. These individuals may include members of governing bodies and/or other individuals known to you to be involved in community relations work. Members of the Inspectorate and/or other officers of the Education Department may also be able to offer advice.

4. Some action which can be taken may have an immediate effect:
   (i) The swift removal of graffiti and in this context, racist graffiti, on and around buildings. The Direct Works Department contains a team of staff known as the 'graffiti squad'. They are usually able to remove graffiti of an obscene or racist nature within twenty-four hours of being told of its presence. This facility is made available either by sending a Repair Note to the Area Maintenance Depot of the Direct Works Department or by telephoning the Works Service Unit 223 7222, extension 158

or 153 and following up with a Repair Note to the Depot.

(ii) The prevention of the distribution of racist literature within or at the gates of schools, colleges, youth clubs and so forth.

5. All reports of racist incidents are reviewed twice termly by a group of senior colleagues, which I chair. It is important that we receive reports of incidents so that we may identify any particular trends and, by looking at lessons learnt, be better placed to offer advice should similar incidents arise elsewhere within the service.

6. The procedures outlined in this letter have previously been fully discussed with the teaching associations and have been circulated to non-teaching staff associations for comment.

7. Attached to this letter are copies of a notice which draws attention to reporting procedures as set out in paragraph 2 above. Heads and Principals are asked to post the notice in staff rooms, kitchens, cleaners rooms and so on. The notice will also be published in the Bulletin. Extra copies can be obtained from schools Administration, Crown Square.

8. I am copying this letter to community groups and to union secretaries.

Yours sincerely,

RACIST INCIDENTS

As you know, it is Education Committee and City Council policy to work to combat racism. As part of this policy members of staff of education establishments – all employees – who recognise a situation involving possible racism, are asked to report this to the head of the establishment. The head is asked to take appriopriate action, and report both the original incident and the action taken to the Chair of Governors and the Chief Education Officer.

If you report an incident, and no action has been taken within one month, you may report in writing directly to the Chair of Governors and the Chief Education Officer. 'Incidents' may involve you, or other people, adults or children; racist graffiti are included, and attempts to distribute racist literature.

Please help us to make Manchester a racism-free city.

G. Hainsworth
Chief Education Officer.

Dear Colleague,

RACISM

I sent you a letter on 3 April 1985 about reporting racist incidents, and also in XXX I sent a copy of the Committee's draft statement of intent for a policy on racism. The first letter included the following paragraph:

2. "Whenever a situation with possible racist overtones is recognised, the member of staff involved should report this to the Head of the establishment who should then submit a report in writing to the Chief Education Officer and Chair of the Govering Body. Any action which follows should be reported to the Head of the establishment to the member of staff who raised the issue. If no action has been taken within one month of an incident being reported, the teacher or lecturer involved may report in writing to the Chief Education Officer and the Chair to the Govering Body and ask for action to be taken."

Since circulation, two points have been made:

(a) that "member of staff" should be substituted for 'teacher' in line seven, since the procedure applies to all staff;

(b) how has the advice contained in this paragrah been given to all employees in each establishment?

I attach a notice which includes the amendment, which you may find useful to circulate to staff and attach to notice boards, in staff rooms, kitchens, cleaners' rooms and so on. The notice will also be published in the Bulletin. Extra copies can be supplied on request to XXX.

I am sending copies of this letter to all union secretaries. Between us, I am confident that we can reach all employees of the Education Committee.

Yours sincerely,

As you know it is Education Committee and City Council policy to work to combat racism. As part of this policy members of staff of education establishments – all employees – who recognise a situation involving possible racism, have been asked to report this to the head of the establishment. The head is asked to take appropriate action and report both the original incident and the action taken to the Chair of Goverors and the Chief Education Officer.

If you report an incident, and no action has been taken within one month, you may report in writing directly to the Chair of Governors and the Chief Education Officer.

'Incidents" may involve you, or other people, adults or children, racist graffiti are included, and attempts to distribute racist literature.

Please help us to make Manchester a racism-free City.

G. Hainsworth
July 1985

To: Heads of Establishments
    Chairs, School/College Governing Bodies

Dear Colleague,

RACISM

1. In May 1982 the attention of heads of teaching establishments was drawn to concern over racial tension manifested within, or affecting education establishments. Since that time some colleagues in schools, colleges and other establishments have reported incidents. These reports have been helpful in giving some indication of the extent of the problem though obviously they do not give a comprehensive picture. Particularly helpful have been those reports where the follow up action taken by the establishment has proved to be an example for others to consider when faced with similar issues. I now want to repeat my request to all colleagues that all instances of racism, whether individual or institutional, are reported.

2. Whenever a situation with possible racist overtones is recognised, the member of staff involved should report this to the Head of the Establishment who should then submit a report in writing to the Chief Education Officer and Chair of the Governing Body. Any action which follows should be reported by the Head of the Establishment to the member of staff who raised the issue. If no action has been taken within one month of an incident being reported, the teacher or lecturer involved may report in writing

504

directly to the Chief Education Officer and the Chair of the Governing Body and ask for action to be taken.

3. I will take this opportunity to remind colleagues of advice previously given. It is important to stress that appropriate action should be taken as soon as an example of racism is recognised: there is no need for the head of an establishment to wait until it has been reported to me. In fact, as mentioned above, the most helpful reports are those which describe the action taken subsequently. It will often be appropriate to involve other agencies or individuals. These individuals may include members of governing bodies and/or other individuals known to you to be involved in community relations work. Members of the Inspectorate and/or other officers of the Education Department may also be able to offer advice.

4. Some action which can be taken may have an immediate effect:
   (i) The swift removal of graffiti and in this context, racist graffiti, on and around buildings. The Direct Works Department contains a team of staff known as the 'graffiti squad'. They are usually able to remove graffiti of an obscene or racist nature within twenty-four hours of being told of its presence. This facility is made available either by sending a Repair Note to the Area Maintenance Depot of the Direct Works Department or by telephoning the Works Service Unit 223-7222, extension 158 or 153 and following up with a Repair Note to the depot.
   (ii) The prevention of the distribution of racist literature within or at the gates of schools, colleges, youth clubs and so forth.

5. The action outlined in this letter had previously been fully discussed with the teaching associations and has been circulated to non-teaching staff associations for comment.

6. I am copying this letter to the Chairs of Governors of all establishments and to community groups.

7. Heads and Principals will note that I have enclosed two extra copies of this letter. This is to facilitate wide circulation among the staff of establishments, both teaching and non-teaching.

Yours sincerely,

APPENDIX G

Statment to the MacDonald Inquiry into Racial Violence in Manchester Schools

Identifying Violence in Manchester Schools

As far as we know, there is no method of systematically monitoring violence within Manchester Schools and other educational establishments. Consequently, we have no agreed criteria for identifying violence, we do not know the extent of violence, whether it is increasing or decreasing and most important of all, we have no agreed strategies for dealing with violence except on an ad hoc basis.

Having considered traditional research/survey techniques for obtaining this information and found them wanting, we would like to suggest the following outline proposal for the Panel's consideration. We have restricted ourselves to an outline in recognition of the need for full consultation with all parties from the very beginning.

1. The responsibility for identifying, monitoring and dealing with violence should be owned by each individual establishment. Each establishment, therefore, needs to devise its own policy which meets its own needs and is based on its own particular circumstances. These school based policies would then inform LEA policy development.

2. The definition of violence is problematic. Personal violence reflects the structural and institutionalized violence of society and may be expressed in many forms. Educational establishments are complex hierarchical organisations. Power is invested differentially and wielded differentially. Some violence is condoned, some is not and bullying can exist at many levels. Within such a system both individuals and groups of individuals can feel violated in a number of different ways.

3. "Violence" can occur between the following groups:

    a. Student to staff
    b. Staff to student
    c. Student to student
    d. Parent to staff
    e. Staff to parent
    f. Student to parent
    g. Parent to student
    h. Between staff

    Within each of these groups the variables of race, gender, class, disability, age and sexual orientation must be recognised.

508

4. In the first instance each establishment could set up an umbrella working group which might look like:

Parents

Co-opted members   *Staff*
Headteacher
Governing body   **WORKING GROUP**
Community groups

Students

Representation in these groups must reflect race, gender, disability and sexual orientation

This group should be non-hierarchical and should not reflect the power structures that already exist within the school.

The size of the group could be problematic but it is unlikely that every group would be fully represented. Nevertheless it is important that representatives from all groups should be invited. It may be necessary to consider written representations for example from gay or lesbian parents/students/staff who may not feel safe enough to identify themselves.

5. The task of the umbrella group would be to identify its establishment's

a. *Definition of Violence* – personal, insitutional, structural (physical, verbal, racial, sexual.)

b. *Structures of domination within the school.*
    How is discipline and control upheld in the school?
    Who has power over whom (race over race, social class over social class, men over women, teacher over student, parent over child, headteacher over classteacher?)

c. *System for monitoring violence.* Is there a violent incidents monitor? Are suspensions recorded? Is there any system for monitoring punishment?

d. *Strategies for dealing with violence.* Are these gender linked? Are these age linked? Are these strategies for dealing with victims? What are the school rules about violence?

e. *Techniques for teaching non-violent solutions to conflict.* (See Chief Education Officer's Report February 1987, Peace Education Guidelines).

6. In order to inform this process the umbrella group may wish to subdivide into groups according to particular characteristics, e.g. girls and women (students, parents, staff), ethnic group (students, parents, staff). Sub-groups would address the frame of reference in relation to their own experience and feedback into the umbrella group. These sub-groups could meet with equivalent sub-groups from other establishments forming support networks throughout the City.

7. From this exercise the establishment should be able to determine:

    1. The nature and range of the violence within it.
    2. Its techniques for identifying and monitoring violence.
    3. Its techniques for dealing with violence.
    4. Its need for future development.

    Such a working group would:

    1. Raise levels of consciousness with regard to the nature of violence.
       Empower victims and low-status groups by providing support.
    3. Develop good practice for reducing aggression and violence and develop non-violent solutions to conflict when it does occur.

8. The working group would be expected to complete its task within a time limited period and be in a position to report to:

    1. Its whole community.
    2. Its governing body.
    3. The LEA.
    4. The Equal Opportunities Unit.
    5. The Race Unit.

    It is understood that extensive consultation would take place at all stages.

Leah H Burman
Senior Educational Psychologist

Pauline Collier
Educational Psychologist

Maria L Heffernan
District Senior
Educational Psychologist

Statement to the MacDonald Inquiry into Racial Violence in Manchester Schools

The Implementation of Anti-Racist Policies

Manchester LEA has a long history of producing policy statements in the multicultural and anti-racist field. The pattern of their development over the last 10 years has been described by K. McIntyre and L.H. Burman (1986). Also well documented are the difficulties that LEAs are facing nationally in putting policy into practice (Young and Connolly 1981, Willey 1984, Troyna 1982, Mullard et al 1983). This statement aims to discuss some of the reasons for the gap between policy and practice.

It is considered that a raised level of awareness of the needs of ethnic groups can be observed in Manchester. Many more schools have anti-racist policy statements than were evdident in the Troyna study of 1982. Structural issues are addressed in policy documents central to the development of school curriculum and practice e.g. Reports of the CEO on:

1) Restructuring of Services for Students with Social and Emotional Difficulties.
2) Profiling and Record Keeping.

There are several steps that need to be taken at LEA level to effect change in daily practice. These include:

1) Consultation with community groups, parent and students, before policy statements are produced for Education Committee approval.

2) Discussion and information exchange with other LEAs.

3) Writing of policy statements.

4) Clarification and communication of issues to the receivers of policy statements so that they understand their importance and relevance.

5) Explicit guidelines to assist institutions in identifying areas for change.

6) Careful coordination of all the above.

It may be said that only point 3) has been adequately addressed. Developments have stopped at the policy writing stage. The reasons for this are complex but may be summarised by the following points:

511

1) An over simplified view of the nature of policy making, implementation and coordination.

2) The need for a fuller understanding of the practical implications of theories for structural, institutional and personal change.

3) Confusions about the nature of and necessity for anti-racist work.

4) A failure to address central issues relating to class.

5) Confusions about the meaning of "equal opportunities".

6) The need for a real commitment to change which by its nature in this context means a willingness to share power at all levels.

7) The need to grasp the complexity and variability of local situations, and their implications for policy and implementation.

8) The absence of any real discussion and dialogue about the proposed contents of the policy with the consumers i.e. students, parents, community groups, staffs.

9) The absence of any real communication of policy to the consumers.

10) The absence of support mechanisms for those institutions and individuals who can experience considerable stress when they are faced with backlash either from within or without the institution.

11) The need for whole institution strategies.

The remainder of this statement is devoted to exploring these 11 points in more detail and suggesting some avenues for change.

In order to conceptualise the structural, institutional, and personal issues involved it is necessary to address the origins and maintenance of racism in the context of recent social and political history.

It is argued that British society is made up of a hierarchical class structure. Black people who came to this country to work after the 1939–1945 war found that, as a result of the post-colonial legacy, they were denied opportunities alongside the white working classes. The maintenance of Black people in the lowest levels of society to this day has allowed their scapegoating for the ills of society e.g. crime, housing and job shortages, and has divided the working class (Searle 1977). At the same time Black workers have confronted the latent racism of their fellow workers and joined in collective struggle within the workplace. This collective struggle which recognises that class ultimately unites peoples, is an important part of the historical record of the last three decades (La Rose 1987).

Schools both reflect and shape the nature of our hierarchical society. The purpose and functioning of schooling is to prepare children for their eventual roles in life according to the needs of the economy. Race, class, gender, sexual orientation and disability operate within this ethos as the most important factors determining success or failure. The working classes are trained to offer a semi-literate and compliant workforce to staff industry and the public services. Black labour performs some of the dirtiest most tedious and badly paid jobs, (La Rose 1987), and is heavily over represented in unemployment statistics.

It is important that the links between racism and the class struggle are realised by policy makers, staffs, students and parents in the same way as they have been acknowledged by some Black workers. In Manchester it is not clear that this relationship has been recognised. In a recent Equal Opportunities policy document (in preparation) class related issues have been removed.

Location of race, class, gender, sexual orientation and disability as discrete entities with equal opportunities policies prevents a realistic appraisal of the situation.

Equal opportunities policies tend to analyse separately the difficulties that the identified oppressed groups of race, class, gender, sexual orientation and disability have experienced in gaining access to resources within our society. There are assumptions that these opportunities may be accessible with only small changes in individual and institutional practice. However in a society that is structured so that only a few will have access to resources, far more fundamental changes are necessary before the situation can improve. The exercise of power which is vested in the dominant group of largely white able-bodied middle-class men must be challenged in order to develop an effective strategy for change.

An appreciation of the resistance that is likely to be experienced once these issues are opened up and how to work positively within such a context, is also necessary. Power and advantage are not given up easily (P. Collier 1987). If power is to be devolved then conflict will become an inevitable factor to deal with. "Change involves an uneasy balance between moving too fast and too slow, between taking people with you or leaving them stranded and antagonistic". (G. Weiner 1985). It is still the view of many, however, that a shift of power within the school system is an inevitable and attainable objective. (Dhondy, 1981).

Consideration of the nature of power, its use and abuse and how it may be constructively shared may help to illustrate why there have been major difficulties in putting policy into practice.

It has already been stated that the LEA, schools and support services tend to mirror the nature of society. As such, they are hierarchical systems. Heads of establishments and managers have considerable power. Individual staff lower in the hierarchy have relatively little power and may experience difficulty in making their views heard. Students and parents have even less power. Rules, practices, and curricula are devised by schools. They tend to reflect white traditional middle-class values. Students and parents are expected to conform. Schools can become alienating places for many adults and students who may be unable to identify with these institutions and may not feel valued. Teachers may find that they cannot reach their students and without a structural analysis, are unable to understand why.

Mukherjee (1986) has summarised the way many teachers perceive the context of their teaching roles in ILEA. The following statements are often echoed by Manchester teachers:

"1. Acute tension and suspicion within the hierarchical power-structure.
2. Pastoral care means control and an obsession with discipline.
3. Little or no inter-action between departments.
4. There does not seem to be any coherence of purpose, codes or practices.
5. Hostile students – demoralised teachers – inconsistent and ad hoc controls and sanctions – leading to suspension.
6. Overt and covert racist attitudes without any policy to deal with them.
7. Enormous infrastructure – without any well defined lines of communication – and lack of capacity to make decisions".

Anti-racist policies which are devised in this climate are irrelevant in meeting the needs of those for whom they are supposed to provide. In many circumstances students, parents and teachers are unaware that these policies exist and therefore have no knowledge of their content. Such policy development is dangerous because it maintains the status quo, whilst masquerading as a force for change.

Some students, parents, community groups and staffs are already recognising the influence that they can achieve through meeting in groups and networks, and making their views known. (Dhondy, Beese and Hassan 1981). The publication of Coard's book "How the West Indian Child is made ESN in the British School System" (1970) had a major influence in the development of the Black working-class education movement. Supplementary schools which aim to provide students with a sympathetic and relevant learning experience have demonstrated the possibility of parental control (John 1986).

Community groups e.g. WIOCC have canvassed parents' views and have identified the failure of the school system to address their concerns regarding student under-achievement. Students meet in Youth Clubs and discuss concerns. Many of these we understand currently focus on issues relating to school discipline. Aarten (Association of Anti-Racist Teachers Network) is becoming an important force with contacts across the country.

The LEA must listen carefully to the views that are presented. A shared dialogue needs to be developed where both LEA and the represented group jointly identify aims and objectives in a context of understanding of each other's possible roles for defining and implementing policy. The LEA needs to prove its commitment to change by taking responsibility for its oppressive mode of functioning and by sharing power through a process of pursuing suggested lines of action. Dilemmas will be faced when demands are made to which institutions are opposed. The challenge of justifying beliefs through debate will be necessary and will serve to clarify points of view. In this way an atmosphere of trust and closer working may develop (Young and Connolly 1981).

This process should be mirrored at every point in the education system. Students, parents and staffs need to be empowered in order to negotiate the power structures of the system. Schools, for example, should give more responsibility to students and parents to help question and shape their rules, practices and curriculum content. This should include involvement in radical ways e.g. student groups, parents' groups, school councils, in-service training, sharing of skills. People's individual experiences need to be taken seriously and where a need for change is suggested, this should be considered. (TUBE 1986). Since schools are about educating young people, we need to know how they see themselves, what their views and feelings are, and how they define their place within the education system.

The final point that needs pursuing is the recognition that racism is not a static entity. It changes according to the variability of local situations e.g. Catholic, Protestant schools; Wythenshawe, Gorton, Didsbury catchment areas (Gulam 1986). Dialogue between the institutions and their consumers open up possibilities for grasping this complexity so that the full implications of policy implementation can be realised.

Summary

This Statement considers some of the reasons why there continues to be a gap between policy and practice in the anti-racist field. It is argued that:

1. The LEA, the schools and the support services need to recognise the social role of the education system in the context of British social history and the class structure of British Society.

2. There is a need to move away from the analysis of race as a single strand inequality, and to move towards the creation of key concepts which recognise the structures and processes that produce inequalities shared in differing degrees by many.

3. The LEA, schools and support services need to evaluate the ways in which the education system currently disempowers both its consumers and the staff within it.

4. Because policies are currently produced without a dialogue with students, parents, community groups and staffs, there is a failure to address the real difficulties and complexity of situations that are experienced daily.

5. It follows that policy can only be developed and implemented as a result of collective action between groups and a real dialogue between the LEA, institutions and these groups.

6. Change is a difficult process and power and advantage are not given up easily. Strategies for dealing with conflict and supporting those striving for change need to be developed and promoted throughout the education system.

Leah H Burman   Pauline Collier
Senior Educational Psychologist   Educational Psychologist

Maria L Heffernan
District Senior
Educational Psychologist

516

References

Coard B. (1971). How the West Indian Child is made Educationally Subnormal in the British School System. Beacon Press.

Collier P. (1987). The Disproportinately High Take Up of Resources by Boys in Special Education. M.A. Dissertation.

Dhondy F., Beese B. and Hassan H. (1981). The Black Explosion in British Schools. RTP Publications.

Gulam (1986). The Implementation of Anti-Racist Policies. Internal Paper M.E.C.

Halsey N.N. (1980). Origin and Destinations: Family Class and Education in Modern Britain. Oxford University Press.

John G. (1986). Talk given to Conference on Education and Young Black People. 10.5.86. Published he TUBE/M.E.C.

Karn V. (1983). Race and Housing in Britain: The Role of the Major Institutions in Ethnic Pluralism and Public Policy. (Ed.) Glazer N. and Young K. Policy Studies Institute.

La Rose (1987). Anti-Racism and the New Black Middle Class and British Society in Race Today. June/July 1987.

McIntyre K. and Burman L.H. (1986). The Educational Needs of Black Pupils. M.E.C.

Mukherjee T. (1986). Black Responses to White Definitions in Multi-cultural Education: Towards Good Practice. (Eds.) Arora R. and Duncan C. Routledge.

Mullard C., Bonnick L. and King B. (1983). Racial Policy and Practice in Education. University of London Institute of Education.

Searle C. (1977). The World in a Classroom.

TUBE/MEC. (1986). Report of a Conference on Education and Young Black People.

Troyna B. (1982). The Ideological and Policy Response to Black Pupils in British Schools. Warwick University.

Weiner G. (1985). Just a Bunch of Girls. Open University Press.

W.I.O.C.C. (1985). An Afro-Caribbean perspective on Educational issues in Manchester. Report of the Black Caucus Working Party. (Afro-Caribbean Group).

Willey R. (1984). Policy Responses In Education in Education and Cultural Pluralism. (Ed.) Maurice Craft. Falmer Press.

Young K. and Connolly N. (1981). Policy and Practice in the Multiracial School Policy Studies Institute.

APPENDIX H

Internal Memorandum

From: JC Taylor, E Milroy, A Warm
To: I Macdonald, Macdonald Inquiry

Your Ref:	Our Ref.	Tel. Extn. No.	Date
	I/JCT/MLB		24.9.87

Recommendations to the Inquiry

1. When we gave evidence to the inquiry on 21.4.87, we were asked if we would be prepared to make recommendations to the inquiry which could help in the deliberations and agreed that we would do so.

2. We have spoken to Gus John as a member of the inquiry team in order to clarify the nature of the task and have understood it to be in two sections:

   i) further work we believe to be necessary at Burnage High School in the light of our inspection findings;
   ii) recommendations necessary to combat racism/racial violence in Manchester Schools.

3. I enclose the notes we have prepared. They take the form of brief paragraphs which we hope may form the basis of discussion when we meet you.

   Mr Gulam has been involved in the discussions which have led to these recommendations. His views are included within them and we would be pleased if you could invite him also to join a meeting with you to discuss them.

I. *Recommendations concerning further work we believe to be necessary in Burnage High School in the light of inspection findings*

1. *Relationships with the Community*

   (a) In advance of ethnic monitoring, it would be valuable for the school to make a detailed analysis of the varied communities the school serves by making a trawl amongst the students, thereby giving the scope and size of the exercise;

   (b) white parents must not be forgotten in this exercise;

   (c) a series of meetings would be valuable, building on the work already being done, to find out if links (and of what type) are wanted;

(d) named people should be nominated to service the links;

(e) the setting up of a forum so that governors can meet group representatives;

(f) meetings should be held at times convenient for committees, i.e. evenings and weekends;

(g) the above format should be reviewed after one year.

2. *Anti-racism training in linked primary schools*

(a) Linked primary schools should nominate 'key worker(s)' to focus anti-racist staff development/INSET organised at Burnage High School. This would create a working ongoing relationship between primary and lower secondary school staff;

(b) anti-racist training is part of a process. It does not have a finite end but should have a determined starting point. Too often the process starts too late, usually in the secondary school. The model suggested is one which should have a primary-secondary continuum. Essential to this is that primary schools should address themselves to developing a pastoral curriculum which includes work on aggression, race, support, co-operation, sharing feelings, development of positive self-images, etc. This should be validated via the arrangements suggested in (a) above;

(c) key trainers should be identified in the LEA to facilitate the process;

(d) the Co-operative Group work project currently being developed in primary schools could provide a valuable model for implementation.

3. *Signalling to all staff that anti-racism is on the agenda of the school*

Possible courses of action could be:

(a) stipulating that the capitation allocation made to each faculty involves a percentage for use on this issue coupled with a requirement that each faculty reports back on how monies were spent and action that was taken;

(b) headteacher setting aside a percentage of 'inhouse' GRIST money and "Teacher" days for staff INSET on the issue;

(c) involving of governors and community groups in the enterprise.

4. *Identifying ways in which ethnic minorities of students are given status and recognition in the school and the curriculum*

   (a) ensure that all departments are aware of the dangers of euro-centricity in images; written texts, display materials, etc;

   (b) promote materials and activities which show ethnic minorities people in positive roles, leadership roles, contributory roles;

   (c) look at the role models available to ethnic minority students in terms of career aspirations;

   (d) celebrate the events of each culture centering on the community itself contributing, rather than white teachers on behalf of . . .;

   (e) expect ethnic minority students to take leading roles in terms of prefects, group leadership, etc;

   (f) senior management should monitor departments and student experience systematically. Strengthen the contribution of governors, especially ethnic minority governors, in this respect;

   (g) develop students advocates for ethnic minority groups.

5. *The need for political education – in particular to influence white youth*

   (a) A potent way of combatting racism is to get young people to identify what they have in common with each other rather than what is different. The paper by Gus John to the NAME conference provides a very valuable starting point;

   (b) within the curriculum PSE, English, Humanities and Art, for example, all have a contribution to make in this development, as well as the pastoral curriculum;

   (c) representatives from department/faculties come together to develop strategies in order to enable this aspect of political education to be introduced into the curriculum in a co-ordinated way;

   (d) a developmental step would be to introduce a young people's 'grouse' group. The group would be similar to a democratically elected school council and would make representation to management on issues affecting the wellbeing of the school community. It would also monitor racist incidents/aggression. The school management would need to be duty bound to reply to this group's grievances.

6. *Systematic observation of teachers dealing with ethnic minority students*

   (a) Acknowledge the key role of office staff as often the first contact students have with the school. Office staff need training in dealing with students, often under extreme pressure;

   (b) if teachers are observed by senior management or inspectors, the quality of interaction can be examined, asking such questions as:

       (i)   is there any difference in response rate between ethnic minority and white students?

       (ii)   is material written in a way which included and does not exclude them? How far are students themselves involved in reviewing resources and in contributing to teaching materials?

       (iii)   where students do not seem anxious to participate e.g. in some aspects of PE, are the alternatives in Physical activity explored?

       (iv)   is there positive mutual respect between teachers and students in the spoken and written word?

       (v)   is there any evidence of groups or classes being 'sorted' (albeit inadvertently) on a racial basis, e.g., special needs being confused with ESL needs?

       (vi)   how far are community language materials available to parents especially at critical times of choice like option time, parents' meetings?

       (vii)   do teachers model in their interactions with students the expectations they hold of the way they expect students to relate?

       (viii)   is there any evidence of negative expectation in checks about uniform – or behaviour or general standards which operate adversely on ethnic minority students?

7. *Teacher exchange*

   (a) the purpose would be to combat the insularity of staff at Burnage High School. Teacher exchanges would follow up a recommendation in the CEO's report to Committee on Swann;

(b) exchange should involve Burnage High School staff from Upper and Lower school exchanging with staff from other schools, including primary schools.

8. *An in-depth study of individual staff reaction to the headteachers' anti-racist policy*

(a) use would be made of "Responding to Swann" (NAME) as a springboard;

(b) asking staff to produce a statement/critique, individually and collectively, for the head;

(c) asking the head to produce a paper based on statements from staff and using "Teacher" days to explore ways forward with staff on a "forcefield analysis" model;

(d) use a questionnaire and analysis via C Roberts' work.

9. *Methods of communicating policy matters to staff*

(a) the inspection report recommends that the headteacher reviews and improves the methods of communicating policy matters to the staff;

(b) this task should be done with the senior management team;

(c) methods of communication should be clear, formalised and include meetings with middle managers where discussion may take place in order to clarify policy matters;

(d) headteachers and members of the senior management team should be available to join the meetings middle managers have with staff;

(e) the sequence of meetings should feedback formally and in writing so that proper records of meetings are made;

(f) minutes of meetings should be available to governors.

10. *Management of Transition to Upper School*

(a) does the school have a sytematic induction process for third year students?

(b) are students clear about the ways in which consistent valuing of their cultural or racial differences is carried through into upper school?

(c) how is student success celebrated? – by comparison with others or with the students' best efforts?

(d) are there any parent-tutor group meetings to help parents get to know staff, and the enhanced opportunities of upper school?

11. *Ways in which student power is organised, expressed and incorporated into the school organisation*

   (a) Disputes between students and teachers are often unfair. A highly educated, mature, often middle-class adult debates against an immature, often less articulate young person, in a forum which is seen to be on 'the teacher's side'. Judge and jury is often a member of the school senior management team. This is not fair for the student;

   (b) a student/parent advocacy should be developed. The mechanism could be a teacher or youth worker appointed in each area of the city. The staff appointed would be independent of any individual institution and could be called upon by any parent or young person to act as their advocate in disputes.

12. *Planned residential experiences*

   The quality of relationships between student/teacher and teachers/student can be improved by planned residential experience. Each student should have the opportunity of such experiences. There are three possible avenues:

   (a) in Year I the experience should be part of the pastoral curriculum. Each tutor group with their tutor, Head of Year and some other teacher, should follow a three-day residential course. The theme for the course should be "Friendship". Suitable materials for this course could be extracted from 'Active Tutorial Work' or the new CCDU Health Skill Programme. Good quality relationships determined so early in a young person's school career are often maintained through that young person's school life. Staff will need specific training in residential work if this is to be effective. The LEA is able to provide this training;

   (b) in addition other residential experiences should be developed by the school whenever possible. These experiences should be outside the formal curriculum. Staff should be encouraged to initiate such ventures;

   (c) field courses organised by departments in Upper School should take cognisance of the need for pastoral work as an integral part of any course provided.

13. *An outside perspective on the school*

   It would be valuable to explore the possibilities of a piece of social research carried out through the Planning Department in order to get a perspective on the school within its social and geographical setting. Possible action points would be:

(a) the analysis feedback to the school;

(b) the school asked to respond to public perceptions;

(c) the school asked to undertake an action response to perceptions;

(d) a follow-up analysis made by the Planning Department.

II. *Recommendations necessary to combat racism/racial violence in schools*

This section is shorter, because we believe that what is said about Burnage High School in the recommendations above has application to schools generally. However, there are a number of points that we feel deserve emphasis:

(i)   the concept of student/parent advocates on a linked basis, each serving a group of schools, we feel deserves exploration;

(ii) the 'Parents Shop' works well as a means of providing information to parents. Extension of this service could be very valuable;

(iii) the department should explore ways of working as a model with the 'REEPER' group of parents who are committed to multi-cultural education/anti-racist education as a means of combatting the "backlash" effect;

(iv) all schools should be encouraged to provide parents' rooms/spaces where parents can feel welcome in schools. This in itself has value, but particularly where the step is taken as a move toward inviting active participation in the life of schools, vis-a-vis combatting racism;

(v)   all that is said about curriculum in Burnage has application to other schools. However, other points to emphasise are:

(a) emphasis is needed on staff development/INSET for dealing with multicultural/anti-racism as a cross-curricular theme. this is the language of the Secretary of State for Education's national curriculum consultative document. This type of staff development is needed per se but now needs added emphasis, the danger being that teachers and schools may interpret a nationally imposed curriculum as not requiring the development of anti-racist education;

526

(b) extension of the co-operative group work project through to the secondary stage. As mentioned in I.(5.)(d) above, we believe that the project provides a valuable vehicle for the development of anti-racist education. To extend it would provide a valuable means of addressing the effective needs of pupils at transition;

(c) concerted efforts should be made with Examining Boards to raise awareness that syllabi produced should be rigorously scrutinised in terms of multicultural/anti-racist approaches;

(d) in addition to (c) above, new course development is needed with Examining Boards, which move completely away from eurocentricity, eg GCSE in African History;

(vi) the LEA should further explore strategies for the appointment and promotion of black teachers, ie:

(a) actively to follow up the recommendations in the CEO report to Policy Sub-Committee 16.9.85. on the Swann Report;

(b) more involvement of black teachers on working/planning groups and management courses

(vii) expansion of anti-racism training geared to the needs of staff at all levels within the service as an effective means of educating all staff to understand the process of policy implementation and the part they each have to play in it;

(viii) further refinement of the processes for dealing with racist incidents/aggression at LEA, schools and classroom levels.

Appendices

A.   A private and confidential report of sub-committee to the Board of Governors of Burnage High School (see Chapter 20).

B.   A private and confidential report of the Board of Governors of Burnage High School – 9th September 1985 (see Chapter 20).

C.   Plant Hill – Mr McCorkle's version of events (see Chapter 27).

D.   Plant Hill – Mr Speller's report (see Chapter 27).

E.   Plant Hill Chief Education Officer's letter (see Chapter 27).

F.   Letters and documents on reporting and monitoring racist incidents in Manchester (see Chapter 29).

G.   Burman, Collier and Heffernan report on identifying violence and anti-racist strategies.

H.   Taylor, Milroy, Warm and Gulam's recommendations on anti-racist policies.

INDEX